Cerebral Palsied and
Learning Disabled Children

Cerebral Palsied and Learning Disabled Children

A Handbook/Guide to TREATMENT, REHABILITATION and EDUCATION

By

NANCY C. MARKS, O.T.R., M. Ed.

Educational Consultant and Evaluator
Developmental Therapy Department
Rotary Rehabilitation Center, Mobile, Alabama
Formerly Director of Occupational Therapy
Shands Teaching Hospital and Clinics
University of Florida, Gainesville, Florida

With a Foreword by
HOMER PASCHALL, M. D.
Chief, Orthopedic Surgery
Veterans Administration Hospital
Gainesville, Florida

CHARLES C THOMAS • PUBLISHER
Springfield • Illinois • U.S.A.

Published and Distributed Throughout the World by
CHARLES C THOMAS ● PUBLISHER
Bannerstone House
301-327 East Lawrence Avenue, Springfield, Illinois, U.S.A.

© *1974 by* **CHARLES C THOMAS ● PUBLISHER**
ISBN 0-398-02911-3
Library of Congress Catalog Card Number: 73-7805

Printed in the United States of America
HH-11

Library of Congress Cataloging in Publication Data

Marks, Nancy C
  Cerebral palsied and learning disabled children.
  1. Cerebral palsied children. 2. Mentally handicapped children. I. Title. [DNLM:
1. Cerebral palsy—Rehabilitation. 2. Cerebral palsy—Therapy. 3. Learning disorders—Rehabilitation. 4. Learning disorders—Therapy. WS340 M345c 1973] RJ-
496. C4M28 616.8'36 73-7805 ISBN 0-398-02911-3

FOREWORD

Several years ago I met Nancy Marks as she appeared in the Cerebral Palsy Clinic at the College of Medicine of the University of Florida. It was obvious that she had more than a passing interest in cerebral palsied and learning disabled individuals because of her probing questions which she asked about each child. One of the questions which always followed was "Where can I read about it?" Before long she recognized that she was compiling a sizeable reading list and that in no single volume could she find references to definitions, diagnosis, surgical procedures, bracing, physical therapy techniques, speech therapy techniques, occupational therapy techniques, assistive devices, teaching methods and procedures, etc. She came to me to ask advice about compiling this wealth of information into a form useable by occupational, physical and speech therapists, and special education teachers and students preparing for these disciplines. From this came the concept for this book. Her goals were to assimilate in one volume relative information that could be useful for any student, therapist, and teacher, comprehensive enough to provide understanding of the field, yet not so exhaustive as to be burdensome to the reader. This information has been tempered with her experience. As I reviewed her book, chapter by chapter, it became apparent that she was achieving her objective in a most admirable fashion.

This Handbook is directed primarily towards students and therapists in the health related professions, and special educators, but is comprehensive enough to be of distinct value to the medical student and junior residents in pediatrics, neurology and orthopedics. It will also prove valuable to the practicing physician as a rich source of ready reference material to devices and techniques in the special therapy and education areas in which he is usually not familiar. If one desires more specific information on any of the topics discussed in the Handbook, he will find the bibliography to be an accurate and complete source for additional reading. Mrs. Marks has achieved her goals in providing the student, therapist and teacher with a complete handbook that should stand the test of time and be a most valuable addition to the bookshelf of those engaged in the habilitation and education of a child with cerebral palsy or learning disabilities.

H. A. PASCHALL, M.D.
Division of Orthopedics
College of Medicine
University of Florida
Gainesville, Florida

PREFACE

This is by no means a conventional publication. Therefore, it is well to state at the outset what this book is *not* intended to do. It is not intended to be just another textbook. It is not intended to be a bedside reader for neurosurgeons and orthopedic surgeons. However, it *is* the intent, herein, to gather up and synthesize the myriad bits of information concerning the broad subject of the cerebral palsied/neurologically impaired (learning disabled) child which are scattered hither and yon, and consolidate them into one Handbook. The format then of this Handbook is intended to offer up-dated information on a practical and convenient level. It should be noted that the term *neurologically impaired* is used predominately throughout this text to refer to the learning disabled child (variously identified in other publications as minimally brain damaged, perceptual dysfunction, maturational lag and what-have-you).

The idea of preparing a Handbook of this nature evolved from the author's recognition of a need for a more thorough understanding of cerebral palsy and neurological impairment (learning disabilities) by those who daily come in contact with these children. It is hoped that the book will be of particular benefit to educators, therapists and medical professionals (as well as students preparing for these disciplines) who work with the orthopedically handicapped, neurologically impaired (learning disabled) and the "organic" mentally retarded.[1]

[1] From an educational and treatment standpoint, many common elements exist in providing for other groups of orthopedically handicapped children (i.e. spina bifida, muscular dystrophy, arthritis). In addition, many of the learning and behavioral deviations noted in children with cerebral palsy and the neurologically handicapped (learning disabled) are strikingly similar. "The neurologically handicapped disorder may represent a subclinical form of cerebral palsy" (Paine, 1965), or as depicted recently as minimal cerebral palsy by Illingworth (1963). There is then considerable overlapping of symptomatology—incoordination, inadequate balance, motor planning and fine skilled performance; distractibility, impulsiveness and hyperactivity; strabismus; speech defects; short attention span; confused laterality (referring to ability to distinguish right from left) and mixed laterality (use of hand, foot, or eye); and learning disorders including poor/difficult conceptualization, memory and reading, writing, spelling, and arithmetic skills. It is because of these commonalities that both the cerebral palsied and learning disabled child will be thoroughly analyzed in the Handbook.

The book is organized to present, in successive chapters, the nature of cerebral palsy and learning disabilities, an in-depth look at the significant features of the nervous system as related to educational and habilitation problems, methods of evaluating and managing these problems and practical suggestions for remediation, training and treatment.

It is the wish of the author that the information and guidance she has provided will lighten the load of those dedicated persons who work in one of life's most rewarding vineyards: educating and training the handicapped. "Clearly, if we wish to make human life something more worthwhile than it now seems to be for many people, we must attempt to comprehend the incredible possibilities for development that are present in every child's brain" (Russell, 1959[2]).

Nancy C. Marks

---

[2]References for *Preface* are listed at the end of Chapter 1.

ACKNOWLEDGMENTS

I am indebted to the following individuals whose cooperation and assistance in preparing this book have been unfailing: to Dr. Homer Paschall, Chief of Orthopedic Surgery, Veteran's Administration Hospital, Gainesville, Florida, without whose help and encouragemnet this book would not have been possible; to Miss Anna Deanne Scott, Professor of Occupational Therapy, Boston University, Boston, Massachusetts, for her personal help and guidance throughout the preparation of this book and for her invaluable editorial suggestions; and to Dr. Alice C. Jantzen, Professor and Chairman, Occupational Therapy Department, Shands Teaching Hospital and Clinics, University of Florida, Gainesville, who provided inspiration during my education and thereafter.

I would also like to express my gratitude to Dr. Jorge A. Ferrer, Department of Opthalmology, Shands Teaching Hospital and Clinics, University of Florida, Gainesville, for his instructive guidance in preparing the chapters dealing with visual processes and disorders; to the authors, editors, and publishers who granted permission to use portions of their publications; and to the inter-library loan librarians of both the University of Florida and the University of South Alabama for much valuable assistance.

Finally, and especially, to my husband, Dr. Thomas C. Marks, Jr., whose support, encouragement and assistance have been unflagging.

N.C.M.

CONTENTS

Page

Foreword—H. A. Paschall v

Preface vii

Acknowledgments ix

Chapter

One   Cerebral Palsy 3

Two   The Nervous System 13

Three   Learning: Mechanisms and Disorders 42

Four   Orthopedic Management in Cerebral Palsy 88

Five   Speech and Language Disorders 130

Six   Vision and Its Defects 176

Seven   Visual Impairment and the Learning Environment ... 200

Eight   Pharmacological Approach to Management 229

Nine   Systems of Therapy 246

Ten   Special Adaptations and Equipment 279

Appendix A

Task Level Evaluation 340

Appendix B

Swallowing Patterns for Droolers 360

Appendix C

Sources of Material for Visually Impaired 364

Appendix D

Hand Utilization Techniques for the
Cerebral Palsied Child 374

References 381

Author Index 383

Subject Index 388

Cerebral Palsied and Learning Disabled Children

Chapter One

CEREBRAL PALSY

INTRODUCTION

THE TERM CEREBRAL PALSY IS USED to note any functional deviation, weakness or incoordination, of the *motor* (musculature) system. It is the result of damage to the motor strip of the brain before, at or immediately after birth. Although cerebral palsy may appear to be progressive because of increased deformity resulting from disuse of muscles, muscle spasm, or contractures, it is non-progressive in nature. Once it has occurred, the damage to the brain is circumscribed and stationary. Difficulty in controlling certain muscles is the one common aspect all children with C.P. share. Cerebral palsy is an intricate concept because it involves damage of one or more parts of the brain and is therefore a central nervous system deficit. Since the brain is the center not only of muscular control but also of intelligence, behavior, personality, and many other functions, defects in the motor system are often combined with lesions in other parts of the brain. Mental (intellectual, emotional), perceptual (visual, auditory, association) and sensory (hearing, seeing, feeling) disturbances can co-exist. A diagrammatic view of cerebral palsy (See Fig. 1) may help to clarify this point. The diagram indicates that the C.P. who is primarily *motor* handicapped can also, but not necessarily, be afflicted with *one or more* of the associated disturbances. In conclusion, we may say that the motor involvement is the *principle* disorder which separates the C.P. from the "neurologically impaired (NI)" child. The disorders such as epilepsy or perceptual dysfunction which

3

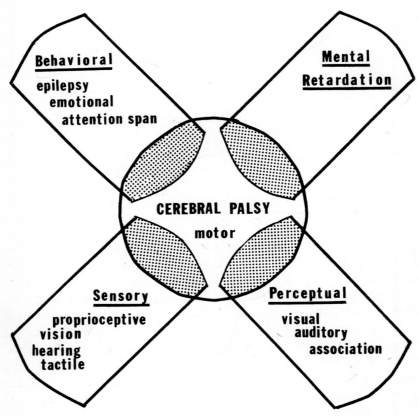

Figure 1. Cerebral Palsy: A diagrammatic representation.

may be present are associated disorders which may as well be found in the neurologically impaired and mentally retarded. The point, however, is that the disorders of movement and posture are the distinguishing factors which justify calling a child "cerebral palsied."

INCIDENCE

A study by Levin, Brightman, and Burtt (1949) reveals an incidence of 5.9 percent per 1000 live births and an actual prevalence of 152 per 100,000 population. Phelps (1950), in reporting the most frequently cited study, indicated that from 6 to 7 children per 100,000 population are born with cerebral palsy each year.

United Cerebral Palsy Association estimates (and Dr. Phelp's figures are not too far removed from this figure) that in the general population an average of about one person below age of 18 is cerebral palsied in every thousand. In a city of 80,000 people there would then be some 80 C.P. children who would need care. Of these, 8 cases (10%) would be so severe that they could not be helped; 8 cases (10%) would be so mildly handicapped they would not require definitive treatment; 64 cases (80%) remain to be helped—they could be restored to some degree of a productive, happy life. It is important for the educator to note, however, that those 10 percent mildly handicapped who may not require *medical treatment per se* could very conceivably be those shadow children who have been variously labeled minimally brain damaged, perceptually handicapped, learning disabled or what-have-you.

Cerebral palsy emerges more distinctly than ever as the foremost crippling agent in the younger age group (Towbin, 1960). This phenomenon should be of increasing interest to the teacher as more and more of these children will become members of the school population. Ironically, this event is a result of improved medical techniques which give life to children who would otherwise possibly have been stillborn. "Although many infants now live through the catastrophic events of the perinatal stage, the prevalence of severe multiple handicaps among them has increased" (Vernon, 1967). Additionally, improved habilitation techniques render a more *normal* life for many of these children who may have otherwise been relegated to an institutionalized or home-bound life. Social advances such as better sanitation, rising material standards of living and improved health education are also factors which encourage the survival of brain damaged children.

ETIOLOGY

Since many different disorders are included under cerebral palsy, there are a diversified number of causes. For purposes of clarity, the factors causing cerebral palsy are generally divided into three principal groups: *prenatal*, those causative factors from time of conception to onset of labor; *perinatal*, from onset of labor to birth; and *postnatal*, after time of birth of child. Each group has several subdivisions of specific causes, however, only the more important factors in each group will be presented.

The *prenatal* group represents cases in which damage to the brain is incurred at some time between conception and the beginning of labor. There is included in this category:

—Congenital factors, or those acquired in utero—rubella[1] or other maternal infections such as mumps, measles (rubeola), influenza.

—Rh blood factor, Kernicterus[2] or jaundice due to Rh blood incompatibility.

—Metabolic disturbances (i.e. diabetes) in the mother.

—Anoxia (oxygen deprivation) due to cord anomalies or maternal anoxia.

—Prematurity. There is general agreement that approximately 33 per cent of all patients with C.P. are prematurely born making this the most common prenatal cause. Prematurity itself may not be the principal cause because such other factors listed above as metabolic disturbances in the mother may lead to a premature birth.

[1]See discussion in Chapter 5 under hearing characteristics and post-rubella children. Perlstein (1952a, 1952b) observed that spasticity is closely related to a history of maternal rubella as well as a history of prematurity, birth trauma and toxemia of pregnancy.

[2]Kernicterus is a pathological condition. Its main cause is erythroblastosis fetalis which is a hemolytic disease of the newborn. Hemolytic disease of the newborn is a condition characterized by jaundice, anemia, enlargement of the liver, spleen and heart. Among the substances in the blood is a group called the "Rh factor" or "Rh antigen." Eighty-five percent of the U. S. population (Lassman, 1951) have Rh positive blood. When Rh+ red blood cells are introduced into the circulation of a person who is Rh—, antibodies are produced to destroy the red blood cells which are incompatible with the RH— blood. If a mother is Rh— and her husband Rh+, the offspring may be Rh+. While the Rh+ fetus is developing, the mother produces antibodies which destroy or damage the fetal red blood cells (hemolysis). This Rh incompatibility is the chief cause of hemolytic disease of the newborn. When the child is born, some of his blood cells are called erythroblasis giving the condition its name (erythroblastosis). The child may subsequently develop anemia and jaundice. It is when the jaundice affects the brain that the condition becomes known as *kernicterus.* One of the major causes of athetosis is kernicterus. The tetrad of symptoms (Perlstein, 1961) in kernicterus consists of 1) athetosis (the most common symptom), 2) difficulty in vertical gaze, 3) enamel dysplaseas of the deciduous teeth, and 4) auditory loss or imperception which occurs in nearly one-half of the patients with kernicterus and may take the form of hearing loss or of an impressive auditory aphasia.

The *perinatal* group are the result of:
—Maternal and fetal anoxia during birth and
—Mechanical injury to the fetal brain and other intercranial damage incurred during delivery.

Postnatal cases are associated with the following causes affecting the brain during early infancy:
—Trauma to head,
—Infections - meningitis, encephalitis,
—Vascular - hemorrhage.

It is important to observe that interference with oxygenation of the brain is a common etiological denominator in cerebral palsy, and plays an important etiological role when considering the C.P. child's total handicap. That is, the nervous system may suffer from lack of oxygen during the prenatal, natal and/or postnatal periods. For instance, during the prenatal period, the young nervous system may suffer oxygen lack due to a variety of maternal illnesses or during the natal period, there may be interference with fetal and/or the mother's respiration or during the actual delivery from mechanical obstruction. "A deficit [of oxygen] for as little as 90 seconds can result in lasting and irreversible consequences" (Montagu, 1962). The structures in the brain which are most sensitive to damage due to anoxia are those which make up the diencephalon—the thalamus and hypothalamus. The thalamus is the major relay station for the transmission of all sensations (except smell). It is here that information is crudely analyzed before being relayed to appropriate cortical areas. The areas with the richest blood supply are most vulnerable to anoxia as blood is the transmitter of oxygen. These areas are the occipital (visual) and precentral (motor) areas of the brain. Thus, gray matter is more susceptible to and particularly dependent upon, oxygen want than white matter. So, the more superficial layers of the cerebral cortex (the gray matter which is the center for higher thought processes) require more oygen than the deep cortical areas. These factors will become clearer after reading Chapter Two dealing with the nervous system.

In general, the fact that all levels of the brain, or that all cells in a given affected area, are not damaged equally is a basis for a hopeful outlook for many cases of cerebral palsy.

DIAGNOSIS AND CLASSIFICATION

Traditionally, the physician has been responsible for diagnosis of cerebral palsy. Classification in C.P. was derived from observable *surface* symptoms and their severity. Criterion for classification is made on *location* and *type* of neuromuscular involvement.

When discussing diagnosis with respect to *location* the following terms are used:

Monoplegia	One extremity, either arm or leg, perhaps hand or foot involved.
Hemiplegia	One side of the body involved with usually the arm and leg on that side being weak and spastic.
Paraplegia	Both legs involved—practically always of the spastic or rigid type.
Triplegia	Involves three extremities, both legs and one arm or both arms and one leg—usually spastic type.
Quadriplegia	Involvement in all four extremities. When the involvement is most severe in the legs, spasticity will predominate; when the most severe involvement is in the arms, they will usually be dyskinetic, including athetoids.

When discussing diagnosis with respect to the *types* of neuromuscular involvement, the classification system most generally used in the United States is the following described by Phelps (1950).

1. Spasticity
2. Flaccid paralysis
3. Athetosis
4. Ataxia
5. Rigidity
6. Tremors
7. Mixed

This system is based upon the predominant clinical manifestations of those observable *surface* symptoms previously mentioned.

1. Spasticity

Spasticity is the result of lesions in Area 6 or combined lesions of Area 4 and 6 of the cerebral cortex, *or* lesions somewhere along the descending fibers of the pyramidal tract.

Area 6 suppresses certain impulses, contractions or stimulations originating in the pyramidal system. When a portion of Area 6 is damaged, suppression does not occur, and the muscles remain in a state of spasticity or tension. In the normal muscular system, the suppressors allow one muscle group to relax when opposing muscles contract, resulting in smooth movement. However, in spasticity, this balance is absent resulting in increased muscle tone, exaggerated reflexes and the presence of a stretch reflex. Muscles which are unable to relax may shorten and flexion deformities called contractures may develop. The child is able to voluntarily move the involved muscles but the pull of spastic muscles causes the movement to be slow and inaccurately performed. In a recent survey, Bowley *et al.* (1969) states that about 75 percent of C.P.'s show spasticity.

2. Flaccid Paralysis

Flaccid paralysis results from lesions in Area 4 of the cerebral cortex or along descending fibers of the pyramidal tract. The chief symptom of flaccidity is weakness as inhibition is the strongest remaining influence on muscle tone. A lesion of Area 4 exclusive of Area 6 is, however, a very rare occurrence.

3. Athetosis

Athetosis results from a lesion in the extrapyramidal system—specifically, the globus pallidus of the basal ganglia. The extrapyramidal system exerts a suppressing, restraining effect on the muscular system and provides a system of coordinated muscle control and automatic movement patterns as a result of influences from the basal ganglia.

These children are characterized by involuntary muscular activity. They walk in a stumbling manner. Their movements are not coordinated or rhythmical but instead consist of writhing, twisting series of movements. They do not follow any sequence. The athetoid is able to pick up an object or put his hand to his mouth but in doing so he goes through these uncontrollable, involuntary movements. These same movements can be noted in the facial musculature in many of these children resulting in facial grimaces which, of course, are uncontrollable. Such facial grimaces are frequently misinterpreted—teachers, parents and others at times may feel that the child is being *defiant,* not taking his work seriously, etc. The movements cease when the child is asleep. As the child makes a conscious effort to perform, the athetoid movements intensify. Emotionality increase these movements also. For instance, when the child becomes excited and anxious concerning a new task introduced in the classroom these movements are often intensified.

Hearing defects are fairly common in this group. Therefore, a subclassification of *deaf athetosis* will be found in much of the literature dealing with the athetoid. This particular problem has important implications for the teacher. This problem, the hearing defect, is often associated with Rh incompatibility. There is often loss of high pitch or high frequency tones with essentially normal hearing in the lower pitch ranges giving the parent and casual observer the impression that the child's hearing is normal. This child often learns to become a lip reader, especially for consonant sounds. Besides having athetosis and hearing loss, these children have limitations of vertical eye motions, either upward or downward, or both, with normal lateral eye motions.

4. Ataxia

Ataxia is a result of a lesion in the cerebellum which normally controls balance and muscle coordination. The ataxic suffers incoordination due to disturbance of kinesthetic awareness of body and/or balance sense. Musculature is often hypotonic. Frequently there is a deficit in normal sterognosis and depth perception. The ataxic child is unsteady in his movements. Nystagmus (jerky movements of the eye) is common.

5. Rigidity

The exact location of the lesion is not known. Diffuse lesions of the brain may produce rigidity. Rigidity is the result of inadequate phase relationship (resistance) between excitation and inhibition of antagonistic muscles. Antagonists are those muscles which act in opposition to each other. Flexors (muscles which bend a limb) are then antagonistic to extensors (muscles which straighten a limb).

Rigidity is a continuous resistance to movement and has been compared to bending a lead pipe. The resistance is similar to spasticity but without a stretch reflex. The main characteristics of rigidity are hypertonicity and slow movements but with no stretch reflex and no involuntary motion.

6. Tremor

Tremor is the result of a lesion in the basal ganglia. There is involuntary, rhythmic, reciprocal movement (trembling or shaking motion). Intention tremor occurs when the child volitionally or intentionally begins a movement, and is absent when muscles are at rest. Nonintention tremor occurs when the extremity is at rest but ceases when the child makes a movement volitionally.

7. Mixed

There is a mixture of two or more of the above types. The most common mixed type is spastic and athetoid.

The following two examples illustrate how the classification system of location and type criterion is implemented in diagnosing C.P. A child may have a diagnosis such as mild spastic hemiplegia. This child would be motorically involved in either both the right arm and leg or the left arm and leg. The involvement would be spastic in nature with little limitation of activity. Or, a child may have a diagnosis such as moderate quadriplegia with mixed spastic and athetoid involvement. This child would be moderately involved in all four extremities so that independent functioning is significantly limited.

REFERENCES

Bowley, Agatha, and Gardner, Leslie: *The Young Handicapped Child,* 2nd ed. London, Livingstone, 1969.

Illingsworth, R. S.: Minimal cerebral dysfunction. In Box, M., and Mackeith, R. (Eds.): *Clinics in Developmental Medicine,* No. 10. Spastics International Medical Publications in Association with William Heinemann Medical Books, Ltd., Lavenham, England, Lavenham Press, 1963, p. 27.

Lassman, F. M.: A clinical investigation of some hearing deficiencies and possible etiological factors in a group of cerebral palsied individuals. *Speech Monog, 18:*130-131, 1951.

Levin, M. L., Brightman, T. J., and Burtt, E. J.: The problem of cerebral palsy. *NY State J Med, 49:*2793-2799, 1949.

Montagu, M. F. A.: *Prenatal Influences.* Springfield, Thomas, 1962.

Paine, R. S.: Organic neurological factors related to learning disorders. In Hellmuth, J., (Ed.): *Learning Disorders.* Seattle, Special Child Publications, 1965, vol. 1.

Perlstein, Meyer A.: Infantile cerebral palsy: Classification and clinical correlations. *JAMA, 149*:30-34, 1952a.

Perlstein, Meyer, A., and Barnett, H. E.: Nature and recognition of cerebral palsy in infancy. *JAMA, 148*:1389-1397, 1952b.

Perlstein, Meyer A.: The clinical syndrome of kernicterus. In Swinyard, Chester A. (Ed.): *Kernicterus in Cerebral Palsy.* Springfield, Thomas, 1961.

Phelps, W. M.: The Cerebral Palsies. In Mitchell-Nelson (Ed.): *Textbook of Pediatrics.* New York, Saunders, 1950, 5th ed., p. 1360.

Russell, W. Ritchie: *Brain: Memory: Learning.* Oxford, Clarendon Press, 1959.

Towbin, A.: *The Pathology of Cerebral Palsy.* Springfield, Thomas, 1960.

Vernon, M.: Prematurity and deafness: The magnitude and nature of the problem among deaf children. *Except Child, 34*:289-295, 1967.

Chapter Two

THE NERVOUS SYSTEM

Introduction

THIS CHAPTER IS DESIGNED To establish a basic foundation in neuroanatomy (or the *structure* of the nervous system) and neurophysiology (or the *function* of the nervous system). With such an understanding, the teacher and therapist will have established a base upon which to build a viable educational and treatment program for the CN/NI child. In similar fashion, a knowledge of the structure and function of the fuel system and ignition system of a car should enable one to better understand what makes a car run or function. Moreover, if we understand the mechanics involved that operate the engine under normal conditions, it follows that we should then be better equipped to repair (remediate and treat) a damaged engine. The following then is a look at the essentials of the structure and function of the human nervous system of most concern in understanding cerebral palsy.

BASIC NEURAL PROCESSES

An understanding of the basic parts of a system and how they function will permit a more adequate comprehension of how the total system functions. The smallest functioning part of the nervous system is the nerve cell, or *neuron*—the fundamental structure of the entire human body. Ten to 14 billion of these microscopic cells form the neural network that act to coordinate, integrate and run all the other systems of the body. The brain has the giant's share of these cells or 90 percent.

The principal function of a neuron is, first to receive stimuli; second, to conduct or transmit these stumli or impulses; and third, to pass this information to other parts in the organism. The definition of a neuron is "a nerve cell body and all its processes." A neuron then consists of one cell body and branches or processes extending for varying distances. The neurons have three parts or, a neuron = dendrite + cell body + axon (Fig. 2). The *cell body* gives the entire unit its life. The *dendrites* are the *tenacles* or feelers—they receive information (electrochemical impulses) from thousands of other neurons and conduct these impulses toward (afferent) the cell body. The *axon* is a single fiber extending from the cell body where all outgoing impulses originate. The axon conducts impulses away from (efferent) the cell body. Just as importantly, however, is the fact that an impulse may not be passed to other neurons along the line. The network of neurons keeps the various parts of the organism in touch with each other and functioning in a coordinated manner permitting appropriate responses to changes in both the internal and external environment. In order for most neurons to be able to discharge an impulse, it depends on incoming signals. However, some neurons can spontaneously fire. The incoming impulses in this instance serve only to slow down or speed up the *self-imposed* firing.

The complex nervous system of man involves chains of these cells arranged so that the end of the process of one cell comes into close relation to the dendrite of another. This is the "network of neurons" referred to previously. A change (stimulus) in the

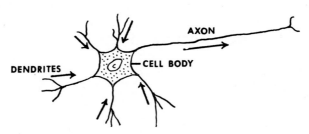

Figure 2. A Neuron = cell body + axon + dendrite.

environment starts a nerve impulse in the protoplasm of one cell in the chain; the impulse travels along the processes (axon) of the cell which initiated it and the impulse passes to the next cell in the chain. Each link in the chain, the nerve cell with its processes, is the neuron.

A closer analysis of this inter-communication system—getting signals from one cell to another—is in order. The vital link in the network is the *synapse*. These are miniscule connections where the axon coming from one neuron is fused or soldered to the dendrites of another neuron. Located at this juncture, the synapse, is a fluid containing ions. These ions are small electrically-charged particles. A pulse travels only to the synapse. It is at this point that the pulse creates an electrical phenomena which releases a chemical. This chemical release permits an impulse to be transmitted on to the dendrite of the next neuron. Sometimes the electrochemical reaction at the synapse does not let the impulse through. The impulse is inhibited from passing on to the dendrite of the next neuron. This inhibition serves, among other things, as a filter. It screens out unnecessary stimuli thus saving the brain from being engulfed with insignificant information. Once an impulse begins traveling on the *wires*, it continues uninterrupted until it reaches the synapse. It is at this point that message changes take place. This may be referred to as the *all-or-none* principle.

If this neuronal network does indeed pervade the entire body (and it does), why is it that damage to the peripheral body parts does not, as a rule, cause permanent neuromuscular damage while damage to nerve cells in the CNS, can, and usually does, cause irreparable damage? The answer lies in the manner in which the neurons are protected against harm. The protection is in the form of an insulated covering called *myelin*. Nerve sheaths (Schwann cell sheath or *neurilemma* sheath) secretes this myelin. Now, here is the partial answer to our question posed above: the neurilemma sheath is found only outside of the CNS or found only in the PNS (peripheral nervous system). It is this sheath that is, at least in part, responsible for nerve regeneration. Therefore, because the neurilemma sheath is not found inside the CNS, there cannot be *regeneration* of damaged neurons. Although the

CNS neurons are myelinated or unmyelinated, the sheaths originate not from Schwann cells but from another kind of nervous
tissue called glial cells. These cells either do not have the innate
ability to regenerate or are not permitted to do so through some
factor unknown to neuroscientists at the moment. Glial cells do
offer structural support to CNS neurons and they *feed* these
neurons. Other body cells receive nourishment from the blood
vessels—but, not so the neurons.

Before leaving this concept of regeneration, it must be noted
that if the cell body is destroyed, the entire neuron ceases operation
because the cell's *life line* is cut off. Although this would, at first
blush, discourage the teacher and therapist's efforts, it is not the
case for as we shall see in another section, the nervous system is
plastic and pliable. Changes and learning can take place as we
will come to see. It is capable of *relearning* despite damage. The
answer to how the nervous system learns will be forthcoming in
the chapter dealing with mechanisms and disorders of learning.

Functionally, neurons are divided into three main groups:
sensory, motor, and interneurons.

(1) Sensory neurons are of two types. First are those which pick
up impulses from sensory nerve endings and sense organs (receptors) and carry them to the central nervous system. These afferent
neurons constitute a characteristic element of the spinal and
cranial nerves. Second are those afferent neurons within the spinal
cord and brain which relay incoming impulses from lower to
higher centers of the central nervous system.

(2) Motor neurons are of two types. First are the ones that conduct impulses from higher to lower centers within the nervous
system. Second, are those that relay the outgoing impulses from
the CNS over cranial and spinal nerves to muscles or glands (both
of which are effectors or motor neurons). These respond by
appropriate activity—the hand grasps a pencil and the heart pumps
blood. Motor neurons like sensory neurons are found both in the
central and peripheral nervous system. The cell bodies, like that
of the sensory neurons, are always housed either in the spinal cord
or in the skull. The processes are either within the CNS or travel
outside where they constitute the PNS. Axons are grouped to-

gether in common connective tissue outside of the central nervous system where they are called nerves.

(3) *Interneurons* (internuncial). These serve as connections or

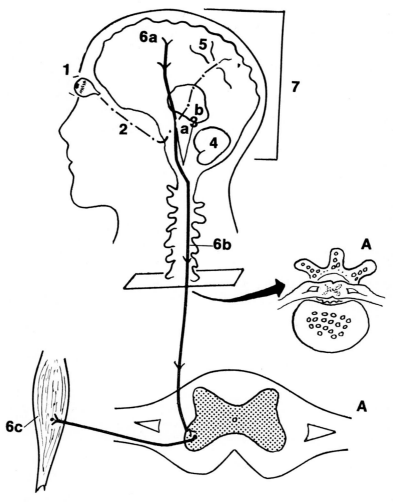

Figure 3. Important Components of Behavior.

1) Receptor, 2) Sensory Nerve, 3) Internuncial process—a. brain stem, reticular formation, b. thalamus, 4) Cerebellum, 5) Sensory strip or area, 6) Efferent mechanism—a. motor strip, b. efferent nerve, c. effector, 7) Cerebrum.

associations between sensory and motor neurons. Both afferent and efferent processes as well as the cell body are located entirely within the central nervous system. The interneurons are of vital importance for they modify messages coming in from the sensory receptors and also judge what messages should be passed on. They filter out unnecessary information.

Discussion thus far has concerned the basic neural processes or the microscopic structures in the nervous system but how do these structures actually operate to produce a response and promote learning? When a child sees something he wants such as a cookie, his response can take one of several forms. He may reach out and grasp a cookie, he may think better of sneaking one and decide he'd better ask permission first; or he may decide to forget it and go about his business. Or, when the child is asked to copy words from the blackboard, he must pick up his pencil, read the words, and write them on his paper. If pricked by a pin on a finger, the hand will quickly withdraw. The mechanism(s) making these and enumerable other behaviors or responses possible may be analyzed through several stages—actually *seven important components of behavior* or responses. Make reference to Figure 3 as you read the following section:

The child must (1) receive information from the environment (such as the sight and smell of the cookie). In this particular diagram, the primary source of stimuli is the visual (exteroceptor). The reception of stimuli is, at any rate, the function of sensing devices called receptors.[3]

[3]There are 3 types of receptors, each being sensitive to a particular kind of stimuli: (a) *Exteroceptors* are divided into two groups: i. the special exteroceptors— taste, hearing, seeing, smelling; and ii. the skin exteroceptors—heat, touch, cold, pain, pressure. The stimulation comes from the external environment; (b) *Proprioceptors* which may also be divided into two groups: i. Those which initially send impulses to the cerebellum such as neuromuscular spindle, neurotendinous spindle (golgi tendon organ), and the vestibular receptors of the inner ear which are sometimes referred to as unconscious (Moore, 1969) proprioceptors; and ii. those receptors which reach the cortex (conscious proprioceptors) such as deep muscle pressure, pain, ligament and vibratory receptors, joint capsules. Both types function by signaling the CNS about balance, posture, muscle movement and tone. The proprioceptors are those sensory end organs which are stimulated by "action of the body itself" (Sherrington, 1907) and; (c) *Interoceptors* which are found in the internal organs of the body. They are sensitive to such sensations as pain, hunger, thirst and blood pressure (Table I). In

The function of the receptors and their afferent nerves (sensory pathways[4]) is to inform the CNS of the stimulating event in the internal and/or external environment. Sensory information is thereby received. These receptors biologically translate or transduce these stimuli (the stimuli is a type of energy such as touch, stretch, pain) into electrical signals called *nerve impulses* which the nervous system ultimately uses as information. The nerve impulses are then (2) conducted by sensory neural pathways (axons of the afferent neuron or nerves) or the impulses may be passed by interneurons to motoneurons (See Fig. 13 in Chapter 4 *Orthopedic Management in Cerebral Palsy*). Returning to Fig. 3, those impulses going to the higher CNS areas do so via (3a) the reticular activating system (3a), thalamus and, (4) cerebellum and to (5) primary and secondary receptive portions of the cerebral cortex[5] (7). The electrical signals are transmitted from the thalamus, reticular formation and cerebellum to the primary areas, then to parasensory or secondary (association) areas which surround each primary receptive area. It is here that our sensations derive meaning (7). The sensations are studied, analyzed and finally action plans are formulated. Simply speaking, the process thus far looks like this: Impulse (1) to sensation (2) to perception (7). Once an impulse has acquired a meaning, the *perceptions* are in some yet unknown manner related to past experiences (memories). Neuroscientists are of the general opinion that the hippocampus (located above the brain stem), thalamus and the amygdala are all somehow concerned with infixing memories. During this whole process, which occurs in a few thousandths of a second, the reticular activaing system continues to play its role by blocking out unnecessary stimuli thus permitting the cortex to perform its analysis.

The plans or commands, thusly formulated, are passed on to the motor strip (6a) which transforms these commands into vol-

[4]Sensory pathways such as the dorsal column-medial lemniscal pathway system which convey tactile discrimination, two-point discrimination, stereognosis, deep touch or pressure, awareness of passive movements, position sense, vibratory sense and weight perception.

[5]The primary and secondary cortical areas will be fully discussed in this chapter.

the chapter dealing with therapeutic systems, we will see that most of the systems attempt to influence, by various techniques, the exteroceptors and the proprioceptors.

untary action. The motor areas of the CNS (Areas 4, 6, 8, Fig. 5) give rise to efferent nerves. It is through these efferent pathways (6b) that electrical signals are carried to the muscles or effectors[6] (6c) in various parts of our body causing them to respond. In Figure 3 the electrical signals are sent to the flexor and extensor muscles of the arm causing them to contract and relax respectively so that the hand can reach for the cookie. Relate this to Figure 13 in Chapter 4, *Orthopedic Management and Cerebral Palsy.*

The voluntary action (behavior) is coordinated by the cere-

TABLE I

RECEPTORS

EXTEROCEPTIVE	PROPRIOCEPTIVE	INTEROCEPTIVE
General	*Unconscious*	
Pain	Neuromuscular spindle a. Nuclear bag fiber	Pain (difuse or nonspecific)
Temperature	b. Nuclear chain fiber	Stretch or cantraction to an abnormal degree
Light touch, light pressure, and crude tactile sense	Neurotendinous spindle Vestibular (labyrinth)	Olfaction[1] Gustatory[1]
Special	*Conscious*	
Vision	Pressure superficial and deep[2]	
Hearing	Vestibular (labyrinth)[2]	
Olfaction[1]	Joint, ligament, fascia, periosteum[2]	
Gustatory[1]	Vibratory Tactile discrimination[3] a. Deep pressure b. Spatial localization c. Perception of size, shape, texture d. Skin drawing and 2-point tactile	

[1]Can be considered as either an exteroceptive or interoceptive type of receptor, according to different authors.

[2]Kinesthetic sense: receptors which let one know where their body is in space. Also called position sense. Consists of those receptors starred and probably others.

[3]Also called stereognosis.

Reprinted with permission from: Moore, Josephine: Structure and Function of the Nervous System. In *Expanding Dimensions in Rehabilitation.* Zamir, L. J. (Ed.) Springfield, Thomas, 1969.

[6]The effectors are of three types: (a) Skeletal muscles such as the muscles in the arms, legs and trunk which are under voluntary control; (b) Smooth muscles in the viscera, glands and walls of blood vessels which are not usually under voluntary control; and (c) Cardiac muscle and glands.

bellum (4) which receives impulses from all the sensory modalities. Likewise, it sends out impulses throughout the brain stem and midbrain to *regulate* descending impulses.

There is another process which plays a most important role in the regulation of behavior. This process is called *feedback* to the CNS, whereby the CNS is informed as to whether the response has actually taken place and what the outcome of that response was. If the CNS is informed that the response has not taken place, then it must issue new orders to the muscles. *Feedback* plays an important role, then, in determining whether behavior should be terminated or continued. There are many such feedback systems operating such as auditory, visual and the gamma loop (motor) feedback system.

To sum up, the child is said to relate to his external surroundings through the following behaviors. (1) *Reflex response* in which there is a definite sensory input and a rather simple yet specific output or response. The child is pinched, he *automatically* withdraws; he smells something peculiar, his nose wrinkles; a light is turned on in a darkened room, his eyes (pupils) constrict. The response is predictable. Reflex activity is involuntary. The child may or may not be aware (conscious) of the activity. The responses are purposeful and adaptive. They are generally necessary then for the individual's protection and well-being. (2) *Voluntary response*—there is input but it is not necessarily categorical or specific. The responses are willed and complex such as playing with an erector set. (3) *Perception*—here there certainly is input, albeit varied, but there may or may not be any observable output or response. We can listen to a classroom lecture or a symphony, or look at a beautiful sunset without any overt response.

Though this view of the response/behavior organization is not complete, it is hoped that Figure 3 and the discussion of that figure will permit deeper insight into this truly complex system. As therapists and educators, it is not our responsibility to be fully knowledgeable of the intricacies but we need to know the basics in order to add legitimacy and give substantial reasons to our training-teaching techniques so that we are not "working in the dark." In short, to help us answer the *whys* of *what* and *how* we work in the classroom and clinic.

GENERAL STRUCTURE OF CENTRAL NERVOUS SYSTEM

Again, some acquaintance with the structural organization of the nervous system is necessary for an understanding of the nervous system's functions. This section will serve to identify and locate the structures to which later reference will be made. The nervous system is divided into a central (CNS) and a peripheral (PNS) portion. The *central nervous system* (CNS) consists of the *brain* and the *spinal cord* (Fig. 4).

The brain is divided into 3 regions: the cerebrum, the brain stem, and the cerebellum.

The Cerebrum consists of two cerebral hemispheres. They

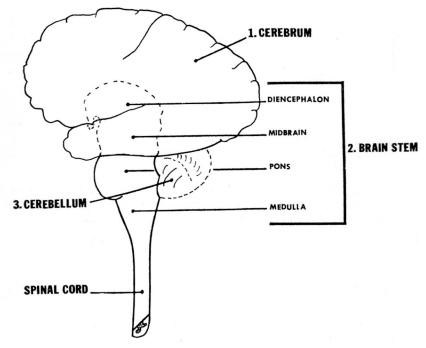

Figure 4. The Central Nervous System.
    A. Brain
        1. Cerebrum (4 lobes)
        2. Brain Stem
        3. Cerebellum
    B. Spinal Cord

are incompletely separated by a fissure and joined together at the bottom of this fissure by the corpus callosum. On the outer surface of the hemisphere lies a layer of gray matter which constitutes the cortex which is 80 percent of the volume of the brain. The cerebral cortex is also the region where sensations receive their final, refined examination and where responses are decided and initiated (Fig. 5, *The Cerebral Cortex: Areas of Cortical Function*). A layer of cerebral cortex 1.3 to 4.5 mm thick covers the surface of the cerebrum. It is estimated to contain an electrochemical network of some ten billion nerve cells. There are six layers in all. This crumpled gray cover is the seat of man's higher faculties: language, abstract thinking, foresight. Beneath the gray matter of the cerebrum lies the white matter. This consists of medullated nerve fibers as well as neuroglia. Three types of myelinated nerve make up the center of the cerebral hemispheres: (i) transverse fibers interconnect the two hemispheres; (ii) projection fibers connect cerebral cortex with the lower portions of the brain such as the basal ganglia and brain stem and spinal cord, and finally; (iii) association fibers connect the various portions of the same cerebral hemispheres. Within the white matter, another gray matter section, the basal ganglia is located.

The Brain Stem consists of the following areas of the brain: Diencephalon, Midbrain, Pons and the Medulla. Found clustered about the brain stem is an automatic gland system necessary to maintain such bodily functions as eating, breathing, emotions, and sex. Some of these glands and suborgans are the thalamus, hypothalamus and hippocampus.

The Cerebellum is located below the posterior section of the cerebrum. It rests and is attached to the brain stem by three bands of connecting fibers. It is composed of two cerebellar hemispheres and a central portion called the vermis. Like the cerebrum, the cerebellum is also covered by a layer of gray matter, the cortex. The cerebellar cortex encloses a deeper mass of white matter. It is here that our responses are *monitored* and orders to correct performance are issued. It is interesting to note that, although the brain makes up only 2 percent of the total weight of the body, it receives 20 percent of the oxygen supply to the body.

We will now look at the structure of the second section of the

CNS, the *Spinal Cord*. The spinal cord is housed in the vertebral column or backbone. The gray matter (the nerve cell bodies of neurons) is centrally placed and surrounded by white matter (the nerve fibers or axons and dendrites). This is in contrast to the cerebral and cerebellar cortices where the gray matter composes the outer portions. From the cord pass 32 pairs of spinal nerves in five groups named according to the area of the vertebral column from which they emerge. The spinal nerves are part of the peripheral nervous system which will be discussed next.

STRUCTURE OF THE PERIPHERAL NERVOUS SYSTEM (PNS)

CRANIAL NERVES. There are twelve pairs of cranial nerves—motor, sensory, and mixed. The cranial nerves which have motor function arise or have their origin within the brain stem. Those with sensory function originate from groups of cells on trunks of nerves or in sense organs such as the eye or ear. The cranial nerves provide most of the sensory information upon which our nervous system acts and to which it reacts.

The cranial nerves are named according to the order in which they emerge from the brain, or numerically, and by names which imply their function or distribution. Table II indicates their designation, type and function.

SPINAL NERVES. As indicated previously, 31 pair of spinal nerves emerge from the spinal cord. These nerves pass between the bony vertebrae which surround the cord and then branch into smaller nerves, the peripheral nerves, which distribute fibers to various parts of the body.

With an understanding of the structure of the nervous system, attention will be focused now on the *functions* of these various structures.

FUNCTION OF THE CENTRAL NERVOUS SYSTEM

Brain

As previously mentioned, the brain is divided into the cerebrum, brain stem and cerebellum. The first division to be discussed is the cerebrum.

TABLE II
CRANIAL NERVES

Location	No.	Name	Sensory Function	Motor Function
Anterior base of brain	I	Olfactory	Smell	—
Midbrain	II	Optic	Sight	—
	III	Oculomotor	Sight	Muscle eye movement & accommodation
	IV	Trochlear	Sight	Muscle eye movement & accommodation
	V	Trigeminal	Pain, cold, heat, touch of eyes, teeth, face	Muscle of chewing
Pons	VI	Abducens	Sight	Muscle eye movement
	VII	Facial	Taste buds & muscles of facial expression	Muscle movement of face
	VIII	Acoustic	Hearing and equilibrium	—
Medulla	IX	Glossopharyngeal	Taste buds	Muscle of swallowing
	X	Vagus	Reflexes of respiration, hunger	Muscles of speech, swallowing
	XI	Spinal Accessory	Palate & neck muscle sense	Movement of palate and neck
	XII	Hypoglossal	Muscle sense of tongue	Tongue muscle movement

Cerebrum

For descriptive purposes, the hemisphere is divided into four lobes: the frontal lobe, the occipital lobe, the parietal lobe and the temporal lobe. Recently, however, a fifth lobe, the limbic, has been cited by some researchers. Divisions and classifications of the cortex have been attempted by many investigators. The most commonly employed system is that of Brodman who labeled individual areas within these lobes. The areas have been used as a reference base for the localization of functional and pathological processes. Some of the principal areas and their functions which should be of concern to educators will be discussed. Frequent reference to Figure 5 will be helpful as you read this portion.

Frontal Lobe (Area 4, 6, 8, 44, 45 and Association Areas)

Area 4—Motor Area (and more recently, 3, 1 and 2 have been added). This area is essential for the execution of voluntary willed muscle movement. Area 4 is the transmitter of the impulse along tracts called the pyramidal system. The purpose and intent of the movement originates in the cerebral cortex just anterior to this area. However, not all impulses arise from the motor cortex (Area 4). As researchers continue to study the brain, revision in our thinking must also continue to take place in accordance with the findings of these investigations. One such change is that it is now believed that less than half of the pyramidal tracts originate in Area 4 (the precentral gyrus). Other tracts (approximately 1/5) arise from Areas 3, 1, and 2 (the postcentral gyrus or sensory strip of the parietal lobe) and the remainder arise, according to Ruch et al. (1965), from still other parts of the cerebral cortex (i.e. temporal and occipital lobes).

After descending into the brain stem, the fibers cross or decussate to the opposite side at the medulla. Again, recent evidence indicates that most of the tracts stop at the pons where they synapse with other tracts. Pyramidal fibers are distributed to voluntary motor nuclei of cranial nerves, controlling, for instance, facial movement; and to motor cells of the spinal cord, controlling leg or arm movement. A series of internuncial elements distribute the impulses to the segments involved in coordinated motor activity. Damage to the motor cortex (Area 4) produces flaccid paralysis.

Area 6 was, in the past, known of as the *premotor* or cortical extrapyramidal system concerned with exerting an inhibitory, suppressing effect on voluntary muscle movement. This system (the extrapyramidal) includes all those descending tracts not part of the pyramidal system. It was in this area that gross muscular movements of the trunk and upper and lower extremities had their origin. This area was thought also to be concerned with the development of motor skills probably of a more complex nature than those represented in the motor area itself. The principal functions of the extrapyramidal system then were concerned with associative movement, postural adjustment, and autonomic (involuntary) integration. Thus, the extrapyramidal system was concerned more with the modulation and coordination of movements than with its initiation. It was believed to have an inhibitory or suppressing effect on muscular activity and to control the complex automatic acts like walking and making facial expressions. Some parts of this system do originate in Area 6; however, recent evidence indicates that the other lobes also contribute fibers to this system.

The extrapyramidal system is now known of as *coeps* (Cortically Originating Extra-Pyramidal System) (Ruch *et al.*, 1965) originating from Areas 4, 3, 1, 2 and 6 as well as other areas. How this is to affect the old concepts about the relationship between damage to the premotor cortex producing spasticity because the inhibitory affect is missing due to damage to Area 6, remains at this point an open question. However, the *coeps* is thought to wield influential powers over the diencephalon, basal ganglion and continues on down much as the pyramidal track possibly with more connections.

Area 8 is concerned with control of conjugate eye movements.

Association Areas

A brief comment concerning *association areas* in general is in order before specific comment is directed to the frontal association area. The association areas are connected with the sensory and motor areas by association fibers. They are of importance in the maintenance of higher mental activities in man. The association areas, according to Gardner (1966), are the most important part of the nervous system as regards mental and emotional processes.

The *frontal* association area has long been known as an area concerned with higher intellectual and psychic functions. It is believed that the frontal association area is essential for such processes as abstract thinking, foresight, mature judgment, and initiative. Studies with animals have indicated that removal of this area is followed by such signs as hyperactivity, inability to learn and difficulty with problems which demand a retention of facts for more than a few seconds such as remembering in which of two cups food has been placed. *Immediate* or *recent* memory is lost—abilities which the animal had as a result of previous learning and/or training are not lost. It is hypothesized that a habit pattern may be formed in the frontal lobes and then shifted elsewhere for long-term retention.

Broca's Area (44 and 45)

This area is the seat of *articulated speech* or motor, expressive speech. A lesion of this area in the dominant hemisphere causes expressive aphasia (motor aphasia). The child is unable to speak intelligibly although he has no paralysis of the lips, tongue or vocal cords. He knows what he intends to say, but cannot form and express words correctly. The words come out in a garbled manner. He has no difficulty understanding others and is able to recognize his own errors.

Parietal Lobe (Areas 3, 1, 2, 5, and 7) (stereognosis and association)

The cortex of the parietal lobe contains the sensory receptive area of the brain together with important association areas concerned with vision and language. The primary sensory cortex areas and their functions are: *Area 3*—pain and temperature; *Area 1*—light touch (two-point discrimination); *Area 2*—proprioception or awareness of direction of movement and position of body and body parts. The arrival of impulses at one of these receptive areas produces well-defined sensations of pain, temperature, touch, or movement, but nothing is conveyed except raw sensory data. Here, an object remains as a meaningless pattern of light; and touching of an object does not disclose any meaning such as shape, size, weight, or texture. To be fully comprehended, the arriving sensory messages must undergo analysis in the extensive cortical zone adjacent to the primary sensory area or the sensory *association area*—Areas 5 and 7. This area has the task of formulating sensory stimuli into object images and of comprehending their meaning. This—the process of *knowing* or gnosis— entails a comparison or association of present sensory data with past experience. Thus, the recognition of objects, a type of *knowing*, is a combination of gnostic sensations of touch, two-point recognition, touch localization and position and joint sense. A child is able to appreciate the form, shape and texture of objects. For instance, he comes to know the *form* of his own body—has a body image, so to speak—by *blending* all the sensory impulses coming to the parietal lobes. Stereognosis is the ability to recognize form and shape. The loss of this sensory ability is called astereognosis.[7]

The disturbances in symbolic thinking which occur if there is damage to this portion of the brain are discussed in Chapter 3, *Learning: Mechanisms and Disorders*. They are of prime significance to the teacher as the parietal lobe has been implicated as an important area of the brain controlling reading ability and related skills such as writing. Disorders of body awareness are also related to parietal lobe defects. In conclusion, we find that parietal lobe damage which results in sensory and perceptual dysfunction is somewhat common in the CP/NI particularly due to the proximity of this lobe to the motor cortex. This entire matter will be presented in the chapter on special learning difficulties as mentioned previously. It is the intent of that chapter to deal with these problems as well as additional learning difficulties, in practical, usable terms answering questions of an educational nature—how

---

[7]Astereognosis is the term applied to the inability to recognize the shape of objects by touch. Poor touch discrimination and defective sensory adaptation may be present in the CP/NI so that the child has difficulty not only discriminating shape but also may show this defect in his inability to discriminate texture, weight, and size. Also present may be the inability to localize touch stimuli (tactile discrimination) whereby the youngster is unable to recognize two stimuli when simultaneously applied when the stimuli are separated by only a small distance.

teachers and therapists may recognize, diagnose, and finally, remediate these difficulties.

Temporal Lobe (Areas 41, 42, 21 and 22 (Association area)

The temporal lobe cortex is mainly concerned with the reception of auditory, vestibular (balance), and olfactory impulses. Also, important word, sound and visual memory patterns are *stored* in this area. Or, more specifically, in Area 41, the auditory receptive center and Area 42, the associative auditory receptive center. Areas 41 and 42 are referred to as the primary hearing areas. Area 41 is the primary receptive area for hearing. Eventually the fibers from the 8th cranial nerve, the auditory nerve, are relayed to this area. Each lobe receives impulses from both ears. Therefore, lesion in one lobe causes partial hearing loss, and lesions in both lobes, deafness.

Again, the association areas (Area 21 and 22) blend the sensory data received thereby playing an important role in symbolic formulation and expression. So, once the impulses reach the brain (the temporal lobe), a complex information-processing job is performed. This processing job is often referred to as *perception—* or the mental process by which significant meaning is given to sensations. See discussion is Chapter Three.

Learning: Mechanisms and Disorders

It is the opinion of many neurologists that auditory and visual association zones impinge upon an extensive area of the temporal lobe in which visual and auditory sensory experiences appear to be placed on tape for storage. It is here that the unknown mechanisms of memory, hallucinations and dreams may be located. One indication of the importance of the temporal lobe in memory function is that removal of both lobes in humans permanently abolishes memory of past experiences.

Damage which involves an area in the temporal lobe called Wernicke's area (Areas 41 and 42 of Brodman), affect the auditory association cortex. In the dominant hemisphere this causes auditory receptive aphasia (sensory aphasia). The child cannot comprehend spoken language. He can speak and hear, but the words are meaningless.

Beginning early in life, nearly every individual trains one hemisphere of the brain more intensively than the other in the processes of association. The left side of the brain usually assumes the leading (dominant) role and the individual becomes right handed. Language function, too, is usually relegated to the hemisphere of motor dominance. Therefore, language is usually dominated by the left hemisphere. Aphasia does not appear unless a lesion is located in the dominant hemisphere. The speech centers of the non-dominant hemisphere can be developed successfully in young brains.

For example, a young right-handed child of three who suffers an injury in the left hemisphere, the dominant hemisphere, will learn to speak successfully again in a year or two because the non-dominant right hemisphere has subsequently been developed. Up to age four, the speech area can be organized in either hemisphere. Aphasia, in its widest interpretation, is an inability to express (communicate) in either reading, writing, or speaking (expressive aphasia); or, it can be an inability to receive meaning from spoken or written communication (receptive aphasia). This inability is caused by cerebral damage. Again, damage in the temporal lobe in the Wernicke area results in receptive (sensory) aphasia. Damage in the frontal lobe in the Broca's area results in expressive (motor) aphasia.

Occipital Lobe (Areas 17, 18, and 19)

The occipital lobe is posterior to the temporal lobe and parietal lobes, but there is usually no definite groove separating them on the surface of the hemisphere. Area 17 is the main visual area where the primary sensation of sight is registered. This area receives impulses from fibers of the 2nd cranial nerve, the optic nerve. Each lobe receives impulses from both eyes, therefore a lesion in one lobe results in contralateral hemianopsia or blindness in one-half of the visual field in the eye opposite to the lobe damaged. Lesions of both lobes results in total blindness. Areas 18 and 19 are the visual association areas. Visual sensations received in Area 17 (the primary cortical center for vision) are

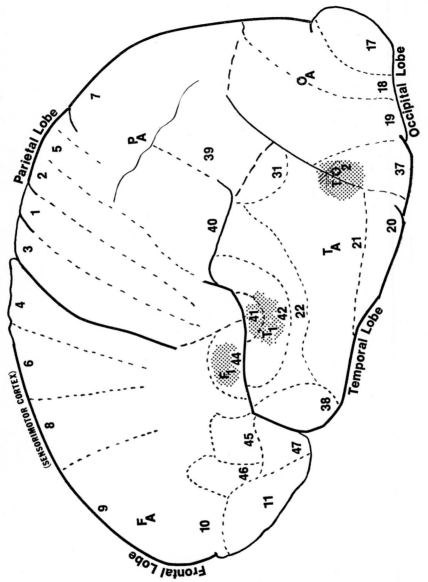

Figure 5. The Cerebral Cortex: Areas of Cerebral Function.
This representation of the cerebral cortex is somewhat modified
after the works and words of Campbell (1905), Penfield (1948), Penfield and Rasmussen (1957), Penfield and Roberts (1959), Nielson

(1962), Brock and Krieger (1963), Nathan (1969) and others. The cortical areas are shown (numbered) according to Brodman (1909) and subsequent workers (Vogt *et al.* 1926) who microscopically studied the cortex and mapped it into areas according to cytological (cellular) characteristics.

Let it be understood that some of the statements or conclusions concerning cortical functions are merely hypothetical while others are more or less proven. Changes have taken place since the original "mapping". For instance, Areas 4 and 6 were regarded as pure motor areas. More recently, however, research indicates that some 20 percent of these areas are concerned with sensory materials as well. This holds true also for the sensory areas 3, 1 and 2. Thirty percent of these areas are now thought to be concerned with motor functions. Concerning localization of cerebral cortex function, it should be understood that as Brock *et al.* (1963) has said, "In attempting to allocate given functional attributes to different parts of the cerebral cortex, neurology has gone through a period of localization of this or that function to this or that area or center." Presently then we see that "the concept of *center* has undergone change and some would rather speak of a higher concentration or specialization of a certain function in a certain area, thus indicating a less rigid restriction of a given function to a given area than is implied by the term *center.*" For concise reviews of other methods of organizing the cortex, see Morgan (1965).

With the reservation that this diagram may not be entirely "precise", it offers theoretical underpinnings which are essential in understanding what happens to the materials that enters the child's "mind". One would want to refer to this Figure also when reading Chapter 3 *Learning: Mechanisms and Disorders.*

CEREBRAL CORTEX FUNCTIONS ACCORDING TO BRODMAN

Areas and Sections

Frontal

4 Motor Area or precentral gyrus

6 Premotor Area

8 Conjugate eye movement

9 or F_A Frontal association area. Higher psychic functions such as abstract thinking, foresight, mature judgement, initiative, memory for recent events, morale and social sense, making it possible for the child to express verbal and non-verbal information in a socially acceptable manner.

Results of lesion: Personality and emotional changes; intellectual changes are questionable (See discussion of Frontal Lobe). More specifically, the effects of lesions may be seen as lack of restraint which may lead to aggressiveness; distractibility and restlessness leading to difficulty in paying attention; emotional instability; lack of initiative which may lead to difficulty in planning a course of action; disorders of memory for recent but not remote events; and indifference.

44 Articulated speech or motor, expressive speech; it is believed that "memory trace" tissues for motor patterns of speech reside here.

F_1 Known as Broca's area. Lesions cause apraxia, aphasia, or motor aphasia.

Parietal

3 Pain and temperature

1 Light touch (two-point discrimination)

2 Proprioception or awareness of direction of movement and position of body.

5 Sensory association area (in conjunction with Area 7)

7 or P_A Stereognosis and Association. Formulation of sensory stimulation into object images and meaning.

39 (Angular gyrus) This area is associated with visual recognition of written, arithmetic and other symbols (such as musical symbols). Contains also the memory center for the printed or written word (Brock, 1963).

Results of lesion: Verbal symbol visual agnosias such as alexia, agraphia, and acalculia or a varied combination (Nielson, 1962). The child may be able to read but does not understand the sense of the symbols (lacks comprehension). If there is no damage to the tactile and kinesthetic region of the parietal lobe, the child will know the letters if they are drawn on his skin.

40 Association area.

Temporal

41 Auditory receptive center.

42 Associative auditory receptive center. Recognition of spoken language.

T_1 Wernicke's Area. A lesion here results in the inability to recognize the spoken word or "word deafness" (auditory verbal agnosia). Wernicke's aphasia is receptive aphasia.

21 and 22 Recall and interpretation of speech; understanding of the spoken word (speech) is developed here.

Result of lesion: lose of verbal recall.

TO_2 (Including Area 37 and the posterior part of Area 21) Related to recall of names and words, and language formulation. This area is associated with forming and storing sound and word memory patterns.

interpreted and integrated into perceptions in Area 18. Area 19 receives stimuli mainly from Area 17. Damage to the association areas results in visual agnosia or the inability to visually recognize and identify objects, although there is no defect in sight.

Having presented the structure and function of one of the three regions of the brain, the cerebrum and its lobes, let's continue now to the second region of the brain, *the brain stem.*

Brain Stem

This portion consists of the diencephalon, the midbrain, pons and medulla which in turn contains ascending and descending pyramidal and extrapyramidal tracts, nuclei of cranial nerves, connections with the cerebellum and the reticular formation.

The *midbrain* is the highest area of the brain stem. It connects the pons and the cerebellum with the hemispheres of the cerebrum. In addition to containing afferent and efferent fiber tracts, it contains nuclei concerned with motor coordination. The nucleus of the 3rd and 4th cranial nerves are located in the midbrain.

Result of lesion: anomia, amnesic aphasia, and formulation defects.

T$_A$ Association area.

Occipital

17 Primary cortical center for vision. This is the pure vision area which receives impulses from the 2nd cranial nerve.

18 Association of "What it is that is seen." The function of this area is recognition (knowing) (Nielson, 1962).

Result of lesion: geometric-optic agnosia or loss or defect in direction sense of lines with visual-space disorientation leading to difficulties in writing, drawing, and inability to discriminate right from left. Also present may be simultanagnosia or the loss of the sense of motion of objects.

19 Visual imagery for objects or association of "How to use what is seen." Found also in this area is activation of "memory traces." Lesion to this area may result in tactile-occipital agnosia or the inability to recognize objects by touch alone; inability to form a visual "image" of the object by touching it.

0$_A$ Visual association area.

Result of Lesion: Visual agnosia and visual association.

Pons. The pons (or bridge) acts as a union between the two halves of the cerebellum and between the medulla and the cerebellum. The nucleus of the 5, 6, 7 and 8th cranial nerves are found here.

Medulla. All the afferent and efferent tracts of the spinal cord are represented here, many which cross over in the medulla. The nucleus of the 9th, 10th, 11th, and 12th cranial nerves are found in the medulla. This is also a center for such bodily functions as respiration and heart rhythm.

Diencephalon. This is composed primarily of the thalamus and hypothalamus which is situated deep in the brain. In preceding sections we have considered the *wiring* of the nervous system —the transmission of information from sense organs into the spinal cord, and the travelling path to higher centers for integration with other incoming information. Much of the proprioceptive information ends in the cerebellum (which we will cover in the upcoming section) where it is blended with data about touch, equilibrium etc. In contrast to cerebellar pathways, *all* of the sensory data which reaches the cortex, except olfaction, pass through the *thalamus,* a common relay center. Here, added fusion and integration occur, combining appropriate information, then shunting these combined messages to different destinations, each sense having its own receiving station in the cerebral cortex. For instance, along the front of the parietal lobe is a long strip of cortex called the somaesthetic area which serves as the primary reception area for touch, pressure, and kinesthetic sense. The thalamus may also be involved in focusing the attention by making certain cortical sensory areas more receptive and others less receptive. The hypothalamus is an area for temperature regulation, water balance, and blood pressure regulation and controls almost all of the endocrine gland functions. Surrounding the thalamus is the limbic system. The major role of this system is to paint our perceptions with various emotional colors such as fear and pleasure. It also helps us to reestablish a more tranquil state after an *emotional* flareup.

A brief description of the *reticular formation* is appropriate here. The reticular formation is, by definition, a net-like series of short interwoven fibers and nerve cells. This net-work of nerve

cells is scattered throughout the spinal cord up through the diencephalon (Ruch *et al.,* 1965; Laursen, 1967). The formation
receives impulses from the spinal cord, the cerebellum, and the
cerebral hemispheres, and basal ganglion and it also sends impulses
to these structures. The formation then not only screens impulses,
it also maintains a two-way *conversation* with the cortex. Practically all of the major sensory pathways then send collaterals into
the reticular formation.[8] Many cells of the reticular formation
project to higher centers in the cerebral cortex by the diffuse
thalamic projection system.[9] These cells play an important role
in wakefulness, conscious states, and attention. The RAS can
block out, depress or emphasize impulses. They form what has
been termed the *reticular activating system* (RAS). Of all the
sensory systems feeding into the reticular formation, the most
powerful in the arousal reaction is the input from the head. Touch
on the face will arouse a person more quickly requiring a less
intense stimulus than visual, auditory, or bodily (somatic) stimulation. Visual stimulation is least effective. The ascending afferent
(sensory) impulses then serve an activating function. There is also
a comparable descending function. The descending influence of
the reticular formation is that of facilitating or inhibiting motor
activity, largely at the level of spinal motor neurons.

It becomes clear that the reticular formation has important
ascending and descending functions and serves as a center for
integration of sensory information (it decides what sense information should and should not be passed on to our minds). The

---

[8]This may be a bit confusing. When discussing the thalamus, it was stated that
this structure is the major relay station of all sensation except smell. However,
sensory information reaches the cortex via two avenues: (1) through the reticular
formation and (2) directly by connections (neurons) from receptors. Regarding (1)
collaterals are sent from the sensory system to the reticular formation as the sensory
impulses are traveling up to the cortex. Concerning (2) receptor neurons synapse in
the thalamus where they are then transmitted to the cortex. Therefore, the RAS
fibers *intercept* the massive influx of sensory impulses coming from the body before
these impulses enter the thalamus. The thalamus distributes the impulses, which
were screened by the RAS, to the regions of the cortex (the proverbial *thinking cap*)
where decision making occurs.

[9]If the reticular formation is damaged or *cut off* (e.g. by anesthetization), sensory
messages reach the cortex but there is no awareness of stimulation or perception
(Brazier, 1963).

RAS also alters motor responses at a reflex level. That is, the reticular formation can deal with some sensory information without the assistance of the higher cortical areas. The RAS does not analyze or interpret, it merely selects or picks out strong or novel stimuli and dampens or blocks out weak and common stimuli. It may follow then that the presence of rich and varied sensory stimulation is essential to the development and maintenance of attentive, effective, and adaptive behavior. This concept is important. Remember, the nervous system soon ceases to react to repetitious, boring, monotonous stimuli. It does, however, react to change and novel stimuli. "Use stimuli for short periods of time . . . constantly change in order to *rev-up* the system and keep it alert and cooperative" (Moore, 1969).

Cerebellum

The third and final division of the brain is the *cerebellum*. Through its precision circuitry, the cerebellum is responsible for muscle synergy or *cooperation* throughout the body. It times and coordinates the action of muscle groups so that movements are performed smoothly and accurately. Voluntary movements can occur without help from the cerebellum. Such movements are, however, clumsy. The importance of timing can be appreciated through the following illustration. A child reaches for a pencil. In so doing, the extensors of the arm contract (or shorten) to straighten the elbow while, simultaneously, the flexors relax. Suppose that the flexors do not relax to a corresponding degree or at the same time. This lack of relaxation would either prevent or make straightening the arm difficult to perform smoothly. Suppose that the flexors did relax, but not until extensor contraction had begun. The result would be a jerky type of reaching movement. One can readily see the importance of timing, for even if muscle power and voluntary control are normal, without timing, movement will be awkward.

In order for the cerebellum to coordinate or modify muscular activity, it needs position and movement information. All sensory modalities, including tactile, auditory and visual stimuli, feed such information to the cerebellum. In addition, the cerebellum receives information from motor and sensory regions of the cerebral cortex. After an evaluation of the incoming afferent information, the cerebellum makes appropriate correction for any mistakes or inaccuracies of muscle activity. This information, in the form of nerve impulses, is dispatched over several routes to reach the voluntary motor system and thereby modifies muscular movements. In summary then, the incoming information must be integrated and coordinated in the cerebellum. One of the peculiarities of the cerebellum is that the efferent fibers which leave the cerebellum make up only one-third as many fibers as the number that enter it. This reduction is made possible by built-in neuron controls which sharpen, fuse and code incoming signals resulting in the transmission of only important messages to muscles. The majority of messages that leave the cerebellum are aimed at the muscles.

Disorders of the cerebellum are manifested chiefly as defects in coordination of muscular activity. With specific reference to cerebral palsy, lesions of the cerebellum will produce ataxia, incoordination and nystagmus.

This concludes a discussion of the brain, one of the two major divisions of the central nervous system. The spinal cord which is the second major division of the central nervous system will be considered next in terms of function.

The Spinal Cord

Like the brain stem, the spinal cord contains the *wires* which carry the *efferent* (descending) impulses from the higher to the lower centers and the afferent (ascending) impulses from the lower to the higher centers. The spinal cord is also a center of reflex action for the trunk and extremities. A reflex is an automatic response to a given stimulus (such as pin prick). The impulse resulting from the stimulus does not penetrate the level of consciousness. Reflexes are fixed reactions, their performance does not require prior experience. From the spinal cord pass 31 pairs of spinal nerves in five groups named according to the area of the vertebral column from which they emerge. The spinal nerves, it will be remembered, were covered under structures of the peripheral nervous system. The spinal cord can be briefly characterized as having a dual role. This part of the nervous system acts as a reflex center and as a conduction pathway to and from higher brain centers.

FUNCTION OF THE PERIPHERAL NERVOUS SYSTEM (PNS)

The second major portion of the nervous system is the Peripheral Nervous System. This portion contains the *spinal nerves* and the *cranial nerves*. The structure of the PNS has previously been presented. Now the functions will be presented. As indicated in the section on structure, the 31 pairs of spinal nerves pass from the spinal cord. After so doing, the nerves branch into smaller peripheral nerves which distribute fibers to various parts of the body. Each nerve splits into a dorsal and a ventral root. The dorsal roots contain afferent (sensory) fibers, some of which innervate the skin, while others innervate organs, tissue and muscles. The ventral roots contain efferent (motor) fibers many of which directly innervate muscle, skin, organs and tissue. At the spinal cord, we find then both motor and sensory functions.

The sensory cranial nerves contain afferent fibers and conduct information from receptors located in the head as well as from receptors in visceral organs such as the heart and pancreas within the body. The motor cranial nerves contain the efferent fibers and innervate various effector organs such as the eye and heart.

Essentially, the peripheral nervous system represents lines of communication about external and internal occurrences, whereas the central nervous system is the center of coordination and the place of determination of the most appropriate ways to utilize (to respond) to the information gathered by the peripheral nervous system. No choice of response is possible without synaptic connections between nerve cells, and these points of connection are contained entirely in the central nervous system.

REFERENCES

Brain, W. D.: *Speech Disorders: Aphasia, Apraxia, and Agnosia,* 2nd ed. Washington, Butterworths, 1965.

Brazier, M.: Role of limbic system in maintenance of consciousness. *Anesth Analg,* 42:748-751, 1963.

Brock, S. and Krieger, H. P.: *The Basis of Clinical Neurology,* 4th ed. Baltimore, Williams and Wilkins, 1963.

Brodman, K.: *Vergleichende Lokalisationslehre der Grosshirnrinde in ihren Prinzipien dargestellt auf Grund des Zellenbaues.* Leipzig, J. A. Barth, XII, 1909, reprinted in 1925, p. 324.

Campbell, A. W.: *Histological Studies on the Localization of Cerebral Function.* Cambridge, Cambridge University Press, 1905.

Gardner, E.: *Fundamentals of Neurology,* 4th ed. Philadelphia, Saunders, 1966.

Laursen, A. Mosfeldt: Higher functions of the central nervous system. *Ann Rev Phys, 29:*543-572, 1967.

Moore, Josephine C.: Structure and function of the nervous system in relation to treatment techniques. Zamir, L. J. (Ed.). *In Expanding Dimensions in Rehabilitation.* Springfield, Thomas, 1969.

Morgan, Clifford: *Physiological Psychology,* 3rd ed. New York, McGraw Hill, 1965.

Nathan, Peter: *The Nervous System.* Philadelphia, Lippincott, 1969.

Nielson, J. M.: *A Textbook of Clinical Neurology,* 3rd ed. New York, Paul Hoeber, 1962.

Penfield, W.: Research. *Nerv Ment Dis Proc, 27:*519-534, 1948.

Penfield, W. and Rasmussen, T.: *The Cerebral Cortex of Man.* New York, Macmillan, 1957.

Penfield, W. and Roberts, L.: *Speech and Brain Mechanisms.* Princeton, Princeton University Press, 1959.

Ruch, Patton et al.: *Neurophysiology.* Philadelphia, Saunders, 1965.

Sherrington, C. S.: On the proprioceptive system especially in its reflex aspect. *Brain, 29:*467-482, 1907.

Vogt, C. and Vogt, O.: Die vergleichend-arkitektonische und die vergleichend-reizphysiologische welderung der Grosshirnrinde unter besonderer Berücksichtigung der menschlichen. *Naturwissenshaften, 14:*1191-1194, 1926.

Chapter Three

LEARNING: MECHANISMS AND DISORDERS

It Has Been Estimated That approximately 100 million nerve impulses reach the CNS every second. Theoretically, each of these impulses could potentially be translated into a learning experience thereby effecting a change in the child's behavior and performance (his experience being tempered by training and teaching). A permanent change in the child's performance must occur before learning is said to have taken place. Experiences such as seeing, hearing, feeling, smelling and tasting (as well as the kinesthetic sensations which accompany movement) are sensations from one's environment (both from without and within): the antecedents producing a response (i.e. conditioned learning; learning of motor skills). They, the sensations, may or may not acquire meaning (cognitive learning—memory, concept formation, recognition of relationships, sequential thinking, generalizing etc.) which all lead to understanding and awareness. As we will come to see, however, the 100 million nerve impulses previously mentioned are not all translated into meaning and, therefore, learning.

Midway between the experience and the final gnosis (knowing, conception, meaning), is a process called *perception* or sensory appreciation (perceptual learning). In general, this process is analogous to the digestion of food. See Table III. Afferent impulses (the food or the raw materials which are used to build cells or meaning) comes from the skin, muscle (mouth), tendons and organs of special sense such as the eyes and ears. The impulses ascend in the spinal cord (the esophagus) to reach the thalamus (stomach). The *food* or impulses are sent on to the various lobes

Raw Materials:

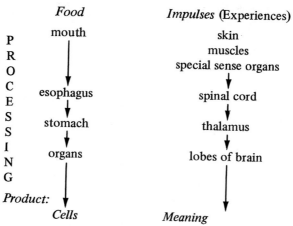

Table III Analogy; Digestion/Perception

in the brain[10] (organs of the body) where they are digested and metabolized or *constructed* into meaningful perceptions or cells.

Indigestion or *sensory and/or perceptual disturbances* occur when there is: (a) faulty sensation or information. This can be caused by defects in the reception stations such as peripheral sensory defects, impaired motor functioning (because a child has motor/musculature involvement, he is unable to properly feel an object in order to form a concept); (b) damage CNS (impairment in one or all of the cerebral lobes); (c) impaired executive function or motor involvement. Relating this to the digestion process, we find that (a) above becomes defects in the reception stations of sensory or motor origin such as structural difficulties in the organs of mastication which lead to imperfections in the food (impulses) received. And (b) becomes damaged internal mechanisms (stomach, pancreas); and (c) becomes kidney, bladder disorders.

In addition, one must not neglect the importance that motivation plays in the overall schema of learning. An interesting com-

[10]The parietal lobe is the cerebral location of sensory discrimination. Each lobe, however, has a more or less specific job to perform as does each organ in the human body such as the pancreas which secretes digestive enzymes.

ment made by Dr. Skatvedt, a pediatrician in charge of a school for cerebral palsy children in Oslo, Norway, has tremendous implications for the successful use of contingency management in the classroom for the cerebral palsy as well as other ortho-pedically handicapped and neurologically impaired children. He states that they have found no correlation between degree of motor involvement, perceptual defects and emotional difficulties. He feels that *drive* is an ingredient that is "sadly lacking" even in children with a normal IQ, without sensory or perceptual difficulties. In addition, he feels that they (the children) have to be pushed in their exercises and school work all the time. "When they come into a learning environment where their problems are understood they do well" (Skatvedt, 1961). If the child is moti-vated, he will desire active involvement which also facilitates learning because experiences, perceptions etc. will become as-sociated with the child's daily-life activities.

In Chapter 2, there was a brief presentation in diagrammatic form (Fig. 3) concerning the six important components in the process required for a response and subsequent learning to take place. Indirect reference was made in step six to 'sensations acquiring meaning.' Also, brief mention was made regarding perception in the discussion of the association areas of the various lobes of the cerebrum. See Figure 5, *The Cerebral Cortex.* But as Teuber (1962) noted, "there is neither an adequate definition of perception nor an adequate neurophysiologic theory to explain it." Popularly defined, however, perception is "the ability to rec-ognize and use visual stimuli [as well as other stimuli] and to interpret these stimuli by relating them to previous experiences (Goldberg, 1968). Or, as this writer prefers, perception is an activ-ity of the mind midway between sensation (i.e. feeling, seeing) and thought (meaning). A process which gives *meaning* to the stimuli. This process—perception—functions as a preliminary to thinking. It is the way an individual organizes, combines, relates and understands or knows the stimuli which are in his environ-ment. The perceptual process is, therefore, another aspect in the learning phenomenom.

The cerebral hemispheres provide us with a mental repre-sentation of the environment within which we live (Nathan,

1969). The amorphous sensory inflow acquires meaning. We come to recognize objects in our environment as meaningful *things* such as furniture, flowers and music. A sensation is perceived in the primary areas of the cortex; reasoning occurs in the secondary association areas. We not only perceive an object as being a pencil, we conclude that it is the pencil we saw someone use to write with yesterday.

We do not yet know much about the connection between the structural brain with its billions of microscopic cells, and the relationship it has with the psychological processes of cerebral function such as learning, remembering, thinking, and having ideas (Halacy, 1969). However, investigators have gained insight into the neural mechanisms of behavior through such techniques as: (a) ablation: removal of a part of an animal's nervous system and studying the resulting impairment, (b) electrical recording: electrodes are placed on the surface of the brain or within the brain thereby providing information about the physical characteristics of messages and the paths these stimuli follow in the nervous system, and (c) electrical stimulation: an electrical current is passed through the brain and responses are observed and measured. Researchers can thereby make a working assumption concerning the functions of various parts of the nervous system. Other methods involve microscopic and biochemical study and techniques of the behavioral sciences. The advances made possible from such studies suggest answers to "Where? in the brain, rather than to How?" (McFie, 1969).

Previously mentioned was the astonishing fact that so many incoming stimuli or potential sources of learning impinge upon the nervous system every second. It becomes obvious that selection and/or reduction of this stimuli is necessary if order is to be made of the chaos. Selection appears to be according to need. That is, when we are hungry all else seems unimportant until we fulfill that need. We have all, at one time or another, been consumed in an interesting book or an intriguing television program and, at the same time, have been able to filter out such distractions as a voice, or the passing traffic and its associated noise. The child's ability to filter out extraneous stimuli and thereby utilize only worthy incoming stimuli (those experiences in his surroundings) is greatly facilitated by his attentional powers. The reticular formation plays a most important part in the attentional aspect required if learning is to take hold. See Chapter Two for an account of this elaborate formation.

The mechanisms involved in learning are complex. In part, perhaps, this complexity arises because there are many kinds of learning such as classical conditioning. As it is not the intention of this *Handbook* to review the psychology of the entire learning arena, the remainder of this chapter will deal with *perceptual learning* and its relationship to the CP/NI child.

A great deal of attention and effort during the past 15 or so years has been directed to certain difficulties attributed to cerebral damage. Many, if not all, of these difficulties can be encountered in these children. Aphasias, apraxias, agnosias and a variety of sensory-motor disorders may be evident. Many names have been applied to these difficulties/disorders such as visual, perceptual, visuo-spatial, or visual-motor impairments, spatial inability, constructive apraxia as well as the auditory perceptual disorders and on and on.

There does not seem to be complete agreement by *experts* concerning differences in the processes involved or the skills required in these various areas. The upshot of this confluence of viewpoints was that the subsequent course of educators and psychologists has become extremely difficult to follow. For instance, Nelson (1962) states that there is, in fact, no distinction between perceptual (visual) and visuo-motor responses. He considers both as perceptual. Abercrombie (1964, p. 12) uses the term 'spatial' (or visuo-spatial) difficulties to include both perceptual and visuo-motor disorders. The difficulties the child encounters are both in perceiving and manipulating what is perceived.

In attempts to eliminate some of the confusion which has been generated over the past few years, our discussion will be limited to three areas:

1. Peripheral perception (reception): sensory, kinesthetic;
2. Central perception (cortical integration): visual, auditory, tactile, proprioceptive;
3. Visuo-motor (executive): eye-hand performance.

The parameters of so limited a discussion will necessitate a more concise presentation than that encountered in the common textbook. Under the heading, SENSORI-PERCEPTUO-GNOSIA STUDIES RELATED TO THE CP/NI CHILD is presented an attempt to draw a picture, or synthesize, the main defects and some of the ramifications of the sensori-perceptuo-gnosias as they pertain to the CP/NI. This section delineates most of the reported studies that relate specifically to the CP/NI child.

Under EXPLANATORY NOTATIONS, implications and suggestions will be made concerning teaching-training techniques and methods. Additional guides will be noted in the Appendix section and in Chapter 10, *Special Equipment and Adaptations*. This manner of presentation is a departure from the more traditional textbook format; however, it is felt to be more meaningful.

Although many words have been written in an attempt to propose the *best* teaching-training methods, the problem of what can realistically be done to ameliorate learning and perceptual aberrations in the cerebral palsied/neurologically impaired child remains largely theoretical. How children will learn most efficiently is a problem at least as old as Socrates. "In 2,000 years no one has come up with an answer acceptable to everyone, including the kids themselves. Thus, we shall probably still be experimenting with teaching gimmicks and arguing about their effectiveness 2,000 years from now" (Oakley, 1971).

Pay particular attention to the section under Some Perceptive Disorders: Definitions, in this chapter. This is a discussion of a more general nature dealing with some common disorders of the perceptual aspects of learning. Many investigations in the area of perceptual disorders are studies made on adults with cerebral lesions. Whether it is safe to assume that the effects of damage will be a carbon copy in the child is open to some question, but "we have to use what clues we can to help us in these difficult studies [of cerebral lesions in childhood]" (McFie, 1969, p. 43).

Throughout this presentation, the reader will find assistance in referring to Figure 5. *The Cerebral Cortex*. When referring to the Figure, bear in mind that as was evidenced in Chapter Two, the two cerebral hemispheres are generally viewed as symmetrical in appearance. Although there is a degree of functional symmetry, many functions are dispersed between the hemispheres in a definite asymmetrical pattern. This phenomenon is known as *dominance,* or the tendency for one of the cerebral hemispheres to have the *majority rule* in certain functions. Possibly the most obvious example of this phenomenon is handedness or lateral preference. As Benson *et al.* (1968) suggests, heredity plays the major role in determining dominance although environmental conditions certainly play their part as well, such as the right handed mother who insists that her youngster is to follow suit. Language is another fine example of lateralization of the human cerebral function. Several studies: Goodglass (1964), Penfield et al. (1959), and Subirana (1958), show that patients demonstrating right hand preference will most frequently have left cerebral dominance for language. That is, the left side of the brain will be dominating the individual's speech if that individual is right handed. (There is much evidence in the literature concerning the frequent presence of aphasia in right spastic hemiplegics). Although it is the common belief that left handed people will have right cerebral dominance for language, at least some authorities feel that approimately 60 percent of left-handed individuals have left hemisphere speech dominance (Goodglass *et al.,* 1964; Roberts, 1969).

Right brain dominance seems to be in evidence for such non-verbal activities as visual-spatial discrimination and learning (spatial perception is organized in the right parietal lobe as well as short-term non-verbal memory). Hécaen (1962) feels, however, as do others, that left brain damage may cause disorders of these functions. For instance, body-schema (e.g. right-left orientation and finger gnosis) is organized in the left parietal lobe as is praxis or purposeful movement. Short-term non-verbal memory is impaired by lesions of the right hemisphere. Long-term memory appears to be unaffected by brain injury. It does appear that damage to the right cerebral hemisphere seems to decrease, to some degree at least, particular nonverbal activities such as visual-spatial perception as opposed to the disorders of verbal activities such as verbal fluency and reasoning which result from left hemisphere damage. From the foregoing, we can clearly state that there is strong evidence to support the idea that there is definite unilateral dominance for certain functions. Some investigators feel that failure or delayed cerebral dominance can be positively linked to certain disorders, which will be discussed, where indicated, under the section: Some Perceptual Disorders: Definitions.

In recent years, investigators of this most intricate nervous structure called the brain, have come to realize a factor which throws optimistic light on the problems resulting from damage. This factor is called *compensation* "by which the human brain tends to make up the deficit by the use of neural mechanisms situated in healthy areas [of the brain], which have a functional similarity to the destroyed part" (Brock *et al.*, 1963, p. 284). This is of particular import when dealing with children who are suspected of or have been definitely diagnosed as having brain damage. The CNS is *over-wired* so that, potentially, there is more than one road, or wired circuit, to a particular point (or more than one area of the brain that can be developed for a particular function). This *road* (fiber(s)) may need only to be used in order to set down a steadfast path . . . as the tracts in a yet unpaved street will soon emerge (when traveled upon) as a useful highway with its ability to transport all kinds of vehicles (information) to their destinations (lobes). It therefore becomes important to establish an 'entrenchment of information' on these pathways (tissues) through such methods as active participation, multistimulation techniques and other procedures such as those espoused by the supporters of the neurophysiological approach to habilitation which are thoroughly presented in Chapter 9, *Systems of Therapy.*

We may see this (the compensation phenomenon) in the case of language. Unilateral brain damage (to the dominant hemisphere) early in life will result in only a transient language loss. Finding that, as Zangwell (1960) states, "At birth the two hemispheres are virtually equipotential in regard to the acquisition of language and dominance may be readily shifted in consequence of early brain injury. Although this plasticity—and hence the possibility of a shift in dominance—appears to diminish rapidly with increasing age, its limits have yet to be defined with precision." The angular gyrus is essential for language development and, according to Benson (1970), myelination in this area is not complete until around puberty or ten to twelve years of age.

In the early years, the first ten or so years, we find that a region of the brain may not have established a particular functional commitment, although it contains most of the *raw materials* (i.e. nerve fibers etc.) on which to establish such function. The verbal and non-verbal skills that would normally be performed by a damaged hemisphere can consequently be developed in the other, or undamaged, hemisphere. Theoretically, the hemisphere is able to not only carry on its own designated function but can as well take on the function of the damage hemisphere.

Again, the fact that the nervous system is plastic or pliable is extremely important to those dealing with training and teaching the CP/NI child. The child cannot *add* to the estimated twenty billion neurons in the brain (Nobach, 1969) that the child is endowed with from birth, nor can damaged CNS neurons actually *regenerate*. There are other phenonmena occurring in this system which permits learning and re-learning to take place. According to Moore (1969), and others, these changes are: (1) dendritic growth, (2) an increase in myelination of neuronal processes,[11] (3) changes at or within synapses and the changing of synapses, (4) collateral growth of axons, (5) new endplate development, (6) growth of new receptor cells replacing old or damaged ones in some systems of the body, and (7) the use of different or less-used neuronal circuits [the *over-wired* concept previously mentioned]. "These regions [and structures] may well be like the proverbial white sheet, waiting to be written upon" (Nathan, 1969).

SENSORI-PERCEPTUO-GNOSIA STUDIES RELATED TO THE CP/NI CHILD[12]

Investigator and Summary of Study

Tizard *et al.* (1954). Sensory impairments were found in 50

---

[11]According to Nathan (1969), up to the age of ten or so, vast areas of the cortex are not yet myelinated; and up to the age of twenty, large areas of the frontal lobes are not yet myelinated.

[12]Only a summary of each study with pertinent findings is presented. See original works for detail.

percent of the children studied (106 were hemiplegics) (see Notation 1).

Most common disturbance found: a) total or partial astereognosis, and b) two-point discrimination. The authors suggest that in some cases at least, these impairments were the main reason the children did not use their affected extremity. Severe sensory loss can, however, be seen with minimal motor defects.

Unimpaired in most children: a) perceptuo-motor (visual-motor) areas (i.e. block design, picture completion, reproduction of design, and memory for design). Children tended to use good extremity in task performance.

Hanson (Abercrombie *et al.*, 1964). Finger agnosia was the only impairment found in diplegics.

Wilson *et al.* (1967). Somatosensory: pressure, two-point discrimination. Forty-nine percent of the cerebral palsied children studied (120 in all) had: a) one or more sensory defects (light pressure on tip of index finger and palm; two-point discrimination. This supports studies by Tizard *et al.* (1954), Hohman *et al.* (1958), and Tachdjean *et al.* (1959). No significant difference was found between the spastics and athetoids. There was a difference as a function of age however: the younger group was more sensitive than the older group on pressure-palm measures and less sensitive on two-point discrimination. (See Notation 2). Results indicate that the presence of one somatosensory defect increases the likelihood of a second defect.

Critchley (1953); Elithorn et al. (1952); Head et al. (1920). Tactile after-images or tactile perseveration which appears to interfere with discrimination and possibly with the child's attentiveness. This phenomenon was found in both groups in Wilson's et al. (1967a) study (i.e. both in the CP group and the non-neurologically impaired). (See Notation 3).

Wilson et al. (1967b). Form discrimination (stereognosis). Studied 120 cerebral palsied (congenital) and 60 non-neurologically impaired controls. Results: a) controls had superior performance, b) athetoids performance in discriminating both size and form did not vary with age. The spastic group showed improved performance with increasing age. This supports Abercrombie's et al. (1964) and Taylor's (1959) findings: athetoids are essentially less impaired than spastics in sensory and perceptual functions, and c) generally, the presence of one defect (i.e. somatosensory) increases occurrence of a second (astereognosis). (See Notation 4 and 5).

Hohman *et al.* (1958). Subjects: 47 children in age group 6 to 16 years with good or better than average IQ. Most common defects found were: a) loss of form discrimination, b) impairment of two-point discrimination, and c) loss of position sense (kinesthesis). The authors suggest that these abilities are cortical (parietal) in locale. Loss of light touch, sharp and dull, hot and cold, measuring ability, wet and dry, rough and smooth are thalamic functions.

Monfraix *et al.* (1961). Results of study: a) disorders in manual perception can be found in all forms of cerebral palsy (occurs with greater frequency and severity, however, in the spastic or rigid rather than in the athetoid), b) somewhat more frequent in right sided spastic hemiplegics, and c) disturbances are probably more common and severe in unilateral than in bilateral cases. (See Notation 6). (See 7 in Explanatory Notations for general comments concerning implications that these above studies have in the teaching-training-treatment triad.

Connors *et al.* (1967). Transfer of information. Subjects: children who all had medical diagnosis of organic brain injury with normal IQ scores. All the children were significantly poorer than severely emotionally disturbed children in transmitting information from touch to vision (the task involved feeling forms as long as the child desired, then pointing to one of the forms displayed on the front of a board which matched that being manipulated). The authors indicate that the brain injured (neurologically impaired) children were slower and actually inspected the figures much longer than their controls. This rules out the possibility that the differences in performance were due to the brain damaged (neurologically impaired) greater 'impulsivity.' The authors conclude that the "rate of information transmission is much slower." Tactile problems were ruled out as these children apparently did not have any peripheral sensory defects. One could possibly assume then that if children without peripheral sensory deficits have these "transmission" problems, children with sensory (peripheral) deficits most assuredly will experience "transmission of information" problems. The authors further conclude that "the deficit lies in the matching of the tactual schemas with the visual schema." (See Notations 8 and 9).

Cruickshank *et al.* (1957). Figure-Ground. Subjects: 211 spastics, 114 athetoids and 110 controls. Administered Syracuse Visual Figure-Background Test. Some of the results: a) both CP groups demonstrated poorer performance than their controls; spastics tended to do poorer than did the athetoids. Performance by the athetoids appeared to vary with age (i.e. the younger children's performance approximated that of the spastics, while the older athetoid's performance approximated that of the controls or the non-handicapped, and b) the spastic children made more responses including reference to background instead of the foreground.

Wedell (1960). Wedell attempted to find the type of CP with which perceptual impairment would most likely occur. Results: a larger number of CP children showed low perceptual ability. Within the CP group: perceptual impairment was found to be associated with spastics rather than athetoids and with bilateral and left-sided spasticity rather than right-sided. This indicates that perceptual impairment may be related to right-sided hemisphere brain damage. This study supports Cruickshank's *et al.* (1957) study.

Cruickshank et al. (1965). Figure-Ground. This is an extension of Cruickshank's *et al.* 1957 study. Subjects: a different group of 401 spastic children. Results: Four major generalizations: 1. As time increases, the ability to perceive figure also increases. [Caution: this may be a negative factor if what the child sees includes details unessential to the learning situation which would result in confusion. Illustrative is the child with eye movement disorder.] 2. Color enhances figure perception. [Indication: the stimulus value of the object to which the child's attention is desired should be increased, and environmental distraction, decreased.] (See Notation 10). 3. Improvement noted when material was presented in a 3-dimensional manner as opposed to 2-dimensional (such as figures painted on cardboard). 4. Structure of visual material is important. More figure perceived when material presentations include large figure on large background. (See Notation 11). See Chapter 7 *Visual Impairment and The Learning Environment* for further studies and implications concerning visual perception.

Studies dealing with auditory perception. Although there is a fair amount of investigation and research in the field of visual perception particularly of the adult, research to study auditory perceptual function in children with cerebral dysfunction as well as the *normal* child have been few despite theoretical evidence that information received auditorially can be subjected to perceptual distortions causing, among other problems, omission and reversals in reading and writing. Hardy (1966) proposed that the fundamental language disorder of children with suspected or actual neurological impairment may be their difficulty in ordering (sequentially) acoustic events, and Eisenson (1969) feels that the underlying problem of aphasic children is that of auditory perception.

Refer to *Perceptual Disorders: Definitions* in this chapter. It is in this section that one will gain a greater appreciation of the relationship that auditory perceptual functions have to the various disorders that may be present in the CP/NI child. To be aware and to have some working knowledge of the auditory process and its disorders will bring us one step further to the successful management in our therapeutic and training procedures.

SOME PERCEPTUAL DISORDERS

Aphasias

The inability to comprehend and use language is commonly termed aphasia. This is the term applied when the disorder is not due to hearing loss, mental retardation, emotional problems, or motor defects in the speech mechanism. When applied under the aphasia umbrella, we find two major categories: (1) sensory receptive (Wernicke), and (2) motor or expressive (Broca's) aphasias. However, "the literature is burdened with many utterly useless terms" (Nielson, 1962).

Broca's aphasia is characterized by: loss of expressive (volitional) speech, comprehension is retained. Associated with this syndrome is usually found a loss of the ability to write (spontaneously or upon dictation) and to copy. Wernicke's aphasia is probably the best known sensory syndrome which is characterized by a loss of comprehension (receptive aphasia as it were or auditory verbal agnosia) of the spoken and of the written word (visual verbal agnosia) and inability to write (agraphia) and paraphasia (jargon, garbled oral or written language). In general, when applied to adults, the term aphasia means a loss of a skill (language) previously acquired. However, when applied to children, we are dealing with a skill which has not been acquired or, at best, the skill has not been fully developed.

The inability to acquire language skills from birth has been called "developmental" or "congenital" aphasia, "specific language disability," "delayed language development" and "congenital word deafness." "Congenital aphasia" seems to be the accepted term. Speech either does not develop or it is delayed. According to Agranowitz *et al.* (1968), aphasia and related disorders in children exist as a result of damage to the language areas incurred prior to birth, at birth or in early years. See Chapter Five, *Speech and Hearing Disorders* for Ingram's interpretation of language disorders such as dysphasia, dyslexia and dysgraphia.

Regarding developmental aphasia in childhood, Paine (1968) feels that this "nearly always includes some degree of receptive deficit as well as an expressive one, and that there is frequently a coexisting peripheral hearing loss and even more often some defect in central auditory transmission or in analysis of the coded transmission at a cerebral level." Rappaport (1964) states that such children have adequate but often not fully normal understanding of what is said, their speech is slow in appearing and is generally limited to one- or two-syllable patterns. See Ingram's *Classification of Common Speech Disorders in Childhood,* Table IX, (number five), as well as Table XV, *Classification of the Developmental Speech Disorder Syndrome,* both found in Chapter Five.

Therapeutic treatment techniques for the congenitally aphasic child possess many of the same principles used with the adult: intensive, repeated, and combined stimulation via whatever channels best reach the child (Johnson *et al.*, 1967).

For a complete treatment synopsis see:

Agranowitz, A. and McKeown, M. R.: *Aphasia Handbook for Adults and Children,* 3rd. ed. Springfield, Thomas, 1968.

McGinnis, M. A.: *Aphasic Children: Identification and Education by the Association Method.* Washington, D.C., Alexander Graham Bell Association for the Deaf, 1963.

Roberts, A. C.: *The Aphasic Child: A Neurological Basis for His Education and Rehabilitation.* Springfield, Thomas, 1966.

Wood, N. E.: *Delayed Speech and Language Development.* Englewood Cliffs, Prentice-Hall, 1964.

Kleffner, F. R.: Aphasia and other language deficiencies in children. In Daley, William T. (Ed.): *Speech and Language Therapy with the Brain-Damaged Child.* Washington, Catholic University of America Press, 1962.

Hortense, Barry: *The Young Aphasic Child.* Washington, Alexander Graham Bell Association for the Deaf, 1961.

Generally, large visual materials and kinesthetic information are used. This is in accordance with the theoretical principle that "one sensory modality may provide more informational redundancy than another" (Goodglass, 1968). Mechanical devices and automated techniques such as the Language Master (Bell and Howell) have been enjoying popularity in dealing with various learning disorders. Reference is made frequently to teaching machines being implemented for this or that purpose but rarely are specifics offered concerning their use and construction. An *electric board,* Figure 6, is one such teaching machine used successfully in training the aphasic child with linguistic problems (Keith, 1967). The machine can, as well, be adapted for other perceptual difficulties. See Chapter 10, *Special Equipment and Adaptations* for specific instructions for construction and use of this machine.

Miller (1968) proposed the term "central dysacusis" to denote the childhood form of *receptive* aphasia or auditory agnosias. According to Miller, this term (central dysacusis, infers an integrative or interpretive level disturbance resulting from a CNS deficit. This deficit may be either genetically determined (prenatal) or peri- or post-natally acquired. According to Wepman (1951), this

ELECTRIC BOARD

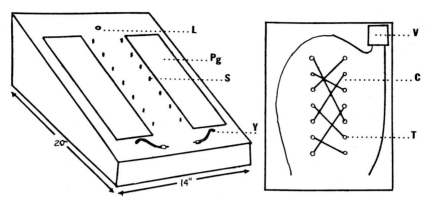

Figure 6. Front (left) and back (right) views of the electric board. Legend: L = Light; Pg = Plexiglas guard; S = Socket; Y = Stylus; V = 6 Volt battery; C = Colored wires used in reprogramming; T = thumb screw. (Reproduced by permission of Dr. Frederic L. Darley and Mr. Robert L. Keith).

language disturbance affects symbolization, concept formation and comprehension or expression of the spoken or written symbol.

Delayed speech and language development results not only from the child's inability to respond consistently to sounds [one of the hallmarks of the receptive aphasic child (Myklebust, 1954),[13] is that their verbal responses are often *ecolalic* in nature—speech is imitated without comprehension], but also, many of these children have poor auditory memory spans possibly due to their characteristic inattentiveness and hyperactivity. Lateral dominance problems are not uncommon and related to this phenomenon we see that "these children often read a printed page with greater ease in the mirror than by looking directly at it." (West, 1947) See Ingram's discussion of the "dysphasic" child in the chapter concerning speech and hearing disorders. See also 12, Explanatory Notations.

Some tests which have been recommended for evaluation of the dysacusic child are: (a) Sequin Form Board (Sequin, 1907);

[13]See this reference for other behavioral symptoms of aphasia in young children.

(b) the Goodenough Draw-A-Man Test, (Harris, 1963); (c) the Bender Gestalt Test (Bender, 1938); and (d) the Marble Board Test (Werner *et al.*, 1939). Also see Bakwin *et al.* (1966) for (d) tests of laterality, handedness, eyedness, footedness and earedness.

Hearing evaluations are important when dealing with children who may be suspected of having aphasia. Many of these children who were thought to be aphasic later turned out to have high frequency hearing disorders. This miss-diagnosis is primarily due to the child's inconsistent response to sounds. A relatively new audiological testing technique, an evaluation of cortical responses to acoustic stimuli recorded by electroencephalograph and analyzed by computers, may be reviewed in Price *et al.* (1966a, 1966b), and Rapin (1964).

A mild retardation in talking, up to two or even two and one-half years, is not unusual. However, the term "expressive aphasia" or "developmental mutism" (See Table XV in Chapter Five) refers to retarded speech development up to three or three and one-half years of age when the delay is not related to organic, brain damage (as in cerebral palsy), intellectual (mental retardation) or psychiatric (autism). Rather, there is a delay in acquiring language function. Some of these children will have learning difficulties in reading, writing and spelling (Ingram, 1965).

Constructional Apraxia

This disorder is referred to as spatial orientation defect, or as optical apraxia. It is important and common in parietal brain damage. It can be defined as a difficulty in putting together, reproducing or constructing, if you will, one-dimensional units so as to form two-dimensional figures or patterns. It is essentially, then, a *manual* defect within the *visual-spatial* domain. Visual *memory* is defective or lost and *praxic* (motor) disturbances are evident. The child will be unable to copy a design, or duplicate a design using sticks, or blocks. When drawing, the child tends to crowd the drawing into a corner, copy may be smaller or larger than the model and the lines are faulty. This child often tries to draw his copy upon the model. Vertical lines are apt to be slanted, horizontal lines tend to tilt up or down. This is most typically seen with a right parietal lobe lesion. The praxic disturbances mentioned are those concerned with motor skills so that *apraxia* is loss of the ability to carry out purposive, skilled acts, even though the sensory and motor systems are intact. Lesions apparently cut off impulses in the association tracts. The idea—the mental formulation of a plan—is correctly formed but mistakes occur in translating the plan into performance.

In addition to defects thus far mentioned, there may be mirror reversals. Aphasic writing defects can be observed which are revealed in formation of letters or numerals: E becomes Ǝ, L becomes ⅃. Up, down, back, front confusions are readily seen. Obviously, jigsaw puzzles are difficult to solve. The child, when asked to drive a nail into a board, may grasp the head of the hammer and hit the nail with the handle. Scissors are difficult to use. In every day living, the defects become apparent in such tasks as dressing, eating, and playing games. Piercy *et al.* (1960) observed that this disability was more frequent and more severe in patients with lesions of the right hemisphere. Constructional apraxia, however, can result from a lesion of either hemisphere but is more severe when the lesion is in the right. According to Brain (1965), constructional apraxia is rarely a pure motor disorder as "he [the child] knows what is meant by copying, since he sets out to do it; but if he is incompletely aware of his errors, his disability must be perceptual as well as motor."

Developmental Dyscalculia

This is a failure to recognize or manipulate number symbols. Especially evident in *mental* arithmetic and in *written* arithmetic. There is poor memory for numbers. The exact origin of this disorder usually cannot be determined. In children who have this difficulty, there is a "prolongation of the time and increase in the amount of energy required to achieve an adequate use of numbers" (Cohn, 1961).

Characteristics: (1) malformed or large number symbols, (2) strephosymbolia or mirror writing, (3) inability to sum single integers, (4) inability to recognize operator signs and to use linear separators, (5) failure to discriminate specific order characteristics of multi-digit numbers, (6) inability to remember and use tables of multiplication, (7) inability to *carry* numbers, and (8) inappropriate ordering of numbers in multiplication and division (Cohn, 1968).

The relation of dyscalculia to finger agnosia has given rise to interesting studies which discuss the close relationship of fingers to counting. Associated difficulties in letter recognition may be pronounced. The dyscalculia child is usually at his worst when the process is purely abstract (mental arithmetic), is better on paper and best if objects such as coins or an abacus are used. There is easier mental handling of *concretized* problems such as adding two actual objects to two more objects rather than adding 2 + 2.

Developmental Dyslexia (congenital word blindness)

A study group of the World Federation of Neurology developed a definition of specific developmental dyslexia:

> A disorder manifested by difficulty in learning to read despite conventional instruction, adequate intelligence and sociocultural opportunity. It is dependent upon fundamental cognitive disabilities which are frequently of constitutional origin.

As indicated by this definition, Developmental Dyslexia is a specific difficulty in learning to read. This difficulty exists in spite of at least average intelligence, and without an obvious emotional disturbance or brain damage, or gross impairment of hearing or vision. The child has difficulty in writing although he may be able to copy well. This inability to write is likely associated with a "memory" for word and letter shape difficulty. They cannot remember what the symbols look like, therefore, the child is unable to spontaneously write the words or letters. There may be damage to those areas of the brain concerned with *visual memory* of words, letters and figures. The child may be prone to spelling errors.

Schonell (1948) noted that these children have one or more of the following difficulties: (1) weakness in discrimination of phonic units, (2) lack of knowledge of common phonic units without actual weakness in discrimination or remembering, (3) a weakness in the discrimination of visual patterned words, especially those visually similar, (4) an unsystematic and irregular attack on words: parts of words (beginnings, middles or ends) being used as a basis of guessing, and (5) an extreme tendency to observe words from right to left or from the middle of the word to the left and showing itself in confusion, partial reversals and complete reversal of small words.

Whether delayed or mixed dominance plays any relationship in this disorder is still unclear (Benson, 1968). There are reports however that poorly established cerebral dominance, leading one to suspect an immaturity in cerebral development, is a source of difficulty in learning to read. These difficulties are assumed in these reports to result in directional confusion which is shown in reversals in reading and writing. Concerning lateral dominance, Zangwill (1962) states that the evidence supports a positive relationship and Silver and Hagin (1967) found an abiding failure among retarded readers to establish a definite lateral dominance. Another source of learning difficulty and reversal tendencies in reading reported in the literature is crossed-eye dominance. But, again, there are conflicting opinions. Johnson (1957) says that right-handedness combined with left-eyedness is a common occurrence among retarded readers. Orton (1928, 1937) found an excess amount of ambidexterity, sinistrality and mixed handedness and eyedness in his subjects. He was also concerned with the manner in which his *word blind* children made reversal (directional) errors, or mirror images (b for d). As well, the children showed tendencies to reverse the order of letters within words or words within sentences. Thus, "the man saw a red dog" might be misread as "a red god was the man" (Ingram, 1960). These same problems were noted also in the children's writing. One is able however to find studies which will support either camp. See Vernon, 1957; Zeman, 1967; Harris, 1958; Stephens *et al.* (1967) for comments from those who do not support the above findings.

As indicated in the speech disorders chapter, some studies (Granjon-Galefret, 1951) feel that the important relationship with specific developmental dysphasia and related disorders (dyslexia, dysgraphia) is not sinistrality or crossed laterality but the delayed or very weak establishment of hand or foot preference. The entire subject has been reviewed by Money (1962) and Critchley (1964).

It has been suggested that developmental dyslexia may be due to brain damage as both categories (dyslexics and the minimally brain damaged) have many features in common: impaired left-right orientation; an increase in the frequency of mixed, crossed or poorly established dominance; the digit repetition test of the WISC is below average; and the number of males is higher (Table IV).

It appears from the literature, however, that more evidence points to a positive family history of similar problems. Therefore, the *cause* would be of an innate, or constitutional, inherited origin as indicated in the definition proposed by the World Fed-

TABLE IV

DIFFERENCES BETWEEN CHILDREN WITH SPECIFIC DEVELOPMENTAL DYSLEXIA AND WITH MINIMAL CEREBRAL DYSFUNCTION*

	Specific Developmental Dyslexia	*Minimal Cerebral Dysfunction*
Abstract and inferential reasoning	Good	Poor
Arithmetical ability	Good, except cannot read printed problems and may have difficulty with mathematical symbols	Poor[a]
Perceptual disabilities	Chiefly for words	Multiple
Attention span	Good	Short
Hyperactivity	Infrequent, unless driven	Common
Visual motor coordination	Often good, but not always	Poor
WISC:		
Similarities	High	Below Average
Block Design	Average or above	Below Average
Full Scale IQ	As good as siblings	Lower than siblings
Verbal vs. performance score	Performance higher than verbal	Verbal higher than performance
Family history	Usually positive	Usually negative[b]

*Modified from McGlannan (1968).

[a]The typical minimal cerebral dysfunctioned child learns to read and by the fourth or fifth grade, reading and particularly spelling, which is mostly memory, are likely to be among his better areas of performance. Mathematics is almost invariably the poorest. The situation with the dyslexic: may be good at mathematics, but disability in reading persists, in many cases, despite the best remedial training.

[b]Although many of the children discussed under neurologically impaired (Minimal cerebral damage, learning disordered or what have you) do not have histories of pre-, at, or post-natal abnormalities, it is significant to realize that many children with cerebral palsy cannot be explained on the basis of any information gleamed from medical histories. This indicates that there may indeed be an *organic* basis to the problems associated with the specific developmental disorders.

(Reproduced from: Paine, R. S.: Syndromes of "Minimal Cerebral Damage". *Ped Clin N Amer, 15*:779-801, 1968.

eration of Neurology study group. Critchley's comment concerning the relationship between minimal brain damage and dyslexia may, however, dampen the spirits of those who support this theory as he says that "it is improbable [that brain damage is the cause] from what we know of resilience or plasticity of the juvenile cerebrum." (Critchley, 1968) Possibly a more acceptable hypothesis concerning *cause* is that of cerebral immaturity.

A somewhat discouraging conclusion is drawn from the literature concerning teaching this child. There does not appear to be one best method or technique for instructing the dyslexic. "This area (dyslexia) has far more theories than firm findings." (Benson, 1970).

See the following for references:

Critchley, M.: *Developmental Dyslexia*. London, Heinemann, 1964. (This contains a full bibliography up to 1964).

Critchley, M:. Is developmental dyslexia the expression of minor cerebral damage? *Slow Learn Child*, 13:9-19, 1966.

Critchley, M.: Some observations upon developmental dyslexia. In Williams, D. (Ed.): *Modern Trends in Neurology*. London, Butterworths, 1967.

Thompson, J. L.: *Reading Disability*. Springfield, Thomas, 1966. (Full bibliography).

Money, J.: *Reading Disability. Progress and Research Needs in Dyslexia*. Baltimore, Johns Hopkins Press, 1962.

Dysgraphia

This, the impaired ability to express oneself on paper (writing), is commonly associated with dyslexia and some aphasias (i.e. dysphasia). The child can copy but cannot write spontaneously. A dysgraphia produced by a left parietal lobe lesion results in defects of language in addition to the writing difficulties. Critchley (1968) states that this term is incorrect, however, when describing a mentally retarded or developmental dyslexics inability or difficulty with writing. The typical dysgraphic person is one who, at one time, has had this ability but due to a brain lesion of the "speech area" (or the middle one-half of the dominant cerebral hemisphere) has consequently lost this ability.

The child's written efforts can be evaluated or analyzed to determine the presence of this disorder. Commonly, one will find an abundance of word repetitions and omissions. Dyslexia may also be present which, as previously noted, is a difficulty in interpretation of meaning of written symbols. It should be noted that it is not at all uncommon to find the *disorders of language* (i.e. dyslexia, dysgraphia and dysphasia) in the same child. Dysgraphia is part of a disorder that used to be called Gerstmann's syndrome. This "syndrome," as Critchley notes, is now out of "neurological favour." See discussion under Gerstmann's Syndrome. Characteristics of parietal dysgraphia: (1) lines may run obliquely rather than horizontally; lines may intersect, or be superimposed (this phenomenon is seen most often in right-parietal lobe dysgraphia in right handed subjects, (2) poor formation of individual letters, and (3) semantic defects (most often found in left parietal dysgraphia).

Gerstmann Syndrome

This disorder was initially described by Gerstmann (1924, 1930, 1940). Although criticized of late (Poeck, *et al.,* 1966), most authorities are in agreement that this syndrome is almost entirely caused by left parietal damage. This syndrome consists of (1) finger agnosia (See Finger Naming Tests) which is an inability to name the fingers and indicate named fingers: (2) left-right disorientation: a failure to appropriately label the right and left sides of the body and space (See 13, Explanatory Notations), and (3) dysgraphia and dyscalculia: a failure to attain the expected level of performance in writing and calculation respectively (Kinsbourne, 1968). The child's performance on some of the WISC subtests (i.e. Block Design, Object Assembly, and Arithmetic) are deficient.

Finger agnosia appears to be the outstanding part of this defect. The child cannot name his own or the teacher's fingers, nor can he pick them out or put them side by side, or point them out on a chart, or move the finger corresponding to the one pointed out on a chart. Of course, not all the symptoms regarded as parietal lobe defects associated with the Gertsmann Syndrome will be noted in each child.

This array of symptoms (1-3 above) has, in the adult, been recognized as indicative of parietal lesions within the dominant hemisphere; however, this is not true in the developmental type. Kinsbourne (1968) notes that "in the developmental Gerstmann syndrome, a certain neural facility is underdeveloped." The localization of this *facility* is not known. Although the cause of this underdevelopment is often genetic, Kinsbourne says that it may alternately be associated with cerebral palsy acquired through perinatal trauma.

Acquired Gerstmann syndrome in children is almost unknown. However, Hermann and Norrie (1958) feel that the difficulty in learning to read and write found in the group of children they studied was caused by the Gerstmann Syndrome of developmental origin. In addition, they pointed out that to elicit the most important element of finger agnosia in children is difficult as their knowledge of finger names is variable. Kinsbourne and Warrington (1964) report, as a result of their normative study, that children of age 7½ reach the requisite criteria on the finger order tests.

There appears to be a selective delay in the ability to recognize, recall and use information regarding the position of some items (i.e. words, letters) in spatial or temporal sequence (See (2) above). Some of these children show spelling difficulties characterized by order errors and poor orientation of their written letters which conceivably can cause an inability or difficulty in learning to write.

The management of such children seems, at present, to be based more or less on teacher preference and not on any proven system or method.

FINGER NAMING. The deficit (finger agnosia), according to Kinsbourne, should be demonstrable in test situations in which finger naming is not involved and demands on verbal ability are minimal. Only one common factor need be observed in the testing situation: all should incorporate the need to utilize information as to relative finger position. A set of such tests was applied by Kinsbourne and Warrington (1962) to a group of patients with finger agnosia as classically defined, as well as to aphasic, right hemisphere and extracerebrally damaged control groups.

Three of these tests are presented below.

1. *Finger Differentiation Test.* Evaluates the subject's ability to allocate touch applied at various parts on the finger surface to one or another individual digit. He is asked to state whether the simultaneously touched loci are situated on the same or on two different fingers (he is not requested to name the finger). In this and the next test the subject places his dominant hand on a flat surface, palm down. The procedure has three phases: demonstration, verification and test.

For demonstration purposes, while the child watches, the examiner touches the patient's fingers in two places (Fig. 7), saying, "Now I am touching two fingers; now I am touching one . . ." After four such trials ("two," "one," "one," "two"), he verifies comprehension: "Now how many fingers am I touching?" If the responses are incorrect, they are corrected. After four consecutive correct responses, the testing proper begins.

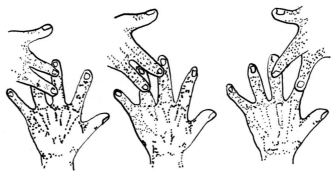

Figure 7. Test 1, finger differentiation test: III ("one"), III and IV ("two"), II and III ("two"). (The drawings in Figures 1, 2, and 3 were previously published in *Brit J. Psychol, 54*:145, 1963.)

The subject closes his eyes. Four consecutive touches are applied, in each case involving the dorsal aspect of the finger tip and of the proximal metacarpal phalangeal joint as follows: IV ("one"), II and III ("two"), IV and V ("two"), III ("one"). The same sequence is then followed on the other hand. A score of six or more correct out of eight constitutes a "pass."

In this and the subsequent test the touches are firmly applied and maintained until a response is given. The subject is

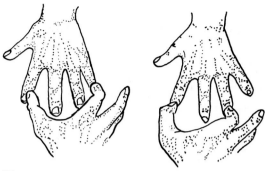

Figure 8. Test 2, in-between test: II/IV ("one"), II/V ("two").

encouraged to reinforce sensory input by slightly moving (wiggling) his fingers.

Should finger differentiation be adequately developed, it becomes relevant to ask, can the subject utilize relative finger position in test performance?

2. *In-Between Test.* The subject is touched each time on two fingers, and he is asked, "How many fingers are there between the ones I am touching?" (Fig. 8). A demonstration phase with eyes open as before is followed by careful verification that the task is understood. Eyes are then closed, and on each hand in turn, touches are applied as follows: II/IV ("one"), III/V

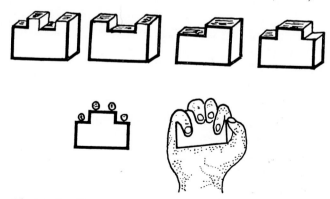

Figure 9. Test 3, finger block test. (Figs. 1, 2, and 3 reproduced by permission of Dr. Marcel Kinsbourne).

("one"), II/V ("two), II/III ("none"). Criterion for pass is again six correct responses out of a possible eight.

3. *Finger Block Test*. No introductory phase is required. Testing commences as follows. Four blocks are placed on the table (Fig. 9): "Do you see these four blocks? I have one more of each. Now close your eyes and give me your hand. I shall place a block in it. Now open your eyes and look at the four blocks on the table; which of these has the same shape as the one in your hand?" Each block is used once in each hand. The subject is cautioned to keep his fingers still and clasp but not manipulate the block. Six out of eight constitutes a pass score.

Significance of the Tests

The tests are not applicable when there is substantial somatosensory deficit affecting the hand. When this is unilateral, an adequate score on the other side excludes finger agnosia, which is, by definition, a bilateral disorder (i.e. one affecting a particular type of information processing irrespective of side of body).

When these tests were applied to the adult groups, failures were recorded in those patients who had finger agnosia, while the aphasic patients and other controls passed with ease. These findings indicate that the finger order tests may be added to the repertoire of methods for detecting finger agnosia and constitute effective procedures which avoid altogether the use of the finger names. This demonstrates the fundamental difference between finger agnosia and aphasic disorders. It also makes these tests particularly suitable for use with children (Kinsbourne, 1968).

Visual Agnosia (central blindness)

There are five areas to be considered under this broad heading: (1) Visual agnosia for objects: inability to recognize objects, although the child is still able to identify symbols, therefore, the child is able to read. Objects can be distinguished in other ways such as by feeling an object; (2) Simultanagnosia: failure to comprehend the meaning of a picture though its individual elements are recognized. This was originally discussed by Wolpert (1924). He described this disorder as an inability to recognize the whole meaning of a picture while details were appreciated. Luria (1959) feels that the main characteristic of this disorder is the visual perceptual restriction to a single object or figure. There is an inability to combine all the parts into an integrated whole. This may be seen in some brain damaged children when they tend to bring a rather complex picture close to their face in an apparent attempt to restrict the visual area so that it is mainly filled with one object. This disability appears to be limited to small objects. The child is therefore able to recognize a human figure, furniture, cars, trees etc. A lesion which causes visual object agnosia not uncommonly also leads to alexia, agraphia, finger agnosia, disorientation for R-L, acalculia and constructional apraxia (Neil, 1968); (3) Visual agnosia for color: the inability to match colors and to arrange them in a graduated series in respect to shade and/ or intensity. This disorder is distinguished from aphasias for colors or inability to name colors; (4) Visual agnosia for space: a general inability to orient oneself in space (the environment) by visual means. Some of the more common disorders of visual disorientation are: (a) disorders in visual localization of objects in space which result from lesions of the afferent visual pathways leading to impaired visual acuity, homonymous hemianopia (displacement of the fixation point,[14] and damage to the central integrative process (this, according to Brain (1965), is the only true visual agnosia); (b) loss of stereoscopic vision, and (c) agnosia for the left half of space. (5) Visual Imagery for objects: inability to draw objects (letters, etc.) from memory. This does not, however, involve loss of object recognition; therefore, there is no "visual object agnosia."

EXPLANATORY NOTATIONS

1. In a more recent publication, Tizard *et al.* (1960) states that over half of the infantile hemiplegics (cerebral defect of perinatal origin) have sensory defects usually taking the form of some loss of peripheral limb sensation. This loss does not usually involve simple sensations such as touch, pain, or temperature unless the thalamus is damaged. Those sensations most often affected, according to Tizard, are discrimination abilities which are

---

[14]See Chapter 6, *Vision and Its Defects* for further clarification of homonymous hemianopia.

affected at the cortical level; i.e. the ability to discriminate shape and texture, position and movement of joints, and the ability to differentiate between touch of one of two points. Tizard further states that, at times, simple forms of thalamic sensations are lost but usually only in the postnatal hemiplegic group. Visual-field defects occur in about a quarter of the hemiplegics.

2. The ability to localize symmetric simultaneously applied tactile stimuli is well developed at 3 years of age (Fink *et al.,* 1953).

3. The occurrence of this phenomenon would appear to be important when dealing with the cerebral palsied. Although this same difficulty may occur in the *normal* child, he has decidedly less outside and/or inside interference operating when coping in the classroom as opposed to those with which the cerebral palsied must cope. The behavior modification techniques may play a significant role by improving selective inhibition as the child's inattentiveness and/or distractability may be caused by, in addition to tactile afterimages, efforts involved in execution (motoric, visuo-motor involvement). Tactile afterimages constitute tactile perseveration.

4. In this study, form discrimination (stereognosis) was correlated significantly with 2-point discrimination (somatosensory). However, 30 percent showing a stereognosis defect did not show a related somatosensory loss. Wilson (1967a,b) observed that children who named (verbally labeled a form) made fewer form errors than those who did not. This would suggest that 'symbol manipulation' may play a role in stereognosis functions in addition to sensory factors.

A *memory factor* may operate as well. That is, in Wilson's study, many of the CP children made the correct choice spontaneously. But when instructed to "feel them all first" and then pick out the correct form, errors were made. They were unable to name a form which previously had spontaneously been named correctly. The children seemed to have forgotten. This would suggest that a memory factor was hampering the child's performance.

Stereognostic functions may therefore involve kinesthesis (somatosensory), verbal mediation and short-term memory.

Carmean (1967; O'Brien *et al.* 1967) found that it was possible to facilitate or inhibit (depress) the learning of a group of two-choice discriminations in some first, second, and sixth graders by controlling the children's activity after the response was made. Performance was enhanced by having the child name the correct stimulus after each choice. Performance was depressed when the pattern was mixed; i.e. sometimes naming the correct and sometimes the incorrect stimulus.

See Cantor, 1955; Jensen and Rohwer, 1963; Kendler and Kendler, 1961; Pyles, 1932; and Spiker, 1963, for experimental evidence which indicates that verbal mediation (labeling) markedly facilitates learning, retention, and problem solving.

5. See Appendix A, *Task Level Evaluation.*

6. Research of the literature reveals that spastic cerebral palsied children appear to experience more sensory losses than those with athetosis. Spatial orientation difficulties and size discrimination problems seem to have a special affinity for the athetoid, but this child seems to generally escape the sensory disorders which plague the spastic.

7. The implications that astereognosis has in the teaching-training-treatment areas may be: (a) hemiplegic children may demonstrate inattention to objects placed or presented to their involved side, (b) there will be obvious interference with form discrimination learning which is considered by many experts to be an essential pre-requisite to academic achievement, (c) the child may show difficulty manipulaing objects such as scissors, buttons, pencils, puzzles etc. This deficit resulting from sensory impairment would be in addition to the primary motor disability, and (d) possibly interferes with transfer of information from touch to vision. See Connors *et al.* (1967).

There are conflicting reports in the literature concerning results of treatment of sensory disorders. Some reports indicate failure, others report success (Kenny *et al.,* 1962) (Ferreri, 1962). It is undoubtedly fair to state that afferent impulses (sensory experiences) be they social, tactile or didactic must be offered as early as possible and with *variety*. The teacher-therapist-physician should assume that sensory defects may very likely exist. Sensory defects do occur in 50 to 70 percent of all cerebral palsied children. The therapist must involve the affected extremity to its maximum in tasks, attempting not to demand the unobtainable or to nag the child. Such disorders should alert the teacher to the possible need for change of teaching methods and materials. The orthopedic surgeon must consider the sensory loss and realize that it will still be present post-operatively and, therefore, possibly may limit the child's motor performance. The various treatment techniques which will be presented in the chapter dealing with Systems of Therapy depend heavily on sensory modalities.

Box identification as a technique in sensory training. This procedure involves placing a variety of objects in a box, asking the child to manipulate them (with the good hand) and to describe the object. Then, the affected extremity is placed in the box. Place the objects in the involved hand. Having duplicates of the objects outside the box is beneficial as it provides an additional clue (visual). Have child then identify the object. Objects should vary in shape, texture, size, and temperature. Consider such things as the child's attention span and frustration tolerance.

Sensory Story, a multisensory approach to training. This technique was used by Jones *et al.* (1969) to promote and facilitate communication, attention to tactile, auditory and visual stimuli and hand usage in relation to sensory input in the hands. A stage divided into four equal parts and set on a turntable was the book for the story. (This particular stage measured 20 inches in diameter and 9 inches in height). The general procedure involved eleven different objects which corresponded to the story. In this story, objects were used such as balls of clay, a bowl with water and soap, balls, textured material, etc. As the story proceeded, each object was presented at the appropriate time. The children were encouraged to communicate verbally or non-verbally in direct response to the situation or object. Jones sums up the results of the use of the *sensory story* approach by stating, "The three dimensional turntable model, as the book for a nursery school *sensory* story, appeared in this study to be functional and appropriate in encouraging hand usage in relationship to auditory, visual and tactile sensory input, in stimulating communication and in lengthening attention span."

Because the handicapped child suffers from a lack of varied

multisensory experiences as indicated by such authorities as Sayegh *et al.* (1965) "poverty of experiences" and Shere *et al.* (1966) "an impoverished object-environment," this multi-sensory story approach certainly merits at least a trial by teachers and therapists as one possible means of relief to this "poverty of experience," which is evidenced in the life of many hapdicapped children. For, as Schermann (1966) states, "sensations are the child's raw materials for thinking and learning to use all of his senses: visual, tactile, kinesthetic, auditory and olfactory."

The conclusion can well be drawn that sensory modalities used in training should incorporate both cutaneous and proprioception. And, essential to maximum development of motor function, there must be integration of sensory stimuli: visual, auditory, tactile and kinesthetic.

Gibson's (1955) study indicates that sensory acuity can be improved with training. For instance, two-point discrimination was affected by a few hours of training. According to Zaporozhets (1965, 1969), sensory learning can be increased. One training program dealing with manipulation of figures is reported by Zaporozhets. The program included special instructions of using fingers to trace outline of cardboard figures. The instructor stressed changes in the various shapes and counting the sides. After the special training procedures, the children were able to recognize the figures regardless of position.

Gassel and Williams (1963) claim that patients with homonymous hemianopia can, by paying attention, make better use of residual vision on the 'blind' side. This may be done by using what they call "gaze vision," in which the subject gazes straight ahead but pays attention to the hemianopic side instead of the area to which his gaze is directed. Jacobson (1929) was able to help people become aware of muscle tension, as distinct from the cutaneous and other sensations which often accompany muscle contraction, through progressive relaxation. Paying attention is said to be the fundamental basis for perceptual efficiency and learning capacity (Lindsley, 1968).

8. Birch and Belmont (1964) supports the Connors' study previously mentioned. Both feel that intersensory linkages be-

tween touch and vision are significantly impaired in children with brain injury.

9. Developmental changes do occur. While form recognition is almost completely developed by age five, transfer of information regarding size and orientation of figures is later and more gradual (Birch *et al.,* 1963) (Gollin, 1961). Refer also to the studies performed by Zaporozhets (1965) mentioned in Chapter 7, *Visual Impairment and the Learning Environment* regarding eye movements. The method of manipulation or exploration of objects involved in haptic (without vision) perception becomes more thorough and systematic with age (Hoop, 1971). This is supported by various investigations (Piaget, 1948; Zaporozhets, 1965).

The implication which can be drawn here, as well as in the study by Carmean concerning naming the correct stimulus after each choice and in the phenomenon of "after images," is that verbal instructions and comments from the teacher or therapist, and even from the child himself while performing, would appear to be of considerable importance. However, we must be aware of the possible negative effects that the child's language difficulties, if present, may have on the perceptual process. Belmont *et al.* (1968) studied subjects who were cerebrally damaged with aphasia, a cerebrally damaged group without aphasia, and a non-brain damaged, non-aphasic group to determine what the relationship between language is to perceptual processes. The task involved matching an auditory signal (a sharp, percussive 'tap') with a visual dot pattern presented on a 5 x 8 inch card. The authors felt that language, under certain conditions, may be a hindrance in the successful processing of sensory information. Blank and Bridger (1966), in their paper, suggest that verbal mediation plays an important role in sensory and intersensory processing. They studied visual, temporal and spatial integration in children. Results suggest that the use of overt verbalization can result in a deterioration of accuracy in performance. Kahn (1965) seems to support this rather negative finding. He found that the children who counted when being tested were among the worst auditory-visual performers. Kendler *et al.* (1966) found, too, that verbal labeling interfered with performance at the third grade level.

Related to the above comments is the idea of using all the sense modalities to stimulate as many 'learning' channels as possible. Various sensory experiences differ as to their ability to arouse associations (Goodglass *et al.*, 1968). Sensory stimuli may vary in its ability to excite the damaged areas to the 'threshold levels' that are necessary in order to produce an adequate response.

It is known that a blind person can learn to write, print or draw. This indicates that information on spatial relations can be acquired through kinesthetic perception without any visual perception (Brown *et al.*, 1967). At least in some cases, children with visual defects can utilize the avenue of kinesthesis in learning academics. However, a word of caution is in order when dealing with the CP/NI as many of these children have sensory-kinesthetic deficits.

10. Although there is a paucity of systematic inquiry into the effects of stimulus novelty on discrimination learning in children, quite a number of studies have shown that novelty encourages and evokes orienting and attending responses in children. See the following references:

House, B. J., Orlando, R., and Zeaman, D.: Role of positive and negative cues in the discrimination learning of mental defectives. *Perc Motor Skills, 51*:614-618, 1957.

Zeaman, D., House, B. J., and Orlando, R.: Use of special training conditions in visual discrimination learning with imbeciles. *Amer J Ment Def, 63*:453-459, 1958.

Harris, L.: The effects of relative novelty on children's choice behavior. *Child Develop, 2*:297-305, 1965.

Mendel, G.: Children's preferences for differing degrees of novelty. *Child Develop, 36*:453-465, 1965.

According to Brain and Goodenough (1929), preference[15] for color or form stimuli is a function of developmental stages. That is, the preference for form occurs up to age 3, preference for color appears from age 3 to 6, and preference for form reappears from age 7 into adulthood. Perception of white form on black back-

[15]According to Gaines (1971), preference has historically been described as, "children's behavior where one stimulus dimension is consistently selected in the presence of several stimulus dimensions."

ground seems developmentally more primitive than perception of black on white background. Mecham *et al.* (1966) recommends the use of white forms (letters, shapes etc.) on a black background.

11. Orientation of figures appears also to be a factor in perception accuracy. Frequently observed is the child who seems to confuse letters which are similar except for 'spatial orientation': b for d, p for q. When reproducing, or printing, these letters, the child may reverse or rotate them. These observations have led to a great many investigations. For a sampling, see the following references:

Haufmann, E.: Some experiments on spatial position as a factor in children's perception and reproduction in simple figures. *Psychol Forshung, 17*:319-329, 1933.

Davidson, H. P.: A study of reversals in young children. *J Genetic Psy, 45*:452-456, 1934.

Davidson, H. P.: A study of the confusing letters b, d, p, and q. *J Genetic Psy, 47*:458-468, 1935.

Wechsler, D., and Pignatelli, M.: Reversal errors in reading: phenomena of axial rotation. *J Ed Psychol, 28*:215-221, 1937.

Rudel, R. G., and Teuber, H. L.: Discrimination of direction of line in children. *J Compar Physiol Psychol, 56*:892-898, 1963.

Sekuler, R. W., and Rosenblith, J.F.: Discrimination of direction of line and the effect of stimulus alignment. *Psychonomic Sci, 1*:143-144, 1964.

We find from these studies a fact which potentially has usefulness in the classroom, particularly with reading. Developmentally, errors in horizontal orientation are more common and persist longer than errors in vertical orientation. The horizontal or lateral position maximizes the possibility of reversal errors (See Sekular *et al.,* 1964). Furthermore, Nadine and Evans (1969) suggest that the horizontal arrangement of letters necessitates a "sequential search" requiring tracking of both letter and position information. Under the vertical format, a single fixation provides both letter and position information. This eliminates the need for an extensive search pattern in differentiating among words. (This may be particularly relevant to the child with eye muscle disorders). See Figure 10.

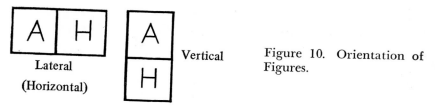

Lateral
(Horizontal)

Vertical

Figure 10. Orientation of Figures.

12. According to Kephart (1971), laterality is "the internal awareness of the two sides of the body and their differences. Laterality must be learned." And directionality is "the projection, into external space, of the awareness of laterality" (right and left, up and down etc.).

13. An example of the word *name* is mirror written in Figure 11.

14. Right-left orientation (a facet of spatial orientation). This very broad concept has attracted a great deal of attention in the literature. As early as 1937 (Orton, 1937), the problem of defective cerebral dominance and its consequent ambidexterity problems was associated with stuttering.

Right-left orientation refers to many types and levels of performances. See Benton, 1959, and Poeck *et al.*, 1967. Therefore, as suggested by Benton (1968), in evaluating right-left orientation, "it is essential that the broad capacity be analyzed into operationally defined components or levels." Whereupon, he has proposed an analysis which consists of five components (A-E in Table V) of right-left orientation.

The ability to perform on the "A" level is a prerequisite to successful performance on the other levels. We then see a hierarchial relationship in the abilities A-E. That is, discrimination

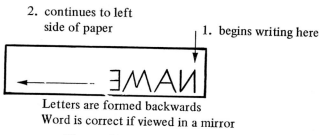

2. continues to left side of paper

1. begins writing here

Letters are formed backwards
Word is correct if viewed in a mirror

Figure 11. Mirror Writing.

TABLE V

SOME COMPONENTS OF RIGHT-LEFT DISCRIMINATION

Orientation toward one's own body

The subject is instructed to:
   A. Point to single lateral body parts on his own body (e.g., his left ear);
   B. Execute double uncrossed commands (e.g., touch his *left* ear with his *left* hand);
   C. Execute double crossed commands (e.g., touch his *left* ear with his *right* hand).

(The subject has his eyes open during the execution of these performances. The same performances are then executed with his eye closed. If the subject cannot or will not keep his eyes closed, he is blindfolded.)

Orientation toward a confronting person

The object of orientation being either the confronting examiner or a frontview representation of a person, the subject is instructed to:
   D. Point to single lateral body parts

Combined orientation toward one's own body and a confronting person

The subject is instructed to:
   E. Place either his left or his right hand on a specified lateral body part of the confronting person (e.g., his *right* hand on the *left* ear of the confronting person).

From Benton, Arthur L.: Right-left discrimination, *Ped Clin N Amer* 15 (3):747, August, 1968.

of the left and right sides of one's own body develops rather slowly. This ability begins about four years of age. At six, there is identification of single body parts related to left and right. From six to nine, the ability to perform "double-crossed command" develops. By nine, this ability should be well established. By twelve, the child should be operating as a normal adult.

A 32-item test, which provides for the assessment of each of these components of right-left discrimination, is shown in Table VI. See also Benton *et al.* (1960). One needs to be cautioned that, as Myklebust (Johnson, 1967) suggests, "an inability to identify body parts may be indicative of a disorder in auditory comprehension."

Benton points out that this evaluation does not exhaust all the possibilities. Other aspects and levels can be evaluated such as (1) naming lateral body parts on self and others: See Head, 1926; Benton, 1959 and Ayers, 1966 and 1968; (2) imitating crossed or uncrossed movements made by the teacher or therapist. See Head, 1926; Ayers, 1968; and (3) locating tactile stimuli. See Benton, 1959; Ayers, 1966. According to Benton, right-left dis-

TABLE VI
BENTON RIGHT-LEFT DISCRIMINATION TEST (FORM A)

(Examiner to Subject, eyes open)

1. Show me your *left* hand.
2. Show me your *right* eye.
3. Show me your *left* ear.
4. Show me your *right* hand.

5. Touch your *left* ear with your *left* hand.
6. Touch your *right* eye with your *left* hand.
7. Touch your *right* knee with your *right* hand.
8. Touch your *left* eye with your *left* hand.
9. Touch your *right* ear with your *left* hand.
10. Touch your *left* knee with your *right* hand.
11. Touch your *right* ear with your *right* hand.
12. Touch your *left* eye with your *right* hand.

13. Point to the man's *right* eye.
14. Point to the man's *left* leg.
15. Point to the man's *left* ear.
16. Point to the man's *right* hand.

17. Put your *right* hand on the man's *left* ear.
18. Put your *left* hand on the man's *left* eye.
19. Put your *left* hand on the man's *right* shoulder.
20. Put your *right* hand on the man's *right* eye.

(Examiner to Subject, eyes closed)

21. Show me your *right* hand.
22. Show me your *left* leg.
23. Show me your *right* eye.
24. Show me your *left* ear.

25. Touch your *right* ear with your *right* hand.
26. Touch your *left* knee with your *right* hand.
27. Touch your *right* eye with your *left* hand.
28. Touch your *left* ear with your *left* hand.
29. Touch your *left* eye with your *right* hand.
30. Touch your *left* knee with your *left* hand.
31. Touch your *right* shoulder with your *left* hand.
32. Touch your *right* eye with your *right* hand.

From Benton, Arthur L.: Right-left discrimination. *Ped Clin N Amer, 15* (3):748, August, 1968.

crimination has usually been assessed along the lines presented in Table V.

Regarding general directional concepts, what is the basis for left and right discrimination? Boone (1965) feels that 'up' 'down' concepts develop as an ultimate result of gravity on the body (therefore, proprioceptive in origin). And, that concepts such as front and back develop as a result of visual orientation ("one's ears are in front of one's head"). Benton postulates that R-L abilities result from sensory excitation from muscles and joints of the two sides of the body (again, proprioceptive in nature) as well as containing a linguistic or symbolic component.

It is not surprising then to see right-left discrimination disorders and body image disorders in the CP/NI child. In fact, "From a clinical standpoint, the most interesting result to date is the indication that impairment in right-left discrimination may be associated with the presence of brain damage in children." (Benton, 1968) Body image disturbance, according to Benson et al. (1968) is a rare occurrence in children. Where reported, the disturbance seems to be limited to those children suffering bilateral brain damage.

It is questionable whether or not R-L discrimination disturbances regarding both the visual perception and directional aspects are causes of reading disability (dyslexia). Again, Benton states, "critical analysis of the pertinent literature shows that there is no substantial evidence for this conclusion." Rather, he feels that "it is a reflection, rather than the cause, of a basic linguistic disability." Or as Rabinovitch (1962) proposed, the difficulty is "in translating perception into symbols."

REFERENCES

Abercrombie, M. L. J.: Perceptual visuomotor disorders in cerebral palsy: A survey of the literature. *Little Club Clinics,* No. 11 Spastics International Med Publications. London, Heinemann, 1964.

Abercrombie, M. L. J., *et al.*: Visual, perceptual and visuomotor disorders in a school for physically handicapped children. *Percept Mot Skills,* 1964.

Agranowitz, A. and McKeown, M. R.: *Aphasia Handbook for Adults and Children.* 3rd ed., Springfield, Thomas, 1968.

Ayers, A. Jean: Southern California Perceptual-Motor Test. Los Angeles, Western Psychological Services, 1968.

Ayers, A. Jean: Southern California Kinesthesia and Tactile Perception Test. Los Angeles, Western Psychological Services, 1966.

Bakwin, H., and Bakwin, R. M.: *Clinical Management of Behavior Disorders in Children.* Philadelphia, Saunders, 1966, pp. 357-363.

Belmont, L., Birch, H. and Belmont, I.: Auditory-visual intersensory processing and verbal mediation. *J Nerv Ment Dis, 147*:562-569, 1968.

Bender, L.: A visual motor test and its clinical use. *Amer Orthop Asso Res Mono 3.* New York, L. G. Lowrey, 1938.

Benson, F. D., and Gerschwind, N.: Cerebral dominance and its disturbance. *Pediatr Clin N Amer, 15* (3):759-769, 1968.

Benson, F. D.: Personal communication. February, 1970.

Benton, A. L.: *Right-Left Discrimination and Finger Localization: Development and Pathology.* New York, Hoeber-Harper, 1959.

Benton, A. L.: Right-left discrimination. *Pediatr Clin N Amer, 15* (3): 747-758, 1968.

Benton, A. L., and Kemble, J. D.: Right-left orientation and reading disability. *Psychiat Neurol, 139*:49, 1960.

Birch, H. G., and Belmont, I.: Perceptual analysis and sensory integration in brain-damaged persons. *J Gen Psychol, 105*:173-179, 1964.

Birch, H. G., and Lefford, A.: Intersensory development in children. *Child Develop Monogr, 28*:3-48, 1963.

Blank, M., and Bridger, W. H.: Deficiencies in verbal labeling in retarded readers. *Am J Orthopsychiatry, 36*:840-847, 1966.

Boone, D. R.: On the other hand: Laterality, dominance and language. *J Kansas Med Soc, 66*:132, 1965.

Brain, W. D.: *Speech Disorders: Aphasia, Apraxia, and Agnosia.* 2nd ed. Washington, Butterworths, 1965.

Brian, C. R., and Goodenough, F. L.: Relative potency of color and form perception at various ages. *J Exp Psychol, 12*:197-213, 1929.

Brock, S., and Krieger, H. P.: *The Basis of Clinical Neurology,* 4th ed. Baltimore, Williams and Wilkins, 1963.

Brown, J. R., Darley, F. L., and Gomez, M. R.: Disorders of communication. *Ped Clin N Amer, 14* (4):725-748, 1967, p. 729.

Cantor, G. N.: Effects of three types of pre-training on discrimination learning in pre-school children. *J Exp Psychol, 49*:339-342, 1955.

Carmean, S. L., and Weir, M. W.: Effects of verbalizations on discrimination learning and retention. *J Verbal Learn Verb Behav, 6*:545-550, 1967.

Cohn, Robert: Delayed acquisition of reading and writing abilities in children. *Amer Arch Neurol, 4*:153-164, 1961.

Cohn, Robert: Developmental dyscalculia. *Ped Clin N Amer, 15,* 1968.

Connors, C. K., and Barta, F.: Transfer of information from touch to vision in brain-injured and emotionally disturbed children. *J Nerv Ment Disease, 145*:138-141, 1967.

Critchley, M.: *The Parietal Lobes.* Baltimore, Williams and Wilkins, 1953.

Critchley, M.: *Developmental Dyslexia.* London, Spastics Society/Heinemann, 1964.

Critchley, M.: Developmental dyslexia. *Ped Clin N Amer, 15* (3):674, 1968.

Cruickshank, W. M., *et al.: Perception and Cerebral Palsy,* 2nd ed. Syracuse, Univ Press, 1965.

Cruickshank, W. M. *et al.*: *Perception and Cerebral Palsy: A Study in Figure Background Relationship.* Syracuse, Syracuse Univ Press, 1957.

Elithorn, A. *et al.*: Some mechanisms of tactile localization revealed by a study of leucotomized patients. *J Neurol Neurosurg Psychiaty, 15*:272-281, 1952.

Eisenson, Jon: Developmental aphasia: Therapeutic implications. In Wolff, P. H., and MacKeith, Ronald (Eds).: *Planning for Better Learning.* Clin Develop Med, No. 33. London, Heinemann, 1969, p. 104.

Ferreri, J. A.: Intensive stereognostic training. *Amer J Occup Ther, 16*:141-142, 1962.

Fink, Max, and Bender, M. B.: Perception of simultaneous tactile stimuli in normal children. *Neurology, 3*:27-34, 1953.

Gaines, Rosslyn: Children's selective attention to stimuli: stage or set? *Child Develop, 41*:979-991, 1971.

Gassel, M. M., and Williams, D.: Visual function in patients with homonymous hemianopia. III. The contemplation phenomenon; insight and attitude to the defect; and visual functional efficiency. *Brain, 86*:229, 1963.

Gerstmann, J.: Fingeragnosie: Eine umschriebene Störung der Orientierung ameigenen Körper. *Wein Klin Wehnschr, 37*:1010, 1924.

Gerstmann, J.: Syndrome of finger agnosia, disorientation for right and left, agraphia and acalculia. *Arch Neurol Psychiat, 44*:398, 1940.

Gerstmann, J.: Zur Symptomatologic der Hirnläsionen im Übergangsgebiet der untern parietal und mittleren Occipitalwindung. *Nervenarzt, 3*:691-695, 1930.

Gibson, E. J.: Perceptual learning. *Psychol Rev, 62*:32, 1955.

Goldberg, H.: Vision, perception, and related facts in dyslexia. In Keeney, A. H., and Keeney, V. T. (Eds.): *Dyslexia and Treatment of Reading Disorders.* St. Louis, Mosby, 1968.

Gollin, E. S.: Tactual form discrimination: Developmental differences in the effects of training under conditions of spatial interference. *J Psychol, 51*:131-140, 1961.

Goodglass, H., and Quadfasel, F. A.: Language laterality in left handed aphasics. *Brain, 77*:521-548, 1964.

Goodglass, H., *et al.*: Sensory modality and object naming in aphasia. *J Speech Hear Dis, 11*:488-496, 1968.

Granjon-Galifret, N., and Ajuriaguerra, J. de: Troubles de l'apprentissage de la lecture et dominance laterale. *Encephale, 40*:385, 1951.

Halacy, D. S., Jr.: *Man and Memory: Breakthroughs in the Science of the Human Mind.* New York, Harper and Row, 1969.

Hardy, W.: Discussion. In Carterette, E. C. (Ed.): *Brain Function,*

Vol. 3, Speech, Language, and Communication. Berkeley, Univ. Calif Press, 109-114, 1966.

Harris, A. J.: *Harris tests of lateral dominances: manual of directions for administration and interpretation,* 3rd ed. New York, Psychological Corp, 1958.

Harris, D. B.: *Children's Drawings as Measures of Intellectual Maturity: A Revision and Extension of the Goodenough Draw-A-Man Test.* New York, Harcourt, Brace and World, 1963.

Head, H.: *Aphasia and Kindred Disorders of Speech.* Cambridge, Univ Press, 1926.

Head, H., and Holmes, G.: Sensory disturbances from cerebral lesions. In Head, H. (Ed.): *Studies in Neurology.* London, Hodder and Stoughton, 1920, vol. 2, pp. 533-638.

Hecaen, H.: Clinical symptomatology in right and left hemisphere lesions. In Mountcastle, V. B. (Ed.): *Interhemispheric Relations and Cerebral Dominance.* Baltimore, Johns Hopkins Press, 1962.

Hermann, K., and Norrie, E.: Is congenital word-blindness a hereditary type of Gerstmann's syndrome? *Psychiat Neurol Basel, 136*:59, 1958.

Hohman, Leslie B., *et al.*: Sensory disturbances in children with infantile hemiplegia, triplegia and quadriplegia. *Am J Phys Med, 37*:1-6, 1958.

Hoop, N. H.: Haptic perception in preschool children. *Am J Occup Ther, 25*:415-419, 1971.

Ingram, T. T. S.: Pediatric aspects of specific developmental dysphasia, dyslexia, and dysgraphia. *Cereb Palsy Bull, 2*:254-277, 1960.

Ingram, T. T. S., and Mason, A. W.: Reading and writing difficulties in children. *Brit Med J, 2*:463, 1965.

Jacobson, E.: *Progressive Relaxation.* Chicago, University Chicago Press, 1929.

Jensen, A. R., and Rohwer, W. D., Jr.: The effect of verbal mediation on the learning and retention of paired-associates by retarded adults. *Am J Ment Def, 68*:80-84, 1963.

Jones, M. H., et al.: Two experiments in training handicapped children at nursery school. In Wolff, P., and MacKeith R. (Eds.): *Planning for Better Learning.* London, Spastics Internat Med Pub, 1969.

Johnson, D. J., and Myklebust, H. R.: *Learning Disabilities.* New York, Grune and Stratton, 1967.

Johnson, M. S.: Factors related to disability in reading, *J Exper Ed, 26*:1-26, 1957.

Kahn, D.: The development of auditory-visual integration and reading achievement. Unpublished doctoral Ph.D. dissertation, Columbia Univ, 1965.

Keith, R. L., and Darley, F. L.: The use of a specific electric board in rehabilitation of the aphasic patient. *J Speech Hear Dis,* 32:148-153, 1967.

Kendler, T. S., *et al.*: Verbal labels and inferential problem solution of children. *Child Develop, 37*:749-763, 1966.

Kendler, H. H., and Kendler, T. S.: Effect of verbalization on reversal shift in children. *Science, 134*:1619-1620, 1961.

Kenny, W. E., *et al.*: Training hands in children with astereognosis due to cerebral palsy. *J Bone Joint Surg, 44A*:1490, 1962.

Kephart, N.: *The Slow Learner in the Classroom.* Columbus, Merrill, 1960.

Kephart, N.: *The Slow Learner in the Classroom,* 2nd ed. Columbus, Merrill, 1971.

Kinsbourne, M., and Warrington, E. K.: A study of finger agnosia. *Brain, 85*:47, 1962.

Kinsbourne, M.: Developmental Gerstmann syndrome. *Ped Clin N Amer, 15*:771-778, 1968.

Kinsbourne, M., and Warrington, E. K.: The development of finger differentiation. *Quart J Exp Psychol,* 15:132, 1964.

Lindsly, D. B.: Neurophysiological basis of attention (Abstract). *Dev Med Child Neurol, 10*:250, 1968.

Luria, A. R.: Disorders of 'Simultaneous Perception' in a case of bilateral occipital-parietal brain injury. *Brain, 82*:437-449, 1959.

McFie, J.: A neuropsychological view of learning difficulties. In Wolff, P., and MacKeith, R. (Eds.): *Planning for Better Learning.* London, Heinemann, 1969.

McGlannan, F. K.: Familial characteristics of genetic dyslexia: Preliminary report from a pilot study. *J Learn Dis, 1*:185, 1968.

Mecham, M. J., *et al.*: *Communication Training in Childhood Brain Damage.* Springfield, Thomas, 1966.

Miller, M. H.: Dysacusis. *Ped Clin N Amer, 15,* 1968.

Monfraix, C., *et al.*: Disturbances of manual perception in children with cerebral palsy. *Dev Med Child Neurol, 3*:544-552, 1961.

Money, J. (Ed.): *Reading Disability.* Baltimore, Johns Hopkins Press, 1962.

Moore, Josephine C.: *Neuroanatomy Simplified.* Dubuque, Kendall/Hunt, 1969.

Myklebust, H. R.: *Auditory Disorders in Childrens A Manual for Differential Diagnosis.* New York, Grune & Stratton, 1954.

Nadine, C. F., and Evans, J. D.: Eye movement of prereaders to pseudowords containing letters of high and low confusability. *Percept and Psychophysics,* 6:39-41, 1969.

Nathan, Peter: *The Nervous System.* Philadelphia, Lippincott, 1969.

Neil, Gordon: Visual agnosia in childhood VI: Preliminary communication. *Dev Med Child Neurol, 10*:337-379, 1968.

Nelson, T. M.: A study comparing visual and visu-motor perceptions of impaired defective and spastic cerebral palsied children. *J genet Psychol, 101*:299-332, 1962.

Nielson, J. M.: *A Textbook of Clinical Neurology,* 3rd ed. New York, Paul Hoeber, 1962.

Noback, Charles R.: *The Human Nervous System.* New York, McGraw-Hill, 1967.

Oakley, Donald: "Including Kids Themselves", *The Mobile Press Register,* September 21, 1971.

O'Brien, G. L., and Carmean, S. L.: Verbalizing and writing as auxiliary responses during discrimination learning. *Psycho Sci, 9*:335-336, 1967.

Orton, S. T.: Specific reading disability—strephosymbolia. *JAMA,* 1094-1099, 1928.

Orton, S.: *Reading, Writing and Speech Problems in Chlidhood.* New York, Norton, 1937.

Paine, R. S.: Syndromes of 'Minimal Cerebral Damage.' *Ped Clin N Amer, 15*:779-801, 1968.

Penfield, W., and Roberts, L.: *Speech and Brain Mechanisms.* Princeton, Princeton Univ. Press, 1959.

Piaget, J., and Inhelder, B.: *The Child's Conception of Space.* New York, Norton, 1948.

Piercy, H., *et al.: Brain, 83*:225, 1960.

Poeck, J., and Orgass, B.: Uber Störungen der Rechts-Links-Orientierung. *Nervenarzt, 28*:295, 1967.

Poeck, J., and Orgass, B.: Gerstmann's syndrome and aphasia. *Cortex, 3*:421-437, 1966.

Price, L. L., and Goldstein, R.: Averaged evoked responses for measuring auditory sensitivity in children. *J Speech Hear Dis, 31*:248-256, 1966a.

Price, L. L., *et al.:* The averaged evoked response to auditory stimulation. *J Speech Hear Res, 9*:361-370, 1966b.

Pyles, M. K.: Verbalization as a factor in learning. *Child Devel, 3*:108-113, 1932.

Rabinovitch, R. D.: Dyslexia: Psychiatric considerations. In Money, J. (Ed.): *Reading Disability.* Baltimore, Johns Hopkins Press, 1962.

Rapin, I: Evoked responses to clicks in a group of children with communication disorders. *Ann NY Acad Sci, 112*:182-203, 1964.

Rappaport, S.R.: *Childhood Aphasia and Brain Damage.* Narberth, Livingston, 1964.

Roberts, L.: The relationship of cerebral dominance to hand, auditory and ophthalmic preference. In Vinken, P. J., and Bruyn, G. W. (Eds.): *Handbook of Clinical Neurology.* Amsterdam, North Holland, 1969.

Sayegh, Y., and Dennis, W.: The effects of supplementary experiences upon the behavioral development of infants in institutions. *Child Develop, 36*:81, 1965.

Schermann, A.: Cognitive goals in the nursery schools. *Child Study, 28*:15, 1966.

Schonell, F. J.: *Backwardness in the Basic Subjects,* 3rd ed. Edinburgh, Oliver & Boyd, 1948.

Sekuler, R. W., and Rosenblith, J. F.: Discrimination of direction of line and the effect of stimulus alignment. *Psychonomic Sci, 1*:143-144, 1964.

Seguin, E.: *Idiocy: Its Treatment by the Physiological Method.* New York, Bureau of Publications, Teachers College, Columbia University, 1907; reprinted from original edition of 1866.

Shere, E., and Kastenbaum, R.: Mother-child interaction in cerebral palsy; environmental and psychosocial obstacles to cognitive development. *Genet Psychol Monogr, 73*:255, 1966.

Silver, A. E., and Hagin, R. A.: Specific reading disability: an approach to diagnosis and treatment. *J Spec Ed, 1*:109-118, 1967.

Dr. Skatvedt's comment in *Child Neurology and Cerebral Palsy.* Spastics Society/Heinemann, 1961, p. 118.

Spiker, C. C.: Verbal factors in the discrimination learning of children. In Wright, J. C., and Kagan, J. (Eds.): Basic Cognitive Processes in Children. *Monog Soc Res Child Develop, 28* (2), 1963.

Stephens, W. E., *et al.*: Reading readiness and eye-hand preference in first grade children. *Except Child, 33*:481-488, 1967.

Subirana, A.: The prognosis in aphasia in relation to the factor of cerebral dominance and handedness. *Brain, 81*:415-425, 1958.

Tachdjean, M. O., and Minear, W.: Sensory disturbances in the hands of cerebral palsied children. *J Bone Joint Surg, 40A*:85, 1958.

Taylor, E. M.: *Psychological Appraisal of Children with Cerebral Defects.* Cambridge, Harvard University Press, 1959.

Teuber, J.: *The Behavioral Basis of Perception,* New Haven, Yale University Press, 1962.

Tizard, J. P. M., *et al.*: Report: Sensory, auditory and speech defects in cerebral palsy. *Cere Pal Bull, 2*:40-44, 1960.

Tizard, J. P. M., *et al.*: Disturbances in sensation in children with hemiplegia. *JAMA, 155*:623-628, 1954.

Vernon, M. D.: *Backwardness in Reading.* Cambridge, University Press, 1957.

Wedell, K.: Variations in perceptual ability among types of cerebral palsy. *Cere Pal Bull, 2*:149-157, 1960.

Wepman, J.: *Recovery from Aphasia.* New York, Ronald Press, 1951.

Werner, H., and Strauss, A.: *Types of Visuo-motor Activity in Their*

Relation to Low and High Performance Ages. New York, American Assoc Mental Deficiency, 1939.

West, R., *et al.*: *The Rehabilitation of Speech.* New York, Harper & Bros, 1947, pp. 196-202.

Wilson, B. C., and Wilson, J. J.: Sensory and perceptual functions in the cerebral palsied: II. Stereognosis. *J Nerv Ment Dis, 145*:61-68, 1967a.

Wilson, B. C., and Wilson, J. J.: Sensory and perceptual functions in the cerebral palsied: I. Pressure thresholds and two-point discrimination. *J Nerv Ment Dis, 145*:53-60 ,1967b.

Wolpert, I. A.: *ges Neurol Psychiat, 93*:397, 1924.

Zangwill, O. L.: *Cerebral Dominance and Its Relation to Psychological Function.* Springfield, Thomas, 1960.

Zangwill, O. L.: Dyslexia in relation to cerebral dominance. In Money, J. (Ed.): *Reading Disability.* Baltimore, Johns Hopkins Press, 1962.

Zaporozhets, A. V.: The development of perception in the preschool child. In Mussen, P. H. (Ed.): European Research in Cognitive Development. *Child Develop Mongr, 30*:82-101, 1965. Chicago, University of Chicago Press, 1965.

Zaporozhets, A. V.: Some of the psychological problems of sensory training in early childhood and the preschool period. In Cole, M., and Maltzman, I. (Eds.): *A Handbook of Contemporary Soviet Psychology.* New York, Basic Books, 1969, pp. 86-120.

Zeman, S. S.: A summary of the research concerning laterality and reading. *Read Specialist, 6*:116-123, 1967.

Chapter Four

ORTHOPEDIC MANAGEMENT IN CEREBRAL PALSY

THE 1970 NINDS RESEARCH PROFILES (1970) estimates that some 750,000 Americans have cerebral palsy. Of these, nearly 37,500, or 5 percent (Inglis *et al.*, 1970), may be benefited by surgical treatment of the upper extremity. A definitive statement concerning numbers that may benefit from surgery of the lower extremities cannot be made. However, the figure is undoubtedly at least twice that noted for the upper extremities (Paschall, 1971). This larger figure results from the fact that lower extremity deformities are more easily corrected because function is grosser. In addition, these deformities are more amenable to successful results as there is less functional demand placed on the lower extremities. Surgery of the lower extremity in cerebral palsy has remained essentially unchanged for many years; i.e. hip adduction contracture is corrected by adductor myotomy and obturator neurectomy. Recent advances in surgical methods and procedures has thrown renewed interest upon upper extremity surgical treatment of the cerebral palsied as will be obvious to the reader later.

Orthopedic management in cerebral palsy consists of surgery and bracing/splinting.

The surgical treatment of cerebral palsy had its origin when, in 1862, Little proposed and taught that the best method of correcting an equinus deformity in a spastic child was by operation, a belief that was found upon the successful subcutaneous lengthening of his own heel cord!

88

Surgical correction of deformities in cerebral palsy must not be confused with techniques used in the treatment of deformities resulting from such neuromuscular diseases as poliomyelitis. For instance, tendon transfers in C.P. are done only to remove a deforming force to a position where it may act only as a tenodesis but should not be expected to perform as a muscle with normal tone. Most deformities, particularly in the lower extremity, are corrected by tendon release or boney operations to block motion or realign joints.

Surgery is indicated most often in the spastic where it is useful to correct a resistant contracture, restore muscle balance, and stabilize joints. In the athetoid, due to their constant motion and equalization of musculature involvement in both agonist and antagonist, contractures usually do not develop. If athetoid muscles are surgically altered, the deforming force may shift to the antagonist group of muscles of opposite function. That is, if hip adductors are released for scissors gait, the abductors (the antagonist) of the hip may be unopposed and lead to a fixed abducted position of the hip. Occasionally, however, surgery may be performed successfully in the athetoid when surgery may decrease such postural contractures as flexion contractures of hips and knees resulting from prolonged sitting.

NORMAL AND SPASTIC MUSCLES, CHARACTERISTICS

All skeletal muscles contain muscle *spindles*. The spindle consists of two parts: the *nuclear bag* (fibers which are attached to the extrafusal muscle at both ends), and the *nuclear chain fibers* (Boyd, 1962). These spindles serve as watchdogs: they monitor length and tension within the muscle. There is general agreement which indicates that this 'length and tension receptor' (the spindles) serves also as an influence over the entire nervous system, including regulating the activity of the alpha efferents (Rushworth, 1960) producing the smooth muscle contraction characteristic of normal function. Gamma motoneuron fibers innervate the small muscle fibers within the spindles thereby placing controls on the muscle's response to stretch. In the normal muscle, the tension of the spindle is held constant or maintained at a certain level (Figure 12). This maintenance occurs regardless of

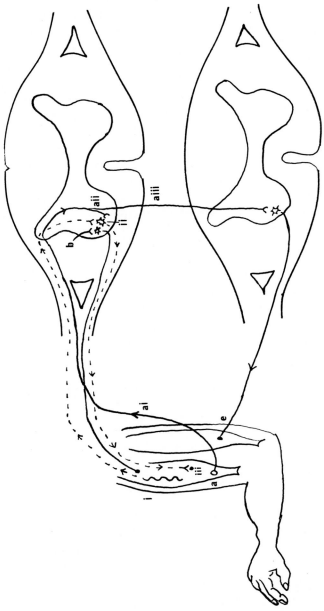

Figure 12.   Alpha-Gamma Loop Reflex System as Applied to Functional Anatomy. A stimulus (i) from a proprioceptive (i.e. annulospiral

the length of the muscle. By maintaining this constant level of *readiness,* the muscle is set to react or act. That is, the muscle spindle is prepared or *biased* through descending pathways which synapse on the gamma motoneuron[16] in the spinal cord. Changes then in the spindle send messages (impulses) to the alpha moto-neuron in the cord (anterior horn) which permits the muscles to contract (Fig. 13). That is, when the muscle is stretched, the spindle is stretched also. Afferent impulses from endings on the annulospiral fibers (Fig. 13) run along the large 1A fibers (4 in Fig. 13). These connect monosynaptically with alpha motoneurons in the anterior horn of the spinal cord which shoots off impulses

[16]It is now the theory that the gamma motoneuron is the main path through which most of the descending pathways pass.

ending of neuromuscular spindle) receptor in the biceps (elbow flexor) is conducted along the axon of the motoneuron where it synapses at (ii), the large alpha motor neuron in the anterior horn. The impulse informs or excites an alpha motoneuron to the biceps (iii) at the motor end plate.

From upper motor neurons (via the pyramidal tracts) come impulses to the Gamma neurons (b) in the anterior horn cell. These stimulate the intrafusal muscle spindles thus causing them to contract and stimulate the annulospiral endings which results in maintaining a constant firing of the Alpha motor neuron (Relate this to "C" under Fig. 13). Golgi tendon organs (a) are stimulated when tension of the contraction or stretch reaches a certain 'critical' point, and/or when they are triggered purposely from the periphery. It is a muscle protector so to speak—when the muscle is 'over-stimulated' the golgi tendon organs, in essence, say "stop, I've had too much." Their afferent firing (ai) produces *inhibition* of the Alpha neurons at (aii). That is, it synapses with an internuncial neuron where an impulse is sent to the muscle that is receiving too much stimulation (the biceps in this illustration). The agonists are thusly inhibited. The afferent firing also sends another internuncial neuron to *facilitate* the antagonistic muscle (elbow extensor (e) in this case) via other spinal cord segments (aiii). The antagonist then is ready to act (contract) should it receive (from the spinal tracts) a message (impulse) to do so. In short, the Golgi tendon organs are muscle tension monitors located in the tendenous attachments of muscles. They fire when a critical tension level is reached. They inhibit alpha neurons to the contracting muscle and facilitate its antagonist. Thus they monitor tension in the muscle which is being stretched or contracted.

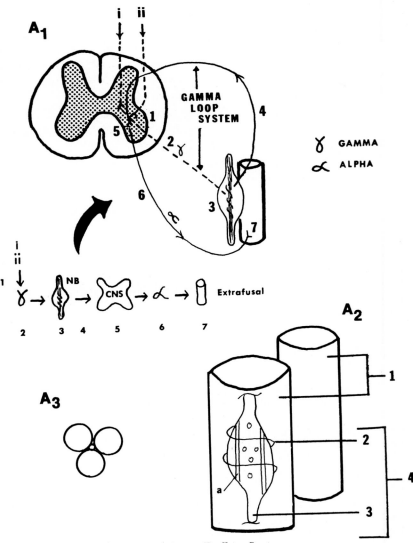

Figure 13. Alpha-Gamma Loop Reflex System

A₁. Alpha Gamma Loop System Diagrammatically Represented. Here we see the descending impulses: supraspinal (ii) and spinal level impulses (i) (see *a* below) synapsing (1) with an anterior horn cell in the grey matter. The impulse then travels along (2) the gamma 1 efferent nerve fibers (via the peripheral nervous system) which in turn causes (3) fibers in the nuclear bag to contract putting a stretch on the neuromuscular spindle (intrafusal muscle—see *b* below) thus stimulating the annulospiral ending (see *c* below). This in turn causes the annulospiral fibers, which are coiled around the nuclear bag, to send impulses over (4) the group 1A afferent fibers which synapse on alpha motoneurons (5) sending impulses over (6) the alpha motor nerve (lower motor neuron) traveling on to the (7) extrafusal muscle fiber (motor end plate) which causes the muscle to contract while, concurrently, the antagonists are inhibited.

The gamma system initiates movement and maintains tone. Muscle tone is a result of continuous (tonic) discharge of the muscle spindle. This occurs even when muscles are not actually moving. Therefore, tone is increased when spindle activity is increased. Thus, the nuclear bag area is stimulated to produce afferent impulses by: (1) stretch (passively) to the extrafusal muscle fibers, and (2) gamma efferent neuron discharge.

a. Gamma motor neurons not only receive impulses from these higher CNS levels but as well receive impulses from exteroceptive, proprioceptive, and interoceptive receptors. This is seen in Figure 12 where, in this example, the stimulus is received by the proprioceptors in the biceps.

b. Skeletal muscles are constructed of two kinds of fibers:

1. Extrafusal. These are contractile muscle fibers. Therefore, their function is to contract or to provide motion. They do not have muscle sensory receptors. The alpha efferent innervates these contractile fibers. The cell bodies of the alpha neurons are housed in the grey part of the spinal cord. Alpha neurons have only a motor supply. They do not have muscle sensory receptors.

2. Intrafusal (neuromuscular spindles). These are located among or between the extrafusal muscle fibers. They consist of at least two kinds of sense organs: (a) Primary endings (annulospiral or nuclear bag), and (b) Secondary endings (flower spray). The gamma efferent innervates the intrafusal (muscle spindle) fibers.

c. "Thus, the spindle maintains tone or a given muscle length that is required for any particular motor task." (Ayers, A. Jean: Occupational therapy directed toward neuromuscular integration. In Willard, H. S. and Spackman, C. S. (Eds.): *Occupational Therapy*, 3rd ed. Philadelphia, Lippincott, 1963.)

A_2. Neuromuscular Spindle

1. Extrafusal muscle fiber (or the voluntary muscle fiber).
2. Annulospiral fiber (Group 1A fibers).
3. Nuclear bag (a) nuclear chain.
4. The Intrafusal muscle (muscle spindle).

A_3. Top view of the extrafusal muscle fibers (the three large circles) and the Intrafusal muscle (one small circle) arrangement.

to the muscle. A stretched muscle contracts (pulls back) in order to prevent lengthening. This is called the stretch reflex (Liddell *et al.*, 1924, 1925). Inhibitory and facilitatory controls are placed on the spindle system by the corticospinal and other central pathways (through the gamma motoneuron) and by such outside influences as pressure, stretch, temperature and balance (Moore, 1969). For instance, when the skin over a muscle is touched, there is an impulse sent to the muscle spindle (nuclear bag fiber), sending a message along the 1A fibers to the alpha motoneuron to the extrafusal muscle causing changes in muscle tone. [Theoretically then, the skin can serve as an important facilitation/ inhibition mechanism which is the basis for many rehabilitation methods (Rood Technique: See Stockmeyer,, 1967; Rood, 1962.] The entire process is sketched diagrammatically in Figure 13. See also Figure 51, Exteroceptive facilitory-inhibitory responses in Chapter 9, *Systems of Therapy*.

We see then that tension in the normal muscle is maintained on an even keel. However, in a spastic muscle there is an increase in tension in the muscle spindles. These spindles become *hyperreactive* to stretch. The controlling influence of the descending tracts (pyramidal motor tract) in cerebral palsy may have two effects. One effect is weakness and paresis due to decreased stimulation of the alpha-fiber; and secondly, disturbance in the smooth muscle contraction due to the uncontrolled gamma-fiber function. So, alterations of muscle tone and posture may be due to stimulation of gamma efferent, with resultant hypertonia, or to disturbance of inhibitory and facilitory centers in the extrapyramidal system (Samilson, *et al.*, 1964). The function of the higher cortical centers (which is inhibitory) is rendered ineffective when they are damaged. There is a release of their inhibitory function on the gamma efferent. The result is continuous electrical activity so that the antagonistic muscles are electrically active in both extension and flexion. Or viewed another way, the spindles become *tight*, and the normal preparedness level is abolished or disturbed. They then overrespond to stimuli (stretch) setting off impulse bombardment from within the muscle to the spinal cord. This places the alpha motoneurons in a constant state of stimulation. The end result of course is continuous impulse stimulation to the muscle (extrafusal) or a spastic muscle. The muscles most affected are the antigravity muscles: the calf muscles, quadriceps and the biceps (or the flexor group). Conversely, if the muscle spindles are slack, they will fail to respond to stretch unless extreme. This occurs in hypotonia (Blencowe, 1969).

The result of true spasticity is failure of the lengthening reaction of the muscle. Relating this specifically to surgery in cerebral palsy, it is important to note that the stretch reflex, which is hyperactive, can be abolished by destroying any portion of the stretch reflex arc (Swanson, 1968). Therefore, attempts to diminish spasticity include: (a) severing the posterior roots of the spinal nerves thereby cutting off the influx of impulses from the spindles (this, however, results in a flaccid muscle); (b) blocking the small efferent fibers which lead from the spinal cord to the muscle spindle by means of chemical injections such as alcohol (See Tardieu *et al.*, 1968); (c) othopedic surgery: lengthening of the muscle. By so lengthening the muscle, it cannot be overstretched (therefore exciting the stretch reflex) and theoretically the inflow of sensory impulses from the muscle spindles is diminished; and (d) therapeutically by means of physical and occupational therapy.

Samilson and Morris (1964) observed the following on upper-limb electromyograms of patients with cerebral palsy: (1) There is continuous electrical activity of spastic muscles, even at rest. This is termed synchronous activity or cocontraction and is present whatever the functional state of the muscle. For example, the flexor carpi ulnaris is electrically active in extension as well as in flexion, in contrast to the asynchronous or phasic activity of the normal flexor carpi ulnaris which is electrically active only during wrist flexion or grasp; and (2) in a cerebral palsied upper limb, even when at rest, the amplitude of electrical activity increases if the contralateral limb moves actively.

In Samilson's patients, electromyograms *after* surgical procedures on the upper limb seemed to suggest some restoration of asynchronous or phasic activity of the muscle groups tested, flexors becoming active primarily in flexion, and extensors in extension.

It is appropriate to close this section by saying that most surgeons prefer to operate after the period of rapid growth unless a deformity seriously interferes with more conservative treatment procedures. Surgical procedures in children with cerebral palsy are predicated on close adherence to the physiological principals summarized in this section.

LOWER EXTREMITY SURGICAL PROCEDURES

Foot

The common deformities of the foot seen in the spastic cerebral palsied child are: (1) equinus, (2) valgus, (3) varus, (4) talipsis calcaneus, (5) clawing of the toes, and (6) adduction deformities of the forefoot or any combination of these. Because the latter three deformities are rather rare phenomenon, the author's efforts have been centered on equinus, valgus and varus deformities.

EQUINUS DEFORMITY. By definition, equinus means downward; however, functionally, it is the elevation of the heel with weight bearing on the toes; or simply, *walking on the toes.* In young children, below the age of five, equinus deformity of the foot can usually be prevented by daily manual stretching of the triceps surae with or without bracing. Unless a brace is worn at night until skeletal maturity, the deformity will recur, just as it may recur after surgery. It recurs during growth because the tibia grows in length faster than the muscle. Surgical correction of equinus should be postponed, if possible, until this period of rapid growth is complete.

Surgical correction of equinus is basically of two methods: either by (1) neurectomy of the tibial nerve to either the gastrocnemius or soleus, or (2) by lengthening of the triceps surae by any of the various standard techniques, such as:

1. Phelps (1951) technique: neurectomy to reduce troublesome clonus (spasm) upon weight bearing. See also Eggers (1952). Technique: neurectomy of branches of the tibial nerve to soleus or gastroc—used when equinus deformity persists after release of patellar retinacula and transfer of hamstring tendons to the femoral condyles.

2. Release (lengthening) of the triceps surae muscle (the gastrocnemius and soleus considered together).

Techniques

a. Silfverskiöld (1923), (Silver *et al.*, 1959). Proximal gastrocnemius recession, heads of origin of gastroc muscle is transplanted to a level distal (below) to the knee with resection of some branches of the tibial nerve.

Postsurgery treatment: After six weeks in a long-leg cast, rehabilitation is initiated.

b. Vulpius (1924) or Strayer technique. Generally, this is the lengthening of the tendon of the gastrocnemius alone.

The Vulpius technique. V-shaped incision into the aponeurotic tendon of gastrocnemius. The original report by Baker (1956) in which was described a modification of the Vulpius operation has been recently (Baker *et al.*, 1970) modified. See also Ingram, 1971.

The Strayer technique (1950, 1958). Distal gastrocnemius recession (lengthening). The retracted proximal part of the tendon is attached to the soleus in this procedure.

c. Lengthening tendo calcaneus. The tendo calcaneus is the Achilles tendon which is the uniting of tendons from gastrocnemius and soleus.

The Strayer procedure is probably the most popular. See discussion on page 1694 in *Campbell's* concerning methods to use with respect to the possible five mechanisms causing the equinus deformity.

VARUS AND VALGUS DEFORMITY. In general, treatment of these deformities is tendon lengthening (rerouting which weakens the musculature or pull) combined with some form of bone stabilization procedure.

Varus deformity in cerebral palsy may be caused by overpull of the tibialis posterior muscle and the other invertor muscles and weakness of the evertor muscles. Valgus deformity may be caused by overpull of peroneal or spasticity of the other evertor muscles and weakness of the invertor muscles (Achilles tendon). Valgus deformity of the heel is usually secondary to tight Achilles tendon as this muscle has its insertion on the lateral aspect of the calcaneus.

To balance muscle power in varus or valgus deformities, the following techniques are utilized:

a. Baker and Hill (1964). Rerouting of tibialis posterior tendon anterior to the medial malleolus. See Baker, Bassett and Dyas (1970), for modifications of this procedure.

b. Tohen et al. (1966). Transfer of extensor hallucis longus and tibialis anterior tendons to lateral of midline of the foot.

Bassett and Baker (1966) and Keats and Kouten (1960) feel that more often than muscle imbalance being the primary cause of valgus deformity, the main factor is contracture of the triceps surae. If such is the case, the first step in correcting the deformity must be release of the contracted triceps surae by an appropriate technique (such as lengthening the tendo calcaneus).

Stablilizing bones: osteotomy of the calcaneus is an additional procedure to correct this deformity, such as:

a. Silver et al. (1967) reports on calcaneus osteotomy for varus or valgus deformities of the foot in cerebral palsy. The operation is basically a modification of the Dwyer osteotomy (1959, 1960, 1963).

b. Baker and Hill (1964) describe another technique for osteotomy of the calcaneus for correcting valgus deformity.

c. The Grice (1952) subtalar extra-articular arthrodesis seems to be the procedure of choice for valgus deformity especially for children between the ages of four and nine. This procedure is usually performed with or before procedures to correct muscle imbalance.

Knee

Deformity of the knee in cerebral palsy involves musculature that bridge two joints. Namely, the rectus femoris, the gracilis, the biceps femoris, the semitendinosus, the semimembranosus and the gastrocnemius muscles. Therefore, abnormalities of the hip or ankle or both are interrelated problems. Almost without exception, the deformity of the knee is one of flexion. It may be primary or secondary (Pollock, 1960). The primary form is caused by contracture of the hamstring and gastrocnemius accompanied by weak quadriceps muscle. The secondary form develops when a fixed flexion contracture at the hip or marked equinus deformity is present. If the deformities are in the early stages, conservative measures such as daily manual stretching and/or braces should be attempted as the avenue of treatment. When knee-flexion deformity is severe, surgical intervention is necessary.

Possibly the most widely known procedures for correction of knee flexion deformity in cerebral palsy are modifications of the Eggers' hamstring transplant. Modifications of the procedure described in 1952 are listed in: Eggers, 1952; Eggers *et al.*, 1963; and Evans *et al.*, 1966. Also, see Masse and Audic (1968). Evans is quick to note that if the Eggers' procedure as originally described for knee flexion contracture is used, the surgeon may create additional problems. For further modifications see: Pollock and English (1967), Pollock (1962), Keats and Kambin (1962) and Baker, *et al.* (1970). Most authorities cited advise leaving at least one hamstring intact to assist knee flexion and to lessen the tendency to genu recurvatum.

If the child has walked for a long period of time with the knee in flexion, the patellar tendon may have elongated. Patellar advancement may then be necessary. This procedure enables the quadriceps to extend the knee completely.

Techniques

a. McCarroll (1949); McCarroll *et al.* (1943); Baker (Roberts *et al.*, 1953). Recently, Baker *et al.* (1970) reported a modification of the Chandler procedure. The new procedure has relieved considerably the need for bracing.

b. Chandler (modified by Lewis, 1947).

Also, see Eggers (1950).

Tendon Lengthening.

a. Green and McDermott (1942).

b. Z-plastic lengthening of hamstring.

When there is a fixed flexion-adduction deformity of marked degree at the hip, the tight muscles are released by surgical operations as described by Soutter. (See under *Hip* in the following section). No attempt should be made to correct an equinus deformity, surgically, at this stage for, "Experience has shown that after a muscle slide operation at the hip or a hamstring transplantation, with or without a gastrocnemius slide at the knee, the equinus deformity will be almost fully corrected without any need to lengthen the heel cord by surgery." (See p. 251, Pollock, 1960).

Hip

Four types of deformities at the hip are common: (1) flexion-internal rotation, (2) adduction, (3) flexion, and (4) subluxation and dislocation.

Muscle imbalance or poor habits regarding positioning (posture) are the most frequent causes of deformities of the hip in cerebral palsy. These positions are flexion combined with internal rotation, adduction and flexion. In addition, the hip may become subluxated or dislocated when adductors, flexors and internal rotators are all severely spastic or rigid. "Every cerebral palsied patient with appreciable involvement of the lower limbs should be considered to have abnormal hips until proved otherwise" (Baker *et al.*, 1962). Deformities of the *Hip*—briefly discussed. Again, the reader is reminded that the near-exhaustive references provided at the end of this chapter supply a comprehensive investigation of the extensive literature on each particular subject area.

1. FLEXION-INTERNAL ROTATION DEFORMITY. This deformity is caused by spastic internal rotators (tensor fascia femoris and anterior fibers of the medius and minimus) which pull against weak or flaccid external rotators, resulting most frequently in the typical *scissors* gait. The common sitting position of the cerebral palsied child is a "reversed tailor position" which is a habitually poor position encouraging development of this deformity. Evans (1966) comments, "Internal rotation is the most enigmatic of problems relating to the lower extremity."

Techniques

a. Baker *et al.* (1964). Semitendinosis transfer used when deformity is mild to moderate with no fixed contractures.

b. Soutter (1914). Performed when deformity is severe. Gluteus medius and minimus are detached from outer face of ilium and the origins of sartorius and rectus are released.

c. Yount (1926).

d. Barr (1943). Anterior border of the origin of tensor fascia latae from anterior superior spine detached and turned backwards so that it acts as an extensor rather than as a flexor.

e. Durham (1938). For internal rotation deformities—division of anterior fibers of gluteus medius and minimus close to the greater trochanter.

According to Pollock (see p. 245, 1960), the results of these muscle-releasing procedures are on the whole disappointing because the glutei are weakened thus allowing adduction deformity to recur.

Rotation osteotomy is the procedure of choice for resistant or fixed rotational deformity. (See *Campbell's*, p. 1712).

2. ADDUCTION DEFORMITY. Some authorities (Silver *et al.*, 1970), (Pollock, 1962) feel that adduction contracture of the hip is the most frequent deformity in cerebral palsied children. The deformity is caused by spastic adductors which pull against normal, weak or flaccid abductors. The mildly involved child is able to walk independently although the legs are medially rotated and flexed at the hip and knees. If the child is severely involved, he may still be able to walk with outside support (crutches, long-leg braces with pelvic band) but his gait may be of the *scissors* type.

The procedures of choice for surgical correction of this deformity are adductor tenotomy and obturator neurectomy.[17] See Barnett (1952), Banks and Green (1960), Silver and Simon (1957), and Silver *et al.* (1966) for surgical procedures and comments.

Banks and Green (1960) offer a synopsis of indications, procedures, and results concerning adductor myotomy and obturator neurectomies for the correction of adduction contractures of the hip.

Generally, post-surgery treatment consists of immobilization in a long-leg plaster-of-Paris cast with wide abduction bar for six weeks. If subluxation is present, some type of abduction apparatus

[17]Neurectomy: A system of selective motor nerve resection (division or partial excision) for correction of deformities of spastic cerebral palsy. The procedure attempts not to paralyze the muscle or muscle group but to, instead, produce in the stronger muscle a loss of power sufficient to result in improved balance and hence increased capability for muscle training. Common usage: (a) branches of obturator nerve for adductor muscle spasm of hip; (b) branches of tibial nerve for spasm of the plantar flexors of foot; and (c) some cases of spastic pronation of the forearm and flexors of the wrist.

is used for six months or more as a night splint. The abduction apparatus can consist of a bivalved long-leg cast with abduction bar; Denis-Browne splint attached to a high shoe, with a wide bar; long-leg braces with an abduction bar to be worn at night. Silver and Bracken (1970) have designed a simple hip abduction splint. As the designers point out, "It has been found to be of particular value in the spastic child with accompanying athetoid movements . . . eliminates mechanical irritation of the legs and feet . . . it also avoids the soiling and unpleasant odours encountered in the use of postoperative long-leg plaster-of-Paris casts for the child who has not acquired urinary and/or bowel control."

3. Flexion Contracture of The Hip. Iliopsoas muscle is of prime importance when considering this deformity. Although the Mustard procedure (iliopsoas transfer) is used effectively with the spina bifida or myelomeningocele (for a paralytic dislocated hip), there does not seem to be mention in the literature of actual use of this procedure with the cerebral palsied. Baker *et al.,* (1970) has performed the Mustard operation, modified, in 12 cases. Eleven of the cases have shown definite improvement. See Figure 14 for a description of the procedure used in the transplantation of the iliopsoas muscle.

Sharrard (1964) suggests that lenghtening or tenotomy of the iliopsoas is a good procedure for spastics. Evans, too, (See p. 135, Evans, 1966) has found this to be a good procedure for spastics. See also Bleck et al. (1964) and Bleck (1966), concerning results he obtained following iliopsoas tenotomy for correction of hip flexion contractures.

4. The Subluxating and Dislocated Hip. There seems to be a dirth of information in the literature on this particular problem. In common use, however, is the varus osteotomy as a surgical corrective measure. This appears to be the accepted procedure (Mortens, 1965) (Lamb *et al.,* 1962).

All accounts discussing this problem in the literature agree that the best treatment for dislocated hip in the spastic is prophylactic. Therefore, the problem is preventable.

Baker (Hill *et al.,* 1966) uses a modification of Mustard's iliopsoas transfer, when abductors and extensors of the hip are weak, to prevent later deformity of the hip through balancing

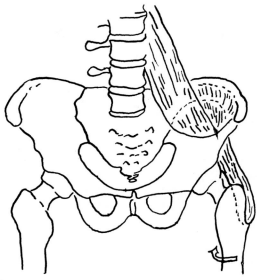

Figure 14. Transplant of the iliopsoas muscle. The tendon and muscles are passed through a posteriorly placed window in the wing of the ilium. The window is cut as far back as possible to allow placement of the transplant into the posterior aspect of the trochanteric area of the femur to assist the hip extensors.

The arrow illustrates that the hip has been internally rotated to show the position of the insertion of the tendon into the posterolateral aspect of the greater trochanter. (Reproduced with permission from: Hill, L. M., Bassett, F. H., and Baker, L. D.: Correction of adduction, flexion and internal rotation deformities of the hip in cerebral palsy. *Develop Med Child Neurol, 8:*410, 1966.)

muscle power and restoring normal femur alignment. See also Phelps' references for his descriptions of three varieties of acquired hip dislocations and surgical procedures thereof including varus osteotomy of the femur, and adductor tenotomy (Phelps 1959, 1951). Pollock and Sharrard (1959) suggest that the true incidence of hip dislocation in cerebral palsy is about 5 percent.

UPPER EXTREMITY SURGICAL PROCEDURES

The hallmark of concern when discussing orthopedic management in the upper extremity is the function and mobility of the hand. The typical disabling position of the upper extremity (which impedes the functional capacity of the hand) includes flexion of the elbow, fixed pronation of the forearm, flexion deformity and ulnar deviation of the wrist and a variety of deformities of the fingers and thumb.

An effective orthopedic management program requires a painstaking study of the factors and barriers involved in the child's deformity(s) of the upper extremity. The pre-operative study must include evaluation of these factors and barriers. A functional profile, then, must be compiled to include evaluation of (1) motor involvement. Are there fixed contractures? What is the status of grasp-release? Does the child have voluntary control over grasp-release? Speed of performance must be considered. Degree of muscle imbalance must be assessed. Are there unstable joints of finger and thumb? To what degree is spasticity and paralysis or weakness present? (2) Sensory involvement. The evaluation in this area must include tactile, kinesthetic, and proprioceptive sensation; and (3) Age, intelligence and motivation of the child.

Because the sensory status of the hand is so important in determining prognosis after surgery, a study by Tachdjean and Minear (1958) will be briefly mentioned. Forty-two percent of 96 cerebral palsied children studied had one or more sensory defects in the hand. Stereognosis was most frequently lost, followed by two-point discrimination and position sense. They reported a higher incidence of sensory defects in children with spastic paralysis than in those with athetosis. To emphasize further the importance of the sensory status of the hand when considering surgery of the upper extremity, DeJong (1958) comments that, "sensation and motion are interdependent and that severe motor disabilities may follow impairment of sensory functions." Several areas must be considered in a sensory evaluation of the hand. (a) *Stereognosis.* Ask the child to identify familiar objects such as a pencil, spoon, key, ball, safety pin. Make certain, however, that the child has seen the object before testing him (blindfolded or vision otherwise occluded) and that he is able to name the object for you. If the child is unable to recognize by sight, you may be dealing with a disordered visual and/or auditory function. Those in authority do not, however, agree as to the actual degree of importance stereognosis plays in successful surgical results. (b) *Two-point discrimination.* Touch the child with two pencil points at varying distances apart on dorsum and palmer surfaces of hand and fingers, and forearm. (c) *Position sense.* With vision again occluded, place the child's hand and fingers in a variety of positions. (See Chapter Three, *Learning: Mechanisms and Disorders,* for an in-depth discussion concerning perceptual disorders). (d) *Sharp-dull sensations.* Simply touch the skin with a pin, the rounded end for dull. Caution must be taken as, "some children at age 3, with average or better performance on psychological tests are able to respond to part of the sensory evaluation; others will not be able to give reliable answers until they are 5" (Goldner *et al.,* 1966). Also, see *Task Level Evaluation,* Appendix A, for specific performance skills and age levels. A more thorough and in-depth discussion concerning sensory impairment in cerebral palsy can be found in Chapter Three, *Learning: Mechanisms and Disorders.*

Again, as with the stereognosis aspect, there does not appear to be complete agreement among the professionals regarding the importance of intelligence as it relates to upper extremity surgery. *Intelligence,* as measured by standard means in severely handicapped individuals is often misleading. Mental deficiency, as measured by the intelligence quotient, is not a contra-indication to surgical treatment, if the willingness and ability to cooperate are present (Samilson *et al.,* 1964). One result concluded from Samilson's experience with 128 operations on the upper extremities of 40 patients with cerebral palsy, interestingly enough, was that some of the biggest gains occurred in patients with comparatively low intelligence quotients. On the contrary, others feel that "a poor candidate for surgery is a severely retarded child or one with an IQ below 70" (See *Campbell's* Vol. I). The child's *motivation* is often considered the *most important* prerequisite for successful surgical treatment of the upper extremities. When all is said and done, however, the average case in which successful surgery can be expected is usually an intelligent, cooperative, spastic hemiplegic patient who has a volitional grasp and release pattern and reasonable sensibility in the hand (Swanson, p. 1129, 1968).

The aim of surgery in the upper extremity is to improve function and appearance. Cosmetic improvement is particularly important if a hand has been yielded useless and can, through surgery, be positioned for more appealing appearance. Generally, no child should have surgery until he is old enough to have had sufficient opportunity to benefit from splinting and other conservative care. If these measures have failed, surgery is by all means indicated. A rule of thumb: 6 to 7 years old is the youngest for cerebral palsy surgery of the upper extremity; 2 to 2½ years old for lower extremity surgery (Paschall, 1971). Time indications for various types of procedures: (a) Soft tissue operations to correct flexion deformity of wrist and pronation deformity of forearm probably indicated earliest; followed by, (b) myotomies; then, (c) tendon transfers; and even later, (d) arthrodesis.

Elbow

If biceps are spastic and triceps normal or weak, tendon lengthening of spastic muscle is performed. If triceps are spastic, and flexors weak, partial neurectomy of triceps is indicated. See Carroll *et al.* (1951), and Carroll (1958), for procedure consisting of biceps lengthening, division of the brachialis fascia, and transfer of the flexor origin from the medial epicondyle to the ulna. Samilson (1964) reports that his experience with releases of elbow flexors from medial epicondyle of the humerus were disappointing.

Wrist and Fingers

The most frequent deformities in the upper extremity in spastic paralysis consists of flexion deformities of the wrist and fingers (Figure 15). The contracted flexor muscles prevent extension of the wrist and are ineffective themselves in grasp because of the tension in the extensor muscles and limited motion of flexors. The deformities are both functionally disabling and, in addition, cosmetically displeasing. This deformity is usually accompainied by pronation of the forearm, flexion of the elbow and thumb-in-palm deformity.

Surgical procedures consist of releasing the origins of (a) pronator and flexor muscles, (b) myotomies, (c) tendon transfers, (d) tendon lengthening, and (e) arthrodesis, which is sometimes help-

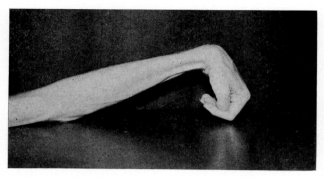

Figure 15. Flexion deformities of wrist and fingers.

ful at the proper age. In general, no surgery is performed before the age of seven.

RELEASE OF FLEXOR-PRONATOR ORIGIN. This procedure may improve the appearance and function of a hand with severe flexion deformities of the wrist and fingers. Release of the flexor-pronator muscle origin from the medial part of the epicondyle and ulna is effective in the correction of wrist and finger flexion contractures and for the relief, as well, of elbow-flexion contractures and pronation contractures. This release procedure is not indicated when passive range of motion (ROM) corrects the deformity and assumes the flexed position during grasp. In this case, transfer of flexor carpi ulnaris to wrist extensor is more useful and less extensive.

Techniques

See Inglis and Cooper (1966); and William and Haddad (1967).

POST-SURGERY TREATMENT. Generally, at 3 weeks the cast and sutures are removed. A splint is applied (Fig. 16), which is worn for 3 months both day and night removing only for therapy. This is a dorsal cock-up splint which essentially maintains the hand in extension but does not interfere with finger function. Occupational and physical therapy is continued as necessary. A night splint is worn until full growth is reached. Regarding flexion deformities of the fingers, the principle flexor is the flexor digitorum superficialis. This deformity is usually associated with flexed and pronated wrist.

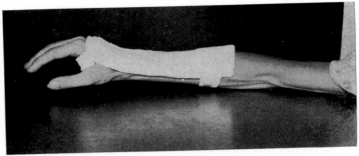

Figure 16. Dorsal cock-up splint constructed of plaster-of-Paris.

Recessing flexor muscle origins gives a shorter resting or postural length; thereby, decreasing strength and spasticity. It will be remembered that in a normal muscle, the degree of tension is related to the length of the muscle when it contracts: the greater the length, the stronger the muscle and, therefore, the greater is the pull or tension.

Again, as is usually the case, conservative measures should be attempted first. That is, stretching of muscle contractures, either manually or through splinting.

Swanson (p. 1134, 1968). Flexor muscle origin are released in the forearm. (Also see Inglis and Cooper, 1966). The proximal attachments of the flexor muscles are sectioned and allowed to move distally. Releasing the pronator in the procedure also improves the frequently associated pronation deformity (Fig. 17).

POST-SURGERY TREATMENT. The extremity is kept in the extended position for approximately 3 weeks. Physical and occupational therapy are the initiated, with the child wearing a modified pancake splint when he is not in treatment (Fig. 18a, and Fig. 18b). The splint is worn for 3 to 6 weeks. In addition, the splint is worn at night for 3 months.

FLEXOR CARPI ULNARIS TRANSFER. As the flexor carpi ulnaris is the most powerful wrist flexor, it is the muscle of choice for this transfer (Boyes, 1962). The flexor carpi ulnaris is transferred dorsally around the ulnar border of the forearm. It is then attached to extensor carpi radialis brevis or longus. Attaching to the extensor carpi radialis brevis gives more control for dorsi-flexion motion; attaching to the extensor carpi radialis longus gives more

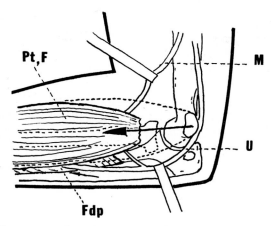

Figure 17. Flexor muscle origin release in the forearm. The proximal attachments of the flexor muscles are sectioned and allowed to move distally. The nerve supply is left intact. Legend: Pt, F = Pronator teres and Flexors; M = Median nerve; U = Ulnar nerve; Fdp = Flex. digit. profundus.

(Reproduced with permission from: Swanson, Alfred B.: Surgery of the hand in cerebral palsy and muscle origin release procedures. *Surg Clin N Amer, 48*:1132, 1968.

effective (a) pulling direction for supination and (b) correction of ulnar deviation as this tendon, the extensor carpi radialis longus, is in a more radial position. The purpose of this procedure is to remove the deforming force that pulls the hand into ulnar deviation and flexion thus promoting supination (to 20 degrees) to the forearm and extension of the wrist (to 15 degrees). The universal indication for this procedure is the presence of pronator-flexion deformity of the wrist with difficulty in active extension of the wrist and fingers with poor supination. For the procedure

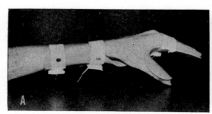

Figure 18. Modified pancake hand splint (a) on hand, (b) off hand.

to be effective, there should be reasonable finger control, passive flexibility of the hand, wrist, and forearm; and a favorable diagnostic profile. Fixed deformities (of pronation and wrist flexion) should be corrected before the transfer either by surgery and/or splinting and therapy. When active supination is present presurgically, the muscle may be carried through the interosseous membrane instead of around the ulnar side of the forearm, thus preventing it from acting as a supinator.

Techniques

Green and Banks (1962). (Fig. 19).

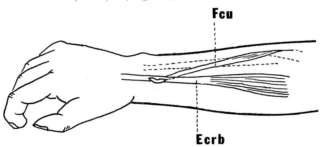

Figure 19. Green procedure for transfer of the flexor carpi ulnaris subcutaneously to the extensor carpi radialis brevis. Legend: Fcu = Flexor carpi ulnaris, Ecrb = Extensor carpi radialis brevis. (Reproduced with permission from: Swanson, Alfred B.: Surgery of the hand in cerebral palsy and muscle origin release procedures. *Surg Clin N Amer, 48*:1131, 1968.

POST-SURGERY TREATMENT. As previously mentioned, the first order of events is to rid the upper extremity of fixed deformities; therefore, after correction of pronation and flexion contractures by releasing pronator teres and flexor group (flexor carpi ulnaris is not released, all others are permitted to *slide*), (1) the extremity is placed in plaster for 3 months to allow stabilization, (2) then exercises to re-educate finger and wrist extension are indicated since they have been over-pulled for so long, and (3) active exercise for supination. After another 3 months, if supination and extension is not sufficiently good, flexor carpi ulnaris is transferred to extensor carpi radialis.

The treatment procedures for the actual flexor carpi ulnaris transfer are as follows: The cast is bivalved soon after surgery to prevent swelling and exercises are begun out of the cast 4 or 5 days post-operatively. Wearing of the bivalved cast is continued on a daily basis for at least 6 weeks. The cast is worn between therapy—time out of cast is gradually increased. As soon as the hand is well controlled, the cast or splint is worn only at night. Splint or cast may, however, still be necessary during the day to support wrist in dorsiflexion for several weeks or months until good balanced function is established. The splint used is the dorsal cock-up splint with an opponens bar (basic long opponens with C-bar).[18]

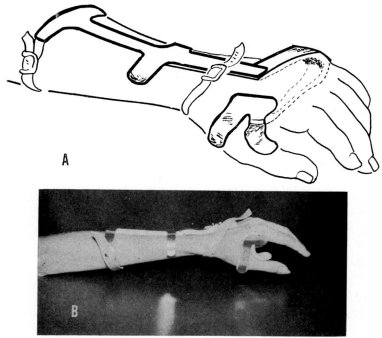

Figure 20a and 20b. Basic long opponens splint with C-bar. (Reproduced with permission from Rancho Los Amigos Hospital Downey, California).

[18]The basic long opponens splint with C-bar or the dorsal cock-up splint with an opponens bar (Stamp, 1962). This may, as indicated, be worn on a part-time basis during "convalescence" to prevent tendency for the wrist to drop into flexion (Figs. 20a, and 20b).

The exercises are aimed at educating muscles in their new pattern. It is not like muscle education as seen in the polio patient. In treatment of the child with deformities resulting from such neuromuscular diseases, the therapist tells the child to concentrate on what the muscle *used to do,* then the child will gradually see that when he *thinks* of what the muscle formally did, it will do the new motion. That is, if the muscle was a wrist flexor, the polio patient *thinks* wrist flexion and the wrist extends. Gradually, the patient will become accustomed to the new motion. In the muscle transfer case (referring to the cerebral palsied), the child must be *taught* the *new motion.* Work is toward supination, wrist extension, grasp and release. As the flexor carpi radialis remains intact, the flexor carpi ulnaris transfer to wrist extension will bring the wrist up to approximately 15 degrees of extension.

"In our experience, transplantation of the flexor carpi ulnaris is the single best procedure to improve function of the wrist and hand in cerebral palsy. It aids dorsiflexion and supination and, at the same time, preserves active motion of the wrist" (Green and Banks, 1962).

Fusion of The Wrist. This procedure is indicated only if active extension of the fingers is sufficient while the wrist is held rigidly in a position satisfactory for fusion. This position, because it eliminates the tenodesing effect on the extensor tendons (present during active wrist flexion), may result in the complete loss of extension of the fingers. If grasp and release can occur with the wrist in the fused position, then arthrodesis is indicated (Samilson et al., 1964).

To determine if hand function can be improved by wrist fusion: Immobilize wrist in a cast or splint in various positions and observe function of the fingers. Fusion is delayed until the child is at least 12 years old (ipiphysis of the distal radius will be damaged otherwise). The wrist is fused in slight flexion and ulnar deviation.

Useful Techniques

a. Brockman-Nissen (*Campbell's,* p. 1198, 1971).
b. Gill-Stein (Stein, 1958).

Thumb-in-Palm Deformity. Probably the most common de-

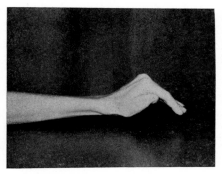

Figure 21. Thumb-in-palm deformity.

formity found in the thumb is the thumb-in-palm deformity which consists of one of two positions: the thumb-in-palm position, (Fig. 21)., and the thumb position of tight adduction (the thumb is held tightly against the side of the index finger). Figure 21 shows the thumb-in-palm position before surgery with flexion of the MCP joint (metacarpophalangeal joint) of the thumb. Spasticity is present in the flexor pollicis longus, and the first dorsal interosseus muscles (causing web space spasticity) leaving weak thumb extensors, abductors and opponens. Figure 22 shows the post-surgery thumb as performed by Goldner (1955, 1961) in which spasticity of thumb web has been released and the MCP joint of

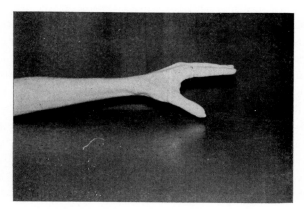

Figure 22. Post-surgery thumb as performed by Goldner (1955, 1961). Web space spasticity released and MCP joint of thumb is arthrodised.

the thumb has been arthrodised. The thumb now stays out of the palm. The flexor carpi radialis and the flexor carpi ulnaris have been transferred to the weakened extensor digitorum communis allowing full extension of the fingers and improving pinch and grasp.

This deformity prevents the thumb from performing its function in grasp and pinch; and, in addition, interferes with the performance of the other fingers. It has been said that the lack of thumb function reduces the hand's usefulness by 50 percent (Inglis *et al.*, 1970). The goal then in surgical treatment is to achieve sufficient abduction of the thumb.

Techniques

A combination of several procedures are usually indicated in this deformity.

a. To release thumb: myotomies in the palm are performed when contracture or moderate spasticity of the intrinsic muscles is noted. See Figure 23. Swanson (1968), Matev (1963).

Myotomy of the adductor pollicis is considered better than tenotomy as it releases the first metacarpal but does not allow hyperextension of the MCP joint (*Campbell's*, p. 328, vol I, 1971).

Myotomies may be sufficient. If not, other procedures may be indicated as follows:

b. If adductor pollicis and first dorsal interosseus are tight and contracted, release of the insertion of these muscles and deepening of the thumb web space are performed through a Z-plasty procedure (Inglis, p. 267, 1970).

c. Lengthening of the flexor pollicis longus tendon combined with fusion of MCP joint for flexion contractures of the interphalangeal joint of the thumb. Lengthening the flexors (and adductors) permits them to still function as flexor (and adductor) of the thumb but because they have been lengthened they will be weakened, allowing extension and abduction. Thusly, the thumb is out of the palm.

d. Tendon transfers. Transfer of the flexor carpi radialis to the extensor pollicis longus to assist in both thumb extension and abduction (Goldner, 1961). Transfer of the flexor carpi radialis to rerouted abductor pollicis longus to assist in thumb adduction.

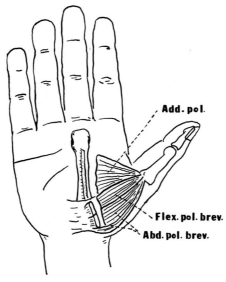

Figure 23. Intrinsic muscle origin release for the thumb. Adductor pollicis, transverse head and portion of oblique head, flexor pollicis brevis, and two-thirds of the abductor pollicis brevis are released. The attachment of the first dorsal interosseus to the first metacarpal may also be released in depths of the wound if necessary. The motor branches of the ulnar and median nerves are spared. (Reproduced with permission from: Swanson, Alfred B.: Surgery of the hand in cerebral palsy and muscle origin release procedures. *Surg Clin N Amer,* *48*:1134, 1968.

Transfer of the sublimis tendon of the ring finger may be performed if opponens is weak (Carroll, 1958). Or, if active abduction and extension of the thumb is weak, the brachioradialis tendon transfer is done coupled with metacarpophalangeal joint fusion to prevent hyperextension (Swanson, 1968). (Fig. 24).

e. Arthrodesis of the MCP joint. This procedure is indicated after transfer of the flexor carpi radialis to the extensor pollicis brevis with pre-existing hyperextension of the first metacarpophalangeal joint.

Capsulorrhaphy of the thumb at the MCP joint can be performed successfully in children who have hyperextension deformity of this joint (Swanson, p. 1133, 1968).

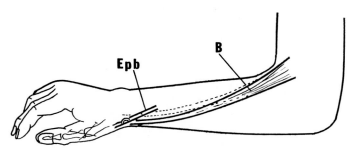

Figure 24. Brachioradialis transfer to the extensor pollicis brevis or longus or the abductor pollicis longus. Stabilization of the metacarpophalangeal joint of the thumb is usually necessary with this procedure. Legend: Epb = Extensor pollicis brevis; B = Brachioradialis. (Reproduced with permission from: Swanson, Alfred B.: Surgery of the hand in cerebral palsy and muscle origin release procedures. *Surg Clin N Amer, 48*:1134, 1968.

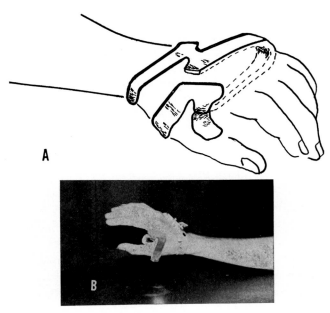

Figure 25a,b. Short opponens splint with C-bar. (Drawing of this splint and drawing of the basic long opponens splint with C-bar were produced with permission from Rancho Los Amigos Hospital, Downey, California.)

Post-surgery treatment. In order to hold first metacarpal (not phalanges) in wide abduction and opposition, a cast is applied. At three to six weeks, the cast and sutures are removed. At this time, a splint (Fig. 25a,b, Short Opponens with C-bar) is applied to hold the thumb in this same position. If tendon transfers are necessary, the cast is retained for six weeks.

SWAN NECK DEFORMITY OF THE FINGERS. The swan neck deformity can be quite disabling. However, it occurs infrequently

TABLE VII

SYNOPSIS OF ORTHOPEDIC SURGERY
IN CEREBRAL PALSY

Lower Extremity	*Major Procedures*
Equinus	1. Neurectomy (branches of tibial nerve)
	2. Release of triceps surae
	a. distal transplantation gastrocnemius
	b. lengthening gastroc tendon alone
	c. lengthening tendo-calcaneus
Varus-Valgus foot	1. Osteotomy
	subtalar bone block (e.g. Grice Procedure)
	2. Tendon transfers
	3. Tendon lengthening - release tricep surae
Knee flexion contracture	1. Lengthening tendon
	2. Tendon transfer (e.g. Modification of Eggers Procedure)
Hip adduction contracture	1. Adductor myotomy
	2. Obturator neurectomy
Hip flexion-internal rotation	1. Division or recession of tensor fascia latae
	2. Division or recession of iliopsoas
	3. Tendon transfers
Subluxating hip	1. Varus osteotomy
Fixed rotational deformity	1. Rotational osteotomy
Hip flexion contracture	1. Tendon lengthening
	2. Iliopsoas tenotomy
Upper Extremity	
Pronation of forearm	1. Release of flexor-pronator origin
Elbow flexion contracture	1. Tendon lengthening
Ulnar deviation	1. Lengthening flexor carpi ulnaris
	2. Transfer of flexor carpi ulnaris
Wrist flexion with ulnar deviation	1. Transfer of flexor carpi ulnaris
Thumb-in-Palm	1. Myotomy
	2. Tendon transfer
	3. MCP fusion
	4. Tendon lengthening
Swan neck	1. Sublimis tenodesis

relative to the other deformities of the upper extremities. The deformity is caused by muscle imbalance and secondary ligamentous and capsular relaxation at the proximal interphalangeal joints (PIP joints), thus allowing the joints to hyperextend.

Technique

a. Swanson (1968). Sublimis tenodesis of the proximal interphalangeal joint. Generally, the procedure consists of drilling a hole in the first phalanx. The flexor sublimis tendon is then pulled up through the hole, and a button is placed on it. It is held for four weeks in order that the tendon can scar down. The profundus remains; therefore, the finger is still able to flex.

BRACES AND SPLINTS

Braces and splints are used primarily to prevent deformity by maintaining a more satisfactory position, to reinforce weak structures, to facilitate preoperative evaluation, and post-operatively, to maintain the corrected position, and as an aid in training and rehabilitation.

PREVENTION OF DEFORMITY. By far the most common deformity in the spastic cerebral palsied is the *equinus deformity* of the ankle. The child with a tight heelcord may require a short-leg brace only at night as walking during the day may provide enough stretch to the tendon to prevent a fixed contracture from developing. Care, however, must be taken to see that the child is able and/or willing to bring the heel down to the floor. A dynamic brace is used in an attempt to aid dorsi-flexion or toe-off thereby preventing a deformity. The dynamic force is supplied by a spring (klensak ankle). Passive bracing to prevent equinus is supplied by a control stop at the ankle or by bending the upright lateral bar at intervals. A short-leg brace is used to *control* or maintain inversion or eversion of the foot by bending the uprights and/or using a T-strap. For instance, to maintain the foot in a more everted position in order to prevent a varus deformity, the upright is placed on the inner side of the leg and the T-strap on the outer side of the foot. A double upright long-leg brace with a pelvic band, hip joints and locking knees with knee pads may be used to *prevent contractures* such as flexion of the knee when spastic hamstrings are overactive. Braces are used to prevent a *scissors gait* from causing fixed knee and hip deformities. Another example: In this category are *twisters* which are proximally attached to the pelvic band and distally attached to either the proximal portion of a short leg brace or to shoes (if the child does not require a brace). These are used to control and prevent medial femoral rotation. The Miller twister (Stamp, p. 1467, 1962) is a cable device, a coiled spring, with plastic covering to reduce damage. Rotation can be increased or decreased by adjustment of the twisting force at the insertion of the cable. Use of a *pancake hand splint* to prevent fixed flexor contractures of the wrist and fingers is indicated early for the spastic hand (Fig. 18b). The splint holds the wrist, fingers, and thumb in proper position, i.e. the wrist is maintained in as much extension as can be tolerated, fingers in almost complete extension, and the thumb is out of the palm. (See discussion of the use of this splint also under preoperative evaluation and postoperative management). The pancake splint is indicated when the deforming force, i.e. flexor spasticity, is not too severe. It is used preferably as a night splint. The short opponens splint with C-bar, Figure 25a, is used to prevent *adduction contractures* of the thumb. The two final examples in this section are the *basic long opponens splint* with C-bar which is used to prevent wrist flexion contractures. See Figure 20a,b, and Figure 63.[19] Also, Figure 26, the *Australian hand splint* (Stamp, 1962) can be used to prevent a wrist flexion contracture. This is, in effect, a simple cock-up splint which requires no straps to hold it in place. The amount of wrist extension can be controlled by bending the dorsal wire. It is possible to add an opponens bar (dowl) or such eating utensils as a fork and spoon or a writing aid such as a pencil.

Bracing, and splinting, of course, is used only as tolerated by the child. It is important to note that splinting and bracing should most frequently be combined with physical and occupational therapy so that the child can be taught through purposeful use of the extremity to maintain the correction achieved by bracing and splinting.

[19]See Chapter 10, *Assistive Devices and Special Equipment*: Combined ADL-long opponens orthosis.

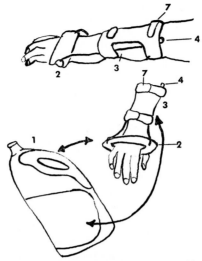

Figure 26. Plastic Handle-Coat Hanger Hand Splint (Australian hand splint).

Method and Materials.

1. Select correct size bottle handle to fit natural resting position of hand and wrist. (The handle is from a plastic clorox bottle).

2. Insert coat hanger wire through plastic bottle handle (20″ of wire). Bend and shape wire with pliers leaving 8″ showing on both sides.

3. Cut pattern to fold over ends of coat hanger wire as well as cover the forearm.

4. Loop wire ends ½-inch back.

5. Cover wire with ½-inch fold over plastic material.

6. Use Scholl's adhesive-backed ⅛-inch sponge-covered felt to face forearm and hold plastic material over wire.

7. Fasten straps with velcro, snaps or ties around wrist and forearm. (Reproduced with permission from: Slominski, A., and Griswold, P.: *Help Us Help Ourselves.* Cerebral Palsy Clinic, Indiana University Medical Center, Indianapolis, Indiana.)

Some authorities (Kendall *et al.*, 1966) are of the opinion that using braces and splints to correct existing contractures is contraindicated for the following reasons: (a) Long-term follow-up has shown that the contractures are altered very little by such treatment, (b) stretching with appliances frequently *triggers off* an excessive stretch reflex with undesirable effects on the rest of the extremity or trunk, and (c) surgical correction is more rapidly effective. In defense of bracing and in contradiction of point (b) above, sustained stretch (which results from bracing) *breaks through* the myotatic reaction and seems eventually to raise the threshold from its appearance, perhaps by producing elongation of the tendon (Fuldner, 1960). The golgi tendon organ releases the muscle. This is the *give* that is felt after one feels the stretch reflex. The golgi tendon organ is a protective mechanism within the muscle protecting the muscle from becoming overstretched. In effect what the golgi tendon organ is saying is, "I give up, go ahead and stretch me. I cannot resist any longer." Most orthopedic surgeons appear to be of the opinion that corrective bracing is ineffective and ultimately surgery will be necessary.

PREOPERATIVE EVALUATION AND POSTOPERATIVE MANAGEMENT. Splinting is utilized to temporarily place an extremity or joint in the position which it is hoped will be attained by surgery. They are thus used to determine if the pending procedure is likely to be successful. Postoperative bracing may be necessary if recurrence of the original condition is to be prevented. An example of postoperative bracing can readily be seen for equinus deformity. In this case, a short leg brace is used throughout the growth period to maintain correction achieved through surgery. The long opponens hand splint with C-bar (opponens bar) is used to protect the flexor carpi ulnaris tendon transfer by supporting wrist in dorsiflexion. Or, the pancake splint is used after muscle recession operation for finger flexion deformity and the dorsal cock-up splint is used to maintain hand in extension after release of flexor muscle origins in wrist flexion deformity.

Presurgically, splinting may be used to determine the ability of the child to perform grasp and release when the wrist is stabilized in a satisfactory position for wrist fusion.

TRAINING. Of importance is the use of bracing to assist in ambulation training by stabilizing individual joints. Double long-leg braces with pelvic band are used for the child with flexor spasm at the knee joint, weakness of the hip extensors, usually without marked spasticity or of mild to moderate spastic involvement. Bracing or splinting is used in the upper extremity to stabilize the wrist in as normal a position as possible during training of the fingers. Bracing of the trunk is used to prevent weak musculature from interfering with sitting and use of the upper extremities. Increasing strength of neck muscles can also be aided by first bracing the weak trunk musculature. Illustrative is the modified Boldrey brace and the hinged head halter (Halpern *et al.*, 1970). The modified Boldrey brace gives rigid support and is used to control head posture placing the head in a more functional "position of reference" permitting more effective use of, or training of, the upper extremities. The hinged head-halter is used almost exclusively with the athetoid (Paschall, 1971). Bracing in the upper extremity can aid in controlling a motor pattern by directing motion. An example of this form of bracing may be seen in the bracing of an athetoid to control *overflow* motion (Figs. 27, 28, and 29).

Figure 27. Upper Extremity Control Brace.

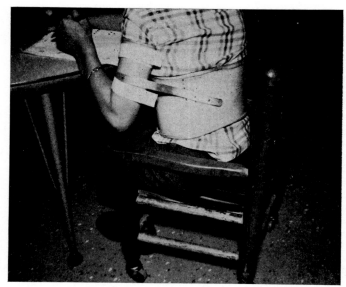

Figure 28. Athetoid child wearing upper extremity control brace while writing.

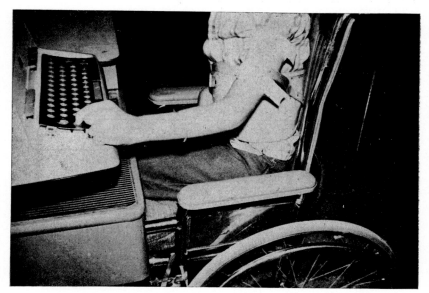

Figure 29. Athetoid child wearing upper extremity control brace while typing.

TABLE VIII

GLOSSARY

Arthrodesis. Surgical fusion of a joint to render it immobile.

Equinus. Downward such as walking on toes.

Genu. The knee.
      a. genu varus: bow-leg deformity.
      b. genu valgus: knock knees.

Incision: The act of cutting.

MCP. Metacarpophalangeal joint.

Myotomy. Incision of a muscle; a functional lengthening which weakens the muscle.

Neurectomy: Excision of a nerve.

Neurotomy. Severing nerve.

Osteotomy. Surgical cutting of a bone.

Recession. Surgical division to lower the insertion of a muscle.*

Recurvatum. Backward bending; a curvature backwards.

Resection. Surgical removal (i.e., excision) of a portion of any tissue such as a nerve or muscle.

Tenodesis. Tendon fixation; suturing the proximal end of a tendon to the bone.

Tenotomy. Incision of a tendon.

Transplant. To transfer tissue from one part to another; a tendon transplant reinforces a weak muscle and/or corrects a deformity.

Triceps surae. Gastrocnemius, soleus and plantarus considered together.

Valgus. Turned outward, away from midline of the body.

Varus. Turned inward toward midline of the body.

    Common Surgical Procedures.

Eggers. Transplant of hamstring tendons to the femoral condyles to improve hip extension and to decrease knee flexion.

Grice. Subtalar extraarticular arthrodesis for paralytic valgus deformity.

Mustard. Ilipsoas transplant to the greater trochanter for hip abductor paralysis.

Sharrard. Transiliac posterior transfer of the ilipsoas for hip extensor paralysis.

Soutter. Subperiosteal recession of the tensor fascia latae and sartorius muscles for hip flexion contracture in poliomyelitis.

Stöffel. Selective motor neurectomies to decrease spastic contractures.

*lengthening or dividing tendon or muscles reduces pull therefore reduces their deforming influence.

RESOURCES

Baker, L. D.: A rational approach to the surgical needs of the cerebral palsied patient. *J Bone Joint Surg. 38A*:316, 1956.

Baker, L. D., Bassett, F. H., and Dyas, E. C.: Surgery in the rehabilitation of cerebral palsied patients. *Dev Med Child Neurol, 12*:330-342, 1970.

Baker, L. D., Dodelin, Richard, and Bassett, Frank H., III: Pathological changes in the hip in cerebral palsy: Incidence, pathogenesis, and treatment. A preliminary report. *J Bone Joint Surg, 44A*:1331, 1962.

Baker, L. D., and Hill, Lowell M.: Foot alignment in the cerebral palsy patient. *J Bone Joint Surg, 46A*:1, 1964.

Banks, H. H., and Green, W. T.: Adductor myotomy and obturator neurectomy for the correction of adduction contracture of the hip in cerebral palsy. *J Bone Joint Surg, 42A*:111, 1960.

Barnett, H. E.: Orthopedic surgery in cerebral palsy. *JAMA, 150*:1396, 1952.

Barr, J. S.: Muscle transplantation for combined flexion-internal rotation deformity of the thigh in spastic paralysis. *Arch Surg, 46*:605-607, 1943.

Bassett, Frank H., III, and Baker, Lenox, D.: Equinus deformity in cerebral palsy. In Adams, John P. (Ed.): *Current Practice in Orthopaedic Surgery.* Vol. 3, St. Louis, Mosby, 1966.

Bleck, E. E.: Management of hip deformities in cerebral palsy. In Adams, John P. (Ed.): *Current Practice in Orthopaedic Surgery.* Vol. 3, St. Louis, Mosby, 1966.

Bleck, E. E., and Holstein, A.: Iliopsoas Tenotomy in Spastic Paralytic Deformities of the Hip. Presented, meeting of American Academy of Orthopaedic Surgeons, Chicago, 1964.

Blencowe, Susan M. (Ed.): *Cerebral Palsy and the Young Child.* London, Livingstone, 1969.

Boyd, I. A.: The structure and innervation of the nuclear bag muscle fiber system and the nuclear chain muscle fiber system in mammalean muscle spindles. *Phil Trans, 245B*:1, 1962.

Boyes, J. H.: Selection of a donor muscle for tendon transfer. *Bull Hosp Jt Dis, 23*:1-4, 1962.

Campbell's Operative Orthopaedics, 4th ed. Crenshaw, A. H. (Ed.) St. Louis, Mosby, 1963, vol. I.

Campbell's Operative Orthopaedics, 5th ed. Crenshaw, A. H. (Ed.) St. Louis, Mosby, 1971, vol. II.

Carroll, R. E.: The treatment of cerebral palsied in the upper extremity. *Bull NY Orthop Hosp, 3*, December, 1958.

Carroll, R. E., and Craig, F. S.: The surgical treatment of cerebral palsy—the upper extremity. *Surg Clin N Amer, 31*:385-396, 1951.

DeJong, R. D.: *The Neurologic Examination*, 2nd ed. New York, Hoeber, 1958.

Durham, H. A.: A procedure for the correction of internal rotation of the thigh in spastic paralysis. *J Bone Joint Surg, 20*:339-344, 1938.

Dwyer, F. C.: Osteotomy of the calcaneum for pes cavus. *J Bone Joint Surg, 41B*:80-86, 1959.

Dwyer, F.C.: a) Osteotomy of the calcaneum in the treatment of grossly everted feet and special reference to cerebral palsy. Societe Internationale de cherurgie Orthopedique et de Traumatalagie, Huitieme Congress. New York 1960, pp. 892-897.

Dwyer, F. C.: The treatment of relapsed clubfoot by the insertion of a wedge into the calcaneum. *J Bone Joint Surg, (Br.) 45B*:67, 1963.

Eggers, G. W. N.: Surgical division of the patellar retinacula to improve extension of the knee joint in cerebral spastic paralysis. *J Bone Joint Surg, 32A*:80, 1950.

Eggers, G. W. N.: Transplantation of hamstring tendons to femoral condyles in order to improve hip extension and to decrease knee flexion in cerebral spastic paralysis. *J Bone Joint Surg, 34A*:827, 1952.

Eggers, G. W. N., and Evans, E. B.: Surgery in cerebral palsy, an instructional course lecture. The American Academy of Orthopaedic Surgeons. *J Bone Joint Surg, 45A*:1275-1305, 1963.

Evans, E. B.: The status of surgery of the lower extremities in cerebral palsy. In Urist, Marshall R. (Ed.): *Clinical Orthopaedics and Related Research.* Philadelphia, Lippincott, 1966, vol. 47.

Evans, E. B., and Julian, J. D.: Modifications of the hamstring transfer. *Dev Med Child Neurol, 8*:539, 1966.

Fuldner, Russell V.: Lower extremity bracing in cerebral palsy. *Dev Med Child Neurol, 3*:34-38, 1960.

Goldner, J. L.: Reconstructive surgery of the hand in cerebral palsy and spastic paralysis resulting from injury to the spinal cord. *J Bone Joint Surg, 37A*:1141, 1955.

Goldner, J. L.: Upper extremity reconstructive surgery in cerebral palsy or similar condition. In *Instructional Course Lectures: The American Academy of Orthopaedic Surgeons.* St. Louis, Mosby, 1961, vol. 18, pp. 169-177.

Goldner, J. L., and Ferlic, D. C.: Sensory status of the hand as related to reconstructive surgery of the upper extremity in cerebral palsy. In Urist, Marshall R. (Ed.): *Clinical Orthopaedics and Related Research.* Philadelphia, Lippincott, 1966, vol. 46, pp. 87-92.

Green, William T., and Banks, Henry H.: Flexor carpi ulnaris transplant and its use in cerebral palsy. *J Bone Joint Surg, 44A*:1343, 1962.

Green, W. T., and McDermott, L. J.: Operative treatment of cerebral palsy of spastic type. *JAMA, 118*:434, 1942.

Grice, D. S.: An extra-articular arthrodesis of the subastragalar joint for correction of paralytic flat feet in children. *J Bone Joint Surg, 34A*:927, 1952.

Halpern, D. et al.: Training of control of head posture in children with cerebral palsy. *Dev Med Child Neurol, 12*:290-305, 1970.

Hill, L. M., Bassett, F. H., III, and Baker, L. D.: Correction of adduction, flexion and internal rotation deformities of the hip in cerebral palsy. *Dev Med Child Neurol, 8*:406, 1966.

Inglis, Allan E., and Cooper, William: Release of the flexor-pronator origin for flexion deformities of the hand and wrist in spastic paralysis. A study of eighteen cases. *J Bone Joint Surg, 48A*:847, 1966.

Inglis, Allan E., Cooper, William, and Bruton, William: Surgical correction of thumb deformities in spastic paralysis. *J Bone Joint Surg, 52A*:253-268, 1970.

Ingram, A. J.: Miscellaneous affections of the nervous system. In Crenshaw, A. H. (Ed.): *Campbell's Operative Orthopaedics*. St. Louis, Mosby, 1971, vol. II.

Keats, S., and Kambin, P.: An evaluation of surgery for the correction of knee-flexion contracture in children with cerebral spastic paralysis. *J Bone Joint Surg, 44A*:1146-1154, 1962.

Keats, Sidney, and Kouten, Joseph: Early surgical correction of the planovalgus foot in cerebral palsy. Extraarticular arthrodesis of the subtalar joint. In Urist, Marshall R. (Ed.): *Clinical Orthopaedics and Related Research*. Philadelphia, Lippincott, 1968, vol. 61.

Kendall, P. H., and Robson, P.: Lower limb bracing in cerebral palsy. *Clin Orthop, 47*:73-76, 1966.

Lamb, D. W., and Pollock, G. A.: Hip deformities in cerebral palsy and their treatment. *Dev Med Child Neurol, 4*:488-498, 1962.

Lewis: *Practice of Surgery*. Hagerstown, Prior, 1947.

Liddell, E. G. T., and Sherrington, C. S.: Reflexes in response to stretch (myotatic reflexes). *Proc roy Soc Med, 96*:212-242, 1924.

Liddell, E. G. T., and Sherrington, C. S.: Further observations on myostatic reflexes. *Proc roy Soc Med, 97*:283-297, 1925.

Little, W. J.: On the Influence of Abnormal Parturition, Difficult Labour, Premature Birth, and Asphyxia Neonatorum, and the Mental and Physical Condition of the Child, Especially in Relation to Deformities. *Trans Obstet Soc London, 3*:293, 1862.

McCarroll, H. R.: Surgical treatment of spastic paralysis. *American Academy of Orthopaedic Surgeons Instructional Course Lectures*. Ann Arbor, Edwards, 1949, vol. 6.

McCarroll, H. R., and Scwartzmann, J. P.: Spastic paralysis and allied disorders. *J Bone Joint Surg, 25*:745, 1943.

Masse, P., and Audic, B.: Critical evaluation of Eggers' procedure for relief of knee flexion spasticity. *Dev Med Child Neurol, 10*:159-163, 1968.

Matev, Ivan: Surgical treatment of spastic "thumb-in-palm" deformity. *J Bone Joint Surg, 45B*:703, 1963.

Moore, J. C.: *Neuroanatomy Simplified*. Dubuque, Kendall/Hunt, 1969.

Mortens, J.: Orthopaedic operations in the treatment of children with cerebral palsy. *Dan Med Bull, 11*:22-28, 1965.

National Institute of Neurological Disease and Strokes Research Profiles: 1970. *Summary of Research at the NINDS.* U. S. Dept. of Health, Education, and Welfare, 1970.

Paschall, Homer. Chief of Orthopaedic Surgery, Veterans Administration Hospital, Gainesville, Florida. Personal communication, 1971.

Phelps, W. M.: Treatment of paralytic disorders exclusive of poliomyelitis. In Bancroft, F. W., and Marble, H. C.: *Surgical Treatment of the Motor-Skeletal System.* Philadelphia, Lippincott, 1951.

Phelps, W. M.: Prevention of acquired dislocation of the hip in cerebral palsy. *J Bone Joint Surg, 41A*:440, 1959.

Pollock, G. A.; Knee deformities in cerebral palsy. *Cereb Palsy Bull,* 2:248-253, 1960.

Pollock, G. A.: Surgical treatment of cerebral palsy. *J Bone Joint Surg.* *44B*:68, 1962.

Pollock, G. A., and English, T. A.: Transplantation of the hamstring muscles in cerebral palsy. *J Bone Joint Surg, 49B*:80, 1967.

Pollock, G. A., and Sharrard, W. J. W.: In Illingsworth, R. S. (Ed.): *Recent Advances in Cerebral Palsy.* London, Churchill, 1959, pp. 286-329.

Roberts, W. M., and Adams, J. P.: The patellar-advancement operation in cerebral palsy. *J Bone Joint Surg, 35A*:958, 1953.

Rood, M.: The use of sensory receptors to activate, facilitate, and inhibit motor response, autonomic and somatic in developmental sequence. In Sattely, C. (Ed.): *Approaches to Treatment of Patients with Neuromuscular Dysfunction.* Study Course VI, Third International Congress, World Federation of Occupational Therapists. Dubuque, Brown, 1962, pp. 26-37.

Rushworth, Geoffrey: Spasticity and rigidity: An experimental study and review. *J Neurol Neurosurg Psychiat, 23*:99-118, 1960.

Samilson, R. L., and Morris, J. M.: Surgical improvement of the cerebral palsied upper limb. *J Bone Joint Surg, 46A*:1203-16, 1964.

Sharrard, W. J. W.: Posterior iliopsoas transplantation in the treatment of paralytic dislocation of the hip. *J Bone Joint Surg, 46B*:424-444, 1964.

Silfverskiöld, Nils: Reduction of the uncrossed two-joint muscles of the leg to one-joint muscles in spastic conditions. *Acta Chir Scand, 56*:315, 1923-1924.

Silver, Caroll M., and Bracken, B. C.: A simplified hip abduction splint for use in cerebral palsy. *Dev Med Child Neurol, 12*:77, 1970.

Silver, C. M., and Simon, S. D.: Operative treatment of cerebral palsy involving the lower extremities. *J Int Coll Surg, 27*:457, 1957.

Silver, Caroll M., and Simon, Stanley D.: Gastrocnemius muscle recession (Silfverskiöld operation) for spastic equinus deformity in cerebral palsy. *J Bone Joint Surg, 41A*:1021, 1959.

Silver, C. M., Simon, S. D., and Litchman, H. M.: The use and abuse of obturator neurectomy. *Dev Med Child Neurol, 8*:203, 1966.

Silver, C. M., Simon, S. D., Spindell, E., Litchman, H. M., and Scala, M.: Calcaneal osteotomy for valgus and varus deformities of the foot in cerebral palsy. A preliminary report on twenty-seven operations. *J Bone Joint Surg, 49A*:232, 1967.

Soutter, Robert: A new operation for hip contracture in poliomyelitis. *Boston Med Surg J, 170*:380, 1914.

Stamp, W. G.: Bracing in cerebral palsy. *J Bone Joint Surg, 44A*:1457-76, 1962.

Stein, I.: Gill turnabout radial graft for wrist arthrodesis. *Surg Gynecol Obstet, 106*:231, 1958.

Stockmeyer, S. A.: An interpretation of the approach of Rood to the treatment of neuromuscular dysfunction. In Bouman, H. D. (Ed.): *Am J Phys Med, 46* (1):900-956, 1967.

Strayer, L. M., Jr.: Recession of the gastrocnemius. An operation to relieve spastic contracture of the calf muscle. *J Bone Joint Surg, 32A*:671, 1950.

Strayer, L. M., Jr.: Gastrocnemius recession. Five-year report of cases. *J Bone Joint Surg, 40A*:1019, 1958.

Swanson, A. B.: Surgery of the hand in cerebral palsy and muscle origin release procedures. *Surg Clin N Amer, 48*:1130, 1968.

Tachdjean, M. O., and Minear, W.: Sensory distrubances in the hands of cerebral palsied children. *J Bone Joint Surg, 40A*:85, 1958.

Tardieu, G., Tardieu, C., Hariga, J., and Garnard, L.: Treatment of spasticity by injection of dilute alcohol at the motor point or by epidural route: Clinical extension of an experiment on the decerebrate cat. *Dev Med Child Neurol, 10*:555-568, 1968.

Tohen, Z., Alfonso, Carmona, Joaquin, P., and Barrera, Juan Rosas: The utilization of abnormal reflexes in the treatment of spastic foot deformities. A preliminary report. In Urist, Marshall R. (Ed.): *Clinical Orthopaedics and Related Research*. Philadelpiha, Lippincott, 1966, vol. 47.

Vulpius, O., and Stöffel, A.: *Orthopaedische Operationslehre*. Stuttgart, Enke, 1924.

William, R., and Haddad, R. J.: Release of flexor origin for spastic deformities of the wrist and hand. *Southern Med J, 60*:1033, 1967.

Yount, C. C.: The role of the tensor fascia femoris in certain deformities of the lower extremities. *J Bone Joint Surg, 8*:171-193, 1926.

Chapter Five

SPEECH AND LANGUAGE DISORDERS

THIS WILL NOT BE A TREATISE ON therapeutic techniques of
speech and hearing disorders. There are many fine publications available dealing with that subject. Rather, this chapter
will be a discussion of the *specifics* of some of the common speech
and hearing disorders and problems encountered in the CP/NI.
Reference will be made throughout this section to some of the
specialized therapy techniques. Given this understanding, it is
hoped that the reader will subsequently be armed with some
practical information upon which to build a viable treatment/
training program. Until one has theoretical underpinnings of a
problem, one cannot realistically nor successfully proceed to *alter*
that problem.

As the damage to the cerebral palsied child is so variable in its
nature, it is not surprising to find that most of the speech defects
found in this population are of a neuromuscular nature affecting
the muscles of articulation, phonation and resonation as well as
respiration. In addition to the motor portions of the brain,
damage may involve other specialized areas of the brain dealing
with communication or those areas which serve as perceivers, in-
terpreters and abstractors. In the discussion concerning the neurologically impaired or the minimally brain dysfunctioned child,
our focus on communication difficulties will primarily be centered
on disturbances in the development of particular language functions identified as developmental dysphasia, dyslexia and dysgraphia. This entire subject is fully covered in Chapter 3, *Learning: Mechanisms and Disorders.*

130

CLASSIFICATIONS OF SPEECH DISORDERS

Ingram (1964) feels that establishing a classification of speech disorders is important for two reasons. (1) It indicates the nature of the speech disturbance (thereby giving guidelines for logical, usefully directed speech therapy), and, (2) it may facilitate controlled study of the effects of the therapeutic program. This author would add a third dimension, (3) such classifications as the one proposed by Ingram in Table IX can serve as a useful tool for communication between disciplines by offering an anchor for discussion which is precisely what will transpire in the next few pages. The Table will be utilized as our point of reference and as an anchor for the discussion which is to follow. Ingram feels that the classification of speech disorders used for general purposes is useful for patients suffering from cerebral palsy (Ingram, 1964).

Although there are many references in the various texts dealing with speech and language disorders in the cerebral palsied and brain dysfunctioned child, they are unfortunately of a cursory nature. To circumvent this somewhat perfunctory handling of a complex subject, we will first discuss Table IX in specific CP/NI terms. Secondly, a more general explication will be presented. The aims of both the specifics and generalized comments are to render the subject comprehensible in terms of significance and depth of the overall problem which will result in a bastion for successful therapy.

Discussion of Table IX

(1) Dysphonia: disorders of voicing, chronic loss of voice. Found in no more than 4 percent of children with speech defects. Found occasionally in the *dyskinetic* child.

The source of energy for phonation is found in the thoracic (chest) cavity consisting of ribs, clavicle, sternum, scapula (shoulder blades), and the spinal cord. The diaphragm is both the floor of the thoracic cavity and the ceiling of the abdominal cavity. The lungs and trachea are both housed in the thoracic cavity. The larynx (voice box) provides the vibration for phonation.

(2) Dysrhythmia: involuntary interference with the normal rhythm of speech (resulting in stammer, clutter). A common disorder in children. The number of children who stammer or hesitate because of neurological damage is small. However, there is a high percentage of cerebral palsied children within this group; common in the dyskinetic; occurs in a high proportion of ataxic children (See Table X).

(3) Dysarthria: defective speech which is attributable to abnormalities of the organs of articulation. According to Brain

TABLE IX

CLASSIFICATION OF THE COMMON SPEECH DISORDERS IN CHILDHOOD

1. Disorders of voicing (Dysphonia).
    (a) With demonstrable disease of the larynx.
    (b) Without demonstrable disease of the larynx.
2. Disorders of rhythm (Dysrhythmia).
    (a) Clutter.
    (b) Stammer or hesitation.
3. Disorders of articulation with demonstrable dysfunction of articulatory apparatus (Dysarthria).
    (a) Due to neurological abnormalities.
        Cerebral palsy.
        Suprabulbar palsy.
        Lower motor neurone lesions.
    (b) Due to local abnormalities. [anatomical/structural]

Jaw and Teeth	Hypomandibulosis.
	Other malocclusion.
Tongue	Tie.
	Tongue thrust.
Lips	Cleft lip (only).
	Other.
Palate	Cleft (with or without cleft lip).
	Other.
Pharynx	Large pharynx (palatal disproportion).
	Acquired disease.
Mixed.	

4. Disorders of articulation without demonstrable dysfunction of articulatory apparatus (Secondary Speech Disorders). [speech sounds are acquired late]
    (a) Secondary to hearing defect.
    (b) Secondary to mental retardation.
    (c) Secondary to psychogenic disorders.
    (d) Secondary to dysphasia due to brain damage.
5. The Developmental Speech Disorder Syndrome (Specific Developmental Speech Disorders). (See chapter three.)
    (a) Involving language development and articulation.
    (b) Involving articulation only.
        [See Table XV.]
6. Mixed Cases.
7. Unclassified and Other.

(Reproduced with permission. From Ingram, T. T. S.: A description and classification of the common disorders of speech in children. *Arch Dis Childh*, 34:444, 1959.)

TABLE X

TYPE AND SEVERITY OF SPEECH DEFECTS IN 67 DYSKINETIC[a] CHILDREN
BY AETIOLOGY AND INTELLIGENCE[b]

I.Q.	Total	Im-paired hearing	Re-tarded only	Dys-arthria only	Dys-rhythmia	Not exclusive categories			No speech	Severity		
						Re-tarded+	Dys-arthria+	Dys-rhythmia+		Mild	Mod.	Severe
Rhesus Incompatibility												
90-110	5	4	0	1	0	2	4	4	0	1	3	1
70-90	4	3	0	0	2	1	2	2	0	2	2	0
50-70	12	8	2	0	0	6	2	2	4	0	2	6
−50	2	2	0	0	0	0	4	0	2	0	0	0
Total	23	17	2	1	2	9	12	8	6	3	7	7
Approx. %	100	(72)	8	4	8	39	(52)	35	26	14	30	30
Birth Injury												
90-110	16	0	0	4	1	2	11	10	0	8	6	2
70-90	11	1	0	2	1	1	7	7	1	3	4	3
50-70	15	3	1	0	0	8	9	8	4	1	3	8
−50	2	0	0	1	0	1	1	1	0	0	0	1
Total	44	4	1	7	2	12	28	26	5	12	13	14
Approx. %	100	9	2	16	5	27	(63)	(59)	12	27	29	31
All patients	67	21	3	8	4	21	40	34	11	15	20	21
Approx. %	100	31	4	12	6	31	59	51	16	22	30	31

[a]Term used to describe children in whom involuntary movement rather than actual paresis are the major cause of physical handicap. Movements are choreoid, *athetoid*, tremulous or dystonic. Also found is sudden involuntary increases in muscular tonus, "tension", in dystonic children.

[b]Only a small percent of the dyskinetic children have normal speech. In this series (67 patients) three-quarters or 75 per cent had complex speech defects comprising combinations of dysarthria, dysrhythmia and retarded speech development. ( ) indicate some interesting percentages.

(Reproduced with permission. Ingram, T. T. S. and Barn, J.: A description and classification of the common speech disorders associated with cerebral palsy. *Cereb Palsy Bull*, 3:57-69, 1961.)

TABLE XI

TYPES OF SPEECH DISORDER IN 122 DIPLEGIC PATIENTS BY EXTENT OF LIMB INVOLVEMENT

Extent of limb involvement	No abnormality of speech	No speech	Dysarthria only	Retardation only	Dysrhythmia only	Dysphasia only	Not exclusive categories				Total
							Dysarthria + other speech defects	Retardation + other speech defects	Dysrhythmia + other speech defects	Dysphasia + other speech defects	
Paraplegia	22	1	6	6	1	1	13	13	2	1	49*
Triplegia	2	0	3	1	0	0	3	3	0	0	9
Tetraplegia	6	21	16	8	1	0	14	13	3	3	64**
Total	30	22	25	15	2	1	30	29	5	2	122
Approx. %	24	18	20***	12	2	1	24***	23	4	2	100

*Speech disorders are more prevalent and severe in children with arm involvement than they are in children with only leg involvement [i.e. paraplegia].

**In general, the children with the most severe and extensive paresis of the limbs showed the most defective intelligence and the greatest retardation of speech development.

***Compare to Table X.

(Reproduced with permission. Ingram, T. T. S. and Barn, J: A description and classification of the common speech disorders associated with cerebral palsy. *Cereb Palsy Bull, 3*:57-69, 1961.

TABLE XII
TYPE OF SPEECH DEFECT IN 69 HEMIPLEGIC CHILDREN (46 WITH CONGENITAL AND 23 WITH ACQUIRED HEMIPLEGIA) BY INTELLIGENCE

| I.Q. | No speech disorder | Retardation only | Dysarthria only | Dysphasia only | Dysrhythmia | No speech | *Not exclusive categories* | | | | Total |
							Retardation + other defects*	Dysarthria + other defects*	Dysphasia + other defects	Dysrhythmia + other defects	
90+	12	2	0	2	1	0	3	2	0	2	21
70-90	8	5	0	0	0	0	3	3	0	0	16
50-70	3	11	0	0	1	0	5	4	6	6	23
—50	0	8	0	0	0	1	0	0	0	0	9
Total	23	26	0***	2	2	1	11	9	6	8	69
Approx. %	34	38**	0***	3	3	1	16	13	9	12	100

*Retardation of speech development; Dysrhythmia
**Found in all but 2 of the congenital; found in all of the acquired hemiplegics
***Dysarthria is inevitable in the bilateral hemiplegic
(Reproduced with permission. From Ingram, T. T. S., and Barn, J.: A description and classification of the common speech disorders associated with cerebral palsy. *Cereb Palsy Bull*, 3:57-69, 1961.

TABLE XIII
SEVERITY OF SPEECH DEFECTS BY SIDE AND AETIOLOGY OF HEMIPLEGIA IN 69 PATIENTS

| Aetiology | Right Side | | | Left Side | | | Grand Total |
	Congenital	Acquired	Total	Congenital	Acquired	Total	
No speech defect	10	4	14	5	4	9	23
Mild defect	6	2	8	7	2	9	17
Moderate defect	6	5	11	3	1	4	15
Severe defect or no speech	4	3	7	5	2	7	14
Total	26	14	40	20	9	29	69

Note: Speech disorders are found more frequently in children with acquired and congenital *right* hemiplegia than in those with acquired and congenital *left* hemiplegia.
(Reproduced with permission. Ingram, T. T. S. and Barn, J.: A discription and classification of the common speech disorders associated with cerebral palsy. *Cereb Palsy Bull*, 3:57-69, 1961.

(1965), disorders of the articulatory mechanisms are (a) anatomical abnormalities or articulatory structures [such as cleft palate], (b) dysphonia, (c) dysrhythmia (clutter and stuttering), and (d) dysarthria.

(4) Secondary: disorders attributable to physical or psychological disorders without abnormalities of the structure or function of the articulatory mechanism usually taking the form of slow speech development. (a) Post-rubella characteristics: High-frequency hearing loss (a significant number of post-rubella athetoids demonstrate high frequency hearing loss). Hearing impairment was found in only three of 122 diplegic children in Ingram's study (See Table XI). (b) Mental retardation: In Ingram's (1960) study, simple retardation of speech development was the *most common* cause of speech disorders in: (i) hemiplegics, see Table XII, also Table XI. This would concur with Crothers and Payne's (1959) findings. Overall, however, normal speech is more commonly found in children with hemiplegia (Table XIII; (ii) in diplegics (Table XI); and (iii) in the ataxic which was commonly found in association with dysarthria and dysrhythmia. (d) As dyslexia and dysgraphia is thoroughly discussed in another chapter, our main concern in this section will be with dysphasia. Ingram feels that the major manifestations of dysphasia (as well as dyslexia and dysgraphia) in the young child is retarded acquisition of speech therefore articulatory de-

TABLE XIV

FREQUENCY OF DYSARTHRIA IN 49 DIPLEGIC PATIENTS WITH A HISTORY OF FEEDING DIFFICULTIES* OR PERSISTENT DROOLING OF SALIVA IN INFANCY

	No. with feeding difficulties and/or drooling of saliva	No. with no speech	No. with dysarthric speech	No. with speech not showing dysarthria
Paraplegia	14	0	10	4
Triplegia	3	0	3	0
Tetraplegia	32	15	16	1
Total	49	15	29	5
Approx. %	100	30	60	10

*Found frequently in bilateral hemiplegics and quadreplegics as well.

(Reproduced with permission. Ingram, T. T. S. and Barn, J.: A description and classification of the common speech disorders associated with cerebral palsy. *Cereb Palsy Bull*, 3:57-69, 1961.

velopment is retarded as is learning to read and write. Ingram (1960) classified dysphasia in childhood as:

I. *Congenital,* originating, therefore, prenatally. There are two etiological types. (a) Familial: this type of dysphasia is *specific developmental.* These children show no demonstrable abnormality of the brain. There is often a family history (therefore, may be genetically determined) of dysphasia, dyslexia and dysgraphia as well as ambidexterity and sinistrality or "crossed laterality."[20] (See Table IX). (b) *Congenital brain abnormality:* this type of dysphasia is *developmental.*[21] These children do demonstrate brain abnormalities such as cerebral palsy (most commonly right-sided hemiplegia; epilepsy; or abnormalities on psychological tests, electroencephalography and on encephalography.

II. *Acquired.* This type of dysphasia is developmental from age 1 to 2; childhood type or mixed (Guttmann, 1942) from age 4 to 8; and Adult type from ages 12 upward. Manifestations of dysphasia (as well as the other two dys-problems) are much the same whether disorder is due to brain damage or of a familial origin. Males are often more affected than females (Ingram 1959a).

(5) Specific Developmental (developmental dysphasia and related disorders): Most common cause of abnormal speech in the general population. Therefore, proportionately, we find significant numbers of CP/NI affected. Brain (1965) would tabulate these disorders as: (1) Aphasia; (a) Developmental receptive

---

[20]Studies concerning laterality and its significance in children are at best conflicting. Such authorities as Orton (1937) who found an excess of left handedness in children with developmental dysphasia (as well as dyslexia and dysgraphia) to Hallgren (1950) and Hermann (1959) who both found no correlation between poor laterality and poor reading achievement. Another theory was offered by Granjon-Galifret and Ajuriaguerra (1951). They proposed that the important association is the delayed or weak establishment of hand or foot preference. Although evidence of poorly developed cerebral dominance is not constantly found in all patients with specific developmental dysphasia, dyslexia and dysgraphia, it is present in a significantly large proportion (Ingram, 1960). Language development may as well be affected: omissions of words, confusion of word order, inability to find words, grammar, sentence structure and aility to express complex ideas may be impaired, comprehension may be impaired. Most of these children have completely normal speech by the age of 9 or 10. Writing difficulties may be evidenced as well.

[21]Comprehension of speech is generally the first manifestation of developmental dysphasia to improve; articulation is the last to disappear.

SEVERITY	DESCRIPTION	OTHER TERMS	
Mild	Retardation of acquisition word sounds. Language normal.	Dyslalia	
Moderate	More severe retardation word sound acquisition and retarded spoken language development. Comprehension normal.	Developmental expressive dysphasia.	
Severe	Still more severe retardation word sound acquisition and spoken language development. Impaired comprehension of speech.	Developmental receptive dysphasia Word deafness. Auditory imperception.	Developmental mutism
Very severe	Gross failure of speech development. Impaired comprehension of language and significance of other sounds. Often apparent deafness.	Auditory imperception. Central deafness.	

(Reproduced with permission from T. T. S. Ingram: Speech disorders in childhood. *Ped Clin N Amer, 15*:611-626, 1968.)

Table XV Classification of the Developmental Speech Disorder Syndrome

aphasia (word deafness or auditory imperception frequently of a familial etiology); (b) Developmental expressive aphasia, and (c) Acquired aphasia. (2) Developmental disorders of reading and writing (dyslexia and dysgraphia respectively). See Table XV and Table XVI.

(6) Mixed cases: "those in which more than one cause of de-

TABLE XVI

PRINCIPAL LANGUAGE AND SPEECH DISORDERS IN CHILDHOOD AND CAUSES

1. Disorders secondary to deafness.
    (a) Peripheral deafness.
    (b) Central deafness.
2. Disorders of the articulatory mechanisms.
    (a) Anatomical abnormalities of the articulatory structures,
    (b) Dysphonia,
    (c) Dysrhythmia— (i) cluttering, (ii) stuttering,
    (d) Dysarthria.
3. Aphasia.
    (a) Developmental receptive aphasia,
    (b) Developmental expressive aphasia,
    (c) Acquired aphasia.
4. Developmental disorders of reading and writing.
5. Disorders of environmental origin.
6. Disorders associated with mental abnormality.

(Reproduced with permission. Brain, Lord: *Speech Disorders: Aphasia, Apraxia and Agnosia,* 2nd edition. London, Butterworths, 1965.)

fective speech is present—for example, children with cleft palate and deafness, which often results from the otitis media to which they are liable. A very high proportion of children with cerebral palsy and defective speech fall into this category. Children with choreoathetosis may show a mixture of dysarthria, dysrrhythmia and secondary speech disorder due in part to deafness and in part to mental retardation. The analysis and classification of the various causes of defective speech is especially valuable in such complex cases. It becomes possible to assess the contribution that each abnormality is making to the total clinical picture of the speech defect. This in turn puts therapy on a more rational basis than is often the case" (Ingram, 1959).

(7) Unclassified and Other: This category, according to Ingram, is used for children with defective speech in whom full diagnostic assessment has not been possible. It is useful, for example, for children whose co-operation in the testing of hearing is limited and in whom no definite assessment of hearing or mental ability can be made.

For purposes of clarity, the speech and language problems associated with the cerebral palsied should fall into the four general categories: Articulatory disorders, retardation of language development, breathing and voice disorders and hearing deficits. While not of a particularly current nature, many excellent sources are available dealing with this area which remain, in many instances, applicable. There is no virtue in duplicating efforts. Therefore, the stated purpose of the following section is to impart to the reader only pertinent, improved and/or amended information that will be of practical assistance and significance. In short, information will be updated in the following discussions.

DISORDERS OF ARTICULATION

CEREBRAL PALSY SPECIFICS RELATED TO ARTICULATION. These disorders are almost inevitable in bilateral hemiplegics; uncommon in hemiplegics as an isolated disorder (Table XII). Causes of articulatory problems are generally of two origins: neurological and anatomical/structural (Table IX).

In general, speech problems resulting from a disturbance in neuromuscular control are known as dysarthria. This may be defined as a difficulty in the articulation of words which may include the motor employment of muscles of respiration and vocalization as well as the lips, tongue and throat (Penfield and Roberts, 1959). In Travis' *Handbook of Speech Pathology* (1957, p. 54) dysarthria is described as a "disorder of articulation due to impairment of the part of the central nervous system [brain, cerebellum, medulla oblongata] which directly controls the muscles of articulation." Characteristically, consonants predominate the sounds or groups of sounds which are faulty. Ingram pointed out that those consonants which are usually acquired last by normal children are the most frequently distorted consonants. In dysarthria associated with cerebral palsy, according to Mysak (1959), there is often found (in addition to the more familiar symptoms noted above, "complicating released or retained infantile oral reflexes such as rooting, mouth opening and chewing reflexes." In *Diseases of the Nervous System* (1955), Brain states simply that "dysarthria is a disorder of articulation." In dysarthria due to upper motor neuron lesions (as in spasticity), Brain indicates the possible associated symptoms of disturbed palatal and pharyngeal reflexes and of impaired voluntary control over emotional expression. We find then that damage to the CNS may result in: (1) abnormal reflexes which results in incoordination of voluntary movement, and (2) weakness of the muscles of articulation. Brain adds a third dimension which is ataxia due to cerebellar deficiency (Brain, 1965).

It is not uncommon to find feeding difficulties (Table XIV) associated with both neurological and anatomical/structural involvement of the lips, mandible, tongue and palate. Chewing or mastication (as well as the other vegetative functions of breathing, sucking and swallowing) are basic muscular functions related intimately with speech production. Reference to this point is made in nearly every article and text written in the area of speech and language disorders. Typically, the characteristic position of the mouth of the cerebral palsied is open. That is, the jaw is depressed; or, converesely, a tightly approximated jaw is seen. Palmer (1948) describes an anomaly, the "mandibular facet slip," which occurs when "various muscular contractures of an aberrant sort" interferes with jaw depression "by a simple hinged movement." By a "compensating pull from the external pterygoids," the jaw is slipped from its sockets, resulting in a depressed jaw and slow, clumsy, ineffective movements," or, "associated with the writhing labial movements of the athetoid are involuntary contractions of the other facial muscle, notably the zygomatieus . . ." (Berry *et al.*, 1956).

Achilles (1955) lists among the functional anomalies frequently found in cerebral palsy: athetotic involvements of the tongue and/or mandible, frequent or constant involuntary elevation and/ or depression of the mandible, involuntary facial movements and facial grimaces, abnormal function of chewing, sucking and swallowing, and drooling (all involving the muscles of mastication or chewing to some degree). The examples are inexhaustible and we need no further citings to be convinced that this close relationship does indeed exist. Let's take a closer look at the muscles that are primarily concerned with chewing. These muscles attach to the mandible and are often known as the muscles of mastication. The four muscles of mastication are: the masseter, the temporal, and the two pterygoid muscles (the lateral and the medial). These muscles are responsible for the bite and for the side-to-side chewing movements.

The *Masseter Muscle* (Fig. 30). The masseter muscle covers most of the ramus of the mandible or the lower jaw. This muscle has two parts which are actually blended. Part *s* originates from

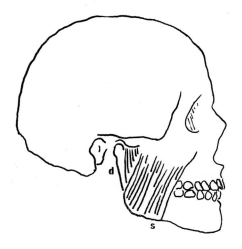

Figure 30. Masseter Muscle.
Legend: s = superficial fibers
d = deep fibers
(Reproduced with permission. Hollinshead, W. Henry: *Textbook of Anatomy*, 2nd ed. New York, Harper and Row, Publishers, 1967.)

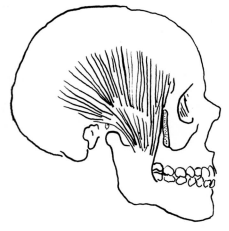

Figure 31. Temporal Muscle.

approximately the anterior two-thirds of the lower edge of the zygomatic arch extending downward and slightly posteriorly. Part *d* arises from the entire deep surface of the zygomatic arch, extending straight downward. The muscle attaches or inserts on almost the entire side (lateral) surface of the ramus of the mandible.

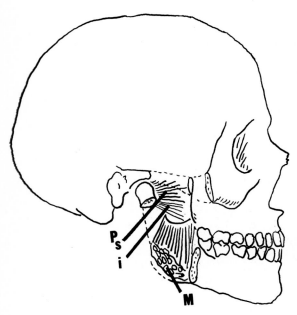

Figure 32. The pterygoid muscles after removal of the temporal and masseter muscles, the zygomatic arch, and most of the posterior part of the mandible. Legend: **P** =Lateral Pterygoid Muscle, superior head of muscle (s) and inferior head (i); **M**= Medial Pterygoid Muscle. (Reproduced with permission. Hollinshead, W. Henry: *Textbook of Anatomy*, 2nd ed. New York, Harper and Row, Publishers, 1967.)

The *Temporal Muscle* (Fig. 31). This muscle is quite a large muscle somewhat in the shape of a fan which covers much of the side of the head. It arises from the temporal fossa (Fig. 33) and comes together and attaches onto the coronoid process (externally).

The *Lateral Pterygoid Muscle* (Fig. 32). This muscle is located under the masseter and temporalis. The muscle runs almost straight (horizontally) backwards where it inserts into the mandible. It originates by two heads from the infratemporal fossa (Fig. 33) and the lateral pterygoid plate. It inserts into the neck of the mandible.

The *Medial Pterygoid Muscle* (Fig. 32). This muscle partly covers (and is partly covered by) the inferior fibers of the lateral pterygoid. Most of the medial pterygoid muscle originates on the medial side of the lateral pterygoid plate. The muscle fibers go downward, posteriorly, and laterally to find its insertion on the inner side of the ramus of the mandible.

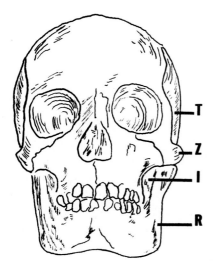

Figure 33. Anterior View of Skull.

Legend: T = Temporal fossa; Z = Zygomatic arch; I = Infratemporal fossa; R = Ramus.

(Reproduced with permission. From Hollinshead, W. Henry: *Textbook of Anatomy.* 2nd ed. New York, Harper and Row, Publishers, 1967.)

Figure 34 is shown to give perspective to the relationship of the four muscles of mastication.

Function of the muscles of mastication can be seen in diagrammatic form in Figure 35. The masseter, temporal and medial pterygoid muscles close the jaw. The masseter and temporal both abduct (deviate the jaw to the same side). The pterygoid abducts

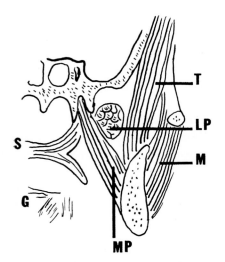

Figure 34. Schema of half of frontal section close to angle of jaw.

Legend: S = Soft palate; G = Tongue; T = Temporalis; LP = Lateral Pterygoid; M = Masseter; MP = Medial pterygoid.

(Reproduced with permission. From Hollinshead, W· Henry: *Textbook of Anatomy,* 2nd ed. New York, Harper and Row, Publishers, 1967.)

to the opposite side (working together then to produce the grinding movement of chewing). Temporal muscle (posterior fibers) are the main retractor of the mandible (pulls the jaw back after it has been jutted forward); and is primarily responsible for maintaining the resting position of closure of the mouth. Lateral pterygoid protracts (pulls forward) the jaw. Alternating action of the two lateral pterygoids (one on each side) moves the jaw from side to side. The important functions of the lateral pterygoid: helps to open the mouth.

The presence of abnormal reflexes in the cerebral palsied may interfer with voluntary control of the speech mechanism. Conversely, although there is some question (Berry *et al.,* 1956) concerning the premise that in order for speech sounds to occur the chewing, sucking and swallowing reflexes must be developed,[22] (Lencione, 1966) and others feel that "there is good reason to believe that the oral reflexes having to do with the vegetative functions involved in feeding must be developed if they are weak (as opposed to hyperactive) in the cerebral palsied. "Articulatory movements which require higher integrated motor activity are more adequately performed when infantile oral reflex behavior

[22]See Dr. Martin F. Palmer's article: Studies in clinical techniques, II. Normalization of chewing, sucking and swallowing reflexes in cerebral palsy: A home program. *J Speech Dis, 14:*415-418, 1947.

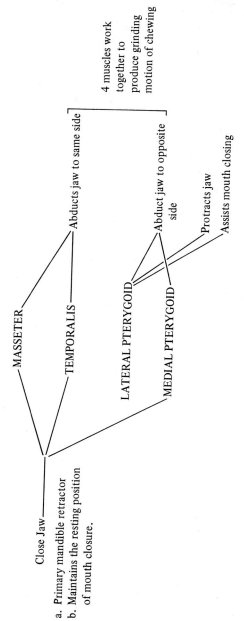

Figure 35. Functions of the Mastication Muscles.

has been inhibited" (Mysak, 1963). The general working assumption and opinion, however, is that there must be control over the chewing, sucking, and swallowing movements before normal speech can develop. Additionally, the occurrence of other abnormal reflexes such as the asymmetric tonic neck reflex or "startle reflexes" may interfer. In this case, the interference is in the form of increasing extensior tone of the jaw, tongue and breathing muscles (Mecham, p. 53, 1966). Reference is commonly made to this point (i.e. abnormal reflex involvement either hypo- or hyperactive in nature) but rarely are any specifics for ameliorating these problems given. The suggestions which follow are applicable to this problem and will be inserted at this time to give the reader food for thought: to excite more normal swallowing (about two swallows per minute), Mysak (1963) recommends (a) stimulating the back of the tongue or palate with a small tongue depressor, (b) directing a small stream of water from an eye dropper against the posterior pharyngeal wall while the head is in a moderate dorsiflexion, and (c) encouraging gentle token coughing. In addition, he recommends the following to weaken involuntary movement and overactive smiling and laughter reflexes which complicate the athetotic dysarthria. The therapist should *desensitize* these reflexes through regular and periodic handling of sensitive thoracic head and neck areas and follow up with resistance of the accompanying involuntary movement. To suppress retained or released infantile oral activity (i.e. cephalic, rooting, lip, mouth opening, biting and suckling reactions) Mysak suggests excitation in combination with the prevention of reflex emergence by the therapist as the chief means. For example (a) if the lower lip depresses and the jaw deviates when the angle of the mouth is stimulated (rooting reflex), the therapist should apply the stimulus and physically prevent the response from taking place, (b) if the mouth opens in response to a visual stimulus (such as a bottle or a finger), the therapist can provide the adequate stimulus and hold the mouth closed (thereby resisting the undesired motion). Two or three periods daily of such attempts at *reflex weakening* is recommended. See Appendix B, *Swallowing Patterns for Droolers,* for additional therapeutic procedures dealing with reflex problems in speech and language.

The *release phenomenon* seems indeed to be a hindrance and is a causal factor in dysarthria in the cerebral palsy. The appearance of this phenomena usually indicates that the higher (inhibitory) centers of the brain have been damaged permitting the lower (therefore more primitive) systems to gain control. The primitive reflexes have been *released* or set free from control and instruction from the higher inhibitory controlling command. Normally, the more primitive reflexes of the spinal cord and brain stem are absorbed or modified by the basal ganglia and cerebral cortex. This higher control results in smooth, coordinated movements. For instance, when damage occurs above the brain stem level (therefore cutting off control from this point up) what remains are those reflexes of brain stem origin.

Because the importance of reflexes in speech therapy of the cerebral palsied (as well as the physical and occupational therapies) is now widely recognized (Crickmay, p. 103, 1966), the therapist should be aware and knowledgeable of the reflexes and their normal and abnormal presence. Such awareness will aid in both evaluation and treatment (See Appendix A). In her book, *Speech Therapy and the Bobath Approach to Cerebral Palsy,* Crickmay offers a comprehensive presentation of the neurophysiological method of treating the speech problems inherent in the cerebral palsied child. She describes in detail, the three principles[23] of the Bobath approach as each specifically relates to speech therapy. See also Mysak (1959) in which he outlines the neurophysiological approach to dysarthria of the cerebral palsied on the therapeutic principles of Bobaths. Also, a detailed account of the theory and procedures of reflex inhibition therapy can be found in Mysak's 1963 publication.

There has been a spurt of vigorous interest in the newer methods of therapy, reflex facilitation and inhibition techniques, in the treatment of neurologically impaired children. All these methods have a neurophysiological basis; most of the approaches attempt to influence sensory input in order to affect motor out-

---

[23]The three main stages in this approach: (1) Inhibition (via reflex inhibiting postures) of pathological and abnormal reflexes; (2) Facilitation of developmentally more mature movements; and (3) Performance of movements under the voluntary control of the child. (See Ch. 9 *Systems of Therapy*).

put, and each abides by the normal developmental sequence. One such approach (Rood, 1962) seems to bare particular relevance for the speech and occupational therapist as it is concerned with the chewing, sucking, swallowing, respiration and speech problems found in the neurologically impaired child. The Rood approach identifies two major sequences in motor development which are distinctly different and yet inseparable because of their interaction one upon the other (Stockmeyer, 1967). These two sequences are those of skeletal function and vital functions. The vital functions sequence encompasses those involved with eating, respiration and speech. The steps to the ultimate skill, speech, are (1) inspiration; (2) expiration (one and two interact to give respiration); (3) sucking; (4) swallowing; (5) phonation (controlled expiration); (6) chewing, and finally, the *skill* level of the sequence, (7) speech articulation. According to this interpretation, speech (the motor act) is dependent upon the coordinated movements of steps one through six. The interested reader is urged to examine Appendix B which is a presentation of the techniques adapted after Rood as they are applied to those steps enumerated above concerning sucking, swallowing, chewing and ultimately, as it were, with speech articulation.

As suggested by Lencione (1966), probably no other investigator has contributed more information concerning the articulatory or speech-sound status of the cerebral palsied as that of Irwin (See 1955, 1957a, 1957b, 1957c, 1960, 1961c and 1963a). In addition, we find reports and investigations of a more recent vintage from Irwin: See 1967a, 1967b, 1967c, and 1968. In 1967, Irwin published a paper offering a pertinent study of a series of speech tests constructed for use with the cerebral palsied and the mentally subnormal child. The purpose of this study was to determine the *reliability* of these tests for their diagnostic as well as predictive quality.

The following tests were included in the report:[24]

1) an integrated articulation tests (1961a. 1961b)
2) a short articulation test of ten difficult consonants (1966, 1961c)
3) a parallel form test of sound discrimination (1965, 1963b)

[24]References are under Irwin unless otherwise indicated.

4) a parallel form test of abstraction (Hammil, 1967; 1964)
5) a test of the vocabulary of use (1966b)
6) a test of the vocabulary of understanding. The Peabody Picture Vocabulary Test (Dunn, 1959) was used for this purpose.

The tests, together with the methods of their construction, may be found in the original studies. The records of a total of 1,890 children from six to sixteen years of age were used to determine the reliabilities of the six speech tests (Table XVII and Table XVIII). Irwin proposed that in view of the results presented in the Tables XV and XX, it may be concluded that the tests both separately and as a whole posses substantial reliability for use with speech handicapped children ranging in age from six to sixteen years as well as for non-handicapped elementary school children.

It is recommended that those interested in the speech problems of the cerebral palsied child review the original articles. The articles from *Cerebral Palsy Journal* and *Cerebral Palsy Review* can be obtained from: The Cerebral Palsy Journal, 2400 Jardine Drive, Wichita, Kansas, 67219.

Irwin's "Manual of Articulation Testing for use with Children

Tests	Position	Subjects	N	r	PEr	Method
Consonant	Initial	CP	265	.95	.01	Kuder-Richardson
Consonant	Medial	CP	265	.97	.01	Kuder-Richardson
Consonant	Final	CP	265	.92	.01	Kuder-Richardson
Vowel	Initial	CP	265	.89	.01	Kuder-Richardson
Vowel	Medial	CP	265	.91	.01	Kuder-Richardson
Consonant	Initial	MR	162	.91	.01	Kuder-Richardson
Consonant	Medial	MR	162	.86	.01	Kuder-Richardson
Consonant	Final	MR	162	.55	.04	Kuder-Richardson
Vowel	Initial	MR	162	.75	.02	Kuder-Richardson
Vowel	Medial	MR	162	.91	.01	Kuder-Richardson

Calculated by formula: $PEr = .6745 \sqrt{\dfrac{1-r^2}{N}}$

With two exceptions, the coefficients stated are within the acceptable range.
*See Irwin, 1961a.

(Reproduced with permission. From Irwin, Orvis C. and Korst, Joseph W.: Summary of reliability coefficients of six speech tests for use with handicapped children. *Cereb Palsy J.* 6-7, July-August, 1967.)

Table XVII Reliability Coefficients of an Integrated Test of Articulation*

TABLE XVIII

RELIABILITY COEFFICIENTS OF
FIVE SPEECH TESTS*

1. Tests	Subjects	N	r	PEr	Method
Consonant. (Short)	CP	333	.87	.01	Kuder-Richardson
Sound Discrimination	CP	260	.90	.01	Parallel Form
Sound Discrimination	MR	76	.81	.01	Kuder-Richardson
Abstract	CP	142	.95	.01	Parallel Form
Abstract	MR	97	.90	.01	Kuder-Richardson
Abstract	Blind	94	.90	.01	Kuder-Richardson
Vocabulary of Use	CP	76	.93	.01	Hoyt
Vocabulary of Use	CP	71	.94	.01	Hoyt
Vocabulary of Use	MR	61	.82	.03	Hoyt
Vocabulary of Undst.	Educable	371	.83	.01	Alternate Form
Vocabulary of Undst.	Trainable	220	.84	.01	Alternate Form
Vocabulary of Undst.	CP	20	.97	.01	Alternate Form
2. Five tests	CP	31	.83	.04	Test-retest
Five tests	Aphasic	38	.86	.03	Test-retest

* (2) through (5) in previously listed tests.
All the coefficients of reliability in the table are within the range of acceptibility.
(Reproduced with permission. From Irwin, Orvis C. and Korst, Joseph W.: Summary of reliability coefficients of six speech tests for use with handicapped children. *Cereb Palsy J*, 6-7, July-August, 1967.)

with Cerebral Palsy" (1961a) consists of consonant (four short tests) and vowel (one short test) articulation. The purpose of the combined tests which is called the Integrated Test of Articulation is: measurement of phonetic articulation consisting of 86 items. It is chiefly a diagnostic test but can be used to measure progress through retesting procedures.

Specifics of the test include (a) used in ages three to sixteen, (b) employs verbal stimuli (the word list is read to the child, the child repeats the word one by one as they are pronounced by the examiner), (c) classification of responses on the record sheet include: substitution, omission, distortion, no response and neutral (the child's response to the word is too distorted to approximate the stimulus word). The Manual consists of a complete discussion of tests; articulation test forms; and eight pages demonstrating administration and interpretation of one test form. The Manual may be ordered from the Cerebral Palsy Journal. See Irwin (1968) for a detailed illustration of the practical application of the test described in the Manual.

By administering this test to 147 children enrolled in various speech centers, Irwin found the following factors operating in the speech of these children:

1. Sex differences are not present,
2. The coefficient of correlation of chronological age and articulation scores is .18,
3. The coefficient of correlation of mental age and articulation scores is .27,
4. The coefficient of correlation of IQ's and the scores is .45,
5. Initial and medial consonants in words are significantly more frequent than final consonants,
6. Medial vowels in words are more frequent than initial vowels,
7. Spastics make a higher mean score on the test than athetoids,
8. While paraplegics make higher scores than quadriplegics and hemiplegics the tendency is not significant,
9. There is no significant difference between the mean scores of right and left hemiplegics,
10. There are significant differences among the children when classed according to degree of involvement,
11. There are significant differences between the means of

mild and severe and between moderate and severe quadriplegics, of ehmiplegics and of paraplegics,

12. The results of administering the integrated test to an additional group of 147 subjects confirm the findings of the
preliminary studies on the articulation of children with
cerebral palsy.

DISORDERS OF BREATHING

The mechanisms of breathing have been thoroughly described
with clarity in many books. Briefly, however, there are three parts
necessary to produce sound: source of energy, vibrating body or
column of air, and a resonating system.

(1) The respiratory system provides the energy (breath stream)

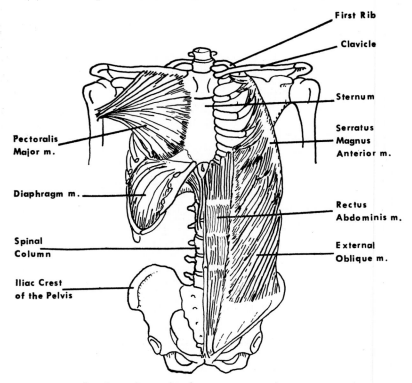

Figure 36. Muscles of respiration.
(From G. Paul Moore, Organic Voice Disorders, © 1971.
Reprinted by permission of Prentice-Hall, Inc., Englewood Cliffs, New
Jersey.)

(Fig. 36 and Fig. 37). When the rib cage is expanded, the diaphragm is contracted and pushed down. A vacuum is created and the air pushes in (inhalation) rather rapidly and is exhaled rather rapidly. Normal breathing consists of 18 respirations per minute. For speech, however, quick inspiration and the gradual releasing of air stream is required. There is a tonus established between the muscles of the diaphragm, rib cage, and pharynx, to allow slow air escapage. Abdominal muscles are also involved in this process.

(2) The larynx, or the vibrating system which provides phonation.

(3) Resonating system which alters or modifies the passage of air to produce different sounds (vowels, diphthongs, and conson-

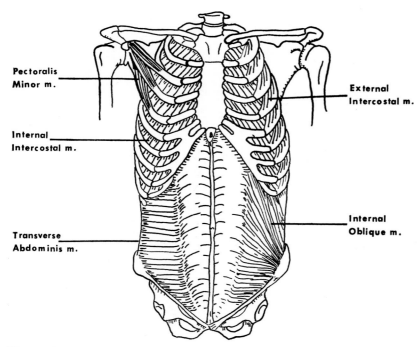

Figure 37. Muscles of respiration.
(From G. Paul Moore, Organic Voice Disorders, © 1971. Reprinted by permission of Prentice-Hall, Inc., Englewood Cliffs, New Jersey.)

ants). This system consists of the throat (pharynx), the mouth (oral cavity) and the nose (nasal cavity).

Breathing disorders in the cerebral palsied may be due not only to damage to the motor cortex affecting muscles which control pharyngeal, laryngeal, and respiratory function but may involve damage to the brain centers (hypothalamus) which regulate the rate and rhythm of respiration. The hypothalamus which lies near the basal ganglia may be affected particularly in the athetoid as a consequence of damage to the latter—usually due to cerebral anoxia at birth (Koven, 1954). And, in the spastic cerebral palsied where the damage is more likely to be in the motor cortex, there is lesser possibility of damage to the central respiratory mechanisms (Blumberg, 1955). Wolfe (1950) feels that the greater incidence of speech problems of all types (including breathing and voice disorders) in athetoids is due to the fact that almost 100 percent of them have some type of speech mechanism involvement. See Palmer (1954) and Achilles (1955, 1956) for a description of the abnormal breathing patterns found in the "brain-damaged child."

Comment is inserted at this point concerning three additional sources for therapeutic speech handling of the cerebral palsied. For a thorough explanation of the techniques, refer to the original works.

THE WESTLAKE METHOD. The general rationale behind this approach to speech habilitation: When movements can be initiated on a voluntary level, the child is ready to learn these movements for use in speech production. The child is evaluated to determine his function on a vegetative level (can he move his tongue to touch a lollipop) and on a voluntary level (can he move his tongue on command). This treatment approach is compatible with the Phelps' method (1948, 1940, 1941) which was one of the first proposed systems of therapy for the treatment of children with cerebral palsy. Stressed in the Phelps "muscle reeducation" system is treatment of individual muscles. There are three main categories or headings to the Westlake principles of therapy: (1) Psychological and social readiness for speech; (2) Physiological readiness for speech. Stressed in this phase are muscle education techniques and various exercises. Following the Phelps' method, equipment is used such as braces and sandbags. Emphasis is also placed on relaxation techniques particularly for the athetoid. Included are specific breathing, blowing, tongue and lip exercises; (3) Direct speech training. The child is led from the involuntary movement stage by watching in the mirror and helping the action with the hands. Later, a more structured approach is implemented such as learning words from a notebook. This is similar, again, to the Phelps' technique in that it builds from passive motion to active assistive to active motion. (See: Westlake 1951a, 1951b, 1961).

THE CASS METHOD. This method is characteristic of a more traditional approach to therapy (Cass, 1965).

THE HOBERMAN METHOD. This method encompasses some of the specific applications of various approaches such as Bobath, and PNF techniques proposed by Kabat and Knott (1953, 1956) in which the spinal cord and subcortical motor centers are stimulated by such techniques as resistance to motion; pressure and stretch; Rood techniques; traditional techniques such as passive relaxation and progressive relaxation as taught by Jacobson (1929). Included also are some aspects of the Westlake (1951) techniques (Hoberman et al., 1960).

In concluding this portion, it would behoove the therapist to note a bit of philosophy proposed by Davies (1964), "therapy is the treatment of the whole person, governed by intellectual, emotional and physical factors. Because apathy is a real danger in the long-term treatment . . . success is perhaps the keynote of therapy—building incentive for further achievement, however small."

DISORDERS OF HEARING

There is indeed an intimate relationship between speech and hearing as it can be said that a child learns to talk as he hears. Deafness (of almost any degree) arrests the normal development of speech and language, since the "primary receptive avenue is disrupted and the sensory motor servomechanism is seriously altered" (Nober, 1967). It would be difficult to state the exact number of cerebral palsied children with hearing loss. Estimates range from about 5 percent to as much as 40 percent. However, the results of one rather comprehensive investigation may add perspective to hearing deficits evidenced in the cerebral palsied and may be considered symbolic of the problem. In a group of 1,293 cerebral palsied children, Hopkins *et al.* (1954) found hearing defects in 7.2 percent of the spastics, 18.4 percent of the ataxics and 22.6 percent in the athetoids. Percentages and estimates aside, there is no doubt that there is a higher prevalence of deafness among cerebral palsied children than in the general population (Gerber, 1966; Nakaono, 1966).

The problem simply stated is this. In addition to those hearing disorders which are particularly prevalent in the cerebral palsied (those associated with *kernicterus* (Rh factor) and *maternal rubella*), these children are in no way shielded from those elements which may inflict hearing problems in "normal" children such as upper respiratory infections and/or infectious diseases such as mumps. It can be said then that the cerebral palsied suffers double indemnity. It is no wonder that the incidence in children with cerebral palsy is much higher than in the general population. This is particularly true of the athetoid who undoubtedly experiences greater problems in oral communication than do the other subgroups of cerebral palsy.

Gerber (1966) investigated the hearing deficiencies among sub-groups of cerebral palsied children. The study included 56 cerebral palsy and 18 non-cerebral palsy children who were used as controls. The breakdown of the cerebral palsied children and percent of hearing loss are as follows: Spastics (total of 26): 50 percent had hearing loss; Athetoids (total of 26): 75 percent had hearing loss. The athetoids were further separated into two groups: (a) non-Rh athetoids (total of 17): 50 percent had hearing loss; (b) Rh athetoids (total of 9): 100 percent or *all* the *erythroblastotic (Rh factor)* athetoids were hearing impaired. Gerbor states that "the Rh athetoids had significantly poorer hearing than other athetoids by nearly 20 dB." The non-kernicterus children were not significantly different from the spastics. Generally, the cerebral palsied children were found to have thresholds on the average of 15 dB below the non-cerebral palsied children. Aside from the hearing-loss data derived from this study, Gerber makes a very interesting and salient point, "it is not motor pattern (i.e. spastic) which is distinguishing from an auditory viewpoint, it is the etiology . . . a classification system based upon etiology would in all probability have greater predictive value for the habilitation of hearing impaired, cerebral palsied children."

It is a well-established and documented fact (Barr *et al.*, 1961; Sheridan, 1964; Gerber, 1966) that deafness as a consequence of *maternal rubella* is a frequent occurrence. The greatest risk of maternal rubella, in fact, is deafness, according to Campbell (1961) and Jackson *et al.* (1958). According to Masland (1967) and Perlstein (1955) the major etiologies of cerebral palsy are anoxia, maternal rubella, prematurity, obstetrical complications, jaundice (especially when related to complications of Rh factor), toxemia, and postnatal infections (such as meningitis). Correspondingly, according to Vernon (1967a, 1967b, 1967c, 1967d, and 1967e) four of the five leading causes of deafness and their respective prevalences are: meningitis, 8.7 percent; complications of Rh factor, 3.7 percent; prematurity, 17 percent; and rubella, 4 to 80 percent.

GENERAL INFORMATION

To form the kindergarten and prepare the soil for our discussion, we will quickly review the salient bits of information regarding hearing in general.

ANATOMY AND PHYSIOLOGY. There are three parts to the hearing mechanism: (1) the ear: the receiver of stimuli or the transducer (changes energy), (2) the neuro pathway: transmission line from the ear to the brain, and (3) the auditory cortex: the decoder in the brain. The ear (1) consists of (a) the outer part (the pinna and canal or the external auditory meatus), (b) the middle ear which encloses a chamber housing the three smallest bones in the body or the malleus (hammer), incus (anvil) and the stapes (stirrup), and (c) the inner ear called the cochlea which is actually the true end organ of hearing or the tranducer of energy. This function is performed by the organ of Corti housed within the cochlea. The organ of Corti changes the form of energy from mechanical to neural energy. Hair cells in the organ of corti are stimulated by fluid activity. These hair cells are connected by nerve endings which bundle together to form the 8th cranial nerve.

TYPES OF HEARING LOSS. In general, there are several types of hearing loss (sometimes referred to as dysacusis): (a) Conductive. Site of lesion is in the outer or middle ear. The most common cause in children is otitis media or inflammation of the middle ear; (b) Sensory (cochlear). Site of lesion is in the inner ear or cochlea. Maternal rubella is the common cause of sensory hearing loss in the cerebral pasied child; (c) 8th nerve disorders. Site of lesion is of course the 8th nerve. A common cause in children is infectious disease such as meningitis; (d) Central hearing impairment (central dysacusis). Site of lesion is the auditory cortex. This entire area is covered in Chapter 3, *Learning: Mechanisms and Disorders;* and (e) Functional or non-organic. No site of lesion. This is a simulated hearing loss as the hearing mechanics function adequately. Caused by psychological disturbances.

Some accounts anatomically dicotomize hearing loss into two types: or, (1) Conductive. Typically, a conductive loss is characterized by a decrease in the intensity levels of all sounds, particularly in the low and middle frequencies; and (2) Perceptive (sensorineural). The perceptive losses are of two kinds (i) Peripheral. Here the defect is in the cochlea, or the cochlear section of the acoustic nerve. Characteristically, the loss is *selective*. That is, the deficit does not affect the entire cochlea or nerve throughout; but rather, the loss is commonly limited to that portion of the cochlea where the *high frequency* sounds are seated. Sounds such as f, v, s, sh [f]; zh[3]; th[θ]; th [ʒ]; t; d; p; k; and g are in this category. These determine intelligibility or, broadly considered, "the frequencies below 1,200 cycles provide most of the carrying power energy and emotional colour of speech" (Fry, 1957) while those above 1,200 cycles are concerned with intelligibility. The phenomenon of recruitment further complicates the peripheral perceptive type of loss. The second type of perceptive hearing loss is (ii) central (cortical deafness). Site of lesion or defect in this type is in the primary auditory areas (cortex or brain stem) which affects *recognition* of sounds. This defect is not to be confused with that of interpretation which is the function of secondary auditory areas in the temporoparietal cortex such as Wernicke's area (Fig. 5). A defect or lesion in the secondary areas causes auditory aphasia and is discussed in the chapter dealing with Learning Disorders.

DEGREE AND EXTENT OF HEARING LOSS. See Table XIX. PHYSICS OF SOUND. Sound is the movement of molecules in a medium (air). The characteristics or parameters of sound are: (1) Rate. This parameter measures the molecular compression and rarefraction (or pushing together) per unit of time which equals the *frequency* of vibrations or the number of vibrations per second. Frequency or *pitch* is measured in *Hertz* (Hz). The ear is capable of receiving frequencies from sixteen of these vibration cycles or Hz (16 complete compression/rarefractions per second) to 16,000 Hz per second; or, 16 (low pitch) to 16,000 Hz. This equals the total hearing range of the ear. (2) *Intensity.* This is the strength, loudness of the vibrations and is measured in decibles (dB).[25] A decible is a unit of physical intensity or power. The average dB of speech is 60 dB. The range is from 0 to 140 dB. And, finally, the last parameter is (3) Spectrum (the quality or timbre). This is the combination of frequency at differing intensities. Therefore, frequency and intensity provide for the spectrum in sound.

The ear ordinarily does not hear a single frequency of vibration at a single intensity which is a *pure* tone. There are combinations of frequencies at varying intensities in real life. It is this combination of frequencies with different intensities that provide different kinds of sounds. So the ear is capable of providing appropriate information to the cortex for differentiation of about one-third of a million different sounds.

SOME DEFINITIONS. *Anacusis:* deafness (profound or complete). *Discrimination:* as it applies to dysacusis of the peripheral type, diminished discrimination is difficulty in discerning differences in phonetic elements due to cochlear or retrocochlear pathology. *Diplacusis:* double hearing. *Dysacusis:* a symptom associated with hearing difficulties. Two types of dysacusis are (1) peripheral dysacusis which includes diplacusis, recruitment, phonemic regression, diminished discrimination and (2) central dysacusis including the auditory agnosias and receptive aphasias. *Hard of Hearing:*

---

[25]If a child has a 40 dB loss at 1,000 hertz, this means that for the child to just hear the sound it must be 40 dB above the intensity at which a normal adult would be able to hear this same sound.

Severity	Decible Range	Implications
Normal acuity	0–20 dB	No difficulty with normal conversation under ordinary circumstances or three feet at 60 dB
Mild	20–40 dB	Difficulty hearing normal conversation if greater than 10 feet from source. Needs preferential seating in the classroom. May not need hearing aid. Hearing loss due to mumps may affect only one ear—seating to the good ear.
Moderate	40–60 dB	Difficulty if greater than five feet from source of normal conversation. Usually has speech problems; requires special training such as hearing aid or aural rehabilitation. May be able to function in normal classroom.
Severe ⎤	60–80 dB	Difficulty in greater than one foot. Requires special education facilities, and school for deaf or residential school.
Anacusis		
Profound ⎦	80–up dB	Difficulty hearing normal conversation.

Table XIX Degree and Extent of Hearing Loss

denotes enough residual hearing left so that child would not require special school but would be able to develop adequate language and speech with a hearing aid and therapy. *High frequency loss:* an auditory defect with a trace of normal hearing in the low frequencies. There is a decrease exceeding 35 decibles at one or more of the higher frequencies. *Hypocusis:* hearing loss. *Phonemic regression:* excessive discriminatory loss suggestive of degeneration of neural pathways of higher auditory centers therefore a hearing aid may be useless as amplification cannot improve intelligibility (Nober, 1966). *Recruitment:* a disproportionate increase in loudness sensation associated with poor discrimination and hypersensitivity to small increases in intensity and frequency. *High Frequency Deafness* (variously referred to as high tone deafness, partial nerve loss, congenital dysacusis, and the *ski slope* audiogram).

This is the most frequent type of hearing loss that is found in the cerebral palsied child.[26] This type of hearing loss is characterized by "ow, ow, ow, ow," for "how now brown cow" (Sortini, 1965). This type of loss in the cerebral palsied is due to *Rh incompatibility* (kernicterus) which results in a loss pronounced in the higher frequencies. It will be remembered that Rh incompatibility leading as it may to kernicterus is one of the factors observed by Perlstein (1952a, 1952b) as one of the three common etiological findings in the athetoid (the others being a history of anoxia and breech delivery). This child is often referred to as a "deaf athetoid" which is merely a cliche as most of these children are not actually deaf but, rather, have a partial hearing defect with aphasoid-like characteristics and/or specific auditory insensitivities.

Keats (p. 320, 1965) described it this way: "High frequency deafness seems to occur more often in a special type of athetoids ... ataxic component frequently associated with defective upward gaze movement of the eyes. ... Such a child can usually be easily distinguished from the other athetoids as they seem to have more involvement in the upper extremities, the head and the neck ... they over use their eyes, constantly watching the lips of the speaker when talking. Their speech defect comes from a hearing loss not in the form of decreased hearing but a pitch defect which cuts out the "s," "t," "th," and "f," "g," and "k" sounds."

The site of lesion is apparently still in the arms of debate. One school of thought places the pathological blame to a defect of the cochlear nuclei of the brain stem or mid-brain or in the cochlea itself. Hardy (1961) feels that, "There is no evidence,

---

[26]Marked high-frequency hearing impairment must be considered as a potential sequela of prematurity, anoxia in the prenatal or perinatal period, postnatal respiratory stress and Rh incompatibility (Matkin, 1968).

as yet, that there is any causal relationship between kernicterus associated with the Rh factor and lesions of these conductive and receptive stages of the auditory system (from external canal through the cochlea by way of the oval window). That lesions may exist here concurrently is taken for granted. More important in the present context is the situation at the level of the auditory nuclei, low in the pons. It is at this point that the lesion relating to kernicterus has been identified in recent histopathologic studies . . . higher in the structure of the brain stem and mid-brain are several important junctions: the lateral lemniscus, the inferior colliculus, and the medial geniculate body of the thalamus. Presumable, a breakdown at any of these three transmissive way-stations would more or less seriously interfere with the transmission of auditory information."

Hardy continues by questioning whether the organic changes involve hearing or listening or both. "At the thalamic level and out into the cortical areas lies extensions of this neural transmitting system and the projection areas. The auditory cortex is the apogee of the organ of Corti. These are complex processes having to do with the refinements of discrimination, of maintaining a temporal pattern of complex harmonic structure, of closing a self-monitoring system whereby the individual recognizes the details of familiar auditory information. If there is developmental lack or damaged tissue in the pertinent corticothalamic regions so that temporal patterns of this order cannot be perceived, then one would expect to see the effect of drastic dysfunction in terms both of auditory organization and of language-learning, association, and recall. At the high integrating levels of audition and language-learning, the principal function to be developed is some aspect of a conditioned response. When the system operates with marked variability, as is usually true with brain-damaged children, conditions are not right for the ready establishment of conditioned responses, and one is apt to see clinically a wide divergence of reactions of sound, particularly speech sounds. All this is part of the experience that is called hearing."

Gerrard (1952) reported that "up to 80 percent of the cases of kernicterus have complete or partial deafness, with particular involvement of the high frequencies." Blakely (1959) believes that "the lesion is in the cochlea" (the organ of Corti is within the cochlear structure), as he found that his subjects demonstrated recruitment. However, to further muddle the hearing problems of the kernicterus child, those on the other side of the argument feel that lesions occur in higher auditory areas resulting in aphasic-like characteristics.[27] The majority of children in Cohen's (1956) study had symptoms suggesting the mixed receptive and expressive types of aphasia. He further indicated that the clinical picture of the child with kernicterus includes "poor feeding, difficulty in head control, often has a persistence of the tonic neck reflex, shows evidence of ataxic as well as athetosis, and eyes show difficulty in supraversion." As well, Byers *et al.* (1955) has suggested that there may be a higher level of perceptual involvement than the cochlear nuclei.

The major psychological, audiological, educational, and physical characteristics of 1,468 deaf children who attended or were given preadmission evaluations at the California School for the Deaf in Riverside, over a 12 year period ending in 1964, were investigated by Vernon (1966). Of these children, 69 or 4.7 percent were cerebral palsied. This is 15 to 17 times the expected rate in the general population (Vernon, 1970). Some interesting results from the study concerning the Rh factor and its relationship to deafness in general and as it specifically affects the cerebral palsied were obtained. There were forty-five educationally deaf children (hearing loss 65 dB or greater in the 500-2,000 cps range ASA 1951) of 3.1 percent of the total (1,468) whose etiology of deafness was complications of Rh factor.[28] Results were as follows:[29]

1. Cerebral palsy was found in over half (or 51.1 percent) of these forty-five children (Table XX.) Of the 69 cerebral palsied, 23 or 33.3 percent were Rh deaf which may be indicative of the fact that complications of Rh factor are the leading cause of com-

---

[27]Paine (1968) feels that the disease leaves an organic damage to the basal ganglia, the nuclei of the brain stem, and the hypocampus, thus causing motor and perceptual defects but few behavioral disorders.

[28]The hearing loss in the cerebral palsied was 78.9 Hz (ASA, 1951) in the better ear for speech range (500 to 2,000 Hz).

[29]See Table XX for a summary of the results as they specifically relate to the cerebral palsied child.

bined conditions of deafness and cerebral palsy. All the cerebral palsied in this study (Rh deaf) were athetoids.[30]

2. Twenty-three percent of the Rh group was classified aphasic (as opposed to only one of the 63 genetically deaf children). Perhaps the most important factor about deafness and Rh factor is that aphasoid disorders and central nervous system lesions are often present in addition to hearing loss (Cohen, 1956; Hannigan, 1956; Myklebust, 1956; Rosen, 1956; and Vernon, 1967). Take note from Table XX that in Vernon's study 51.1 percent of the Rh deaf children were cerebral palsied.

3. The Rh group showed the greatest behavioral evidence of neurological impairment: the primary pathology was in the general area of visual motor perception.[31]

4. Relative to the other four etiological groups, there was not an atypical prevalence of emotional maladjustment.[32]

5. The Rh children had more residual hearing than any of the other four groups (based on pure tone audiometry). Performance on written language, speech, and speech reading did not, however, reflect this. It is Vernon's opinion that there appears to be pathology of auditory perception or integration and symbolization of sound that reduces the effectiveness of the ability to respond to auditory input.

Characteristically, the child with a high frequency loss (which is ability to hear normally or nearly so in the lower frequencies) will be able to respond to many sounds in his environment and to speech containing vowel sounds. Further, he usually responds when called by name "because he can hear lower-pitched speech (Matkin, 1968)." We find that his responses to sound are irradict. Referring to Table XXI, *Frequency Continuum,* we find that

---

[30]At least 80 percent of the Rh children had noticeably poor coordination, but only where there was gross motor involvement was a diagnosis of cerebral palsy made.

[31]However, based on individually administered performance type intelligence tests (WAIS and WISC Performance Scales or Leiter International Performance Scale, 1948) the mean IQ for the cerebral palsied tested (63) was 83. Almost *half* or 29 had average or better intelligence. Those deaf and cerebral palsied due to Rh factor or to prematurity—mean IQ of 88; postmeningitic—IQ of 80 which was the lowest. Many of these postmeningitic children were spastic hemiplegics.

[32]The post-rubella children had the most psychological maladjustment (Table XX).

TABLE XX

SUMMARY:[a] RESULTS OF VERNON'S (1966) STUDY WHICH RELATE
SPECIFICALLY TO THE CEREBRAL PALSIED CHILD

Four Etiologies of Deafness[b]

	Rubella		Prematurity[c]		Meningitis		Rh Factor		Total	
	Total Sample	Percent Handicapped	Total Sample	Percent Handicapped	Total Sample	Percent Handicapped	Total Sample	Percent Handicapped	Total Sample	Percent Handicapped
Prevalence of CP	104	3.8	113	17.6	92	9.7	45	51.1	354	15.8
ASSOCIATED DISABILITIES										
Vision		66.6[d]								
Aphasia		66.6	Aphasia[e]	71.4	Orthopedic	80.0	Aphasia[f] Visual Motor Perception Difficulties	43.7		
Educational failure[g]										
Emotional Maladjustment										

[a] For a complete report, the reader if referred to the original report (Vernon, 1966 and 1970).

[b] Differences in sample sizes exist because it was not always possible to obtain valid diagnosis of the presence or absence of each of the physical anomalies on every child.

[c] The fact that almost one in five prematures has cerebral palsy deserves attention in view of the increasing prominence this etiology is playing in deafness (Vernon, 1967). It is essential that the teacher and therapist be aware of the ramifications of prematurity which Vernon feels is "heretofore overlooked problem". Approximately 17 percent of the deaf school age children are premature and more than two-thirds are multiply handicapped (Vernon, 1967).

[d] Emotional disturbance runs a close second with 50.0 per cent; cataracts were a common visual problem.

[e] Criterion for aphasia: a marked difficulty with language greater than that expected due to deafness or level of intelligence.

[f] Visual disturbance found in 33.3 per cent.

[g] The postrubella children had the greatest prevalence of educational failures and emotional maladjustment and had an overall below-average academic achievement—followed by prematures and those having complications of Rh factor.

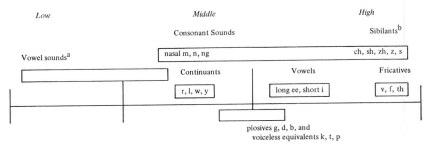

Low	Middle	High
	Consonant Sounds	Sibilants[b]
Vowel sounds[a]	nasal m, n, ng	ch, sh, zh, z, s
	Continuants	Vowels	Fricatives
	r, l, w, y	long ee, short i	v, f, th
	plosives g, d, b, and voiceless equivalents k, t, p	

[a] aw strongest intensity (dB)

[b] ee weakest intensity (dB)

Sounds can be classified into 3 categories:
1. Vowels: 15 in number; voiced, continuants
2. Diphthongs: 6 such as *ai*sle, pl*ou*gh
3. Consonants: 25 (phonemes) such as *sh*e, *ch*ick, *r*un, *d*og, *k*id.

Table XXI Frequency Continuum

the consonants are the sounds most frequently affected in high-tone deafness. The vowels have a higher decible intensity than do the consonants so that this child tends to respond to speech containing vowel sounds. The speech problems resulting from high frequency deficits are due of course to the distorted or filtered auditory input. This faulty input results, consequently, in faulty output such as omission of many consonant sounds. The difficulty a child encounters who has an auditory processing defect (auditory symbolic or language imperception) should ring a warning bell for educators. This child may better be served through a tactile and/or visual educational approach.

Hearing Characteristics, Post-Rubella Children

Rubella or "German measles,[33] although a mild childhood disease, gains importance through its effect on the fetus in utero.[34]

[33]Rubella was first known as "Rothlen" which was the term used by German physicians 150 years ago to describe a new disease (Doctor *et al.*, 1970) which subsequently came to be known as German measles. Then in 1866, Veale (1866) proposed the term "rubella." This is distinguished from measles or rubeola.

[34]When a pregnant woman has rubella, the virus affects the fetus via her bloodstream. "Here the sensitive and rapidly multiplying cells of the unborn infant are attacked" (Ward *et al.*, 1968). As was mentioned in the chapter concerning vision, the problem may be made more complex by the fact that the virus has the unfortunate capability of staying *alive and well* in the infant for several months causing possible damage to the infant during early development.

From previous epidemics, it has been estimated that about 15 to 20 percent of infants born to mothers who have the disease in the first 3 months of pregnancy will have some kind of easily discernible malformation (Sight Saving Review, 1971). For instance, the results of the 1963 to 64 epidemic were as follows: 30,000 abortions and stillbirths; 20 to 40 thousand infants had serious damage by the disease; an additional 10,000 children had mild to moderate handicaps. "With impaired sensory systems of sight and hearing, the two main avenues of learning are closed to the rubella-damaged child" (Doctor, *et al.*, 1970). The most recent concensus concerning the occurrence of deafness in post-rubella children places the figure between 12 to 19 percent. One need only perform some simple mathematics to determine the approximate number of children which survived the 1963 to 64 epidemic having hearing deficits.

The four main problems related to the rubella syndrome are: (1) cardiac malformations, (2) eye disorders (See Ch. 6 *Vision and Its Defects*), (3) physical and mental retardation, and (4) loss of hearing.

Hearing losses in these children are usually bilateral. The audiograms are flat or assymmetrically curved, having their highest thresholds at the extremes of the pitch range (Barr *et al.*, 1961; Doyle, 1953; Jackson *et al.*, 1958; and Levine, 1961). The hearing problem is further complicated by a factor which Vernon (1966) noted in his study of 1,468 children previously mentioned. Of the total, 129 children were *post-rubella deaf* cases. He found 21.9 percent of this group or one in five, had a double language handicap of severe hearing loss and aphasoid involvement. By contrast, 23 percent of the Rh group was classified aphasic; 66.0 percent of the cerebral palsied children had aphasoid characteristics (Table XX). It is essential to remember that in post-rubella children there is a high probability that lesions exist in parts of the brain and central nervous system[35] which are related to central perceptual hearing problems (Barr, 1968; Vernon, 1967). Accordingly, Vernon warns that care must be taken when considering a child with post-rubella deafness as a potential hearing aid wearer

---

[35]In Vernon's study, approximately 47 percent of the post-rubella children's Bender-Gestalt were judged "pathological".

because "central nervous system lesions may cause amplification to be painful and, in general, psychologically traumatic" (Vernon, 1966). He also suggests that when discussing the problem some of these children seem to have in tolerating sounds, reference is being directed to the peripheral phenomenon called recruitment or "the loudness of tones appears to increase more rapidly than normal . . . (the) loudness may be only a matter of five or ten decibles but it produces a sensation of much greater loudness than it would on the normal ear" (Berry *et al.*, 1956). Referring to the question of tolerance alluded to in Vernon's report, Hodgsdon (1967) says that "it has not been established that central nervous system lesions, in the presence of peripheral hearing loss, are responsible for reduced tolerance for amplified sound." Quite the contrary according to some investigators (Jerger, 1960; Davis *et al.*, 1965; Hodgsdon, 1967) who feel that just the opposite or "derecruitment" (an abnormally slow growth of loudness) may occur as a result of damage to the central auditory pathways.

Because there seemed to be considerable disagreement concerning the pros and cons of hearing aids and the benefit thereof to post-rubella hearing impaired children, Hodgsdon (1969) prepared an evidential report suggesting that post-rubella hearing impaired children do not have undue tolerance problems for amplified sound and could therefore benefit from hearing aids. Forty-three post rubella children were studied. The general conclusion drawn was that the children did not appear different from children with sensorineural loss from other causes. However, and this point has particular importance to those interested in the CP/NI, Hodgsdon has been less successful in evaluating the hearing of rubella children with multiple handicaps. He reports, "it is probable that the multiple handicaps will play a part in reducing optimum use of remaining hearing." Additionally, he concludes the report by saying that "many of the rubella children may have poorer auditory function than the audiological evaluation by itself would suggest." Could this not be due to possible central integration dysfunction?

Perhaps we may conclude this section on hearing impairments by referring to a study in 1957 by Woods in which is described the two most common hearing defects in cerebral palsy: (1) High frequency deafness, and (2) Auditory agnosia (or cortical deafness). That parents and professionals alike are frequently so overwhelmed by the combination of deafness and cerebral palsy, "they fail to see and develop the potential which remains" (Vernon, 1970). This familiar bell rings so true in all facets of teaching and training of the cerebral palsied child. The educational philosophy of Vernon (1967) concerning the multiply handicapped deaf child is certainly applicable to the cerebral palsied deaf (or hard of hearing) child: "What is needed are educational-training type programs for these individuals when they are young and vocational services for them as adults. The schools serving them would have to offer flexible experimental type approaches to teaching because the answers about how to educate these youths are not available. Certainly, efforts to adapt existing materials developed in the area of learning disabilities to the deaf children would be a minimal first step."

REFERENCES

Achilles, R.: Communicative anomalies of individuals with cerebral palsy. *Cereb Pal Rev, 16*:15-24, 1955.

Barr, D. F.: Rubella: Implications for amplification. *Nat Hear Aid J, 22*, 1968.

Barr, B., and Lunstrom, R.: Deafness following maternal rubella: Retrospective and prospective studies. *Acta Otolaryngol, 53*:413-428, 1961.

Berry, Mildred F., and Eisenson, J.: *Speech Disorders: Principles and Practices of Therapy.* New York, Appleton-Century-Crofts, 1956.

Blakely, R. W.: Erythroblastosis and perceptive hearing loss. Response of athetoids to tests of cochlear function. *J Speech Hear Res, 1*:5-15, 1959.

Blumberg, M.: Respiration and speech in the cerebral palsied. *Amer J Dis Child, 89*:48-53, 1955.

Brain, Lord: *Speech Disorders,* 2nd ed. London, Buttersworth, 1965.

Brain, R. W.: *Diseases of the Nervous System.* London, Oxford Univ Press, 1955.

Byers, R. K., Paine, R. S., and Crothers, B.: Extrapyramidal cerebral palsy with hearing loss following erythroblastosis. *Ped, 15*:248-254, 1955.

Campbell, M.: Place of maternal rubella in the aetiology of congenital heart disease. *Brit Med J, 1*:691-696, 1961.

Cass, Marion T.: *Speech Habilitation in Cerebral Palsy.* New York,

Hafner, 1965.

Cohen, P.: Rh child: Deaf or "Aphasic?" 2. "Aphasia" in Kernicterus. *J Spch Hear Dis, 21*:411-412, 1956.

Crickmay, Marie C.: *Speech Therapy and the Bobath Approach to Cerebral Palsy.* Springfield, Thomas, 1966.

Crothers, B., and Payne, R. S.: *The Natural History of Cerebral Palsy.* Cambridge, Harvard Univ Press, 1959.

Davies, Ena: Principles of treatment of speech disorders in the cerebral palsied. In Renfrew, C., and Murphy, K. (Eds.): *The Child Who Does not Talk.* Clin Develop Med. London, Spastics Society/Heinemann, 1964.

Davis, H., and Goodman, A.: Subtractive Hearing Loss, Loudness Recruitment, and Derecruitement. A paper presented at the 70th Convention of the Acoustical Society of America, St. Louis, Nov. 3-6, 1965. Abstracted in the *J Acous Soc Amer, 38*:922-923, 1965.

Doctor, P. V., and Davis, F. E.: Educational aspects of rubella sensory deprivation. *Amer Asso Workers Blind,* 1970 Annual Report, Blindness 1970.

Doyle, J. I. H.: A Study of the Relationship between Etiology of Hearing Loss and Audiometric pattern. Unpublished master's thesis, Vanderbilt University, 1953.

Dunn, Lloyd: Manual Peabody Picture Vocabulary Test. Amer Guidance Service, Inc., Minneapolis, Minnesota, 1959.

Fry, D. B.: Speech and language. *J Laryngol, 71*:434, 1957.

Granjon-Galifret, N., and Ajuriaguerra, J. de: Troubles de l'apprentissage de la lecture et dominance latérale. *Encéphale, 40*:385, 1951.

Gerber, Sanford E.: Cerebral palsy and hearing loss. *Cereb Pal J, 27*:6-7, 1966.

Gerrard, J.: Kernicterus. *Brain, 75*:526-570, 1952.

Guttmann, E.: Aphasia in children. *Brain, 65*:205, 1942.

Hallgren, B.: Specific dyslexia. *Acta psychiat scand,* Supple 65, 1950.

Hammill, Don D., and Powell, L. S.: An abstraction test for visually handicapped children. *Except Chil, 33*:646-647, 1967.

Hannigan, Helen: Rh child: Deaf or "Aphasic?" 3. Language and behavior problems of the Rh "Aphasic" child. *J Spch Hear Dis, 21*:413-417, 1956.

Hardy, W. G.: *Kernicterus and Its Importance in Cerebral Palsy.* Springfield, Thomas, 1961.

Hermann, K.: *Reading Disability: A Medical Study of Word Blindness and Related Handicaps.* Springfield, Thomas, 1959.

Hoberman, J. E., and Hoberman, M.: Speech habilitation in cerebral palsy. *J Speech Hear Dis, 25*:111-123, 1960.

Hodgsdon, William R.: Auditory characteristics of post-rubella impairment. *Volta Rev, 2*:97-103, 1969.

Hodgsdon, W.: Audiological report of a patient with left hemispherectomy. *J Speech Hear Dis, 32*:40-45, 1967.

Hopkins, T. W., Bice, H. V., and Colton, K. C.: Evaluation and education of cerebral palsied children. International Council Except Child, Washington, 1954, p. 63.

Ingram, T. T. S.: Paediatric aspects of specific developmental dysphasia, dyslexia and dysgraphia. *Cereb Pal Bull, 2*:254-277, 1960.

Ingram, T. T. S.: The complex disorders of cerebral palsied children. In Renfrew, C., and Murphy, K. (Eds.): The child who does not talk. *Clin Develop Med.*, Spastics Society/Heinemann, 1964.

Ingram, T. T. S.: Specific developmental disorders of speech in childhood. *Brain,* 82:450, 1959.

Irwin, Orvis C.: Phonetic equipment of spastic and athetoid children. *J Speech Hear Dis, 20*:54-57, 1955.

Irwin, Orvis C.: Word equipment of spastic and athetoid children. *Cereb Pal Rev, 17*:13-14, 1957.

Irwin, Orvis C.: A third set of consonant substitution and omission errors in the speech of cerebral palsy children. *Cereb Pal Rev, 18*:11, 1957.

Irwin, Orvis C.: Correct status of a third set of consonants in the speech of cerebral palsy children. *Cereb Pal Rev, 18*:17-20, 1957.

Irwin, Orvis C.: Correct articulation of ten different consonants by children with cerebral palsy. *Cereb Pal Rev, 21*:6-7, 1960.

Irwin, Orvis C.: A manual of articulation testing for use with children with cerebral palsy. *Cereb Pal Rev, 22*:1-24, 1961a.

Irwin, Orvis C.: Correct status of vowels and consonants in the speech of children with cerebral palsy as measured by an integrated test. *Cereb Palsy Rev, 22*:21-24, 1961b.

Irwin, Orvis, C.: A short articulation test of ten consonants for use with cerebral palsied children. *Cereb Pal Rev, 22*:28-31, 1961c.

Irwin, Orvis C.: Difficulties of consonant sounds in terms of manner and place of articulation and of voicing in the speech of cerebral palsy children. *Cereb Pal Rev, 22*:13-16, 1963a.

Irwin, Orvis C., and Jensen, Paul J.: A parallel test of sound discrimination for use with cerebral palsied children. *Cereb Pal Rev, 24*:3-10, 1963b.

Irwin, Orvis C., and Hammill, Donald D.: An abstraction test for use with cerebral palsied children. *Cereb Pal Rev, 2*:3-9, 1964.

Irwin, Orvis C., and Hammill, D. D.: An item analysis of a sound discrimination test for use with mentally retarded children. *Cereb Pal J, 26*:9-11, 1965.

Irwin, Dale O.: Articulation of difficult speech sounds by two groups of retarded children. *Cereb Pal J,* 27:3-7, 1966a.

Irwin, Orvis C.: A comparison of the vocabulary of use and of understanding of cerebral palsied children. *Cereb Pal J, 27*:7-11, 1966b.

Irwin, Orvis C., and Korst, J. W.: Summary of reliability coefficients of six speech tests for use with handicapped children. *Cereb Pal J,* 6-7, July-August, 1967a.

Irwin, Orvis C., and Korst, J. W.: Correlations among five speech tests and the WISC verbal scale. *Cereb Pal J,* 9-11, September-October, 1967b.

Irwin, Orvis C., and Korst, J. W.: A further study of the number and length of sentences in the language of cerebral palsied children. *Cereb Pal J,* 3-4, September-October, 1967c.

Irwin, Orvis C.: Correct status of vowels and consonants in the speech of children with cerebral palsy as measured by an integrated test. *Cereb Pal J,* 9-12, January-Feb., 1968.

Jackson, A. D. M., and Fisch, L.: Deafness following maternal rubella. *Lancelot, 2*:124-144, 1958.

Jacobson, E.: *Progressive Relaxation.* Chicago, Univ Chicago Press, 1929.

Jerger, J.: Observations on auditory behavior in lesions of the central auditory pathways. *AMA Arch Otolaryng, 71*:797-806, 1960.

Kabat, H., and Knott, M.: Proprioceptive facilitation techniques for treatment of paralysis. *Phys Ther Rev, 33*:53-64, 1953.

Keats, Sidney: *Cerebral Palsy.* Springfield, Thomas, 1965.

Knott, M., and Voss, D. E.: *Proprioceptive Neuromuscular Facilitation: Patterns and Techniques.* New York, Hoeber, 1956.

Koven, L. J., and Lamm, S. S.: The athetoid syndrome in cerebral palsy: Part II. Clinical aspects. *Ped, 14*:181-192, 1954.

Leiter International Performance Scale. Leiter, Russell G., Chicago, Stoelting, 1948.

Lencione, Ruth M.: Speech and language problems in cerebral palsy. In Cruickshank, W. M. (Ed.): *Cerebral Palsy: Its Individual and Community Problems,* 2nd ed. Syracuse, Syracuse University Press, 1966.

Levine, Edna: Psychoeducational characteristics of children following maternal rubella. *Amer J Dis Child,* 627-632, 1951.

Masland, R. L.: *NINDB Research Profile: Cerebral Palsy* (No. 13). Washington, US Government Printing Office, 1967.

Matkin, N. D.: The child with a marked high-frequency hearing impairment. *Ped Clin N Amer, 15*:677-690, 1968.

Mechan, M. J., et al.: *Communication Training in Childhood Brain Damage.* Springfield, Thomas, 1966.

Myklebust, H. R.: Rh child: Deaf or "Aphasic?" Some psychological considerations of the Rh child. *J Spch Hear Dis, 21*:423-425, 1956.

Mysak, E. D.: *Principles of a Reflex Therapy Approach to Cerebral Palsy.* New York, Teachers College, Columbia University, 1963.

Mysak, E. D.: Dysarthria and oropharyngeal reflexology: A review. *J Spch Hear Dis, 28*:252-262, 1963.

Mysak, E. D.: Significance of neurophysiological orientation to cerebral palsy habilitation. *J Spch Hear Dis, 24*:221-230, 1959.

Nakaono, T.: Research on hearing impairment in cerebral palsied school children. *International Audiology, 5*:159-161, 1966.

Nober, E.: Articulation of the deaf. *Excep Child, 33*:611, 1967.

Nober, E.: Hearing problems with cerebral palsy. In Cruickshank, W. M. (Ed.): *Cerebral Palsy: Its Individual and Community Problems.* Syracuse, Syracuse University Press, 1966.

Orton, S. T.: *Reading, Writing and Speech Problems in Children.* London, Chapman/Hall, 1937.

Paine, R. S.: Kernicterus. *Clin Proceedings: Children's Hospital, 24*:37-48, 1968.

Palmer, M.: Recent advances in the scientific study of language disorders in cerebral palsy. *Cereb Pal Rev, 15*:3-6, 1954.

Palmer, M. F.: Studies in clinical techniques: III. Mandibular facet slip in cerebral palsy. *J. Speech Hear Dis, 13*, 1948.

Penfield, W. G., and Roberts, L.: *Speech and Brain Mechanisms.* Princeton, Princeton University Press, 1959, p. 8.

Perlstein, Meyer A.: Infantile cerebral palsy: Classification and clinical correlations. *JAMA, 149*:30-34, 1952a.

Perlstein, M. A.: Infantile cerebral palsy. In Levine, S. Z. (Ed.)): *Advances in Pediatrics.* Chicago, Yearbook Publishers, 1955, pp. 209-248.

Perlstein, Meyer, A., and Barnett, H. E.: Nature and recognition of cerebral palsy in infancy. *JAMA, 148*:1389-1397, 1952b.

Phelps, W. M.: Factors influencing the treatment of cerebral palsy. *Physiother Rev, 21*:136-138, 1941.

Phelps, W. M.: Let's define cerebral palsy. *Cripp Child, 26*:3-5, 1948.

Phelps, W. M.: The treatment of cerebral palsies. *J Bone Joint Surg, 22*:1004-1012, 1940.

Rood, M.: The use of sensory receptors to activate, facilitate, and inhibit motor response, autonomic and somatic in developmental sequence. In Sattely, C. (Ed.): *Approaches to Treatment of Patients with Neuromuscular Dysfunction.* Dubuque, W. C. Brown, 1962, pp. 26-37.

Rosen, J.: Rh child: Deaf or "Aphasic?" 4. Variations in auditory disorders of the Rh child. *J Spch Hear Dis, 21*:418-422, 1956.

Sight Saving Review, 40:211-218, 1970-1971 (Winter).

Sheridan, M. D.: Final report of a prospective study on children whose mothers had rubella in early pregnancy. *Brit Med J, 2*:536-540, 1964.

Stockmeyer, Shirley A.: An interpretation of the approach of Rood to the treatment of neuromuscular dysfunction. In Proceedings: An exploratory and analytical survey of therapeutic exercise. *Amer J Phys Med, 46*:900-956, 1967.

Sortini, A. J.: Comments on the 'The education of children with cerebral palsy'. In *Proceedings of the Cerebral Palsy Workshop,* Ste. Adele, Quebec, September, 1965, p. 89.

Travis, L. E. (Ed.): *Handbook of Speech Pathology.* New York, Appleton-Century-Crofts, 1957.

Veale, H.: History of an epidemic of Rotheln with observations on its pathology. *Edin Med J, 12*:404-414, 1866.

Vernon, McCay: Clinical phenomenon of cerebral palsy and deafness. *Except Chil, 36*:743-751, 1970.

Vernon, M.: Multiply Handicapped Deaf Children: The Causes, Manifestations, and Significances of the Problem. Paper given at the International Conference on the Oral Education of the Deaf, New York City, June, 1967.

Vernon, McCay: Characteristics associated with post-rubella deaf children: psychological, educational and physical. *Volta Rev, 69*:176-185, 1967.

Vernon, M.: Meningitis and deafness: The problem, its physical, audiological, psychological and educational manifestations in deaf children. *Larynogoscope, 10*:1856-1874, 1967a.

Vernon, M.: Prematurity and deafness: The magnitude and nature of the problem among deaf children. *Excep Chil, 34*:289-298, 1967b.

Vernon, M.: Psychological, educational, and physical characteristics associated with post-rubella deaf children. *Volta Rev, 69*:176-185, 1967c.

Vernon, M.: Rh factor and deafness: The problem, its psychological, physical, and educational manifestations. *Except Chil, 34*:5-12, 1967d.

Vernon, M.: Tuberculous meningitis and deafness, *J Spch Hear Dis, 32*:177-181, 1967e.

Vernon, M.: "Multiply Handicapped Deaf Children: A study of the Significance and Causes of the Problem." Unpublished doctoral dissertation, Claremont Graduate School and University Center, 1966.

Ward, P. H., and Moore, B. S.: Inner ear pathology in deafness due to maternal rubella. *Arch Otolaryng, 87*:40-46, 1968.

Westlake, H., and Rutherford, D.: *Speech Therapy for the Cerebral Palsied.* Chicago, Nat Soc Cripp Child and Adults, 1961.

Westlake, H.: *A System for Developing Speech with Cerebral Palsied Children.* Chicago, Natl Soc Cripp Child and Adults, 1951a.

Westlake, H.: Muscle training for cerebral palsied speech cases. *J Spch Hear Dis, 16*:103-109, 1951b.

Wolfe, W. G.: A comprehensive evaluation of fifty cases of cerebral palsy. *J Spch Hear Dis, 15*:234-251, 1950.

Woods, G. E.: *Cerebral Palsy in Childhood*. Bristol, John Wright and Sons, Ltd., 1957.

Chapter Six

VISION AND ITS DEFECTS

Approximately 80 To 90 Percent Of An individual's learning occurs through vision. A tenth of the cerebral cortex is required to interpret the complex visual data which it receives (*Life,* 1971). According to Cohen (1962), vision accounts for two-thirds of the three million impulses processed by the brain every millisecond. Barsch (1967) feels that vision is the central position to which "all modes are beholden." To better appreciate and understand the organ that makes such an important contribution to learning, a review of some of the highlights in the visual process and the anatomy of the eye are in order. This review will aid also in understanding the various eye disorders and implications thereof, as they relate to the CP/NI child as well as the normal child.

Vision is a complex process accomplished through the summation of several mechanisms. Refer to Figure 38 as you follow (1) through (7) below:

1. An object (the hammer in this schema) reflects light rays.

2. The light rays enter the eye through the cornea; the amount of light is regulated by the pupil. The rays, which are actually mosaics of dots, then strikes the retina. See Figure 39, *The Anatomy of the Eye.*

3. After striking the retina, the light rays, or 'dots,' are *transformed* via cells called rods and cones[36] from light energy to electrochemical nerve impulses which are transmitted by the rods

---

[36]Rods are sensitive to dim light or they report the black and white of objects; the cones report color information and need stronger stimuli. There are 120 million rods and 7 million cones in each retina.

176

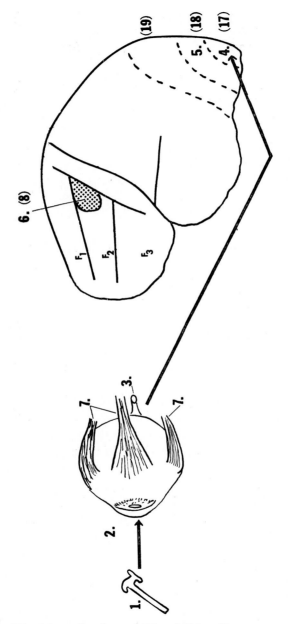

Figure 38. The Transduction of Visual Stimuli.

and cones to the optic nerve. This nerve sends the impulses to,

4. Centers for vision in the occipital lobes of the cerebrum (primary sensation of light is registered in Area 17: the principal visual cortex). This center then transfers the message through the white matter (nerve fibers) of the brain to,

5. The visual perception areas in the occipital lobes through association fibers: Areas 18 and 19, the visual association areas. Area 19 can receive stimuli from the entire cerebral cortex while Area 18 receives stimuli mainly from Area 17. Visual sensations are interpreted and integrated into more complex "perceptions" (the stimuli or *dots* are transformed into meaning)[37] and/or,

6. Command, if necessary, goes to that part of the brain, Area 8, in the Frontal Lobe, concerned with eye movements and pupillary change to

7. Tell the appropriate muscle (extrinsic muscles) to *pull* at the eye.

Eye Muscles (See Fig. 40A)

Voluntary movement of each eyeball is performed by three pairs of *extrinsic eye muscles*. These muscles, in addition, hold the eye in place. There are four rectus muscles and two oblique muscles. As we will see later, if strength of these muscles is not in balance, the equilibrium of the opposing muscle is disturbed producting strabismus. At least one-half of all children with cerebral palsy have eye muscle imbalance, or *strabismus*. In otherwise normal children, the incidence of strabismus is 2 to 5 percent (Pearlstone *et al.*, 1969). The *intrinsic muscles* are the ciliary and pupillary. Function of the ciliary muscle is to support and adjust the lens to near and far vision. The dilator and constrictor muscles (within the iris) adjust the size of the pupil in response to light. See Figure 39, *The Anatomy of the Eye.*

---

[37]It is as though the cortex improves with practice. By continual use of the electrical energy which is repeatedly received, the visual cortex seems to build up a bank full of visual memories. It is to these *memories* that new incoming information is compared, matched, differentiated, defined or decoded. Thusly, "the computer is gradually programmed (Ffooks, 1969)". The theorists today feel that each energy impulse is compared to a "model" and categorized. Perception is achieved by a quick matching performance of the brain.

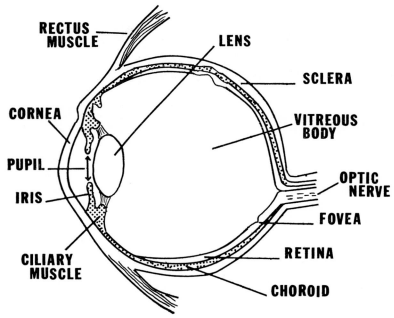

Figure 39. The Anatomy of the Eye.

Nerves

Three cranial nerves control the muscles of the eye. They are: oculomotor nerve (III), trochlear nerve (IV) and the abducens nerve (VI). The chief sensory nerve to the eye is the optic nerve (II). Indeed, the human eye muscles are highly supplied with nerves: one nerve fiber to five or ten muscle fibers. This is compared to one nerve fiber to 120 in the soleus muscle of the leg (Adler, 1959).

Using this information as a foothold, let's consider the relationship that vision has with other functions; and the implications visual defects which occur most frequently in the CP/NI have on the child's performance. The visual problems to be considered are of three general types. Those which, (1) affect the extraocular eye muscles, (2) relate to visual acuity, and (3) relate to perception. These children experience a variety of defects which appear to be related directly to their primary condition (cortical brain damage). And, not to be overlooked, they are

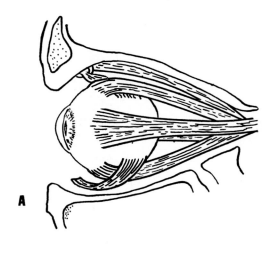

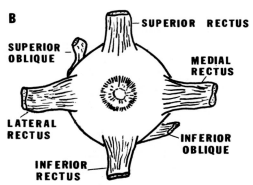

Figure 40. A, Side view of a right eye. B, Front view of a right eye showing extrinsic eye muscles. (From Katzin, Herbert M., and Wilson, Geraldine: *Strabismus in childhood,* St. Louis, Mosby Co., 1968.)

subjected, as well, to those visual defects which occur in the "normal" population such as muscle inbalances and refractive errors of non-cerebral origin, and diseases of the eye.

There would appear to be a variety of causes for visual defects in cerebral palsied children. The site and extent of damage to the brain determines the type of defect. The area of injury may be the cerebral cortex, the mid-brain, the nerves supplying the muscles or the optic nerve. It is plausible, as Guibor (1950a) states, that the "lesions of the cerebral cortex which cause the neuromuscular defect in the other musculature [of the body] may also cause disabilities in the eye musculature." It is the generally considered opinion that there is a genetic factor concerning the cause of refractive errors in the normal population. However, there is some evidence that there is a non-genetic explanation for refraction abnormalities in the cerebral palsied (Sorsby *et al.,* 1962). For instance, neonatal anoxia seems to be correlated with refractive (particularly hyperopic or farsightedness) tendencies (Fantle *et al.,* 1961) but more of this later.

CLASSIFICATION OF EYE DEFECTS

Although not complete, the following enumeration represents a careful screening of the apropo literature which the author feels reflects the most pertinent and common visual defects associated with the CP/NI child.

1. Defects of Extrinsic Ocular Muscle Function
   strabismus
   conjugate deviations
   nystagmus
   dyskinesia of eye muscles
2. Eye Structure Irregularities: Genetic or Environmental.
   cataract
   retrolental fibroplasia
   corioretinitis, e.g. toxoplasmosis
   optic nerve atrophy
3. Refractive Errors.
4. Visual Preceptual Defects (to be discussed in Chapter 7.)

Discussion. Attention will be focused upon what investigators consider to be the most common eye defects seen in this population: *strabismus* and *refractive errors* and their relationship to learning. Throughout the discussion, an attempt is made to synthesize this information and apply it directly to the situation found in the classroom and in habilitation. Strabismus, or squint, is imbalance of the extrinsic eye muscles with loss of coincidence of both visual axes on the object of fixation (more on the actual process involved later). "Indeed it might be held remarkable if the extrinsic ocular muscles escaped implication in a condition so protean [i.e. variable] in its manifestation as cerebral palsy" (Smith 1963). Strabismus associated with cerebral palsy has been the chief subject of several studies. The assumption that strabismus (squint) is the most common of the ocular lesions found in cerebral palsy (but by no means the only one), is supported by a search of the literature. Incidence figures vary, but probably the most reliable study is that of Douglas (1960) in which he found strabismus present in 37 percent of a large number of children with cerebral palsy. This study was performed in England. Other incidence figures, in the United States, are as follows: Guibor gave 60 percent from a series of 142 cases (1950b); Breakey gave 48 percent (1955); and Schacht gave 43 percent (1957). Another English study, in addition to that of Douglas', performed by Asher and Schonnel (1950) gave an incidence figure of 25 percent. That strabismus is the most common visual defect found is given further support by Schacht's study in which he reported that the most frequent type of ocular defect was that associated with external oculomotor movements (esotropia, exotropia and nystagmus). The next most frequent defect was optic atrophy. Refractive errors were found in 54 percent (myopia with or without astigmatism, and hyperopia with or without astigmatism). The incidence of myopia in this group was considerably larger than that reported in normal children. Schacht feels that the high incidence of prematurity may be a contributing cause to this proportionately higher occurrence of myopia.

According to the direction of deviation, concommittant (or nonparalitic) and incommitant (paralitic), strabismus (squint) are classified as:

1. Esotropia or convergent strabismus (one eye turns inward)—most frequently associated with hyperopia.
2. Exotropia or divergent strabismus (one eye turns outward, sometimes called wall-eyed)—frequently associated with myopia. This becomes more obvious as child grows older. Divergent strabismus tends to increase when the child looks up; decreases when the child looks down. Amblyopia is less common.
3. Hypertropia (one eye turns upward).
4. Hypotropia (one eye turns downward).
   (3 and 4 are commonly called vertical strabismus)
5. Alternating strabismus (one or the other eye turns in). The child will use his eyes alternately since he has equally good vision in each eye.

These conditions are illustrated in Figure 41.

To understand the abnormal, the normal must first be studied. A discussion of the normal function of the eyes will help us appreciate and gain perspective of the effect that strabismus and the other common eye disorders have on the child's ability to see the world as it really is. It is in this section of our discussion that the close relationship between strabismus, refractive errors and visual perception will be investigated.

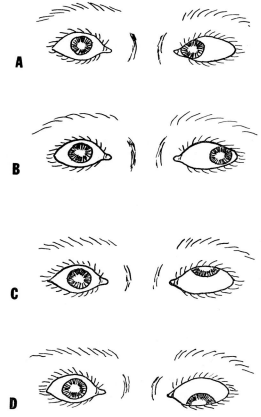

Figure 41. Crossed eyes. Types: A. Esotropia (one eye turned in), B. Exotropia (one eye turned out), C. Hypertropia (one eye turned upward), D. Hypotropia (one eye turned downward).

Normal vision is called binocular, stereoscopic or 3-dimensional vision, a function that requires the teamwork of both eyes or the coordination of the extraocular muscles and the adjustment of such internal mechanisms as the ciliary muscles. Each eye throws an image of the object (light rays from that object) on the retina, or more precisely, on the *fovea*. By a process called *fusion,* the brain makes one picture out of the two relayed images. In addition, the brain gains information called *depth perception* (or stereopsis). Although a child with only one eye (monocular strabismus) can judge depth based on other criteria (i.e. through assistance from shadows and color), the process is much quicker and more efficient with binocular vision. As a result, the child learns about the shape, depth and location of things in the space around him.

Poor binocular vision is probably more detrimental than no binocular vision as the child with poor binocular vision will experience *eye strain* or astenopia characterized by weakness, eye fatique which results in pain, headaches and vision dimness. A child with monocular vision rarely experiences such eye strain.

The effect of one eye turning in, out, up or down as occurs in strabismus, is that the turning eye sees a picture that is much different. Fusion cannot occur and the result is blurred or double vision. To experience this sensation one has only to press ever so lightly upon the lateral or side part of one eye while looking at an object. Because double vision or *diplopia* is confusing to the brain, it will reject one of the images. The image sent by the deviating eye will, therefore, be suppressed. This condition is called *amblyopia.* It has been estimated that the incidence of amblyopia ex anopsia (the full proper term) in the general population is somewhere between 2 and 4 percent. Consequently, between four and eight million people in our country have vision in one eye below the reading level. This condition is curable if detected when the child is very young. "Even if discovered as late as the third birthday, it can usually be cured" (Gunderson, 1970). There are at least two associated defects with regards to strabismus: (1) stereopsis or 3-dimensional vision may be difficult or impossible and (2) the occurrence of amblyopia or dimunition of vision in one eye. If amblyopia occurs, it does so in the turned eye.

In addition to the production of two equal images on the retina, *convergence* and *divergence* of the eyes are essential processes of normal vision. These processes are disturbed in strabismus. As we look from a distant to a near object, our eyes converge; then, as we look from a near object to a distant one, our eyes must move apart, or diverge. The relationship of these processes to refractive errors and strabismus will be discussed later. Convergence and divergence of the eyes is made possible by innervation of the medial and lateral rectus muscles. Injury to the oculomotor and abducens nerves which supplies these muscles may disturb convergence, or divergence respectively and, thus, binocular vision. The oculomotor nerve pulls the eye in; the abducens nerve pulls the eye out.

Another essential to normal vision which is again disturbed in strabismus is *accommodation*. This is the ability of the lens to adjust itself in order to bring far and near objects into focus on the retina. Accommodation is the contraction response permitting the normal eye to look at near objects and the farsighted eye to see distant and close objects clearly. The ciliary muscle affects lens adjustment.

Refraction is another essential to normal vision which is disturbed in strabismus. As rays of light enter the eye, they are refracted or bent by the cornea and lens so that they focus on the retina.

Using the information on normal vision as a background, we will continue our investigation of eye disorders. Looking under (2) of the Classification of Eye Defects, we find genetic or environmentally induced eye structure disorders. Of importance to the CP/NI population are the ocular defects associated with rubella and a disorder called retrolintal fibroplasia. The disorders of the eye associated with rubella usually include cataracts, lesions of the retina, clouding of the cornea not necessarily associated with glaucoma and usually small eyeball size.

Rubella infants are not only infected with the virus in utero but after birth continue to experience damage. The most characteristic ocular anomaly is a cataract, which may be unilateral or bilateral and is frequently associated with microphthalmia, or abnormal smallness of the eyes (Tate, 1969). Rubella eyes are usually 2 to 3 mm less in each dimension in comparison to the Duke-Elder average sizes. Ackerman *et al.* (1969) indicates that cataracts occur in 8 percent of infants exposed to rubella during the first month of gestation and in 2.5 percent of those exposed during the second and third months. Cataracts result from the rubella virus infecting the lens. Rubella virus may persist in cataractous lens for years after birth (Cooper *et al.*, 1969). It is interesting to note that it is during the fifth and sixth week of gestation when the primary fibers of the lens are being laid down (Duke-Elder, 1963). The diagnosis of cataract can usually be made at birth whereas deafness and congenital heart disease (also associated with rubella) are not always apparent in the newborn (Sight Saving Review, 1971). The reader is asked to read Cooper et al., (1969) concerning treatment (i.e. surgery) of the cataractous eye. Congenital rubella glaucoma may be present at birth although reportedly this anomally is much less common than is rubella cataract. Congenital rubella cataracts and glaucoma are treated surgically "but . . . prognosis is poor . . . the virus persists within the eye, especially within the lens itself and probably leads to poor surgical results" (Sight Saving Review, 1971). It is generally accepted that surgical procedures for congenital cataract be delayed until the child is two years of age.

A high degree of myopia is another manifestation of congenital rubella. O'Neill (1967) reported that convergent strabismus occurred in one-third of a series of culture-proven cases of rubella during the first six months of life and increased to 60 percent by eighteen months of age. Retrolental fibroplasia or detached retina causing total blindness occurs in a small percent of children with cerebral palsy. Infants with retrolental fibroplasia (or retinopathy of prematurity) may be totally blind by the time they are three or four months old. It has been established that this condition is related to the high concentration of oxygen that is used in the program for saving prematures. Note that this condition is due to externally induced causes, not to brain damage.

The third main classification of eye defects is that of *refractive errors*. In a previously cited study by Schacht (1957), we found that 68 percent of those children in his investigation had either gross ocular defects or refractive errors high enough to warrant treatment. Furthermore, Pearlstone (1969) found 43 percent of the cerebral palsied children in his investigation had significant refractive errors.

The results of an investigation by Gardiner (1963) can be seen in Figure 42. This figure shows the incidence of refractive

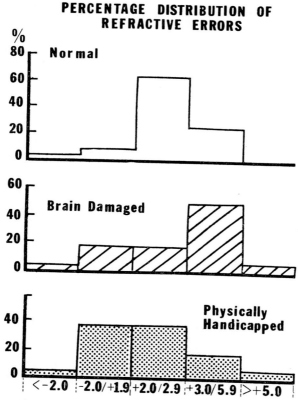

Figure 42. The distribution of refractive errors in normal children, brain-damaged and physically handicapped children. (Reproduced with permission, from Gardiner, P.: Refractive errors and cerebral palsy. In Smith, V. H. (Ed.): *Visual Disorders and Cerebral Palsy*. London, Spastics Society, Heinemann, 1963.

errors in educable brain-damaged children compared with the incidence in children who are physically handicapped from other causes (therefore non-brain damaged). In discussing this figure, Gardiner states that even omitting athetoid children (who are notorious for showing hypermetropia, or vision better for distant objects) there is still a significant difference between the brain-damaged children and the children suffering from other physical handicaps such as hemophilia or arthritis. The conclusion is that hypermetropia is more common in brain-damaged children; myopia (or vision better for near objects) is more common in children physically handicapped from other than brain-damage causes. However, he further comments that both the brain-damaged and otherwise physically handicapped both have more refractive difficulties than the normal. About 25 percent of the brain-damaged children should be considered for glasses as opposed to only 12 percent of the normal population. Glasses are corrective measures used in handling refractive errors. This takes into account only refraction and not other problems such as squint.

Results of the previously mentioned investigation by Fantle and Perlstein (1961) supports Gardiner's study. They further feel that most children with or without cerebral palsy were hyperopic up to the age of nine. After this age, however, the non-cerebral palsied tended to reduce their hypermetropia or they became myopic while those with cerebral palsy remained hyperopic.

Specifically, what are these conditions which prevent the light rays from converging on the retina in a normal manner? The most common refractive problems which cause blurred vision, and, therefore, disrupt binocular vision and visual acuity are: (a) hypermetropia (hyperopia), or farsightedness, in which light rays impinge on the retina before they can focus (Fig. 43B), and (b) myopia, or nearsightedness, in which rays meet in front of the retina (Fig. 43C), and (c) astigmatism, in which the curvature of the lens is unequal. To compare, see Figure 43A, a normal eye in which rays of light come to a focus at the proper place.

It will be remembered that the light rays pass through the cornea, go to the lens which adjusts (or accommodates) by means of the ciliary muscle for the distance from which the object is

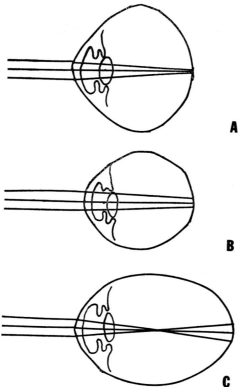

Figure 43. A. Normal eye. The light rays come to a focus at the correct position resulting in good, clear vision. B. Farsighted eye. The light rays strike the retina without focusing resulting in blurred vision, and C. Nearsighted eye. The light rays focus in front of the retina resulting in blurred vision. The infant's eye is like *B* (small) so that all infants are farsighted but as the child grows so do his eyes. At the age of seven or thereabouts, the child's eyes reach the normal size as in *A*. And, if the eyes continue to grow, the result would be a nearsighted eye as in *C;* and, likewise, if the eye stopped growing, the result would be a farsighted eye.

being viewed. These light rays then reach the retina. If the eye is a little short (farsighted eye) or too long (nearsighted eye), the rays do not focus on the retina, resulting in either hypermetropia or myopia.

Referring back to the portion concerning accommodation, we found that this process was a contracting response permitting the normal eye to look at near objects, and assisting the farsighted eye to see a distant and, even more, a close object clearly. The nearsighted eye cannot be helped by this process of accommodation to make a distant object clearer (that is, without the aid of glasses). Why? When the ciliary muscle contracts, the light rays are pulled forward and, as can be seen in Figure 43C, the problem in the nearsighted eye is that the light rays are too "forward" already. The rays would meet even further in front of the retina. Just as a camera can take sharp, clear pictures at different distances by changing lenses or by changing the distance between lens and film (retina in the case of the eye), in the eye, this function is performed by changing the curvature of the lens by means of the ciliary muscle.

When the eyes accommodate they also tend to converge. This is the process whereby both eyes shift their lines of vision toward each other in order to look at a near object. Accommodation prevents blurred vision and, convergence prevents double vision (diplopia).

If a farsighted child has imperfect accommodation or an eye muscle abnormality, the result will be as follows: The eyes will accommodate (or focus, which is the contraction response of the lens permitting the eye to look at near objects), the child's line of vision will no longer meet the object, the eyes may overconverge, and cross. The extraocular eye muscles are unable to move the eyes to permit the lines of vision to converge on the near object. In general, the bearing that refractive errors have on strabismus is this. The farsighted eye tends to develop convergent strabismus. That is, excessive accommodation which occurs in the farsighted eye frequently means excessive convergence, resulting in esotropia. This type of squint commonly commences between the ages of two to six before fusion is fully developed or when accommodation is first seriously demanded. This is the period when the child becomes attracted to, and interested in, near objects such as books, and toys. Secondly, the nearsighted eye tends to develop divergent strabismus. As the need to accommodate is not as great as in either the farsighted or normal eye, the ciliary muscles become weak and underdeveloped as there is less demanded of them. It is important to note that refractive errors are fatiguing and, as stated, definitely limit visual acuity.

Visual acuity has been mentioned previously and should, at this point, be explained in some detail. It is important to determine if the child is capable of central fixation (i.e. can the child use the fovea which is that part of the retina that sees best). Visual acuity is measured with the E chart. The results of this test are expressed as a numerical fraction such as 20/20. This is a comparison between what the person being tested can see as compared to the amount a normal person can see. The first number, 20, represents the distance between child and chart or 20 feet. If a child's visual acuity is 20/100, he is able to read only as far as the line a normal sighted person can see at 100 feet (the child being tested is sitting only 20 feet from the chart). Normal vision is 20/20 which is not usually attained until the child is about five years old; a one year old child is a little less than 20/100, by age of two years it is only about 20/40. Therefore, if the child can match the smallest line of E's (Fig. 44), his vision is 20/20 in that eye. The use of pictures probably provides the most practical and earliest means of visual acuity testing. A chart developed by Österberg (1936) in Denmark has been used with success as have those published by Allen (1957).

Figure 44. Visual acuity testing using the E Chart. The child's vision is said to be 20/20 if he is able to match the smallest line of E's. It is 20/200 if he can match only the top line, etc.

THE IMPORTANCE OF EARLY RECOGNITION AND TREATMENT

There are some rather compelling reasons for early recognition and treatment of eye disorders. Developmentally, vision develops to its maximum degree of efficiency over a long period of time beginning at three months and extending to five years. The incidence figures of eye disorders stated previously would be only one indication for and argument of the importance of at least a routine ophthalmologic examination of every child with cerebral palsy or suspected cerebral palsy or neurological impairment. To add fire to this concept of early recognition and treatment, it is sobering to note that less than 1 percent of normal children, *but* 53 percent of the brain damaged, have strabismus at birth (Deaver, 1959). It is well known that amblyopia is a frequent result of strabismus and may be alleviated or prevented by adequate early treatment (Schacht, 1957). The best treatment for amblyopia is to prevent it through early patching. Refractive errors are known to limit visual acuity and to cause fatigue which lends further support to the importance of early recognition and treatment. Gardiner (1963) says that children with visual defects often "adapt themselves to the defect so that adults may fail to notice the child's inability to see accurately."

It is obvious that visual defects make learning difficult particularly for the physically handicapped child. In addition to the physical involvement, the special senses are often defective in these children. Such other defects as hemianopia[38] (Tizard *et al.*, 1954), defects of hearing and sensation (tactile) are common and may necessitate an even greater reliance on vision. Clear vision and lessened eye fatigue are especially desirable as learning for this child is difficult enough.

Concerning evaluation of visual defects in the cerebral palsied child, Gardiner (1963) states, "Too often, people fail to look for other defects because the physical defect already diagnosed is bad enough." He continues by sharing an example which occurs all

[38]Hemianopia is a visual field defect in which a segment of the field of vision is missing in both eyes, due to a single lesion in the optic pathways. As the pathways travel a considerable distance in the brain (from the eyes to the back of the head), it is not surprising that they are involved in cerebral palsy (Fig. 45).

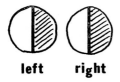

left   right

Figure 45. Right homoymous hemianopsia due to lesion of the left side of the brain.

too often. "In view of the child's mental deficiency, it was a waste of time to give him glasses [referring to a previous eye examination performed by another physician]. I saw this child at school later; his IQ was high, as was his myopia, and when he was given glasses, his morale, behavior and work improved greatly."

Why neglect the visual status of handicapped children: Too often the search for visual defects is neglected because of the feeling that the disorder already diagnosed is "bad enough". Another factor which seems to interfere with opthalmologic examination is the idea that the child's cooperation is necessary to evaluate the ocular muscle balance and refractive errors. This is an unfortunate misconception. "With a little patience and effort we have been able to diagnose and treat disabilities of refractive and ocular muscle balance in severely handicapped children" (Pearlstone, 1969). He reports having success in examining children as young as two years of age for muscle coordination and refractive errors. Denhoff (1967) offers a brief outline for eye examination in the one year old child with cerebral palsy. Opthalmologic examinations can be satisfactorily performed with such children if one is not in a rush, if there is no pressure and concern for time. Hurrying the process will only result in increased tremor, inability to cooperate, and an increase in speech difficulties.

SPECIFIC TREATMENT PROCEDURES OF SOME COMMON EYE DEFECTS

Strabismus

1. Corrective glasses to a) improve the vision, and b) decrease the *accommodative component* of the deviation by correcting refractive errors and thereby cause the squint to be partially or totally corrected.

2. Surgery on the muscles to re-align the globes.

3. Patching the better eye to prevent loss of vision in the deviating eye.

4. Non-surgical means such a) atropine and strong miotic eye drops, and prism glasses. Strong miotics stimulate or facilitate accommodation which is needed for sharper vision without the requirement or need of a strong CNS impulse that would also cause convergence, and b) exercises.

Aims of treatment are, of course, good vision in each eye, a cosmetically appealing eye, and normal fusion or binocular vision. The aim of surgery is to correct the position of one eye in relation to the other. Surgery on extraocular muscles does not affect visual acuity. Nearly every child can benefit from eye exercises. Regarding children with strabismus, Katzin (1968) says that "almost every child can be made to see well, and almost every pair of eyes can be made to appear straight, but good binocular vision is more difficult to attain, particularly in children who are older than 6 years of age."

In the infant, treatment consists of (a) for alternating strabismus: surgery as early as possible starting at six months, (b) for monocular strabismus: amblyopia is first treated by patching followed by surgery. In both cases, results in monocular and binocular vision are better and more frequent the earlier surgery is performed (Ferrer, 1971).

SURGERY. There is a difference of opinion among physicians regarding the most opportune time to perform surgery. Some surgeons operate on children at six months, others wait until two-and-one-half to three years of age when they feel cooperation is possible. In the latter case, during the interim, glasses are worn and, if amblyopia exists, constant patching of the straight eye is implemented.

Before the strabismus can be corrected by surgery, the vision in the squinting eye should be encouraged in order to normalize visual acuity. "If the squinting eye is amblyopic or if its acuity of vision is defective, it should be forced into use by occluding the sound eye" (Duke-Elder, 1963).

Looking more intensely now at one of the important treatment means for strabismus, surgery, we find that surgical procedures are performed on muscles on the outside of the eyeball, not on the internal *seeing* portions. See Figure 40, *Extraocular Muscles of the Eye*. There are two general surgical procedures:

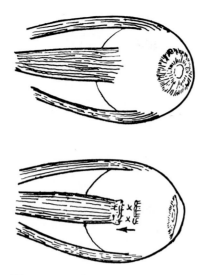

Figure 46. A recession or lengthening operation on the lateral rectus muscle (right eye). (From Katzin, Herbert M., and Wilson, Geraldine: *Strabismus in childhood,* St. Louis, Mosby, 1968.)

(1) Recession (retroplacement). The muscle action is being weakened by moving the muscle back from its original attachment (Fig. 46), and (2) Advancement or resection. This procedure is designed to increase the action of an ocular muscle, by a) resection —a piece of the muscle is cut out, thus shortening the muscle (Fig. 47), and b) advancement—brings the attachment of the muscle

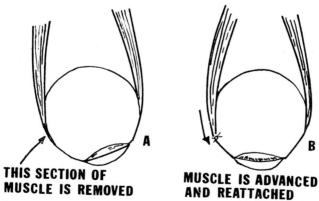

THIS SECTION OF MUSCLE IS REMOVED

MUSCLE IS ADVANCED AND REATTACHED

Figure 47. In A the lateral rectus muscle of the right eye is to be shortened, or resected. B shows the section removed and the muscle advanced and re-attached. (From Katzin, Herbert M., and Wilson, Geraldine: *Strabismus in childhood,* St. Louis, Mosby, 1968.)

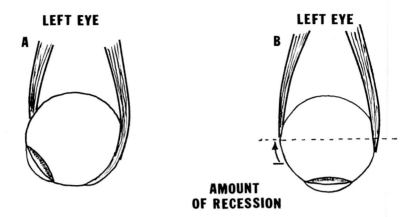

Figure 48. A, Esotropia with the left eye turned inward. B. Recession of the medial rectus muscles. (From Katzin, Herbert M., and Wilson, Geraldine: *Strabismus in childhood,* St. Louis, Mosby, 1968.)

further forward on the eyeball. Surgery of esotropia, for instance, may be performed on the medial rectus muscle. The function of this muscle is to pull the eye inward. The procedure—bimedial recession or setting each medial rectus muscle back on the eyeball so as to lessen the inward pull—permits the lateral muscle to exert its function of pulling the eye out more effectively (Fig. 48). Another approach might be to resect both lateral rectus muscles which would increase their action.

Postoperative treatment is of two general methods. One method is called orthoptic training. This treatment is given until sufficient powers of fusion have been developed. This may be required for a year or even longer. The other method is merely to adjust the strength of the glasses.

Cataract and Glaucoma

For treatment procedures see the discussion under Ocular Defects of Rubella.

Refractive Errors

The farsighted child with esotropia (accommodative convergent squint): By using a retinoscope (once atropine drops have relaxed the ciliary muscles), the opthalmologist measures the correction the child requires. Glasses will be prescribed when the child is old enough. The glasses will relieve the need for excessive accommodation. This will decrease over-convergence. In milder cases, eyedrops are used to stimulate ciliary muscles to contract. Accommodation efforts are decreased, as are efforts at convergence. If the only cause of the child's crossed eyes is his farsightedness, using glasses to correct the farsightedness will straighten the eye. However, in the cerebral palsied, the crossed eyes may be due to brain damage. If such is the case, glasses used to correct the farsightedness will correct only part of the problem. That is, the so-called accommodative component will be treated; however, the neuromuscular involvement will still be present.

The nearsighted child who has exotropia—in this case, the ciliary muscles become weak as there is less required of them. Glasses are used to force the eye to accommodate normally using the weak ciliary muscles. If glasses alone do not work, surgery may be necessary.

AMBLYOPIA OR POOR VISION. This is a "lazy" eye which occurs in the turned eye to prevent double vision. In normal vision, fixation occurs when the image falls on the fovea. This is normal or central fixation. Early in life, an amblyopic eye may develop *eccentric fixation*. That is, the objects are viewed by only a part of the retina (a part other than the fovea). The newest form of treatment for amblyopia, particularly with eccentric fixation, is called *pleoptics*. Pleoptics basically act by stimulating the fovea so as to increase its dominant value as compared to the rest of the retina. Its aim is to increase visual acuity, and, when absent, to develop central fixation. Once this is achieved, the good eye is patched which forces the amblyopic eye to develop to its potential. This ingenious treatment being complicated, expensive, time consuming and relatively unrewarding is practically given up currently, since it requires a high degree of cooperation on the part of the child. It is particularly unsuitable for the cerebral palsied. The old patching method is considered to be the best treatment either for prophylaxis or as a curative measure (Ferrer, 1971).

Another exercise, orthoptics as a treatment modality in strabismus is comparatively not as new as pleoptics. Orthoptic exercises as previously mentioned, are used to fight suppression and to increase fusion. Postoperatively, the exercises are used to reinforce fusion.

As Gesell (1953) has noted, "some children with both neuromuscular symptoms of cerebral palsy and blindness [as well as other visual defects] are potentially normal mentally, but absence of vision [and/or defects of vision] isolates the infant [and older children] from his environment, and this isolation may retard intellectual and personality development." It is indeed extremely desirable for teachers and therapists to be aware of the importance that vision plays in the child's life. We must not only be aware of this but we must develop an understanding of the entire visual process and its relationship to learning.

REFERENCES

Ackerman, B. D., Taylor, W. F., Ingman, M. J., *et al.*: Diagnosis and treatment of congenital rubella. *GP, 40*:136, November, 1969.

Adler, F. H.: *Physiology of the Eye, Clinical Application*, 3rd ed. St. Louis, Mosby, 1959.

Allen, H. F.: A new picture series for preschool vision testing. *Amer J Ophthalmol, 44*:38, 1957.

Asher, P., and Schonnel, F. C.: A survey of 400 cases of cerebral palsy in childhood. *Arch Dis Child, 25*:360-79, 1950.

Barsch, R. H.: *Achieving Perceptual-Motor Efficiency*. Seattle, Special Child Publications, 1967.

Breakey, A. S.: Ocular findings in cerebral palsy. *Arch Ophthalmol, 53*:852-856, 1955.

Cohen, S. A.: Applying a dynamic theory of vision to teaching reading. *J Dev Reading, 6*:15-25, 1962.

Cooper, L. Z., Ziring, P. R., Ockerse, A. B., *et al.*: Rubella, clinical manifestations and management. *Am J Dis Child, 118*:18, July, 1969.

Deaver, G. G.: The child handicapped by cerebral palsy. *Va Med Mon, 86*:681, 1959.

Denhoff, Eric: *Cerebral Palsy: The Preschool Years*. Springfield, Thomas, 1967.

Douglas, A. A.: The eyes and vision in infantile cerebral palsy. *Trans Ophthalmol Soc UK, 80*:311, 1960.

Duke-Elder, S. (Ed.): *System of Ophthalmology*. St. Louis, Mosby, 1963, vol. III.

Fantle, E. W. and Perlstein, M. A.: Ocular refractive characteristics in cerebral palsy. *Am J Dis Child, 102*:36, 1961.

Ferrer, Jorge A.: Personal Communication. Department of Opthalmology, Shands Teaching Hospital and Clinics, University of Florida, Gainesville, 1971.

Ffooks, Oliver R.: Neurophysiology and assessment of visual function in children. In Gardiner, P., MacKeith, R. and Smith, V. (Eds.): *Aspects of Developmental and Paediatric Ophthalmology*. London, Spastics Society/ Heinemann, 1969.

Gardiner, P.: Refractive errors and cerebral palsy. In Smith, V. H. (Ed.): *Visual Disorders and Cerebral Palsy*. London, Spastics Society, Heinemann, 1963.

Gesell, A.: Developmental diagnosis and supervision. In McQuarrie, Irvine (Ed.): *Brennemann's Practice of Pediatrics*. Hagerstown. Prior, 1953, vol. I.

Guibor, G. P.: Some ocular deviations in cerebral palsy. In *Proceedings of the Scientific Sessions of the American Academy of Cerebral Palsy*, Feb. 17-18, 1950a.

Guibor, G. P.: Eye defects seen in cerebral palsy. *Crippled Child, 28*: 4, 1950b.

Gunderson, Trygul: Early diagnosis and treatment of strabismus. *Sight Saving Review, 40*:129-136, 1970.

Katzin, H. M. and Wilson, G.: *Strabismus in Childhood*. St. Louis, Mosby, 1968.

Life. Part II—The amazing cells that command our bodies—The Brain. October 1, 1971.

O'Neill, J. F.: Strabismus in congenital rubella. *Arch Ophthalmol, 77*:450, 1967.

Österberg, G.: A sight-test chart for children. *Acta Ophthalmol, 14*:397, 1936.

Pearlstone, A. D. and Benjamin, R.: Ocular defects in cerebral palsy. *Eye, Ear, Nose, Throat Mon, 48*:437-438. 1969.

Schacht, W. S. et al.: Opthalmologic findings in children with cerebral palsy. *Pediatrics, 19*:623-628, 1957.

Sight-Saving Review, 40:211-218, Winter 1970-1971.

Smith, V. H.: A survey of strabismus in cerebral palsy. In Smith, V. H. (Ed.): *Visual Disorders and Cerebral Palsy*, London, Spastics Society/Heinemann, 1963.

Sorsby, A., Sheridan, M. and Leary, G. A.: Refraction and its components in twins. *Spec Rep Ser med Res Cound*. No. 303, London, 1962.

Tate, H. R.: Congenital rubella syndrome. *Eye, Ear, Nose, Throat Mon, 48*:671-679, 1969.

Tizard, J. P. M., Paine, R. S. and Crother, B.: Disturbances of sensation in children with hemiplegia. *JAMA, 1551*:628-632, 1954.

Chapter Seven

VISUAL IMPAIRMENT AND THE LEARNING ENVIRONMENT

THE AIMS OF THE EDUCATOR AS WELL AS the therapist working with a child with visual impairment are to minimize the consequences of that impairment, and to ameliorate and improve the use of the child's existing vision. By so doing, we will be giving the child an opportunity to acquire information and learning at his highest efficiency level.

Healthy communication between teacher:therapist:opthalmologist is of paramount importance. This is indeed a double-highway. Those working with the child in the education-habilitation environment must secure from the opthalmologist any pertinent information concerning the child's visual status. For instance, what difficulties remain after correction? However, we need also to be aware that many children without obvious visual impairment often go undetected by parent, teacher, therapist and opthalmologist. Similarly, the importance of the child's visual impairment may not be fully appreciated. These are the children whose visual handicap has been interfering with learning as they are unable to derive full benefit from the education being provided. It is, therefore, incumbent upon the teacher and therapist to be aware of the possibility that such disorders exist. In fact, the incidence of visual disorders particularly in the cerebral palsied is rather large.

The following is a list of some considerations to keep in mind when planning methods and materials for the visually impaired child.

1. Does the child have binocular vision?

2. Eye movement. Is there full range-of-motion from left to right, up and down. Paralysis of muscles, nystagmus and difficulties of fixation may be present.

3. If strabismus is present, what type?

4. To what degree does the eye-muscle defect impede eye function. Can the child scan, can he fixate at intervals along a line of print, or on a specific object, are movements jerky or slow? All these factors influence to some degree the sequence in which images are received on the retina.

5. Visual acuity status. To what degree are refractive errors present?

6. Does the child have adequate neck and trunk musculature to permit proper head control?

7. Are there any peripheral field defects present which may result in *tunnel vision?*

It becomes evident that one role of the educator and therapist is to be aware of and attempt to estimate the effect a visual disorder may have on the child's performance. If a visual problem is suspected, by all means make a referral for an ophthalmological examination. If the problem has been previously diagnosed, channel the above questions to the opthalmologist. The information derived from him can be of great assistance and guidance in realistic program planning both in the classroom and in the rehabilitation clinic, as well as in the home.

The purpose of the following section on *techniques and modifications* is to (a) provide a rather concise reference source for materials and methods that can be utilized by the teacher:therapist, and (b) provide suggestions as to techniques as they relate specifically to the cerebral palsied/neurologically impaired child.

Special methods for the visually impaired may more precisely or more accurately be called special equipment and materials. The visually impaired may not be able to use a regulation pencil for writing but he may be able to write by means of a braille writer and/or a modified typewriter with special enlarged print. He may not be able to use regulation textbooks but may be able to utilize such *special* materials as braille editions, records or tape recordings. At any rate, this entire matter will be discussed as this section proceeds.

There appear to be two general approaches in this area. One, through the use of mechanical aids and devices, changes can be made in the physical environment. The second deals more directly with the child. The aim here is to develop the child's residual abilities and senses in a compensatory fashion.

A word of caution. *Special methods* require *special considerations* when working with the CP/NI child but particularly with the cerebral palsied. Considerations must be given to disorders of manual perception. Such disorders are somewhat prolific in the spastic cerebral palsied.[39] The use of braille may be contraindicated in a child who has this type of tactile sense involvement. A study by Jones (1960) lends credence to this. Results of her study were similar to those found by other investigators in that a large proportion, or 75 percent, of the children she assessed had sensory deficits. One or more of the three following areas were either lost or impaired: stereognosis or form discrimination; two-point discrimination; and position or passive motion sense.

A further limitation regarding C.P. children would be upper extremity motor involvement. In the brain damaged, one again would need to be aware of possible sensory impairments. And particularly with the C.P., intellectual performance may be depressed further hampering the use of braille. Be aware of such factors. The interested reader may wish to consult *Perceptual Factors in Braille Word Recognition* (Research Series No. 20). Carson Y. Nolan and Cleves J. Kederis, 178 pp. 1969. This book is the result of several years of study of the braille system as a communication process by the American Printing House for the Blind. The primary finding was that the braille code is perceived one character, or cell, at a time which apparently is an often debated subject. This publication is available through the American Foundation for the Blind.

Special methods are not only numerous and varied but may be difficult to locate. In addition, once located and secured, they

[39]See Chapter 3 *Learning: Mechanisms and Disorders* for an in-depth investigation concerning peripheral and central perceptual disorders.

may not be suited to the child's particular needs. The teacher spends a great deal of time in procuring and preparing special materials to be used in the classroom unless he is fortunate enough to enjoy the services of a resource or itenerant teacher who will provide specialized and adapted material. The intent, therefore, of the following section is to provide a basic guide to sources of information and materials that will be of value to the teacher and therapist who is faced with the challenge of providing the optimum learning environment for the visually impaired orthopedically handicapped/neurologically impaired child. The term visually impaired may be confusing. From an educational-training point of view, a legally blind child is one who has a visual acuity of 20/200 or less in the better eye after the best possible correction. A partially seeing child has visual acuity of 20/70 or less in the better eye after correction.

SPECIAL EQUIPMENT AND MATERIALS

Braille

Although the number of blind CP children is small, the classroom teacher may find the following discussion useful with other blind (or partially seeing) NI children. However, before presenting the sources and types of braille materials available, a word of description about the braille system is in order. This system of raised dots uses as a foundation a cell composed of two vertical columns, each having three dots and each dot being numbered:
1 •   • 4 . The use of the dots can be appreciated through the
2 •   • 5
3 •   • 6
following examples: *a* is represented by the number one dot or • ; *b,* by number one and two dots or, ⦂ ; *c,* by numbers one and four dots or, •• ; *k,* by numbers one and three dots or, ⦂ . So that the word *cab* would appear • • • ⦂ . In order to simplify reading and to conserve space, certain words or groups of letters which appear somewhat repeatedly are indicated by special characters called contractions. The word *and* is represented by the contraction ⦂ • (or, by dots 1, 2, 3, 4, and 6); *the* appears as ⦂ • (or, by dots 2, 3, 4, and 6).

There is almost an overabundance of braille materials. Because of the need for and the wide distribution of braille book users, it is suggested that the teacher refer to one of the following catalogs. The first step is to check a catalog or submit a request to a clearing house or union catalog. *The General Catalog of Braille Publications* is the most extensive catalog. This is available through the American Printing House for the Blind. The APH is a major source of textbooks in braille and large print. In addition to the catalogs of braille publications, also available are tangible materials (slates, maps, paper, etc.), large print publications, music publications, recorded aids, and vacuum-formed, plastic-plate braille. Information concerning texts located at other sources may be obtained from their textbook consultant. Check the clearing houses and union catalogs if you do not find materials suited to your needs. The clearing houses and union catalogs serve two main purposes: (1) they avoid duplication; and (2) they serve as information centers. The mechanics involved are: First, consult catalogs listing braille books. Secondly, if the material is not available from these sources in the form you need, write the APH to determine if the material is available through another source. In this inquiry, specify title, authors, publishers, copyright date, and form in which the book is desired. Third, if the book is available, contact the appropriate source. If it is not available, you may attempt to have it transcribed by a volunteer braillist. Remember, the *General Catalog* is the union catalog of all textbooks that have been transcribed into braille. Also, the *Union Catalog of Hand-Copied Books,* Library of Congress, Division for the Blind and Physically Handicapped is another central information source for braille books. This union catalog has catalogued only library books and general reading; no textbooks are catalogued.

If you find that you need the services of a braillist, an intention report should be submitted. These forms are available on request from the APH. An intention card is placed on file at the Printing House, and remains a part of their records until a Completion Report is filed. This form, also, is available through the APH. When completed, the report should be submitted so current information may be available to others who may be in need of the same material.

Many states are in the process or have developed state and regional registry-depositories. At present, there are thirty-two *regional libraries*. Through these libraries, the Division for the Blind of the Library of Congress circulates braille books, talking books, large type and taped editions. Attempt first, then, to locate materials at the local or regional level. You may be able to acquire your materials from a larger school district with an existing program or from your local State Department of Education.

To requisition materials from the APH, the public school should send their orders on the APH order blank in duplicate to their state department of education which will approve the order and send one copy to the Printing House. The Printing House then will ship the order directly to the school systems. To order APH catalogs request order forms from the State Department of Education or the APH. Information about free instructional materials for registered visually handicapped students may be obtained from your State Education Department.

Braille Book Review is a magazine published bi-monthly for the Library of Congress by the American Foundation for the Blind. It is distributed free to persons who borrow from regional libraries. Its primary purpose is to announce the availability of new press braille books and hand-copied braille books (produced singly by volunteers) to borrowers. In addition, news items about other braille materials and their sources are included. Sample copies of *Braille Book Review* may be requested from the American Foundation for the Blind, Inc.

Another bi-monthly magazine, *Talking Book Topics*, is published under the same arrangement. Its primary purpose is to announce the availability of new talking book records and magnetic tapes to borrowers. Information is given about each new book along with a short description of the contents. In addition, selected bibliographies, articles, and brief news items about literature and activities in library services for the blind and physically handicapped are included. Each issue of this magazine also includes a soundsheet recording (a flexible plastic disc) of news, articles, and new talking book titles and their short descriptions. This soundsheet may be played on any phonograph or talking book machine at 8⅓ rpm. Sample copies of *Talking Book Topics* may be requested from the Foundation.

CATALOGS. Every two years, three catalogs of currently available press braille books and talking books are published, one listing adult talking books, one adult press braille books, and one juvenile press braille and talking books. The book information and descriptions are reprinted from the published issues of *Talking Book Topics* and *Braille Book Review*. All current catalogs may be requested from the regional libraries or from the Division for the Blind and Physically Handicapped, Library of Congress, Washington, D. C. 20542. Catalogs are not available from the American Foundation for the Blind, Inc.

INDEXES. In the alternate, even-numbered years that catalogs are not issued the December issues of *Talking Book Topics* and *Braille Book Review* contain author-title indexes of all talking books and press braille books, respectively, announced during the preceding year. The February issue of *Braille Book Review* each year contains an author-title index of all the hand-copied braille books announced during the preceding year. No cumulative catalog of hand-copied books is published.

MAJOR BRAILLE PRESSES AND PUBLISHERS. (See Appendix C).

VOLUNTEER BRAILLE TRANSCRIBING. It may become necessary to solicit the resources of volunteer services to fully meet the textbook and other material needs of the cerebral palsied/neurologically impaired child with impaired vision or blindness. Volunteer transcribers may be a part of a small local club or group, or may be members of a national volunteer group. A free directory is available upon request listing volunteer braillists whose service may be available in your local area or community. The directory is: Volunteers Who Produce Books, The Library of Congress.

Auditory Materials

The auditory area warrants special attention as this is a promising channel of information input for the visually impaired or blind child. Again, auditory (both peripheral and central) functions may be impaired in the CP/NI and his performance in this area should be assessed before relying on this learning channel to supplement his visual learning. In visually impaired children, the ears may provide the primary avenue for learning.[40] It is interesting to note that the incidence of ophthalmological deficiencies in young school aged deaf children is about twice that found for children with normal hearing (Crane *et al.*, 1954; Sloan *et al.*, 1952).

The teaching of the skill to listen is a primary concern of those working with the CP/NI child with or without visual handicaps. Bischoff (1967), performed an experiment using an adapted form of the Listening Test of the Sequential Tests of Educational Progress. The results of this study showed that both instructional groups used in this experiment increased their listening efficiency significantly (the non-instructional groups showed an actual decrease). He concluded that teachers should become aware that listening efficiency is a skill that can be improved by listening instruction lessons and that with increased skills, recorded material could effectively supplement reading media presently used in the classroom.

The Talking Book is a special long playing phonograph record. This record is played on a Talking Book machine or approved record player. The Talking Book machine may be used with or without earphones. These play records (discs) at 8½, 16⅔, or 33⅓ rpm. Both the book machines and reading materials are available on loan without charge (application should be made to either: The Library of Congress, Division for the Blind and Physically Handicapped, Washington, D. C.; or, to your local regional library of the Library of Congress.) Your local library may be of assistance in obtaining talking books. Some states have sources such as Division of Work with the Blind, or the Library for the Blind.

Partially seeing children have a reading rate of 106 words per minute (Nolan, 1959). This slow rate, considerably less than half that of their seeing peers, makes the use of recorded material

---

[40]See Chapter 5 *Speech and Language Disorders.*

such as Talking Books with about 180 to 200 words read per minute, advantageous to partially seeing students. The Talking Book may be used by the handicapped of all ages.

TAPE RECORDINGS. Magnetic tapes are available with similar materials as the Talking Books. These can be borrowed under the same procedures as are the Talking Books. However, they are not supplied by the Library. Catalogs listing tapes are available from the same source. The application should be accompanied by a brief statement describing the child's physical disability. Certification of his eligibility can be made by a medical doctor, optometrist, registered nurse, and teacher. The agency will send a machine and forward a registration card to the appropriate regional library, which will circulate talking book recordings to the reader. The adapted Sony 105 is recommended for the tapes available from the American Printing House for the Blind. Recording for the Blind, Inc., 215 East 58 Street, New York, New York 10022, has over 10,000 titles on discs 16⅔ rpm, or tapes 3¾, 1⅞ ips., 2 or 4 track to be borrowed at no cost by any blind elementary, high school, college, graduate student, or adult needing educational material. Qualified borrowers may request and have recorded any text not available.

Visual Materials

LARGE TYPE MATERIALS. Size of print and type has received much attention in the literature. The two types of print most widely used in books for the partially sighted child is 24-point (for 20/160 visual acuity) and 18-point. For the sake of comparison, pica typewriter print is 12-point type. Normally, books for children of age 7 to 8 have 18-point (20/20); and for age 9 to 12 they have 12-point (20/80). Nolan (1959) stated that both of these type (24- and 18-point) were read with equal reading speed. He also found that regulation textbook letter type was read more rapidly than an experimental type which was supposedly more legible. Throwing additional light on the use of enlarged type is a study by Mueller (1962). His investigation concerned the effects of illustration size on test performance using the Peabody Picture Vocabulary Test. The plates used in the PPVT are available in two sizes: 5 x 7 inches used in the regular published edition and 8½ x 11 inches. The results show that children with mild visual impairments (20/70 to 20/200) did not show any difference in their performance by using the two different sizes of the test. Those in the lower (20/200 to 10/200) visual group (10/200 being regarded "as the least degree of vision which is generally useable in reading ink print,") showed significant gains when the larger plates were used. Mueller concludes that the PPVT was appropriate for use with visually limited children, and, in addition, he suggests that the results of his study may be applicable to type size and indicated that children with vision better than 20/200 derive little benefit from large type. (Peabody Language Development Kits have been found to have real possibilities for development of visual and auditory skills with the handicapped.) An opthalmologist, Fonda (1966) states that large type is indicated in the following situations:

1. When distant vision ranges from 20/200 to 10/200,
2. When the patient cannot read 12-point (pica typewriter) at 2 inches from the eye,
3. When a greater reading distance is mandatory, for example, for mathematics, and
4. When a child insists that large type is more comfortable and easier on his eyes.

There was a period when ophthalmologists cautioned against use of the eyes with respect to many types of visual handicaps. Today, however, they recommend visually handicapped children use their sight without special restrictions no matter how closely material or objects must be brought to the eye. Lowenfeld (1971) lends support to this by stating that many of these children "are able to read print, large type or even regular size, if they can bring it close to their eyes or use magnifying glasses, as they are now encouraged to do."

See Appendix C for a list of publishers who produce large type textbooks for visually limited children of elementary and high school age.

MICROFILM DUPLICATION AND ENLARGEMENT SERVICES. Commercial microfilm firms perform an expensive, but worthwhile, service. They offer single or multiple copies of books in many sizes of type enlargement. If the book requested has already been filmed by the company and is listed in its catalog, prices will be lower. In addition to acquiring books from the firms, one can also send a book to be microfilmed and enlarged. See Appendix C for names and addresses of microfilm firms.

TANGIBLE EDUCATIONAL AIDS. This is an area in which teachers spend an unduly amount of extra time in preparation of materials because very often these aids appear not to be available from commercial sources. See Appendix C for a list of agencies which prepare tangible educational aids and materials.

SPECIAL ADAPTATIONS AND CONSIDERATIONS

In addition to the special equipment and materials previously reviewed, it is now time to consider special adaptations and considerations which are peculiar to the specific needs of CP/NI youngsters.

Children with ataxia are known to become dizzy and possibly nauseated after a period of concentrating on their desk work. It has been found helpful to present materials singularly: one word or one picture or one object at a time. The child should be encouraged to frequently look away from his work. When presenting letters, words or numbers, it is suggested that they be enlarged and presented at eye level. Because close work causes dizziness, present materials at a distance of possibly ten feet or more.

Remember that the child's efforts to overcome muscle weakness (therefore, the inability to converge the eyes for binocular vision) may result in fatigue even if the actual visual acuity in each eye is fairly normal (Dunsdon, 1952; Goldberg, 1959). The fatigue factor may discourage reading. In addition, there will be: (a) delay in the eye movements from left to right as in following lines of print; and right to left as in going from the end of one line to the beginning of the next; and (b) a delay in refixating during the movements (or, in stopping to look at a word again during the reading of a line). One of the causes (both primary and as a precipitating factor) of reading disability proposed by Schonell (1948) is related to visual defects. The difficulties may be inefficient and slow *perceptual movements* producing an inability to concentrate upon visual forms of words leading to structural and order inaccuracies in words and/or letter perception. The nervous strain imposed by defective vision may lead to emotional irritation causing an unsuitable attitude towards reading and learning in general. The specific visual defects noted by Schonell were myopia, hypermetropia, and squint. Implications for the teacher would be: (a) shorter work periods, (b) use books (and other materials) in which more than the average space is left between lines or words, and (c) use slotted shields placed over the page so that all but the line actually being read is occluded.

Problems associated with nystagmus would appear to be numerous. However, these children seem to make adjustments and function better than one might predict. Although nystagmus does interfere with fixation, eye motion does stop at least momentarily, and this is the point when the child sees best. This *stopped moment* of the eye is referred to as the *neutral position* or that place where the nystagmus is less. Therefore, this is the point visual acuity is at its maximum. This neutral position varies from child to child. It may occur directly in front of or to either side. Each child appears to take advantage of this neutral position by fixating in accordance with this point thereby diminishing, controlling and/or adjusting to the nystagmus. The child may fixate laterally (i.e. turn his head to one side or the other so that he is able to see those things in front). Or, the child may hold a book or other materials to one side or the other to take advantage of this point where the nystagmus is lessened. In other children, nystagmus frequently lessens with convergence of the eyes and, therefore, the child will hold objects as close as possible.

The teacher may need to help the child locate that point by determining the best position for that particular child. In any event, the teacher should permit and, even encourage, head positioning and object placement.

In association with the high incidence both of sinistrality in hand and eye dominance and of cross-laterality, there is a tendency to make *reversals*. Such as (a) confusion in recognition of letters, particularly those alike in shape but different in orientation: "b," "d," "p," and "q," and (b) series of letters or words are mis-read, a word is read backwards or transposed: "was" for "saw." According to Dunsdon, this coupled with convergence defects presents a strong case for teaching, from the beginning, a cursive style of writing.

The literature concerning the use of programmed instruction with normal children is immense. This is not the case with children who have special learning difficulties. It would appear that programmed instruction may offer special advantages for the CP/NI child particularly those with visual problems. The materials are presented at an individual rate, the method of presentation (frames) may be less confusing visually.

Handwriting is often a real problem, particularly for the CP child with visual difficulties. Paper with thick or vivid lines can be obtained which will help the child stay on the line. Large-type or regular typewriters can be utilized possibly by the fourth grade.

As suggested by Berger *et al.*, (1970), "alphabetized shoe boxes containing small items (shoestring, stamp, stocking, satin, sucker, etc., in the *s* box) may be used for beginning phonics, tactile discrimination, concept and vocabulary building. . . . Story books with covers (cut-out felt, rough burlap, etc.) and pictures (objects such as dime store items attached to the page)" provide a little spice for the beginning or early reading stages. Such procedures will aid the child in shape and texture discrimination if he is a possible candidate for reading braille.

Although not alluded to previously, the occurrence of color blindness is to be considered a possible additional *visual defect*. There does not appear to be any direct reference in the literature regarding color blindness in the cerebral palsied or neurologically impaired child. However, recent studies of mentally retarded children have found that the rate of color blindness is much higher in this group than in the intellectually normal population. In addition, the male-female ratio for color blindness is nearly equal. Archer (1964) and Krause (1967) have estimated that more than one in 5 educable retarded children are color deficient. This is compared to about one in 12 normal males and one in 100 normal females. Archer found a prevalence rate of 28.97 percent in 1,008 educable mentally retarded children in Colorado. Krause found a prevalence rate of 22 percent in 609 educable retarded subjects in Tennessee. Other studies have resulted in a smaller percent. O'Connor (1957) found 13.3 percent in sampling over 100 mentally retarded males (See also Kratter, 1957, and Tredgold, 1947). However, the fact remains that color blindness does occur with an increased frequency in this population. One may therefore hypothesize that there may exist an equivalent increased prevalence of color blindness in the CP/NI population.

Color blindness is defined as the inability to discern one or more colors. Two types of color blindness are: (1) monochromatism or the complete inability to discriminate different hues and saturations although perception for brightness is not affected; and (2) dichromatism or perception of only two of the three basic hues (red, green, or blue). There is then either red blindness, green blindness, or blue-yellow blindness. Total color blindness results in all colors being seen as shades of black, gray and white.

What is the relationship of color to learning? Perception of space and form can be achieved both through seeing (visual perception) and touching (tactile perception). However, perception of color is the function of only the retina. If the retina cannot be affected by light stimulation and therefore is unable to send the stimulus to the cortex, color vision is absent (or, at any rate, distorted). Color has long been considered important in the learning process. It is used to increase attention, and reactions. We live in a world that constantly uses references to color: "blue Monday," "pick up the red ball," "it is green like grass," etc. The use of color in making associations certainly performs an important function in learning: "give me two red apples."

Although many color blind persons in the general population indeed are able to overcome this deficiency, color blindness may further impede the already defective learning processes at work in the CP/NI child. The use of color-dependent instructional techniques and materials may penalize such a child. If, in fact, the studies of Archer and Krause cited above can be applied to the CP/NI child, or even if smaller numbers are involved as in the normal population studies, screening programs should be developed as a regular routine in the educational system. Regarding tests of the pseudoisochromatic type, Adam *et al.*, (1967) states that, "generally [they are] accepted as quite satisfactory for the detection of color-vision defects in the red-green region of the spectrum." The accepted method to test for color blindness in the United States is the use of the H.R.R. Pseudo Isochromatic Tables (Ferrer, 1971). This does not necessarily apply to the mentally handicapped. Comprehension and attention span may interfere with obtaining reliable results on such tests.

Concerning the blind child with brain damage, an interesting discussion on treatment techniques for this child can be found in an article by Brachelis (1961). For this child, Brachelis recommends "training in a relatively stable environment or background. And within this background, there should be varying stimuli in the foreground." This varying stimuli is provided by novel situations. Stimuli that are too repetitive may result in a *saturation* effect. That is, "after awhile the external stimulation is not experienced" (Solomon *et al.,* 1961). Brachelis feels that providing novelty situations not only "allows the child to develop patterns of strategy in which he can in new situations more readily interpret and adapt to environments which differ [but] it [novelty stimuli] prevents the effect of saturation with unvarying stimuli."

These recommendations do not differ from those that could and should be applied to the CP/NI who are normally sighted. However, according to Brachelis, an inconsistency exists in that the brain damaged child needs a structured environment but blind children need extra stimulation. It would appear that remedial instruction which would make use of this child's remaining sense modalities and the development of body image and self concept, can be structured and, at the same time, achieve its goals. Use of techniques and procedures such as consistency, sequential presentation, active participation, overlearning, minimal change in concepts and activity, simple to complex principles, accurate and immediate feedback, repetition, and limiting work periods on new activities, will be sufficient to structure the environment and, also provide adequate "stimulation."

For detailed information concerning treatment programs for the blind mentally retarded child the interested reader is referred to:

1. The Edward R. Johnstone Training and Research Center. An educational program for blind retarded children which is

divided into three parts: management, academic and motor. See: Cicenia, E. F.; Belton, J. A.; Myers, J. J., and Mundy, G.: The blind child with multiple handicaps; A challenge. Part II. The educational program. *International J Ed Blind, 14*:105-112, 1965.

2. Walter E. Fernald State School. An open end curriculum where the blind retarded advance at their own rates. Generally, the steps involved are initially play therapy and then sense training classrooms (basic discrimination skills, travel techniques, social interaction, and speech). The next step is the kindergarten (basically the same as the sense training classroom with more emphasis on social training and for the more advanced.) A readiness program in braille or enlarged print is introduced at that time. Then the academic classroom is introduced. See: Tretakoff, M. I., and Farrell, M. J.: Developing a curriculum for the blind retarded. *Amer J Ment Def, 62*:610-615, 1958.

3. Mansfield Training School. Social adjustment is the primary goal. Secondarily, some traditional academic and recreational activities are introduced. See: Deleo, G. M., and Boly, L. F.: Some considerations in establishing an educational program for the institutionalized blind and partially sighted mentally subnormal. *Amer J Ment Def, 61*:134-140, 1956.

4. Sunland's classroom program. This program is for high trainable blind retarded. Emphasis is placed on the development of sensory perception, social and neuromuscular skills. Methods and materials are generally the same as those implemented with sighted retarded children of comparable intellectual levels. See: Williams, D.: Sunland's program for the blind. *Mental Retard, 2*: 244-245, 1964.

EYE DISORDERS AND PERCEPTION/VISUO-MOTOR SKILLS

The information in the literature concerning the relationship of visual disorders and perceptual and visuo-motor disorders in brain-injured adults far outweighs that for children. The pausity of information regarding eye defects and the consequent effects on perception and learning in children (particularly the CP/NI child) in no way lessens its importance. Abercrombie (1960) attacked this "scarcity" problem with vehemence when she stated, "most studies of perception, however, fail to give any report of the condition of the eyes, and though it is probable that gross defects were absent or were allowed for, it is possible that less obvious disorders were present and relevant."

In the well-known and frequently cited studies of Cruickshank *et al.,* (1957), no opthalmological data are given. However, the data resulting from a recent study by Beakey *et al.,* (1968) supports the view that cerebral palsied children have a greater number of visual defects than the non-brain damaged and that there is a strong relationship between oculo-motor or visual defects and visual-perceptual deficits. According to Hebb's (1949) speculations, eye movements contribute constantly and are essential to such perceptual integration tasks as recognition and discrimination and differentiation of forms and shapes. And, Piaget (1952a, 1952b, 1953) maintains that visual stimulation sets off action, and therefore is a primary stimulus for development of intelligence.

Before continuing, an understanding of the terms visuo-motor and visual perception will enhance one's digestion of the present discussion. *Visuomotor* functions (the adjustment of the eye and the hand in relation to the object of fixation) are movements under visual control requiring the coordination of eye and hand. Such skills are revealed in tasks requiring copying a figure, or constructing a design out of blocks, or possibly even dressing. That is, tasks concerned with manipulation in three-dimensional space and possibly with the body orientation in space. *Visual perception* has to do with tasks involving ability to match or memorize shapes, to interpret pictures, to distinguish a figure from a background. Or, those tasks that can be performed without the combined use of the hands.

It has been shown that animals can perceive differences between shapes (Sutherland, 1961). But can these animals write or draw (visuomotor) the shapes they *perceive?* We find that the child moves with purpose in an attempt to make contact with something external to his body, be it reaching out, touching and feeling an object, or moving a book in order to reorient the printed page. Such performance is not purely motor but visuomotor. Teachers must attempt to determine the nature of the child's difficulties in order to utilize the proper teaching methods for as Abercrombie (1964a) says, "It may be the careless equating of the two [visuo-motor and perceptual difficulties] that is responsible for some teaching practices which attempt to teach spastic children to perceive better by practicing visuo-motor tasks." If the child's powers of perception are intact and the problem is visuo-motor, then he (the child) is able to realize his error. This child many times can be observed trying to correct his mistake: he realizes his mistake but motorically has difficulty or is unable to correct the mistake, or has difficulty executing the motion initially. Perceptual difficulties can be detected by asking the child to match shapes etc.; visuomotor difficulties can be ascertained by asking the child to construct shapes (i.e. drawing or building).

Leading authorities in the field of education, psychology, opthalmology and optometry do not seem to be in complete agreement as to the relationship ocular defects have to reading retardation and other academic skills. Some regard reading retardation as primarily due to an inadequacy of central neural functioning (organization of visual stimuli); others relate it to ocular deficiencies. Prechtl (1963) studied 50 children aged 9 to 11. He classified them as having choreiform syndrome. By using electro-oculogram (EOG) recordings during reading, he was able to correlate errors in word recognition with involuntary eye movements in 90 percent of the cases he studied. The main purpose of a research study by Annapolle (1971) was to determine the status of binocular vision skills in relation to developmental dyslexia. He is of the opinion that "binocular vision problems (heterophorias, fusion instability, and poor oculo-motor control) are the major visual factors in developmental dyslexia." Benton (1968) found in a seven-year study, in an attempt to evaluate the role of binocular vision in dyslexia, that 77 percent (77%) of the total in his study (or 1,155 children with specific reading problems) were found to have a binocular control abnormality.

Abercrombie *et al.*, (1963a) would agree with this when she points out that, "the more accurately a child can direct his eyes to a target, and the longer he can maintain fixation when required, the less will be the proportion of time that irrelevant images occupy the retina and particularly the fovea, and the quicker he will learn to perceive." However, in the case of the cerebral palsied child who is likely to have ocular defects or, at any rate, ocular motor retardation, this child may be slowed down in his learning because "they are working on noisy channels" (Abercrombie, 1963b). She argues that since early learning is dependent upon the soundness of visual functioning, cerebral palsied children with visual disorders are highly vulnerable to problems interfering with the acquisition of academic skills. A very interesting study was performed by Abercrombie *et al.* (1963) in which she investigated, by means of electro-oculographic recordings, the primary types of horizontal version movements (saccadic and pursuit) of the eyes. Total time spent off target was also scored. The experimental work was done at a school for physically handicapped children. The first task required the children to fixate on dots (seven in total). When requested by the examiner, the child visually moved on to the next dot. When he reached the end of the row, he went back to the beginning, and repeated. This is similar to the tasks involved in reading (i.e. moving from one word to the next along a line of print). In the second experiment, the child was asked to follow an electric train which moved backwards and forward into and out of a tunnel. The children were asked to fixate on the tunnel entrance while the train was hidden. The child was thusly expected to demonstrate clean movements from left to right and steady fixation (on the tunnel entrance). The performance of the cerebral palsied was the poorest (in comparison to the physically handicapped non-brain damaged children and the normal children). Of the cerebral palsied children whose eye movements were recorded (some of the cerebral palsied children's records were not scorable due to such factors as inattentiveness), 50 percent were more irregular than those of normal children. Figure 49a shows the pursuit movements of a normal child aged ten years when the eyes are following an electric toy train moving from left to right, stopping in a tunnel, and from right to left as it moves backwards out of the tunnel; the eyes are on target most of the time. Figure 49b shows the movements of a cerebral palsied child aged seven years, with irregular runs and unsteady fixation on the tunnels. Another interesting and educationally pertinent finding was that a greater number of the cerebral palsied children showed "directional bias" in per-

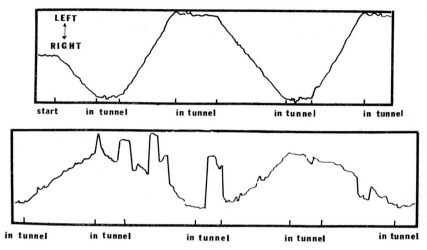

Figure 49. Pursuit movements (following a train) and fixations, (at entrance to a 'tunnel') of *a.* (at top) normal, and *b.* (lower) cerebral palsied child. (Reproduced with permission from: Abercrombie, M. L. J.: Eye movements and perceptual development. In Gardiner, P., MacKeith, R. and Smith, V. (Eds.): *Aspects of Developmental and Paediatric Ophthalmology.* London, Spastics International/Heinemann, 1969, No. 32.

formance (i.e. eye movement was better in the left to right direction on the pursuit task). Abercrombie found a correlation between performance and mental age. As she suggests, this supports the thought that even in the absence of obvious eye disorders, the eye muscles may be retarded in attaining full development of control just as cerebral palsied children tend to be retarded in other motor skills.

In 1964, Abercrombie and her associates (1964b) reported on the work performed with physically handicapped children. They found that within the spastic group there was a definite relationship between the presence of squint and special difficulties on two tests, the maze subtest of the WISC and the figure background test of Frostig *et al.* (1961). The children with squint had a particularly difficult time with the second part of the figure background test (the embedded figure part in which the child is asked to outline the kite-shaped figures). This somewhat supports her contention in 1960 that those children with squint do have problems in "sorting out figure from background."

As educators and therapists, it would be safe to make a working assumption that the problems encountered by the child who may have an ocular muscle imbalance, either a tendency for or the actual state of, will be more apt to lose his place while reading, or possibly skip a line, or find it necessary to reread the same material. This all adds up to a most frustrating, distressing experience. Such difficulties would affect other skills as well as arithmetic. The gravity of the importance of eye movement disorders regarding the perception and reproduction of spatial relationships is stressed again by Abercrombie (1970) when she says that "it is to be expected that any disorder of eye movement would affect perceptual development and more general mental development, because it would reduce the input of relevant information."

The results of a study by Jones *et al.* (1966) indicates how important vision is to the acquisition of academic skills. The study was done to analyze factors of visual acuity and eye movements in relation to reading speed and comprehension in cerebral palsied adults. The subjects (14 spastics and 14 athetoids) were divided into two groups: Group I were those whose comprehension scores on the Gates Test of Reading Ability were at or above the sixth grade level, and Group II were those whose scores fell below this level. The two groups were subdivided as follows: Subjects whose grade level of reading speed was at least the same as their comprehension grade and those whose speed fell a grade or more below their comprehension score. A summary of the findings are: There was a definite relationship between disordered eye movement and slower reading speed. Specifically, the frequency of disordered eye movement in those with lower speed than comprehension was 75 percent and in those in which speed and comprehension was equal was 35 percent. The average number of fixations in both groups was similar (22-26). As might be expected, there were more fixations in persons with lower comprehension (with equal speed) than in those with higher comprehension (with equal speed). Left-handedness was observed in 75 percent in Group II and 38 percent in Group I. Visual acuity was normal in all the Group I subjects, and only slightly impaired in Group II. Hearing loss was more frequent in Group I. There was an especially high degree of refixations in spastics with evidence of abnormal eye movement.

In sum, we see that the results of squint and heterophoria are: (1) perceiving a confused, inconsistent pattern: double vision or outline confusion may occur, or the object may be in a different place from one moment to the next, and (2) binocular stereoscopic vision may be absent which only serves to compound the child's difficulties in whatever learning situation he is undertaking. One of the most important functions of the eye muscles is in searching or exploring the field of vision to find important targets (Abercrombie, 1969). The ability to move the eyes from one fixed point to another is called saccadic movements. The interested reader is encouraged to refer to a study by Yarbus (1967). The importance of saccadic movements to measuring size of objects is discussed in this article as well.

That perceptual development is heavily dependent upon eye (as well as hand) movements gains further support from experiments that were done by a group of Soviet researchers (Zaporozhets, 1965). These investigators contend that unconditioned reflexes in the infant which respond to stimulation of sense organs are important for subsequent sensory perceptual development. Of these reflexes, the most important are the "orienting-exploratory" responses; that is, hand movements (touching, manipulating) and eye movements (such as tracing, object and figure contours). Zaporozhets says that the function of these movements is to "investigate the object and form a copy—an adequate image of the object—by reproducing its features or forming a *likeness* of it." These movements must have practical elements. Simply translated, this means that as a result of the child's active involvement, he is able to experience reality in the form of (1) a product (house made of blocks, a figure made from sticks, a drawing of a design) and (2) a solution (placing geometric objects in appropriate slots, constructing a puzzle). Such "concrete objective modeling," according to Zaporozhets, is most important to "the development of cognitive processes in general and perceptive processes in particular" (Zaporozhets, 1965).

In the perceptual development process, the child proceeds

from the pure executive act of looking at an object to orienting and modeling activities (constructing, copying, reproducing, drawing). Essential then to the development of visual discrimination (to name but one perceptual task) are perceptual-motor experiences. Coming back to eye movements in particular and their relationship to perception, it is interesting to note an experiment performed by the same researchers mentioned above (Zaporozhets) in which eye movements of children at various age levels were filmed. Figures were shown on a screen. The children were asked to look at the figures so that they could later recognize them. In children ages three to four years, the eyes fixated mainly on the central portion of the shape with only an occasional wandering to the edges of the figure. At four to five years, although eye movements were still mainly within the figure, more time was spent near the edges of the shape. At the age of five to six years, the eyes began to trace the edges or periphery of the figures. At six to seven years of age, the eyes traced the edges as if to reproduce or draw the form with the eyes. At the age of five, most of the children were able to recognize the figure which was not the case with the younger children. According to this theme, to identify a figure requires only the ability to fixate on a few parts of the figure. But to reproduce the figure, a *differentiated* tracing of the outline is necessary. That is, a finer visual investigation is necessary. This implies (and supports Abercrombie's findings) that eye movement disorders not only hamper figure identification but possibly have a serious detrimental effect on shape and figure reproduction.

Binocular stereoscopic vision provides information about the relationship an object has to its surroundings in space. It plays an important part in discriminating the object (figure) from the surroundings (background). The child with monocular vision sees essentially a "flat" world. See Ogle (1963) for examples of how binocular vision improves discrimination. The implication drawn is that the difficulties seen in children with cerebral palsy in interpreting pictures and figure-ground performance may be related to inefficiencies of binocular stereoscopic vision. As binocular vision makes depth perception "automatic" or instantaneous, not having this facility would seem to place an additional burden on the CP/NI child who is already, or may be, multiply hindered. The removal of this additional problem would justify surgery to correct ocular deviations. It is suggested by Abercrombie (1960) that squint with its consequent absent binocular vision may not only cause figure-ground problems but may also be the cause of the child's inattentiveness.

Refractive errors do not seem to pose as serious a problem as the other ocular deficiencies discussed. Most opthalmologists seem to feel that these errors play a rather limited role in the skill of reading. Once refractive errors are corrected (with glasses) there would appear to be less visual discomfort and therefore increased ability to concentrate. Visual acuity would also obviously be improved.

In conclusion, we can say that, by definition, perception is an activity of the mind midway between sensation and thought (meaning). Perceptual disorders then are of central origin. But by implication, there must be a precursor (sensations), something for the mind to give meaning to. The precursor or antecedent to perception which we have been discussing is the sensations (impulses) from the eye. It will be remembered that some 80 to 90 percent of all our information about the world comes to us through our eyes. If a faulty or distorted sensation from the child's visual arena is sent to the brain for interpretation and meaning, one can only expect a disorganized and meaningless perception to result. (This can also be said with regard to other sensory input approaches such as tactile impressions and kinesthetic input.) Eye defects contribute significantly to visual-perceptual and visuomotor problems in the CP/NI child. "It is probably no accident that the English language uses the term 'I see' to mean 'understanding.' Let us make certain that the eye, the great window of the mind, is properly cared for at all professional levels" (Halstead, 1971).

GLOSSARY

Accomodation For focusing (i.e. for getting sharp images when object of fixation changes distances from observer) through the muscle of accommodation (the ciliary muscle) in the eye. It does this by squeezing the lens, which is inside the eye.

Accommodation-convergence relationship Normally, when focusing on something near (accommodating), the eyes also converge so that both foveas point at the near object.

Alternating strabismus Both eyes with same visual acuity deviate.

Amblyopia ex anopsia A lazy eye. An eye with an island of suppressed vision in the fovea. This occurs in the turned eye to prevent double vision.

Astigmatism A refractive error due to the shape of the cornea. When this deformation is spherical, it may be myopia or hypermetropia. When cylindrical, astigmatism. Here rays of light may be focused (or close to) in one meridian and far away in another.

Binocular Anything having to do with the use of both eyes together.

Cataract The clouding, to any degree, of the lens of the eye interfering with the passage of light.

Ciliary muscle The muscle of accommodation. It is inside the eye and focuses the lens in the eye to make vision clear.

Convergence The act of both eyes shifting their lines of vision toward each other. It is normally used to look at a near object.

Divergence The act of both eyes shifting their lines of vision away from each other. Normally used to look at something far away after converging on a near object.

Dyskinesia (of extrinsic eye muscles) Disturbance of voluntary control causing fragmentary or incomplete movements.

Emmetropia A neutral state of refraction. The eyes are not nearsighted, farsighted or astigmatic.

Esophoria (or latent esotropia) Tendency of the eyes to converge too much. This is the tendency toward, not the actual deviation (tropia) being prevented by the force of **fusion** capacity.

Esotropia The actual state of incrossed eyes; one eye turns inward.

Exophoria Tendency of the eyes to diverge too much.

Exotropia The actual state of divergent eyes; one eye turns outward.

Farsightedness (or Hyperopia) A short eye that needs to focus (or accommodate) all the time to see clearly, or needs a plus lens.

Field of vision How far up, down, right, and left an eye can see while looking straight ahead.

Focus Same as with a camera; for an eye to see something clearly, the image must be sharply focused on the retina.

Fovea That part of the retina which is used to read and which sees best; when an eye looks straight at something, it uses the fovea.

Fusion Occurs when the brain superimposes and melts what it sees with each eye thereby producing a single mental image. This melting of the images occurs in the visual cortex (Brodmann's areas 17, 18) of the brain.

Hemianopsia (Hemanopia) A visual field defect in which a segment of the field of vision of each eye is missing, caused by a single lesion in the visual pathways.

Heterophoria (or phoria) A latent squint, with a tendency to deviate, but the axes is held right by fusion.

Hypermetropia See "Hyperopia".

Hyperopia Farsightedness: a short eyeball that has to focus (i.e. accommodate) constantly in order to see.

Hyperphoria Tendency of one eye to be higher than the other.

Hypertropia The actual state: one eye is higher than the other.

Hypophoria Tendency for one eye to be lower than the other.

Hypotropia The actual state: one eye is lower than the other.

Line of Vision Visual axis; when the eye looks straight at something, the line of vision is pointed at it.

Monocular Having to do with one eye only.

Myopia Nearsightedness.

Nearsightedness Myopia or a long eye that is too long to be in focus except for things that are close to it.

Nystagmus Short, rapid, rythmic involuntary oscillation of the eyeball usually affecting both eyes and associated with imperfect vision. "Non-symmetric" cases can get benefit from surgery.

Ophthalmologist (or oculist). A physician specializing in the care of the eye and its structures. A medical doctor having received an M.D. and serving an internship in general medicine and surgery. He takes additional training in ophthalmology. In addition to prescribing glasses and contact lenses, the ophthalmologist diagnoses and treats all eye disorders.

Ophthalmology That branch of the medical sciences dealing with the structure, function and diseases of the eye.

Optic nerve The seeing nerve of the eye; a bundle of nerve fibers that connects the retina with the brain.

Optometrist One who is a specialist in optometry. He receives an O.D. degree from a school of optometry which enables him to examine the eyes and prescribe eyeglasses or contact lenses or exercises but not drugs or surgery.

Orthoptics Visual training to develop binocular vision.

Phoria See "Heterophoria".

Pleoptics Visual training to develop better monocular (visual acuity and central, foveal, fixation) vision.

Pursuit movements The ability to follow a moving target in all directions of visual gaze.

Recession An operation in which one of the muscles that moves the eye is placed farther back on the eyeball to make its effect less powerful.

Refraction The process by which refractive errors are measured for correction with eye glasses.

Refractive error The nearsightedness, farsightedness, or astigmatism of an eye.

Resection An operation in which one of the muscles that moves the eye is shortened to make its (the muscle's) effect more powerful.

Retina The inner lining of the eye, which records the images seen by the eye and sends them to the brain.

Saccadic eye movements Shifting from one point of fixation to another.

Squint Strabismus, tropia, heterotropia.

Strabismus Imperfect muscle balance with non-latent eye deviation. Either permanent or intermittent, at far or at near, horizontal or vertical.

Suppression The process by which the brain disregards what one eye sees because that eye is crossed and is causing double vision. The eye can be turned out, up or down.

Visual acuity The measurement of how much an eye can see with its best vision, using the fovea. Normal is 20/20.

REFERENCES

Abercrombie, M. L. J.: Perception and eye movements: Some speculations on disorders of cerebral palsy. *Cereb Palsy Bull,* 2:142-148, 1960.

Abercrombie, M. L. J., Davis, J. R., and Shackel, B.: Pilot study of version movements of eyes in cerebral palsied and other children. *Vision Res, 3*:135-153, 1963a.

Abercrombie, M. L. J.: Eye movements, perception and learning. In Smith, V. H. (Ed.): *Visual Disorders and Cerebral Palsy*. London, Spastics Society/Heinemann, 1963b.

Abercrombie, M. L. J.: Perceptual and visuomotor disorders in cerebral palsy. *Clin Develop Med,* No. 11. London, Spastics Society/Heinemann, 1964a.

Abercrombie, M. L. J., Gardiner, P. A., Hansen, E., Jonckheere, J., Lindon, R. L., Solomon, G., and Tyson, M. C.: Visual, perceptual and visuomotor impairments in physically handicapped children. *Percept Mot Skills, 18*:561, 1964b.

Abercrombie, M. L. J.: Eye movements and perceptual development. In Gardiner, P., MacKeith, R., and Smith. V. (Eds.): Aspects of Developmental and Paediatric Ophthalmology. *Clin Develop Med,* 32. London, Spastics Society/Heinemann, 1969.

Abercrombie, M. L. J.: Learning to draw. In Connolly, K. (Ed.): *Ciba Foundation Study Group on Mechanisms of Motor Skill Development*. London, Churchill, 1970.

Adam, A., Doron, D., and Modan, R.: Frequencies of protan and deutan alleles in some Israeli communities and a note on the selection relaxation hypothesis. *Amer J Phys Anthropol, 26*:297-306, 1967.

Annapolle, L.: Vision problems in developmental dyslexia. *J Learn Dis, 4*:77-83, 1971.

Archer, R. E.: *Color Discrimination and Association of Educable Mentally Retarded Children.* Unpublished doctoral dissertation, Colorado State College, 1964.

Beakey, A., Wilson, J., and Wilson, B. C.: The relationship between visual disorders and visual-perceptual deficits in cerebral palsy (Abstract). *Develop Med Child Neurol, 10*:251, 1968.

Benton, Curtis, D., Jr.: In Keeney, A. H. and Keeney, V. T. (Eds.): *Dyslexia and Treatment of Reading Disorders.* St. Louis, *Mosby,* 1968.

Berger, A. and Kautz, C. R.: Sources of information and materials for blind and visually limited pupils. *Elem Eng, 18*:1970.

Bischoff, R. W.: Improvement of listening comprehension in partially sighted students. *Sight Sav Rev, 37*:161-165, 1967.

Brachelis, L. A.: Symposium-self-image: A guide to adjustment: II. Some characteristics of sensory deprivation. *New Outlook Blind, 55*:288-291, 1961.

Crane, M., *et al.*: *Screening School Children for Visual Defects.* St. Louis, Children's Bureau, US Dept. Health, Education and Welfare, 1954.

Cruickshank, W. B., Bice, H. V. and Wallen, N. E.: *Perception and Cerebral Palsy.* New York, Syracuse University Press, 1957.

Dunsdon, M. I.: *The Educability of Cerebral Palsied Children.* London, Newness, 1952.

Ferrer, Jorge A.: Personal Communication. Department of Opthalmology, Shands Teaching Hospital and Clinics, University of Florida, Gainesville, 1971.

Fonda, G.: An evaluation of large type. *New Outlook Blind, 60*:296-298, 1966.

Frostig, M., Lefever, D. W. and Whittlesey, R. B.: A developmental test of visual perception for evaluating normal and neurologically handicapped children. *Percept Mot Skills, 12*:383, 1961.

Goldberg, H. K.: The ophthalmologist looks at the reading problem. *Am J Ophthalmol, 67*:280, 1959.

Halstead, Ward, as quoted, in part, by Annapolle, L.: Vision problems in developmental dyslexia. *J Learn Dis, 4*:77-83, 1971.

Hebb, D. D.: *The Organization of Behavior: A Neuropsychological Theory.* New York, Wiley, 1949.

Jones, M. H.: The management of hemiplegic children with peripheral sensory loss. *Ped Clin N Amer, 7*:765-775, 1960.

Jones, M. H., Dayton, G. D., Jr., *et al.*: Pilot study of reading problems in cerebral palsied adults. *Dev Med Child Neurol, 8*:417-427, 1966.

Kratter, F. E.: Color blindness in relation to normal and defective intelligence. *Am J Ment Def, 22*:436-441, 1957.

Krause, I. B.: A study of the relationship of certain aspects of color vision to educable mentally retarded children. Unpublished. United States Office of Education Grant Number OEG2-6-08528-1593, 1967.

Lowenfeld, Berthold: Psychological problems of children with impaired vision. In Cruickshank, W. M. (Ed.): *Psychology of Exceptional Children and Youth,* 3rd ed. Englewood Cliffs, Prentice Hall, 1971.

Mueller, M. W.: Effects of illustration size on test performance of visually limited children. *Except Child, 29*:124-128, 1962.

Nolan, C. Y.: Readability of large types. A study of type size and type styles. *Internat J Ed Blind, 9*:41-44, 1959.

Ogle, K. N.: Special topics in binocular spatial localization. In Davson, H. (Ed.): *The Eye.* London, Academic Press, 1963, vol. 4, p. 349.

O'Connor, N.: Imbecility and color blindness. *Am J Ment Def, 22*:83-87, 1957.

Piaget, J.: *The Origins of Intelligence in Children.* New York, International Universities Press, Inc., 1952a.

Piaget, J.: *The Child's Conception of Number.* London, Routledge and Kegan Paul, 1952b.

Piaget, J.: How children form mathematical concepts. *Sci Am,* 1953.

Prechtl, H. F. R.: Prognosis and research needs in dyslexia. In Money, J. W. (Ed.): *Reading Disability.* Baltimore, Johns Hopkins Press, 1963.

Schonell, Fred J.: *Backwardness in the Basic Subjects,* 7th impression. London, Oliver and Boyd, 1956.

Sloan, A. and Rosenthal, P.: School vision testing. *Arch Ophthalmol, 48*:428, 1952.

Solomon, P., Kubzansky, P. E. *et al.*: *Sensory Deprivation.* Harvard University Press, 1961.

Sutherland, N. S.: *The Methods and Findings of Experiments on the Visual Discrimination of Shapes by Animals.* Cambridge, Heffer, 1961.

Tredgold, A. A.: *Mental Deficiency.* London, Balliere, Tindall, and Cox, 1947.

Yarbus, A. L.: *Eye Movements and Vision.* New York, Plenum Press, 1967.

Zaporozhets, A. V.: The development of perception in the preschool child. In Mussen, P. H. (Ed.): European Research in Cognitive Development. *Soc Res Child Develop Monog, 30*:82-101. Chicago, University of Chicago Press, 1965.

Chapter Eight

PHARMACOLOGICAL APPROACH TO MANAGEMENT

T HE PHARMACOLOGICAL AIDS USED IN THE management of the cerebral palsied/neurologically impaired child represents but one of the approaches in a comprehensive rehabilitation program. "In order of importance, drugs must be selected to control convulsion; allay fear and anxiety; reduce hyperkinesis; favorably influence spasticity, dyskinesia, or imbalance; and help adjustment within the family, such as in sleeping, eating and behavior" (Denhoff *et al.*, 1960).

Our discussion will follow within this hierarchy-of-importance frame work set forth by Denhoff. The concentration will be on drugs as they relate to control of seizures, relaxation of muscles and amelioration of behavior problems with essential comments concerning effects of the drugs.

SEIZURE CONTROL—ANTICONVULSANTS

Convulsions or convulsive tendencies (seizures, epilepsy) are present in 60 percent or more of the cerebral palsy cases. Generally, reports in the literature indicate a much higher seizure occurrence rate in hemiplegic cerebral palsy. Churchill (1968) reports that in his study of hemiplegic cerebral palsied, the non-epileptic groups (and not the epileptic group) had a preponderance of right hemiplegia. However, studies by Crothers and Paine (1959), Perlstein and Hood (1955) and Malamud *et al.* (1955) have strongly indicated that epilepsy occurs more fre-

229

quently in acquired than in congenital hemiplegia. Approximately one-third of the children in most cerebral palsy clinics have hemiplegia. Of the children with hemiplegia, 25 percent are acquired postnatally (Carter *et al.,* 1967). Approximately 50 percent of these (with acquired or acute hemiplegia) will subsequently develop recurring seizures. Carter additionally feels that seizures which are associated with hemiplegia may be resistant to anticonvulsants. Severe intellectual impairment is most commonly observed when the hemiplegia is complicated by seizures refractory to anticonvulsants.

As all types of convulsions may be encountered in the CP/NI population, a review of the definitions and classifications of epilepsy follows.

Epilepsy—Definition and Classification. Denhoff (1967) classifies seizures into two broad categories:

1. *Cerebral* (cortical; major motor seizures). These are localized or generalized evidenced by motor, sensory, autonomic (i.e. heart pounding), psychical (illusions and hallucinations), loss of consciousness and automatism (amnesia for short periods) (Penfield *et al.,* 1954). Motor seizures are characterized by a spread of movement down the body, generalized or focal. "Sensory seizures are characterized by a variety of forms: somatosensory (tingling or numbness of an extremity), visual (changes in light or color intensity), auditory (buzzing or humming sounds), vertiginous (dizziness), or olfactory (disagreeable odors)" (Denhoff, 1967). A sensory seizure also may be described as autonomic, psychical, or automatism.

2. *Centrencephalic* (the seizure activity arises subcortically; minor motor seizures). These are evidenced as petit mal, myoclonic, grand mal or psychomotor.

In general, epilepsy is characterized by sudden, transient alterations of brain function. These seizures are usually associated with motor (involuntary increases or decrease of muscle tone and movement), alterations of sensation (including auditory and visual illusions and hallucinations), disruption of autonomic functions (visual and vegetative), behavioral or psychic symptoms (hyperkinesis, aggressiveness), and often accompanied by impairment of consciousness or memory. If frequent seizures are occurring, even when they are of a very minor type, there is likely to be a period, before, during and after the attack, when the function of the brain is impaired (Gordon, 1967). The following classification includes only the most commonly encountered types of epileptic seizures.

Grand Mal (major motor). There is typically a motor or sensory aura preceding the actual attack. This aura may consist of a certain odor, a visual image, or a memory flash. Also preliminary to the attack will be staring or deviation of the eyes. Loss of consciousness usually follows associated with convulsions. The child lies rigid for possibly 1 to 2 minutes with muscles in a mild tonic state (fine, rapid twitching). A clonic period follows in which there is more violent, rapid twitching, followed by deep sleep lasting from 1 to 4 hours. When awake, the child is usually somewhat confused, has a headache, and is frequently aware of muscle soreness.

Petit Mal. These seizures are characterized by a minor attack without conspicuous convulsive movements. Characteristically, the child stops (does not actually fall), stands and stares momentarily. During this time, his voluntary (purposeful) movements are interrupted. These seizures frequently consist of fleeting, momentary loss of consciousness. The seizures may be so fleeting (usually lasting up to 15 to 20 seconds), in fact, that no one, not even the child himself, may be entirely aware of it. There is no preceding aura or post-seizure sleepiness or confusion. This type is rare in a child before the age of four (onset is most frequently between 4 to 7 years). As many as 100 such attacks a day may occur.

Akinetic (minor motor). This type is sometimes referred to as drop or *salaam* seizures characterized by a sudden loss of muscle tone when the child slumps a bit before catching himself or recovering right after his body touches the ground. There are no convulsions and no loss of consciousness associated with this.

Myoclonic. A minor motor seizure. There are brief, involtary contractions of limbs or muscles without loss of consciousness. Some authorities include this under the *Petit Mal* type of seizure.

Psychomotor (temporal lobe). Manifestations of this type seizure vary. There may be incoherent speech; staring; smacking of the lips and chewing movements; hallucinations; outbursts of temper and personality changes; and purposeful but inappropriate movements of extremities such as picking at clothing. Confusion and amnesia commonly occur. It has been postulated that "equivalent states" exist in which the child exhibits a behavior disturbance rather than the classical convulsion (Chusid *et al.,* 1969).

Focal or *Jacksonian.* This is a motor or sensory seizure due to a disturbance of a portion of the motor cortex. The seizure may be limited to the appropriate area of the body (relative to the area of the cortex which is irritated). The seizure may spread to other cortical areas with consequent involvement in corresponding body areas. Consciousness may not be lost.

Table XXII summarizes drug anticonvulsant medications used in cerebral palsy.

TABLE XXII

ANTICONVULSANT MEDICATION USED IN CEREBRAL PALSY
MEDICATION

Generic Name	Trade Name	Average Dosage
1. Cerebral Seizures		
Primidone	Mysoline® (Ayerst)	125-1000 mg nightly
Diphenylhydantoin	Dilantin® (Parke Davis	32- 300 mg nightly
Metharbital	Gemonil® (Abbott)	50- 200 mg t.i.d.
Phenobarbital		32- 200 mg t.i.d.
Methylbarbituric Acid	Mebaral® (Winthrop)	32- 200 mg t.i.d.
Methylphenylethyl hydantoin	Mesantoin® (Sandoz)	50- 200 mg t.i.d.
2. Centrencephalic Seizures		
Ethosuxamide	Zarontin® (Parke Davis)	250- 500 mg t.i.d.
Trimethadione	Tridione® (Abbott)	150- 600 mg t.i.d.
Paramethadione	Paradione® (Abbott)	150- 600 mg t.i.d.
d-Amphetamine sulfate	Dexedrine® (SKF) or	5- 10 mg b.i.d.
1-Amphetamine sulfate	Benzedrine® (SKF)	10- 20 mg b.i.d.
3. Mixed Types		
Phensuximide	Milontin® (Abbott)	250- 500 mg t.i.d.
Ethotoin	Peganone® (Abbott)	250- 500 mg t.i.d.
Phenacemide	Phenurone® (Abbott)	250- 500 mg t.i.d.
	Diamox® (Lederle)	250- 500 mg t.i.d.

(Reprinted with permission. Denhoff, Eric: *Cerebral Palsy — The Preschool Years.* Springfield, Thomas, 1967.)

DISCUSSION OF ANTICONVULSANT MEDICATION

1. *Cerebral seizures (cortical, major motor)* (Refer to Table XXII)

Mysoline (primidone). Denhoff states that Mysoline in addition to Dilantin and Gemonil are the drugs of choice in controlling cerebral seizures. Shanks (1961) in his discussion concerning seizures in children (not cerebral palsied particularly) feels that, "while primidone has proved effective in many children as an anticonvulsant, its effect on the associated behavior has been disappointing."

REACTION.[41] The most common side effect is drowsiness. Dizziness, diplopia and ataxia observed in some (these symptoms disappear in most cases within several weeks after initial administration). Slurred speech, nystagmus and headaches occasionally observed. Livingston (1966) indicates that in his experience the only antiepileptic agents which commonly cause drowsiness are mysoline, phenobarbitol and bromides.

Dilantin. One of the most effective drugs for the treatment of major motor (grand mal) epilepsy, psychomotor (temporal lobe) epilepsy and non-convulsive epileptic equivalents. Little value in treating petit mal (may increase frequency). Little value in treating minor motor epilepsy.

REACTION. Most frequent—disturbances of equilibrium (ataxia or unsteadiness of gait), and diplopia (double vision) due to overdosage. In addition, drowsiness, dysarthria and nystagmus may also be present.

Gemonil. Perlstein (1950) was the first to report on the use of Gemonil in the treatment of epilepsy. He observed good results in patients with "seizures due to organic brain disease."

REACTION. Relatively free of toxic effects. There may be rash and irritability (See Denhoff, 1966).

Mebaral. Frequently used in place of phenobarbital but "while phenobarbital is the safest of the anticonvulsant medications, it causes irritable behavior when used over a long period of time

---

[41]Much of the discussion concerning reactions of the various drugs is taken from Livingston, Samuel: *Drug Therapy for Epilepsy.* Springfield, Thomas, 1966.

with these children. Mebraral is in a similar category" (Denhoff, 1967).

REACTIONS. Relatively free of toxic effects. Rarely causes hyperactivity and excitation. Drowsiness is rarely seen.

Mesantoin (Mephenytoin). Closely related chemically to dilantin; however, Mesantoin is more toxic (Denhoff, 1966). Effective in major motor seizures, and occasionally for psychomotor seizures. Essentially ineffective in *petit mal* and minor motor epilepsy. Mesantoin and Phenurone are used when Mysoline, Dilantin and Gemonil seem to have no effect (Denhoff, 1967).

REACTION. Drowsiness is the most common side reaction. Ataxia, diplopia and dysarthria observed occasionally as is nystagmus.

2. Centrencephalic (petit mal; minor motor).

Zarontin. This drug is generally used jointly with either Mysoline or Dilantin. Zarontin as well as Tridione and Paradione are most efficacious in centrencephalic *(petit mal)* seizures (Denhoff, 1967).

REACTIONS. Nausea, gastric distress, drowsiness, headaches and dizziness may occasionally be encountered. The results of a study of 25 children (Guey *et al.,* 1967) indicated that the use of Zarontin to control *petit mal* seizures seemed to lower intellectual level taking the form of slowness, perseveration, disorders of memory and spatial functions. In addition, the investigators noted occasional withdrawal and personality constrictions.

Tridione. Exceedingly effective drug for the control of *petit mal* epilepsy. Little effect for grand mal and minor motor seizures.

REACTION. Photophobia (or, abnormal intolerance to light) is the most frequent side reaction observed. A study performed by Sloan and Gilger (1947) indicated that, in their patients, there was a temporary impairment of visual acuity, brightness sensitivity, color discrimination and sensitivity to flicker. Those patients studied for more than three months developed tolerance to these visual effects. (These results pertained to general population not specifically cerebral palsied children). In addition, headache, diplopia, vertigo, increased irritability and drowsiness are occasionally found.

Paradione. Used in those patients with *petit mal* epilepsy. It is the drug of third choice for the control of petit mal by Livingston (1966).

REACTION. Similar to those of Tridione (observed less frequently with Paradione). May, however, cause drowsiness in some cases.

Dexedrine. Controls spells of *petit mal* epilepsy in some (not as effective as Zarontin). Useful also in the management of the hyperkinetic syndrome—See under *Behavior*).

REACTIONS. Relatively free of significant side-effects. Most significant which may occur are increased irritability, restlessness, and insomnia.

3. Mixed Types

Milontin. Reported by Livingston (1966) to be the least effective of Zarontin and Celontin.®

REACTIONS. May observe drowsiness and/or unsteadiness of gait occasionally. Rash has been noted by Denhoff.

Peganone. According to Livingston (1966), this drug "possesses very weak anticonvulsant properties." May be used in mild cases of epilepsy whose seizures are refractory to all the primary anticonvulsant drugs.

REACTION. Relatively free of side effects. Occasionally rashes, ataxia and diplopia have been observed.

Phenurone. The Council on Drugs of the American Medical Association (1961) warns that Phenurone "should be employed only by physicians experienced in the treatment of epilepsy and only in patients whose seizures are difficult or impossible to control with other recognized anticonvulsants."

REACTION. Most frequent is adverse change in behavior or personality (such as destructiveness, belligerence, marked irritability, restlessness, and depression).

Diamox. Used in conjunction with other anticonvulsants. "Successful control may be achieved when it was hitherto difficut" (Peterman, 1952).

REACTION. Anorexia, drowsiness, vomiting, irritability, headache, fatigue, dizziness, enuresis, paresthesia, ataxia, depression, irregular respiration, polyuria, skin rash, abdominal distention and cyanosis (Chao *et al.*, 1961). Denhoff mentions rash as a limiting side effect.

It is interesting to note that drowsiness seems to be a common toxic effect among the effective anticonvulsants.

Phenobarbital. See under Mebaral. Denhoff (1966b) warns that, if possible, the use of phenobarbital should be avoided in children with cerebral dysfunction as, "it tends to produce irritable behavior."

RELAXATION OF MUSCLES

Pharmacological treatment in this area is used primarily as an aid in (not a substitute for) the physical rehabilitation (or habilitation) of the cerebral palsied child. These drugs are used to help the child relax—to decrease hypertonus and abnormal postures— and to relieve and allay emotional tension such as the child's fear of being *stretched* in therapy; or being placed in a group; wearing braces; and gait training. Drugs have their greatest value in the cerebral palsied in helping the child behave so that the therapist (and teacher) can put him to work in a meaningful productive manner (Denhoff, 1966). Unfortunately, a drug with all the desired qualities (i.e. skeletal muscle relaxer as well as one that will favorably influence the child's emotions and attitudes) is yet to be uncovered or discovered. The search does, however, continue. Table XXIV refers to drugs used for their skeletal muscle relaxation properties in the spastic cerebral palsied child. Of late, the use of tranquilizers have come into their own and have been successfully employed in the treatment of cerebral palsy as muscle relaxants. (See Table XXIII).

Discussion of Table XXIII

Keats (1965), referring to chlordiazepoxide (Librium®) and diazepam (Valium®), stated that these drugs are "invaluable aids in brace and cast tolerance and in the post-operative management of children." Hunziker's (1960) results of a study of 168 patients with neuromuscular involvements show that in his experience, at least, Librium was superior to Meprobamate (Equinil®) in

TABLE XXIII

DRUGS USED FOR OVERALL RELAXANT EFFECT
MEDICATION

Generic Name	Trade Name	Average Dosage
Meprobamate	Equinil® (Wyeth) Miltown® (Wallace)	200-400 mg t.i.d.
Carisoprodol	Soma® (Wallace)	150-350 mg t i d.
Emylcamate	Striatran® (Merck, Sharp & Dohme)	100-200 mg t.i.d.
Chlordiazepoxide	Librium (Roche)	5- 10 mg b.i.d.
Benzodiazepin	Valium (Roche)	2.5- 10 mg t.i.d.

(Reprinted with permission. Denhoff, Eric: *Cerebral Palsy — The Preschool Years.* Springfield, Thomas, 1967.)

inhibiting positional and postural reflexes and in blocking the spinal reflexes. Plum and Thorn (1961) stated that Librium was the "most effective drug" they had employed in the past ten years. It is interesting to note the results of a study performed by Keats (1965). This investigation involved a study of Librium in a group of 86 children with cerebral palsy ranging in ages from three to sixteen. The series included 36 spastics, twenty-three with rigidity, seventeen athetoids, eight ataxic and two flaccid cases. Among the important conclusions drawn are the following:

1. Chlordiazepoxide (Librium) is tolerated by the spastic type of cerebral palsy patient better than by the other groups. (The results of therapys in this group were not, however, as good as those in the rigidity and athetoid types).

2. Athetoid and ataxic patients cannot tolerate high doses.

3. The drug improves the emotional status of the cerebral palsy child and aids his progress in the physical therapy schedule. They became more cheerful; lost their fear and apprehension.

4. It exerts a muscle relaxant effect in the rigidity groups.

5. The drug may improve involuntary movements in the athetoid group.

6. Chlordiazepoxide worsens gait and motion in the ataxic patient.

REACTIONS. Ataxia, nausea and vomiting, drowsiness, and fatigability. Keats concludes by saying that, "the fact that roughly half of the group received both physical and psychological benefit from Chlordiazepoxide without experiencing side effects seems truly remarkable." Librium's advantage over other drugs is, according to Denhoff (1967), its beneficial anticonvulsant action combined with its calming effects on behavior.

Diazepam (Valium). Another tranquilizer which has been found useful in the cerebral palsied child with spasticity and athetosis. Diazepam is regarded by some authorities as the most effective remedy at present available for relief of spasticity (Lancet, 1970). In addition, "in animal studies it is about five times more potent than Librium in muscle relaxant activity and tranquilization, and ten times as strong as Librium as an anticonvulsant" (Denhoff, 1967). Keats (1965) studied the effects of diazepam on ninety children with cerebral palsy including: forty-one with spasticity, twenty-one with rigidity, twenty with athetosis, four with ataxia, two with flaccidity and mixed spasticity-athetosis in one. Results: Diazepam was most effective in the athetoids, not proving useful in children with spastic and ataxic forms of cerebral palsy, and questionably useful in those with rigidity. The major side effects were drowsiness and ataxia. Phelps (1963) also found diazepam to be more effective in athetoids than in spastics. And, the somatic effect appeared to be more marked than the psychic effect. It is interesting to note that tranquilizing drugs seem to be of more effect in reducing muscle tone in the athetoids. As mentioned previously, emotional factors seems to increase muscle tone in the athetoid thus triggering off involuntary movements. Perlstein (1958) offers this rationale for the use of tranquilizing drugs in this group: "These drugs act on the sub-cortical mid-brain reticular areas and/or in their descending pathways and may reduce the emotional and other alerting triggers which increase tone and tension." Refer to the following for additional investigations in the use of diazepam in the treatment of cerebral palsy:

Denhoff, E., Cerebral palsy—a pharmacologic approach. *Clin Pharmacol Ther, 5*:947-954, 1964.

Denhoff, E.: Diazepam (Valium) in cerebral palsy. *Rhode Island Med J, XLVII*:429-441, 1964.

Engle, H. A.: The effect of diazepam (Valium) in children with cerebral palsy. *Develop Med Child Neurol, 8*:661, 1966.

Keats, S., Morgese, A., and Nordeund, T.: The role of diazepam in the comprehensive treatment of cerebral palsy children. *Western Med,* 4:22-25, 1963.

Phelps, W. M.: Observations of a new drug in cerebral palsy athetoids. *Invest Med,* 4:22, 1963.

Rapp, S., and Carter, C. H.: Use of a polygraph to measure spastic activity in athetoid patients. *J New Drugs,* 6:49-54, 1966

Meprobamate. Major advantage of Meprobamate, according to Denhoff, is its usefulness "in emotionally disturbed athetoids with epilepsy. It can be used to replace Thorazine® when the latter is contraindicated because of seizure activity."

Carisoprodol (Soma). This drug has been used widely to reduce muscle spasm (Spears, 1960). Wood's (1962) study indicated more improvement in athetoids than in spastics. The side effects reported in this study include drowsiness and irritability.

TABLE XXIV

DRUGS USED FOR MUSCLE RELAXATION IN CEREBRAL PALSY

	Medication	
Generic Name	*Trade Name*	*Average Dosage*
Mephenesin	Tolserol® (Squibb)	250-500 mg t.i.d.*
Mephenesin Carbamate	Tolseram® (Squibb)	250-500 mg t.i.d.†
Chlorzoxazone	Paraflex® (McNeil)	250 mg t.i.d.‡
Methocarbamol	Robaxin® (Robbins)	250 mg t.i.d.§

*32 per cent effectiveness
†Similar to Tolserol
‡While it appears to be nontoxic, office studies have not demonstrated that this drug possesses unequivocable muscle relaxant properties when used in cerebral palsy.
§Although drug-placebo studies have not been done, in office practice its action has been like mephenesin.
(Reprinted with permission. Denhoff, Eric: *Cerebral Palsy—The Preschool Years.* Springfield, Thomas, 1967.)

BEHAVIOR AND DRUGS

Drugs which may have an ameliorating effect on hyperkinetic behavior disorders of organic etiology (characteristics so commonly associated with the CP/NI child) are shown in Table XXVI. When discussing pharmacological management, it is necessary to dicotomize hyperkinetic or organic behavior from such behaviors as fear and anxiety (Table XXV)—the products of environmental factors. However, a complete disassociation cannot be made as

TABLE XXV

DRUGS USED FOR ANXIETY AND FEAR REDUCTION
IN CEREBRAL PALSY

Medication		
Generic Name	*Trade Name*	*Average Dosage*
Chlorpromazine	Thorazine (SKF)	10-25 mg t.i.d.
Thioridiazine	Mellaril ® (Sandoz)	10-25 mg t.i.d.
Thioxanthene*	Taractan ® (Roche)	10-25 mg t.i.d.

*Similar to thorazine in its tranquilizing abilities. Used for mood depressions and muscle hypertonia and dystonia.
(Reprinted with permission. Denhoff, Eric: *Cerebral Palsy—The Preschool Years.* Springfield, Thomas, 1967.)

"emotional problems arise as hyperkinesis creates a host of sec-ondary environmental problems" (Denhoff, 1967). We may find one feeding on the other. Consequential to the child's brain damage, he may be unable to control his behavior. He may be tense and rigid; he may even resist the teacher, therapist and family. Environmental responses to such behavior may only in-tensify or reinforce his acting out. Or, the child may withdraw which again may produce displeasing antisocial behavior. The delineation between organic and environmental factors is neces-sary because barbituates (sedatives) often aggravate the behavior disorder of organic origin. At first blush, this would appear to be a seemingly contradictory situation. A possible explanation for this paradox—a sedative actually acting in reverse by aggra-vating or further irritating a child's behavior—is proposed by Gor-don (1967). Because hyperkinetic impulse behavior theoretically, at least, is due to diencephalic dysfunction (brain damage) which ren-ders the system incapable of selecting and/or filtering sensory input, the child may "react first to one stimulus and then to another . . . the effect of barbituate sedation would then be to make an in-efficient function even more inefficient" (Gordon, 1967). That is, any defenses the child may still retain in spite of the brain damage is further weakened through sedation permitting even more bombardment of stimuli to an already chaotic situation. Paine (1968) postulates that "possibly there is some cerebral mechanism for inhibition, that is to say, for selective responsive-ness or unresponsiveness to stimuli on the basis of past experience, which is defective or late in maturing."

The amphetamines (CNS stimulants), according to Denhoff (1967), are ineffectual or have an adverse effect in behavior disturbances without organic components. In the general population, amphetamines (e.g. Dexedrine and Benzedrine) act as stimulants to the central nervous system. These drugs increase one's wakefulness, emotional outlook, and alertness. In children with brain dysfunction, however, amphetamines have somewhat of an emollient effect; that is, they tend to calm down and soothe the hyperactive child. The child is given new abilities. There appears to be a diminution of disturbances to activity, his abilities to attend to tasks is lengthened, his affect is improved, and he is easier to manage as he is less compulsive. He is able to think before doing—his behavior is more stable or as Nellhause (1968) states, "dextroamphetamines and other psychotropic drugs . . . aims at reducing the *neuronal noise.*" Denhoff feels that amphetamines are beneficial also in mentally retarded children with the hyperkinetic syndrome. Also, Dexedrine and Benzedrine have been used successfully in treating epilepsy to counteract drowsiness (Denhoff, 1966). (See also Livingston *et al.*, 1949, for a study of the use of these drugs in the control of *petit mal* and their beneficial affects on behavior). Among the reported side effects of Dexedrine and Benzedrine are difficulties in falling asleep and appetite reduction. In such cases, amphetamines may need to be discontinued. If so, the next four drugs on Table XXVI are recommended by Denhoff as substitutes.

Paine (1968) feels that amphetamines or methylphenidate (Ritalin®) will be of significant benefit to about 50 percent of the children with minimal brain damage. See Whitehouse *et al.* (1963), Eisenberg and Conners (1963) and Eisenberg *et al.* (1965) for studies indicating the efficacy of stimulant drugs in treating hyperkinesis. Ritalin (Methylphenidate) has similar properties to amphetamines having less tendency to produce loss of appetite. In a study of Millichap *et al.* (1968) the effects of Ritalin (Methylphenidate hydrocholoride) were evaluated in 30 children with hyperactivity and learning disorders. The conclusion of this study is that Ritalin in the short-term treatment of children with such disorders has been found to induce "small but measurable improvements" in tests of general intelligence and visual-motor

TABLE XXVI
DRUGS USED FOR HYPERKINESIS AND LEARNING PROBLEMS
IN CEREBRAL PALSY

	Medication	
Generic Name	*Trade Name*	*Average Dosage*
d-Amphetamine sulfate	Dexedrine (SKF)	5-10 mg A.M. and Noon
l-Amphetamine sulfate	Benzedrine (SKF)	10-20 mg A.M. and Noon
Captodiamine	Suvren® (Ayerst)	50-100 mg t.i.d.
Deanol	Deaner® (Rikder)	300 mg once daily for 3 weeks, then 100 mg once daily
		5-10 mg once daily
Reserpine/methylphenidate	Reserpine/ritalin	5-10 mg t.i.d.
Methyl phenidate	Ritalin (Ciba)	10-20 mg t.i.d.

(Reprinted with permission. Denhoff, Eric: *Cerebral Palsy—The Preschool Years.* Springfield, Thomas, 1967.)

perception. But Millichap finally concludes with guarded opinion: "The use of this drug and other therapies in the management of learning disorders must await their evaluation by long-term controlled studies."

For a more detailed, medically-oriented discussion concerning the drugs listed on Table XXVI the interested reader is urged to consult Denhoff's book *Cerebral Palsy. The Pre-School Years,* pp. 64-66, Springfield, Thomas, 1967. In addition, consult the article by Millichap *et al.* (1967) which is a review of the literature concerning drugs used for children with hyperactivity and learning disorders. The results of drug trials are tabulated, giving author, method of trial and side effects. Drugs which are tabulated include Methylphenedate (Ritalin); Amphetamines (Benzedrine and Dexedrine); Deanol; Chlordiazeporide (Librium); Chlorpromazine (Thorazine);[42] Reserpine (Serpasil®); Miscellaneous tranquilizers (Atarax®, Vistaril®, Miltown, Equinal, Prolixin, Taractan®, Sparine®, Librium analogue, (R05-4556); Anticonvulsants (Phenobarbital, Dilantin and Mysoline®).

In conclusion, it should again be strongly emphasized that in attempting to familiarize the reader with the various pharmacological agents (implications for use, reactions, side effects etc.)

[42]In general, it is important to note that Thorazine may produce seizures. In such cases, anticonvulsants would be prescribed along wth the Thorazine.

used with the CP/NI, it was not the purpose to suggest that the reader attempt to apply usage of these agents himself. Use of these drugs must be prescribed by a physician and be administered under his guidance.

A word of caution is in order. Due to the rapid advances in the medical sciences, this chapter will, in all likelihood, be partially antiquated before the book is published. It is self-evident that such advances will ultimately replace much present learning. However, this process appears to be especially true in the case of drug therapy medication. The reader interested in this particular area is therefore advised to seek information on the latest developments to augment the material presented in this chapter concerning the pharmacological management of the cerebral palsied and learning disabled child.

REFERENCES

Carter, S., and Gold, A. P.: Acute infantile hemiplegia. *Ped Clin N Amer, 14* (4) 851-864, 1967.

Chao, D. H. C., and Plumb, R. L.: Diamox in epilepsy: A critical review of 178 cases. *J Pediatr, 58*:211, 1961.

Churchill, J. A.: A study of hemiplegic cerebral palsied. *Dev Med Child Neurol, 10*:453-459, 1968.

Chusid, J. G., and McDonald, J.: *Correlative Neuroanatomy and Functional Neurology.* 13th ed. Los Altos, Lange Medical Publications, 1969.

Crothers, B., and Paine, R. S.: *The Natural History of Cerebral Palsy.* Cambridge, Mass., Harvard University Press, 1959.

Denhoff, E., and Robinault, I. P.: *Cerebral Palsy and Related Disorders.* New York, McGraw, 1960.

Denhoff, Eric.: Cerebral Palsy: Medical aspects. In *Cerebral Palsy Its Individual and Community Problems.* Cruickshank, William M. (Ed.), Syracuse, Syracuse University Press, 1966, p. 81.

Denhoff, E.: Early recognition of cerebral dysfunction in pediatric practice. *Clin Pediatr, 5*:334-341, 1966b.

Denhoff, Eric. *Cerebral Palsy: The Preschool Years.* Springfield, Thomas, 1967.

Denhoff, E., and Holden, R. H.: The effectiveness of chlorpromazine (Thorazine) and cerebral palsied children. *J Pediatr, 47*:328-332, 1955.

Eisenberg, L., and Connors, C. K.: The effects of methylphenidate on symptomatology and learning in disturbed children. *Am J Psychiatry, 120*:458, 1963.

Eisenberg, L., Conners, C. K., and Sharpe, L.: A controlled study of the differential application of outpatient psychiatric treatment for children. *Jap J Child Psychiatry, 6*:125, 1965.

Gordon, N.: The side-effects of antiepileptic drugs (Annotations). *Dev Med Child Neurol, 9*:239-241, 1967.

Guey, J., Harles, C., Coquery, C., Roger, J., and Soulayral, R.: Study of the psychological effects of ethosuximide (Zarontin) on 25 children suffering from petit mal epilepsy. *Epilepsia, 8*,129-141, 1967.

Hunziker, H.: Untersuchungen Über die Muskel-relaxierende Werkung von Librium Ro 5-0690 bei rheumatischen affeklionen. *Ther Umsch, 17*:315, 1960.

Keats, Sidney. *Cerebral Palsy*. Springfield, Thomas, 1965.

Lancet: Diazepam in spasticity. *Lancet,* i ,1161 (Leading article), 1970.

Livingston, E., Kajda, L., and Bridge, E. M.: The use of benzedrine and dexedrine sulfate in the treatment of epilespy. *J Pediatr, 32*:490-494, 1949.

Livingston, Samuel: *Drug Therapy for Epilepsy*. Springfield, Thomas, 1966.

Malamud, N. *et al.*: An etiologic and diagnostic study of cerebral palsy. *J Pediatr, 65*:270, 1964.

Millichap, J., Gordon, F., and Glenn, W.: Treatment of 'Minimal Brain Dysfunction' syndromes: Selection of drugs for children with hyperactivity and learning disabilities. *Ped Clin N Amer, 14*:767-777, 1967.

Millichap, J. G. *et al.*: Hyperkinetic behavior and learning disorders. III. Battery of neuropsychological tests in controlled trial of methylphenidate. *Am J Dis Child, 116*:235-244, 1968.

Nellhaus, G.: What name for 'these' children? *Dev Med Child Neurol, 10*:536-537, 1968.

Paine, R. S.: Syndromes of 'minimal cerebral damage.' *Ped Clin N Amer, 15* (3):779-801, 1968.

Penfield, W., and Jasper, H.: *Epilepsy and the Functional Anatomy of the Human Brain*. Boston, Little, 1954.

Phelps, W. M.: Observations of a new drug in cerebral palsied athetoids. *Invest Med, 4*:22, 1963.

Plum, P., and Thorn, I.: Zur medikamen tösen Behandlung des cerebraen Kinder lähmung. *Annales Paediatrici, 197*:62, 1961.

Perlstein, M. A., and Hood, P.: Infantile spastic hemiplegia. III. Intelligence. *Pediatrics, 15*:677, 1955.

Perlstein, M. A.: The role of drugs in treatment of cerebral palsy. In Illingsworth, R. S. (Ed.): *Cerebral Palsy*. Boston, Little Brown and Co., 1958.

Peterman, M. G.: Treatment of convulsions in childhood. *Am J Dis Child, 84*:409-415, 1952.

Shanks, R. A.: The management of seizures in infancy and early childhood. *Dev Med Child Neurol, 3*:583-590, 1961.

Sloan, L. L., and Gilger, A. P.: Visual effects of Tridione. *Am J Ophthalmol, 30*:387, 1947.

Spears, C. E.: *The Pharmocology and Clinical Usefulness of Cariosoprodol.* Detroit, Wayne, 1960, p. 138.

Whitehouse, D. I., Conners, C. K., Molling, P. A., and Eisenberg, L.: The effects of methylphenidate and phenobarbital in retarded hyperkinetic children. Unpublished manuscript. 1963.

Woods, G. E.: Preliminary clinical trial of carisoprodol in infantile cerebral palsy. *Dev Med Child Neurol, 4*:28-33, 1962.

Chapter Nine

SYSTEMS OF THERAPY

A SYSTEM OF TREATMENT IS A COMPLEX OF ideas used in an orderly procedure in the process of treating a patient. There are many therapeutic methods proposed for treating the cerebral palsied child or the child with brain damage. The various systems can be seen in the following framework: (1) the traditional approach. The aim here is to train muscles in isolation and groups of muscles through somewhat specific exercises, either on the muscle re-education basis or to compensate for involved musculature. There is a heavy emphasis on auxiliary equipment such as braces, splints, pulleys, parallel bars, weights and pulleys; also included in this approach is orthopedic surgery and drugs; (2) Neurophysiological or sensorimotor (central) approach. The aim of treatment involves the exteroceptors and proprioceptors and use of reflexes (inhibition or facilitation via appropriate stimulation) to improve postural and movement patterns; and (3) the Combined (or eclectic) approach. Proponents of this approach do not adhere to any specific regime but, rather, feel that there is no one best method of treatment. Some aspects of all the methods are used in this general method.

There are basic principles common to all the treatment systems which will become evident as the reader studies each of the systems discussed in the following pages. One such basic concept is the fact that most, if not all, of the treatment systems to be discussed are based on developmental orientations. Therefore, a solid knowledge of the normal developmental sequence contributes invaluable assistance to treatment planning irregardless of which system is used. This is the reason for the belabored presentation of the *Task Level Evaluation,* Appendix A. As Denhoff (1960) points out, "the brain-injured child does not follow atypical roads to bizarre maturity; rather he becomes arrested along the road as his deficiencies at various stages become apparent." As is true in the normal child, development of the CP/ NI goes from sensory to motor to perceptual to conceptual stages. According to Huss (1969), the following are principles which are basic to all the various techniques to be discussed. She feels that therapists should use these principles in the treatment of patients in the area of physical dysfunction (cerebral palsy is included).

1. The patient must be progressed through normal developmental sequences and should not attempt to develop fine skills before gross motor patterns are established.

2. Resistance properly applied and graded in total movement patterns enhances motor output.

3. Joint traction produces a flexion response.

4. Joint compression of more than body weight produces an extension or postural response.

5. Quick stretch is facilitory to the muscle stretched while a prolonged, forceful stretch is facilitory to flexors and inhibitory to extensors.

6. Various sensory stimuli influence the motor system and can inhibit or facilitate it depending on the method and area of application. (Table XXVII and XXVIII).

7. The motor system learns through repetition on a subconscious level.

The system descriptions which follow are not intended to include all those that are used in treatment nor should each particular discussion be considered all inclusive. The following represents summaries of some of the more widely used approaches. The reader is encouraged to consult the original works for a more detailed analysis.

THE PHELPS SYSTEM

Phelps (1940, 1941, and 1948) proposed one of the first systems of therapy for the treatment of children with cerebral palsy. This method is based on the ontogenetic plan so that child development scales are used as a preliminary to treatment. Stressed in this system is treatment of individual muscles.

There are two major principles employed in this method. The first, the use of conditioning exercises based on Pavlov's principles and Sherrington's law of reciprocal innervation[43] in order to establish reciprocal motions. The second is the use of Jacobsen's principles in order to develop purposeful movement of the relaxed position. The treatment is started with the least involved extremity and gradually extends to include all the muscles of the body. From relaxation, the child is progressed to motion from the relaxed position, balance, reciprocation, reach, grasp and release, and the adaptation of skills. Contraction or relaxation of muscles is achieved either by the therapist or by such mechanical devices as braces and other supportive equipment as well as by drugs. Phelps employs 15 modalities to assist in developing the cerebral palsy child. These modalities range from massage and the different types of motion principles, to the principle of relaxation as employed in Jacobsen's book on progressive relaxation (1959).

Because the individual muscle is stressed, a thorough muscle evaluation is a prerequisite to treatment planning. Several types of muscles are recognized. (1) Normal muscle. The normal muscle is capable of contracting to the desired degree of tenseness and is able to relax when its antagonist contracts, (2) Spastic muscles. These muscles are hyperirritable, and they react to stretching by contraction which interferes with motion, (3) Flaccid muscle (or, zero cerebral). This muscle lacks power to contract voluntarily. There is pathological overflow. In the cerebral palsy, a stretch reflex may flow over to produce stretch reflexes in other body parts. The strength of the muscles is also evaluated to determine the power each muscle has. After the muscle evaluation, the treatment program is begun.

Brief mention has been made about the use of the fifteen modalities used in the Phelps system. These modalities with a brief description follow.

1. *Massage.* Used to increase power and tone of weak muscles

---

[43]Increase of contraction in one muscle is synchronous with decrease of contraction in its opposng (antagonist) muscle.

by improving circulation and nutrition of individual muscles. This method is actually used very little in the spastic. These movements of massage tend to increase the existing hypertonicity.

2. *Passive motion.* Treatment is more likely to begin with this step. The rationale behind this stage is that before the child can correct an abnormal motion he must first be shown by the therapist how to make the motion without the child's voluntary effort.

3. *Active assisted motion* (follows passive motion). The therapist moves the extremity through a pattern of movement with some help from the child.

4. *Active motion.* The child performs the motion without the therapist's assistance.

5. *Resisted motion.* The therapist manually applies resistance to the child's motion thus the muscle works against the pull of gravity. This technique is used to increase strength in the muscles. Used in the advanced stages of therapy.

6. *Conditioned motion.* The main idea here: conditioning a certain movement so that it will respond to a certain stimulus (command). An example would be singing a specific rhyme to a child for each motion he is to learn during the passive and active assisted steps. It is hoped that the child will automatically perform the motion upon stimulus presentation.

7. *Automatic or confused motion.* This method is used principally for flaccid muscles. The rationale operating behind this stage is that a flaccid muscle can be activated by an overflow of impulses from a resisted motion of another part of the body.

8. *Combined motion.* An advanced modality, two motions or actions are brought together. This modality is used with all types of cerebral palsied. It teaches the child to carry out motions involving combinations of movements at two joints. A child would be taught elbow flexion and shoulder adduction which is necessary for such everyday tasks as self-feeding. It is at this point that occupational therapy is brought into the program if the program is based on the Phelps approach.

9. *Rest, body braces, special equipment* (such as chairs and tables) and other devices are used to control unnecessary or unwanted motion.

10. *Differential relaxation.* This modality is used to reduce

tension and involuntary motion. This is used in treating athetoids and some spastic patients. The child is taught to recognize feelings of tightness and looseness in his muscles. The child is taught by a direct method of sensation of relaxation. This is accomplished by asking the child to tense a group of muscles against resistance; this is followed by sudden withdrawal of resistance and a sudden relaxing of tension by the patient. The sensation of looseness or relaxation is then felt by the child so that he learns the difference between tenseness and relaxation.

11. *Spontaneous motion from the relaxed position.* This modality is used primarily with athetoids. It is voluntary motion at will.

12. *Balance training.* This is a learned function beginning from head balance through upright balancing.

13. *Reciprocation.* This is used in conjunction with the other modalities from the beginning of treatment. It is the ability to immediately reverse the direction of motion.

14. *Reach and grasp.* One of the last steps in treatment.

15. *Bodily skills.* This is the final step in treatment and stresses feeding, dressing, grooming, communication skills.

PROPRIOCEPTIVE NEUROMUSCULAR FACILITATION

This technique is known as the Kabat (1947) technique. His hypothesis is that by means of stimulation of the propioceptive system by using reversal of antagonists, it is possible to stimulate the motor cortex. He states, "In order to restore power in paralyzed muscles one should strive for 'maximal activation of the motor units of the affected muscles with effort'." The techniques for applying The Kabat System were refined by Dr. Herman Kabat and two physical therapists, Knott and Voss (1956).

Proprioceptive neuromuscular facilitation (PNF) is really what most of the facilitation techniques are all about. This method is again developmental. As the name would imply, there is a strong emphasis on the role of proprioception in producing movement. Found in this system is active participation of the child as opposed to passive patterning in the Fay System. It is based on the belief of using spiral and diagonal patterns of movement. The two diagonals of motion for each of the major parts of the body consists of the components of flexion and extension which are always combined with lateral motion and rotation. The receptor mechanism is stimulated (facilitated) through the use of these mass movement patterns producing voluntary movement. Other techniques used (some of which will be discussed in succeeding paragraphs) are stretch, reversal of antagonists, resistance and postural and righting reflexes to *activate* a maximum number of motor units. A common feature of both the Bobath and PNF approaches is the use of *sensory* cues. Reinforcement is aided by stimulation of skin receptors and by verbal commands. Again, the whole idea is to use sensory stimulus to get a motor response. And again, this theory uses maximal resistance. The amount of muscle activity depends upon the percent of motor units excited. There must be something extremely positive about using this technique *(resistance)* to gain a motor response because all the facilitation theories implement it.

Knott emphasizes the use of *repetition* of motion and *goal-directed activities* to facilitate performance. (This is a real plug for the occupational therapist). Spiral and diagonal patterns are one such movement repetition employed in this approach. "Powerful facilitation of the voluntary responses of a paralyzed muscle can be brought about through performance of a mass movement pattern of an entire extremity against resistance" (Kabat, 1952). Some of these patterns are not unlike a pure flexion and extension pattern. In fact, one of the spiral and diagonal patterns is the flexion pattern spiral and diagonal, then to a full extension pattern spiral and diagonal. There are, of course, others such as flexion or adduction combined with flexion and supination and, abduction combined with extension and pronation which is like mixing the synergies of Brunnstrom. Kabat and Knott have put together a book which is entitled *Proprioceptive Neuromuscular Facilitation* which contains about 100 pages of different spiral and diagonal patterns of the upper and lower extremity in which the basic flexion and extension synergies are used and mixed in all the various possible ways.

Principles of the PNF System. Knott bases her methods on the following *principles:* (1) Normal development is cervico-caudal (as in head to tail) and proximal to distal (as in shoulder to hand);[44] (2) Early motor development is reflex. If, in normal development, *reflexes* exist they will be used in treatment to *reinforce* voluntary effort. The child is positioned so that the therapist can manually facilitate movement. That is, so that tonic reflexes like the tonic neck and tonic labyrinthine reflexes can either facilitate or inhibit, assist or resist, the desired motion. In this, then, she agrees with Brunnstrom but does not agree with Bobath. The Bobaths *inhibit* primitive reflexes and get to the others. Brunnstrom and Knott both *use* the primitive reflexes (a baby uses them, therfeore, they are considered normal to development); (3) Early motor behavior (movement) is spontaneous. The baby kicks in flexion and extension. Therefore, Knott is going to use, in treatment, reversing movements such as flexion-extension, abduction-adduction; (4) Developing motor behavior has a sequence. This is seen in Bobath's method (Assessment Chart) and in Rood's ontogenetic motor patterns. These and others, such as Gesell's developmental schemata, has the baby going through certain developmental stages in sequence; (5) As motor behavior develops, there is a shift in dominance between flexion and extension. Flexion and extension takes precedence in development. When sitting flexion is dominant; when standing, extension is dominant. Knott uses this idea of the shift between flexion and extension to encourage an individual. As in the crawling position, she would have the child rock so that he is supporting with extensors and supporting with flexors to be able to shift back and forth from the one to the other; (6) There is overlapping in motor behavior. When a child is developing one skill, development of another skill should begin. Skills are not developed in isolation or one at a time. While the therapist is trying to develop one

---

[44]Moore (1969, p. 17) makes this comment concerning the head-to-tail or cephalocaudal phenomenon:

Dominance or influence of the upper limbs over the lower ones should be remembered when working with patients. In order to obtain the best results, those components of the neuromuscular system which dominate others should be brought under control first, before attempting to achieve control in the less dominant areas. The head and neck have control over the upper limbs and upper trunk. In turn, the upper trunk and limbs have a dominating effect over the lower trunk and limbs. (This can be seen by analyzing the sequence of reflex development).

kind of movement pattern she should also work for other skills; (7) In normal movement, there is balance between agonists and antagonists. This led to a concentration treating or correcting imbalances; (8) Motor learning goes from reflex to voluntary control. Knott would agree with Brunnstrom on this. Knott would first stimulate reflex activity and guide the patient's efforts with some of the other techniques like maximal resistance; (9) Repetition promotes retention of motor learning. Once a response is observed there is a tendency for this response to be repeated. The response may be embedded by repeating the same motion. Repetition of activity and frequent stimulation also develops strength and endurance; and (10) Goal directed activities hasten learning. These then are all the principles that were used to develop the PNF System.

TECHNIQUES EMPLOYED IN THIS SYSTEM. The first one has previously been mentioned:
(1) Spiral and Diagonal Patterns. There are two basic diagonals that are used.

   i. Flexion-adduction and external rotation with the antagonistic extension-abduction and internal rotation as seen in Figure 50A where the right hand goes to the left ear, and Figure 50B where the right hand goes to the right toe.

  ii. Flexion-abduction-external rotation with its antagonistic extension-adduction-internal rotation. It is the same one as the flexion-extension synergies of Brunnstrom, and then reversed. The two basic diagonals can be seen in Figure 50C, right hand to right ear, and Figure 50D, right hand to left toe.

A   **B**   **C**   **D**

Figure 50. Spiral and Diagonal Patterns.
   a. Flexion-adduction and external rotation.
   b. Extension-abduction and internal rotation
   c. Flexion-abduction-external rotation.
   d. Extension-abduction-internal rotation.

(2) Rolling from supine to prone and from prone to supine.

(3) Positioning of patients to facilitate and make movement easier as they (the positions) may use postural reflexes or eliminate gravity etc.

(4) Evaluation is based on assessing developmental patterns rather than any kind of muscle tests or ADL tests. She is looking for a developmental sequence to determine where the child is presently functioning.

(5) From this evaluation, the child is led through the developmental sequence. This is very much like Bobath.

(6) Use of visual cues with the TNR. A child is told to look at body segment that is to be moved and then to look to direction of movement. They are thusly told to look at the hand that is to be moved and then told to look in the direction of movement. Bobath works manually with the child. She would, therefore, actually turn the child's head, shifting the child manually. Knott instructs the individual to turn his own head and shift to the other direction.

(7) Resistance.

(8) Rhythm and Rate. Flexion to extension, this ear to that knee. The movement must be smooth and rhythmical and repeat after itself so that it becomes established in a sequence. Rhythmical movements seem to require less effort. Rate is increased with improvement in function.

(9) One of the biggest contributions of this system is strong verbal commands. Voice commands become very important. If the child is receiving resistance to a pattern, the therapist would say "push" or "pull." This is intended to get the child to concentrate on what he is supposed to be doing. These commands should be goal directed. The therapist would not, therefore, say "extend your arm, flex your arm." Rather, she would tell the child to "reach up to your ear," "touch this pencil," "reach out towards my hand." This gives the child a goal. This goes along with the idea that voluntary movements are Area 4 controlled. Patterned movements are basal ganglia controlled as in walking. Knott is therefore trying to get a subcortical, or a more basic, controlling mechanism working in the child who has damage to cortical control. This kind of movement can very often be ob-

tained if the child is not directed specifically.[45] Rather, when they are directed to accomplish a *pattern of movement,* this is theoretically established in a more primitive brain area (subcortically). It is like asking a hemiplegic to flex his fingers when he is unable to voluntarily perform this task. But in a flexion *pattern,* they are apt to get flexion. Additionally, the motion is more apt to be obtained with strong verbal commands and goal-directed movements.

(10) Auxiliary agents such as cold, electrical stimulation, equipment (pulleys, braces, etc.) are used also in this system.

The therapist may expect to obtain the following kinds of return: Motions that are more primitive on the scale of development. That is, on a phylogenetic (as in human coming from ape) and ontogenetic (as in adult coming from baby) development. The more primitive kinds of movements would likely emerge first such as flexion of the head, shoulder extension and adduction; elbow flexion; internal rotation; ulnar deviation at the wrist and grasp. These are more primitive and therefore more easily elicited in a brain damaged child. The more advanced motions are all the opposites of the primitive movements and, in addition, rotation component like pronation-supination. Of pronation-supination, pronation is the more primitive motion, as the baby is able to do this first. The more advanced motions are: extension of the head, shoulder flexion and abduction, elbow extension, external rotation, radial deviation, release, and supination-pronation.

Brunnstrom Method[46]

This approach developed from the discovery of what actually worked in a clinical setting rather than theorizing that "if this happened, that must have occurred; therefore, we shall try such and such." In the Brunnstrom approach, we see a technique based

---

[45]When directed to perform a specific act or motion, the child is required to "think" which is a cortical function.

[46]For specifics of the Brunnstrom method see:

Brunnstrom, Signe: Training the Adult Hemiplegic Patient: Orientation of Techniques to Patient's Motor Behavior. In *Approaches to the Treatment of Patients with Neuromuscular Dysfunction.* C. Sattely (Ed.). Study Course VI, World Federation of Occupational Therapist (Dubuque, W. C. Brown Book Co., 1962), pp. 44-48.

on reflex training rather than reflex inhibiting. Brunnstrom believes in *using* the *reflexes* not just inhibiting them. The reflexes are used to correct muscular response. The method makes use of whatever exists in the way of the patient's ability to move. In addition to *using reflexes,* she also employs *sensory cues.* Although this approach usually applies to the adult hemiplegic, it can be successfully utilized in the treatment of the child with spasticity. The primary goal is to take the patient at his present level of function and, with *reflex* training, "attempt to provide the wedge which will allow him to progress from subcortical to cortical control of muscle function" (Perry, 1967).

There are four steps in reflex training: (1) *Synergies are elicited on a reflex level.* Synergies are a group of muscles working together. In fetal life, these movement patterns are the first to develop. They are also the first muscular activity to appear after damage to the pyramidal tract. The flexion synergy of the upper extremity contains the following components: retraction (adduction) of the scapula, shoulder abduction, external rotation, elbow flexion, forearm supination, flexion of the wrist, and finger flexion. The extensor pattern of the upper extremity (where the opposites hold true) are: scapular protraction (abduction), shoulder adduction, internal rotation, elbow extension and forearm pronation. Wrist and finger flexion are seen in both patterns. In each of these patterns, one component is said to be the strongest. This is the one that the therapist is most apt to see first; or, the one that is more easily elicited. In the flexor pattern, elbow flexion is the strongest component. In the extensor pattern, adduction of the shoulder (pectoralis major) is the strongest component. The therapist then attempts to elicit these synergies by using the existing reflexes. The goal in this system is to gain control of the flexion and extension synergies so that combinations of these synergies or movement patterns can be used in performing everyday activities.

Some of those reflexes which the therapist might use in her attempts to elicit flexion and extension patterns are:

(1) TONIC NECK REFLEX. If the therapist wants the child to extend his arm, she will turn his head towards this arm. If the therapist is attempting to elicit flexion, she would have the head

turn and look away from the side she wishes the child to flex.

(2) Tonic lumbar reflex. There is a rotation of the trunk. The trunk rotates toward the side the therapist is trying to flex and away from the side she is trying to extend. Or, the arms tend to flex, the legs tend to extend on side toward which the chest rotates.

(3) Tonic labyrinthine. When the child is in the supine position, there is more stimulus or the child is more apt to have increased tone in extension of the extremities. Whereas, if the child is in the prone position, there is more apt to be an increase in tone of flexors of the extremities. If you will think for a moment that when you place a baby down in his crib on his stomach he tends to curl up so that his legs and arms are under him (or flexed). Certain reflexes then are normal during certain stages of development. They gradually become controlled as the child develops higher level reflexes. These reflexes may, however, re-appear as a result of some kind of injury to the brain. This theory or method of treatment *uses* these reflexes just as a baby would use them in learning and going through the developmental sequence.

(4) The fourth kind of reflex that can be used is any one part of the total pattern which is used to assist the other components of that pattern. For instance, in the elbow, the flexors are the strongest. If the child seems to have some elbow flexion, the therapist will encourage this motion which she then hopes will carry over to the shoulder and forearm components.

Sensory stimulation is also used in this approach to elicit synergies. Passive movement is one such sensory technique. The therapist takes the extremity passively through the flexion pattern. Other sensory techniques are stretching, stroking, and tapping (more of this particular subject shortly). Once the therapist has (1) *elicited the synergy,* the next step is to, (2) *capture the motion* synergies, or, get the motions established, consistent and strong. The therapist might repeat the flexion and extension pattern with facilitation. The child is asked to concentrate proximally to distally so that he becomes aware of the motions (synergies or components thereof) and can freely use them. It is during this stage in which the therapist is trying to obtain smooth motion synergies that reciprocal motion and bilateral kinds of motion are very helpful. Sanding activities using the ball bearing skate or a rowing or pedaling motion may be used. Once the motion is *captured* and the child is able to follow through with complete flexion and extension, the therapist wants to (3) *condition* the motion synergies. This involves mixing up the components. That is, instead of always retracting after externally rotating, elbow flexion and forearm supination, the child might be able to retract, abduct, externally rotate and extend the elbow and pronate the forearm. Or, he may be able to adduct and protract, internally rotate and still be able to flex the elbow. The goal in therapy, regardless of the method, is to help the child become functional in a purposeful way. The therapist doesn't want the child to be able only to move his arm in the flexion to extension pattern. She wants him to be able to extend sometimes when abducted, and to flex sometimes when adducted. Just as in muscle reeducation techniques, the therapist passively takes the arm through a motion. It is hoped that this motion will eventually become "active" without assistance. The purpose, then, of this stage is to integrate or mix the motions into more functionally related patterns for such skilled tasks as feeding, dressing and reaching. Reflex components are still in evidence at this stage; however, the therapist is attempting to impose some voluntary control on the synergy. The therapist must select only one new motion at a time. All motions are kept in the pattern except one new motion.

The next stage is that of (4) *complete voluntary control* leading eventually to voluntary hand and finger function which is the last and most difficult motion to retrain in the hemiplegic arm.

Discussion. One phenomenon that Brunnstrom noted is called imitation synkinesis. When a child is attempting to move his involved hand, there are very often involuntary movements in the non-involved hand. These involuntary movements tend to serve as predictors as to where return might occur in the involved hand. If the therapist is trying to develop grasp, the index finger on the other side may flex and the thumb may draw in involuntarily. This may serve as a clue to the therapist as to what she may first try to elicit on the involved side. While the child is concentrating on the involved side, whatever is most apt to start returning will involuntarily occur on the non-involved side due to cross-connections in the spinal cord. This particular reflex training technique is a long-term procedure just as is the Bobath technique. Each step in treatment is established before moving on to the next step. It is most important to check the child's sensory involvement. Prognosis is much poorer with sensory loss especially if the loss is proprioceptive in nature.

Treatment is first directed toward trunk and head control using reflexes (tonic neck and lumbar reflexes, labyrinthine and righting reactions) to *facilitate* reflex postural adjustments. Next, shoulder girdle and hip muscles are stimulated by eliciting synergic actions. Then, attention is paid to the distal parts—the extremities, (the head to tail or cephalo caudle principle). For example, if the therapist is attempting to get a fist open, Brunnstrom has found several techniques to be successful. One such suggestion is: with arms overhead and forearm supinated, the fist tends to open (Fig. 88b, Appendix D). Or, in attempting to close the fist, the reverse is true—with arms down and the forearm pronated, the fist tends to close. In attempting to get the fingers to extend (to get the fist to open) the therapist might pull (extend) thumb back. This occurs frequently in the lives of children at play. When a child has something held firmly in the fist, his friend, by simply pulling his friend's thumb back, will "encourage" his friend to let go of the object being held in the fist. Also see Figures 91c and 91d Appendix D, for additional techniques to facilitate finger and wrist extension.

Other techniques are:

(1) *Proprioceptive stimulation*—a) brisk tapping over the muscle belly, b) resistance (used also in other Systems). Resistance is used on the affected side to give direction to the affected arm. Brunnstrom also believes in lateral facilitation. This is the method of using resistance to the normal side to get a response in the involved side. The rationale is that there are cross connections in the spinal cord. The strong components of a synergy may be resisted to help bring in the weaker ones. Elbow flexion in the flexion pattern may be resisted and the pectorals may be resisted in the extensor pattern. In resisting the strong component, the other components of that particular pattern tend to be elicited.

This phenomenon can be seen when an individual lifts or moves a heavy (resistance) object. Most every muscle that the person owns comes out to help. If the person is lifting something light, not as many muscles are required to perform.

Balance-of-power arguments can of course be raised concerning this point. Those who would support this would contend that one component may become so strong that it becomes a deforming force instead of a means of useful strength. This is possible but in the balance of power the therapist should be working to improve the strength of *all* muscles so that the good get better and so do the weak. The only harm would come when the therapist does not work with both the agonist and the antagonist, c) quick stretch to a muscle to gain a response. For example, if the therapist is going to "quick stretch" wrist extension, she would first push the wrist fast into flexion to put a stretch on the extension tendons. She would then ask for voluntary effort in extension.

(2) *Exteroceptive stimulation*—a) stroking, particularly stroking over the triceps to get elbow extension. Or, in trying to elicit extension of the IP joints of the fingers (extension) brushing over the dorsum of the hand is suggested which tends to encourage or stimulate or facilitate this motion. So it might be that the therapist has a child with his arm clear up in the air, forearm supinated, and at the same time she is brushing the back of the hand then suddenly the hand opens. Then she wonders which of the several techniques worked. The important point, however, is that one or all in combination achieved the purpose. One more achievement in the slow process of habilitation.

The Fay Method[47]

Fay's method is based on the phylogenetic plan which follows the order of normal physical progress found in the race.

Although the cerebral palsied child is unable, much of the time, to produce purposeful voluntary movement, he may retain many of the primitive reflex patterns or automatic spinal reflexes evidenced by such investigators as Sherrington and Babinski in decerebrate animals (i.e. the fish, amphibians, and the reptile).

[47]The term *patterning* has often been applied to this system. The Doman-Delacato system stems from the Fay approach.

Such primitive movements (e.g. the crossed-extension reflex) are possible without a cerebral cortex (decerebrate). Fay postulated that human movement parallels the evolution from the Amphibian, Reptilian and Mamalian eras (swimming, crawling, etc.) Elicitation of these primitive movement patterns is the core of this system. Thus, through stimulation of the proprioceptors through passive movement, the patient's brain is made aware of normal movement patterns and eventual cortical integration is hoped for (Fay, 1954). The aim in therapy is to get these lower-level reflexes coordinated or combined with the undamaged portions of the higher cortical control centers.

The therapeutic program begins with an evaluation of the child's reflex development. Therapy is then initiated at this level *using* the reflexes and automatic responses that are present. These existing movements are stimulated and elicited to inhibit antagonistic muscles, to develop muscles, and ultimately to produce coordinated movements. The first level in developing motor patterns is the fish or amphibian stage. This is the *homolateral pattern*. The rationale for the first step is that due to partial or complete loss of cortical control, the child must depend on the midbrain. Passive exercises are performed which, Fay believes, act on the sensory feedback mechanisms which ultimately leads (spontaneously) to progressively more mature movements. The amphibian crawling movement pattern is elicited by passively moving the extremities and head. The child is placed in the prone position (on his stomach), the arm and leg on one side is made to flex, the face is turned to the flexed arm. As the arm and leg are extended, the arm and leg of the opposite side are flexed, the head then rotates toward that side. This alternating movement is continued with regularity of rhythm until a definite pattern is developed.

The next level in the developmental sequence is called the *homologous pattern*. The head is held in midline with arms performing the flexion sequence, and the legs performing the extension sequence. Progressing next to the *crossed-diagonal pattern* of the reptilian stage. This level is characterized by crossed or contralateral movement patterns. The left arm flexes with the head simultaneously turning toward the left arm, and the right leg flexes. Ultimately, these movements are to be performed without passive assistance. Once the motions in the above steps are established, the child moves on to the quadruped level (all-fours position); and finally, on to the biped stage. Thusly, advanced patterns are developed such as creeping and crawling leading to the upright locomotion or walking stage.

Fay has described procedures for "unlocking" reflexes, i.e. unwanted reflex patterns are diminished or broken up by using specific stimuli. One such unlocking procedure suggested is to passively move the thumb into opposition to decrease finger flexor tone. Unlocking procedures, used repetitively (30 to 50 times) result in reduction of hypertonicity and serve to prepare for activity in total patterns of movement (Page, 825, 1967). See Fay, 1946, for a detailed description of methods to reduce hypertonicity.

BOBATH METHOD

The Bobaths feel that in order to understand their neurophysiological approach to the treatment of the cerebral palsy child, it is necessary to understand their rationale which is based on the concept developed by Walshe. He propounded the idea that the sensory system, by means of external receptors and proprioceptors, can initiate and continually direct willed movement (those activities of the nervous motor mechanism, the pyramidal system, which acts only as a passive common pathway between the sensory system and the cortex). Spasticity (abnormal muscle tone) will distort the function of the proprioceptive system; therefore, by reducing the spasticity, the proprioceptor system will be restored so that it can function normally. That is, pathological reflexes distort distribution of muscle tone. By reducing or inhibiting abnormal reflex activity, muscle tone can be favorably influenced The Bobath Method is based on the theory that any kind of CNS lesion (a cortical lesion), releases primitive reflexes[48] (postural

48There are some reflexes (the moro for instance) that are *inherent* or *built-in*. These remain throughout life but are gradually brought under the influence of higher control centers. They can be seen again especially as a result of brain damage. Other reflexes such as walking, talking and running are automatic or conditioned reflexes which have to be learned. That is, they had to be ingrained into the nervous system before they could become subcortical, or utilized as spontaneous reflex responses. (Moore, 1969, p. 14).

reflexes)[49] from the usual inhibition which is a function of the higher centers. These centers are damaged in the cerebral palsy child. Therefore, their function as inhibitors is also damaged. If there is a lesion in the brain stem or the brain, the reflexes in control are those below the site of lesion because these reflexes are permitted to function unchecked. Depending, then, on the site of lesion, the cerebral palsied child demonstrates primitive reflex patterns of posture and movement and abnormal muscle tone[50] which interferes and distorts normal postural patterns. How the Bobaths propose to *reduce* or *normalize* the abnormal muscle tone that interferes with normal development is what this system is all about.

In normal development, the primitive reflexes are gradually modified (resynthesized) into more mature patterns of movement. For instance, when righting reactions are active, their presence will inhibit tonic reflexes because the righting reactions are developmentally more mature. Brain damage throws up a roadblock; the incoming stimuli are rerouted through lower centers. The stimuli therefore are unable to benefit by the reorganization which is the function of the higher centers. Based on that theory, the Bobath's goal in treatment is to *inhibit* the primitive reflexes

[49]These postural reflexes, by regulating tone throughout the body, help to maintain posture and equilibrium of the body. They are located in the brain stem, midbrain, cerebellum, and basal ganglia. They are stimulated by the sensory end organs in the joints and muscles and also by the labyrinths. When these postural reflexes are allowed to function unchecked, an increased muscle tone or spasticity results. The righting reflexes play an important role here and are stimulated by tactile stimulation on the surface of the body and by optical righting reflexes.

[50]In spasticity, the muscle tone is abnormally high. In the athetoid and ataxic, the muscle tone varies between hypertonicity and hypotonicity. We may find an athetoid child able, in certain circumstances, to show fairly normal postural and movement patterns. However, under stress or when excited through over-stimulation of one sort or another, the child may revert to more primitive movement patterns. The child then, because of this fluctuating muscle tone, is unable to stabilize and maintain body postures and his movements become misdirected and unpredictable. The function of centers in the brain stem and midbrain regulate muscle tone. The Bobaths believe that "abnormal muscle tone is due to the release of these centers in the brain stem and midbrain from the inhibiting influence of the cerebral cortex" (Bobath, 1954). Or, ". . . postural adaptation is a function of reflex mechanisms situated in the brainstem and cerebellum. These mechanisms are not put out of action by higher CNS lesions resulting in syndromes e.g.: hemiplegia, instead appear to become exaggerated and done as a result of such lesion." (Walshe, 1923).

thus producing more normal muscle tone followed by *facilitation* of the higher reactions and reflexes according to a developmental sequence. In particular, the higher reactions which they are working for are righting and equilibrium reactions.[51] The primitive reflex patterns dominate the motor behavior in the cerebral palsied child. Thus, the tonic reflexes of the lower brain stem and spinal cord dominate the behavior of both spastic and athetoid (Bobath, 1959). The release of midbrain righting reactions from basal ganglia control results in some athetoid patterns (Denny-Brown, 1962; Twitchell, 1959).

Bobath's theory is developmental. This is common to all the theories of facilitation implemented in the treatment of cerebral palsy. Being developmental, there must be a way to evaluate the developmental sequence and determine where this normal development has been blocked. The therapist must determine which reactions are a) normal, b) pathological (reactions which are not considered a part of normal development—abnormal muscle tone and coordination); and c) primitive but nevertheless normal (motor development is retarded or those patterns that were, at one time, normal but did not disappear at the appropriate age level). The therapist must determine which movement the child is able to perform voluntarily, and which he can only do involuntarily, or merely as a reflex movement in response to a stimulus. The Cerebral Palsy Assessment chart provides a guide for this process. This Chart from the Occupational Therapy Department of Rancho Los Amigos Hospital[52] has been adapted from assessment charts developed by the Bobaths. It provides a summary of reflex-motor development sequence. The first portion of the chart describes the administration of the test. In addition, it

[51]Righting Reactions are automatic movements. Their purpose is to serve posture adjustment and maintain normal position of the head in relaton to space and to the rest of the body. They include: the neck righting, labyrinthine and body righting reactions. The Equilibrium Reactions are automatic movements whose function is to maintain and regain balance. They begin to appear at 6 months when the righting reactions are fully implanted or developed. The equilibrium reactions gradually modify the righting reactions. These reactions are stimulated by changing the positional relationship between body and space and/or body and supporting ground or surface.

[52]Published in *American Physical Therapy Association Journal, 45*:463-68, May, 1965.

describes a way in which the therapist records her findings. This can be changed to suit but the main thing is that the therapist records in some consistent way. The evaluation determines if the therapist can place the child in a position, if the child can maintain this position, and get into the position unassisted. In general, it assists the therapist in determining to what degree of normal the child is able to function. The form then goes on to describe each of the positions. The test postures and movements are given in stick figure form. The figures begin in the supine position and progress to things that can be done in the prone, then resting on elbows position, going on finally to sitting position, kneeling and standing. This developmental progression is much the same as proposed by such authorities as Gesell. The Assessment Chart, however, records development specifically in stages to be able to check positions. There are some finer gradations incorporated in this chart that are not noted in other developmental schemes. It therefore fills in a few of the gaps in the developmental progression. The Chart not only serves as a guide to evaluation but serves also as a guide to treatment in that it gives the next progression or level towards which the therapist should gear therapy. One point that Bobath stresses about each position is that it has some self-care function. If someone is having difficulty at one of these levels, the therapist might go on to the next two or so; but, generally, if the child is unable to perform on one level, he will begin to falter on the subsequent levels. The therapist then picks up on activities that might help the child to achieve on the level where he begins to have serious problems in performance.

In all tests, the therapist (1) places the child in the test position, (2) the child is then asked to stay in that position, and (3) the child is asked to move into the test position independently.

Having determined the child's level of motor development, the program is begun. The first step in therapy is to inhibit or suppress the primitive reflexes.

"RIP's" or "reflex-inhibiting patterns" are used to inhibit the abnormal postural patterns and to normalize muscle tone. The child is put into positions exactly opposite to the primitive reflex patterns which he demonstrates. These abnormal patterns are changed at some *key points* (which will later be described) and, at the same time, automatic or voluntary functional movements (normal postural reactions) are facilitated (Bobath, 1963). Simplified, flexion is changed to extension, pronation to supination, and adduction to abduction.

From the description given by Bobaths, the following "RIP's" apply to the upper extremities and therefore are of particular interest to the special educator:[53]

1. Extension of the head facilitates extension of the rest of the body.
2. External rotation at the shoulders, tends to inhibit flexion components of the extremities (Fig. 87A, B and C, Appendix D).
3. Internal rotation tends to inhibit extension in the extremity. (Fig. 87D, E and F, in Handling Procedures, Appendix D).
4. Horizontal abduction and shoulder hyperextension tend to inhibit flexion of the neck, arms and hands (also adduction and internal rotation of the legs).
5. Elevating (lifting) the shoulder girdle and lengthening (stretching) the side of the trunk tends to decrease (inhibit) spasticity in the hemiplegic arm.
6. Weight bearing on the hand tends to facilitate extension and postural support. Just leaning on the palm of the hands on the child's desk or on a table tends to increase extension and postural support. It is the same idea as the positive supporting reaction that when the soles of the feet touch any surface the legs tend to extend.

In attempting to gain control of an extremity, the procedure should be from proximal to distal (such as from shoulder to hand). Let's say that the child has elbow and wrist flexor spasticity. The therapist should start proximally toward the idea of relaxing the spasticity in the elbow and wrist. She might then combine some of the above mentioned "RIP's." That is, head extension, external rotation at the shoulder and abduction and hyperextension of the shoulder would be used to put the child in a position where the extremity would tend to relax (the spasticity would be inhibited). The therapist has thusly combined all the "RIP's"

[53]A more descriptive presentation of these and other reflex-inhibiting patterns may be found in Volume 46 of the *American Journal of Physical Medicine*, 1967, "The Bobath concept in treatment of neurological disorders", Sarah Semans, p. 732-785.

starting proximally at the head to shoulder etc. and put each of these in sequence towards reducing the problem in the distal part (wrist and hand) of the extremity. The "RIP's" then are used primarily for relaxing the lower primitive reflexes.

It is important to discuss, more than briefly, some of the finer points concerning reflex inhibition as this is the foundation of the Bobath approach. The following example may cast a more descriptive light on the process of inhibiting primitive reflexes: A child with flexor-type spasticity is (1) placed in the kneeling position back on his heels. What happens? (2) The trunk falls forward (spine flexes), arms adduct and flex, and the head falls down (flexes). In this position the child is unable to extend his hips, raise his trunk, extend arms and move them forward and probably would be unable to raise his head. Reflex inhibition is called upon. The child is: (3) kept in full hip and knee flexion, the spine is extended (thereby counteracting the flexed spine), the arms are moved forward in full extension of elbows, wrist, and fingers (counteracting inward rotation of upper arms and pronation of forearms both of which are flexor patterns) palms are facing each other, head is raised, and ankles are extended. The child is slowly placed in this position and then held by the therapist at *key* points. These *key* points are the proximal body parts such as the *shoulder girdle* or those muscles affecting the head, neck, jaw and rib cage; and the *pelvic girdle* or those muscles about the hip. Bobath refers to the shoulder and pelvic girdle as the source from which movement initiates. By holding the child at the proximal parts, the reflex activity is prevented in the distal parts, permitting normal movement.

Severe spastics are not held in these positions (as they have a hard time as it is moving) but instead, are moved within the pattern such as by rolling from side to side until he is able to do this himself. The athetoid, on the other hand, who moves too much as it is, must hold a posture as long as possible. These new positions may at first cause fear in the child as they are foreign to him. He is all too familiar with the abnormal patterns. However, the child must not be permitted to be released during this period of mounting tension. Bobath stresses this by stating, "If the reflex inhibiting posture (pattern) can be maintained in spite of the struggle, the spasm gradually subsides; the patient feels easier and increasingly more comfortable in this new posture. After the spasm has died away and the patient has adjusted himself to the posture, spasticity is greatly diminished or abolished temporarily" (Bobath *et al.,* 1952). The period during which the reflex activity is being inhibited (while the therapist is maintaining the R.I.P.) will be one of correct sensation from the child's muscles and joints. This period of adjustment means muscle tone becomes more normal throughout the body. In the spastic, there is decreased resistance to passive movement. Abnormal muscle tone will be present until resistance to an RIP is gone. In the athetoid, involuntary movements decrease and may disappear. In the ataxic, tremors are absent. This period of adjustment gradually will become longer. By inhibiting the abnormal reflex activity through the use of the R.I.P.'s, the proprioceptors in the muscles and joints are permitted to send normal, correct sensations to the brain. The child is then able to experience normal muscle tone which, according to Bobaths, "forms the background against which normal movements take place" (Bobath *et al.,* 1952).

The sensory messages which are conveyed through the proprioceptive system to the brain are received without the child's awareness. As the Bobaths state, "The patterns of these new postures are laid down by purely sensory impressions and without the patient's conscious attention" (Bobath *et al.,* 1954). Translated into a practical example, we know that after many months of a mother dressing a child (putting the arm through the hole, the feet into shoes), the child gradually is able to perform these motions himself. It is almost as if these movement patterns were gradually chiseled into the child's brain without the child being aware of it. The movements become automatic.

The Bobaths state that they do not know, conclusively, what role the child's conscious awareness plays in the retention of new sensory learning. However, the Bobaths do feel that his treatment has been "successfully applied to infants and mental defectives, who are quite incapable of conscious co-operation" (Bobath, 1950). Again, the child is gently placed into the "RIP's" and held firmly by the therapist until the tension subsides and the child becomes comfortable in this position—"The therapist must prepare the patient for every movement she wants him to do by *positioning*, not by making patient consciously aware of actions she is striving for" (Perlmutter, 1971). The child is then encouraged to remain in this position under his own steam. This is a gradual process proceeding in the following fashion: the therapist places and holds the child; the therapist places and the child holds; the child assumes and holds "RIP." The *second* stage in therapy is *facilitation* of normal automatic movements (which follows self-imposed control). It is during this stage that the righting reflexes and the equilibrium reactions (the higher, more mature postures) are developed. The therapist progressively lessens her hold on the child, moving her hands from one key point to another until, finally, the child is in complete control. He, therefore, has the ability to inhibit his own reflex activity in an "RIP." If the child should begin to lose control, the therapist must intervene and the process must begin again. It is important to note that progression in determining which "RIP" is to be used next follows the normal sequences of motor development. (Lying, to turning over, to sitting up, to kneeling, to getting balance in sitting and kneeling, to standing and balance). As previously mentioned, the Assessment Chart serves not only as an evaluation tool but also as a treatment guide. The Bobaths believe that it is not possible for activity at any level to be developed to any degree of functional usefulness until the child is secure in his performance at an earlier level.

Regarding the second stage, the Bobaths have suggested a number of facilitation procedures such as:

1. Shifting the child from side to side, backwards and forwards while in sitting, kneeling, and standing positions. This is done to stimulate the appearance of normal, automatic balance reactions (equilibrium reactions).

2. Assisting the child by starting or completing a movement. A movement which a child wants or attempts to perform is aided by the therapist if the motion is not too far beyond his developmental level.

3. Tapping or tickling under the tips of the fingers tends to promote finger and wrist extension. Most of the tapping techniques proposed are for the lower extremities but, in general, as

is described in other methods, tapping over any muscle belly stimulates muscles to respond.

4. Shaking to decrease tone. To open a spastic hand, the proximal part of the arm is put in the best position for opening (horizontal abduction, extension, and external rotation) the distal part of the arm (wrist and hand) is shaken which tends to relax the extremity.

5. Resistance to increase tone. Resistance tends to increase the number of motor units and gives direction to motion and joint (proprioceptive) feedback.

6. Trunk rotation, a sequence of rotational movements. This procedure is usually begun in the supine position and is used to encourage the child to come to the sitting position. Other righting reflexes are elicited by using key points (such as the head and shoulders). To elicit the neck-on-body reflexes, the head would be moved in either rotation with flexion or rotation with extension. (See Appendix A, *Task Level Evaluation* for descriptions of other righting reflexes).

7. Rocking and bouncing. This technique increases muscle tone, facilitates equilibrium reactions.

8. Pretzel work. This just means putting the child in all sorts of positions.

The third stage or phase is a program which she terms "willed movements." These movements are not taught, but seem to appear spontaneously. They occur "when spasticity is reduced or absent and while the limb is placed in a position which by association reactions facilitates this movement."

Briefly, the Bobath method uses basic postural patterns as outlined on the Assessment Chart. That is, the sitting, kneeling, standing sequence. Additionally, they use voluntary movement which is controlled with the above kinds of techniques as well as the RIP's. The child is actually trying to move and simultaneously the movement is either inhibited or facilitated. The therapist and patient then work together, usually on a mat, to get smooth movements usually involving trunk rotation in trying to progress through the developmental sequence of movement. The primitive reflexes are inhibited and higher reflexes ar facilitated to produce smooth movement through the developmental sequence. One final word before moving on to the next facilitation/inhibition technique. Spasticity does not melt away. "Any permanent reduction [of spasticity] depends upon the learning that goes on." The child is able to do something that he was unable to do before spasticity was momentarily inhibited. The child must continue "to do these new things and getting them perhaps on a cortical level after they have learned to do them. Then there is a more permanent reduction in the hypertonus" (Semans, 1967b).

ROOD SYSTEM

Like the Bobath method, the Rood method is based on the hypothesis that it is possible to stimulate the higher centers of the brain through the periphery. The Bobaths state that they are stimulating the inhibitory centers, but Rood is stimulating the stimulator centers. As defined by Rood (1965), this system is "The activation, facilitation and inhibition, of muscle action, voluntary and involuntary, through the reflex arc." The Rood approach capitalizes on a theory of sensorimotor interfacilitation based on neurophysiologic observations confirmed by Eldred and Hagbath (1955). Basic to the Rood system are two concepts: (1) that motor function and sensory mechanisms are interrelated, and (2) that movement and postural responses are actualized or activated without conscious awareness of the response but rather that movement and postural responses should be automatically activated as in normal development. Rood believes that stimuli needs to be present before a response occurs and that stimuli provides feedback during the response. So that after the stimulus is applied, the child performs an activity in order to use the input on a cortical (thinking) level. The child should think about the *activity* not about *how* to move the arm. Lindsley (1960), among others, gives evidence that inflow from the spinothalamic tract (the afferent path on which stimuli from skin receptors travel) go to the reticular-activating system. In earlier chapters, it was shown that the reticular system (as well as other higher centers or systems) has an influence over the gamma efferent fibers which supply the muscles (or more particularly, the muscle spindles). Although the alpha motor neuron is the final common pathway to the muscle, it is preceded and influenced by the gamma motor neuron activity. It follows, therefore, that "general receptors of the skin could have significant influence on the regulation of movement" (Stockmeyer, p. 924, 1967).

A variety of stimuli are utilized in this approach to activate, facilitate or inhibit motor responses. The reader is referred to Stockmeyer (1967) and Rood (1962) for specifics of treatment. The techniques as applied to the vegetative activities such as sucking and chewing can be found in Appendix B.

Briefly, however, "high" and "low" threshold receptors (fibers) are stimulated in accordance with the motor responsibility demanded of them during what Rood refers to as light, heavy and skilled work. Cutaneous (skin) receptors and proprioceptors are stimulated to obtain certain responses. Some of the modalities (stimuli used in treatment) are described below.

For facilitation

(1) Positioning. Reflex patterns are either facilitated or inhibited. See Fiorentino (1971) for a review of reflex pathology; (2) Brushing. Currently little in the way of brushing is apparently being advocated by Rood as she feels that this source of stimuli gives too much stimulation to the "immature nervous system." Instead, a vibrator is used. Vibrating or rubbing the skin causes contraction of those muscle bellies lying beneath the skin area being stimulated and simultaneous inhibition to the antagonists. See Figure 51, relate this diagram to Figure 13 in the chapter dealing with orthopedic management; (3) Icing. Three to five strokes with ice to the dermatone; the area is blotted dry; and icing is repeated two or three times at 10 second intervals; response occurs after 30 seconds. Icing is preceded by brushing. See Chusid and McDonald (1954) for an excellent illustration of the dermatonal areas which, of course, contain sensory nerve fibers for pain, temperature, light touch, tactile sense and proprioception; (4) Pressure (to the muscle belly). Pressures have their effect via the muscle spindles and other proprioceptors. (Fig. 51); (5) Joint compression (facilitates extensors or the postural muscles) and traction (facilitates flexors); (6) Stretch (acts via the gamma system, see Figure 51); (7) Resistance. This is a form of stretch. However, "rather than passively stretching a tighter muscle to increase range,

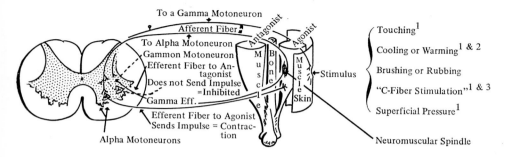

Key: ———Facilitory
‒ ‒ ‒ ‒ Inhibitory

1. Facilitates contraction of underlying muscles & synergists & inhibits antagonistic muscles.

2. Cooling slows down the sensorimotor response. Warming speeds it up.

3. "C-Fiber Stimulation" causes a reverberating circuit. Impulse continues to travel over the circuit long after manual stimulation has ceased.

Figure 51. Exteroceptive facilitory-inhibitory responses.

application of graded resistance to the motion desired is usually more effective . . . [for example] instead of forcefully pushing the jaw shut, give a quick pull in the direction of opening and then resists the closure" (Huss, 1971); (8) Vestibular stimulation such as fast rolling and tilting; (9) Taste (as demonstrated in Appendix B).

For inhibition

Those stimuli used to *inhibit* are: (1) Pressure (applied to a muscle insertion); (2) Slow stroking for three minutes; (3) Pleasant odors (See Appendix B); (4) Slow rolling used until the child seems relaxed; (5) Neutral warmth; and (6) Joint compression (inhibits flexors) with light pressure. Stimuli are thus applied to exteroceptors (skin) and proprioceptors (joint capsules, ligaments, vestibular receptors in the inner ear). See Table XXVII and Table XXVIII. Again, a developmental sequence of motor response is followed in this approach. The steps in the "developmental sequence" of this therapeutic treatment system are referred to as the ontogenetic motor patterns (See Rood, 1962).

Discussion of the various treatment techniques used with the

TABLE XXVII

PROPRIOCEPTORS AND MUSCULAR RESPONSES

Proprioceptors	*Muscular Response*
Neuromuscular spindle	
Nuclear bag fiber	Facilitates homonymous muscle and synergists and inhibits the antagonists.
Nuclear chain fiber	Facilitates flexor muscles and inhibits extensor muscles.
Neurotendinous spindle	Inhibits homonymous muscle and synergists and facilitates the antagonists.
Vestibular	Facilitates muscles involved in maintaining equilibrium —inhibits others.
Pressure	Facilitates homonymous muscle and synergists and inhibits the antagonists.
Joint traction	Relaxes and/or facilitates flexors and inhibits extensor muscles.
Joint compression	Facilitates extensors (postural muscles) and inhibits flexors.
Tactile	Facilitates homonymous muscle and synergists and inhibits the antagonists.

Reprinted with permission from: Zamir, Lelia J. (Ed.): *Expanding Dimensions in Rehabilitation.* Springfield, Thomas, 1969.

TABLE XXVIII

EXTEROCEPTORS AND MUSCULAR RESPONSES

Exteroceptors	*Muscular Responses*
Light touch	Facilitates homonymous muscle and synergists and inhibits antagonists.
Temperature	Same as above. Also cooling slows down impulse transmission. Warming speeds up impulse transmission.
Pain	Avoidance or withdrawal reflex of total body or a part.
Vision	Optic righting reflex. Tracking reflex. Avoidance response. Perception of pleasant relaxes; of unpleasant creates muscle tension.
Hearing	Discordance or loud noise creates muscle tension. Soothing sounds relax. Unexpected noise results in body turning toward the sound.
Smell	Pleasant ordors relax. Noxious odors excite or create muscle tension. Unexpected odors (pleasant or otherwise) excite the nervous system.
Taste	Sweets and favorite tastes relax. Distasteful substances result in an avoidance response and create muscle tension.

Reprinted with permission from: Zamir, Lelia J. (Ed.): *Expanding Dimensions in Rehabilitation.* Springfield, Thomas, 1969.

cerebral palsied child may leave the reader somewhat bewildered. A careful study does, however, produce many commonalities to each approach which lends an equalizing effect to this confusion. It simply boils down to the fact that almost any kind of external stimulus (proprioceptive and exteroceptive) *appropriately* applied *wakes up* or *slows down* muscle movement. Or as Moore (1969, pp. 13-14) cogently states:

> It appears that the abnormal nervous system never has a chance to be conditioned and thus establish meaningful reflex pathways. Current rehabilitation techniques attempt to do this for the nervous system which is incapable of doing it alone. We condition it for the handicapped child by putting in certain *repetitive stimuli patterns.* In turn, if the person is properly *positioned,* these result in properly patterned responses. If repeated enough times, hundreds of times if necessary, there may be improvement. The nervous system must be given a chance to myelinate its pathways and establish new synaptic connections. Then it must reuse these routes repeatedly before results can be achieved. [Nervous pathways and synaptic connections, when used repeatedly, develop and mature]. We attempt to do this conditioning process on a reflex or unconscious basis first. Only later do we attempt to have the patient do it consciously by himself. Further practice (repetition) at the cortical (conscious) level helps to ingrain these responses into the nervous system. The eventual hope is that the behavior will be learned well enough to become subcortical [unconscious] in nature, and thus become an integral part of the nervous system functioning. If these goals can be achieved by repetitive stimulation on the reflex or unconscious level, repetitive stimulation and effort on the conscious level, and conscious repetition over and over until it becomes subcortical response, then we will have made a major step in rehabilitating the damaged nervous system. It is not until new movement patterns or behavioral responses become sub-cortical that we can say that they are a part of the nervous system complement of response patterns.

Although as Tizard (1966) says, "We have no scientific evidence—in the sense of studies with controls—that any one method of treatment of cerebral palsy [or the neurologically impaired] gets better results than any other," one thing is definite: there must be close cooperation and a good working relationship between the therapies, the physician, the teacher, family and community. Planning the child's program requires carry-over. Because a good deal of work should be done in the classroom, it is important for the teacher to be aware of the various treatment approaches which are used in the treatment of these children.

Each of the systems presented are total techniques in and of themselves. The therapist must establish a limit. That is, she may choose to be a purist and use one system to the exclusion of all others; or she may wish to choose "bits and pieces" of one or more of the systems; or she may choose to use one system combined with some ADL training. The therapist should know, within certain limits, what she can expect from the child in therapy. This results by virture of her initial evaluation of the child, psychological and physician's reports. The therapist must establish priorities as to what she believes the child needs in his particular life style. What may be the critical ingredient to the child's progress may very well be the therapist herself. The therapist must be a believer in whatever technique or combination of techniques she chooses to employ. It would behoove all those working in this *vineyard* to listen again to the words of George Washington, "Truth will ultimately prevail when pains are taken to bring it to light."

REFERENCES

Bobath, K., and Bobath, B.: Spastic paralysis: Treatment of by the use of reflex inhibition. *Brit J Phys Med, 13*:121, 1950.

Bobath, K., and Bobath, B.: A treatment of cerebral palsy based on the analysis of the patient's motor behaviour. *Brit J Phys Med, 15*:107, 1952.

Bobath, K., and Bobath, B.: Treatment of cerebral palsy by the inhibition of abnormal reflex activity. *Brit Orthoptic J, 11*:1, 1954.

Bobath, K.: The neuropathology of cerebral palsy and its importance in treatment and diagnosis. *Cereb Palsy Bull, 8*:13-33, 1959.

Bobath, B.: Treatment principles and planning in cerebral palsy. *Physiotherapy, 49*:122-124, 1963.

Chusid, J. G., and McDonald, J. J.: *Correlative Neuroanatomy and Functional Neurology,* 7th ed. Los Altos, Lange Med Publications, 1954, p. 141.

Denhoff, E., and Robinault, I. P.: *Cerebral Palsy and Related Disorders.* New York, McGraw-Hill, 1960.

Denny-Brown, D.: *The Basal Ganglia.* New York, Oxford University Press, 1962, Chapters V, VI, and VII.

Eldred, E., and Hagbath, K. E.: Facilitation and inhibition of gamma efferents by stimulation of certain skin area. *J Neuropsychiat, 3*:644-652, 1955.

Fay, T.: Problems of rehabilitation in patients with cerebral palsy. *Delaware M J, 18*:57-60, (March), 1946.

Fay, Temple: Basic considerations regarding neuromuscular and reflex therapy. *Spastics Quart, III* (3), September, 1954.

Fiorentino, Mary R.: *Reflex Testing Methods for Evaluating Central Nervous System Development,* 6th ed. Springfield, Thomas, 1971.

Huss, Joy: Controversy and confusion in physical dysfunction treatment techniques—clinical aspects. In Zamir, Lelia J. (Ed.): *Expanding Dimensions in Rehabilitation.* Springfield, Thomas, 1969.

Huss, Joy: An introduction to treatment techinques developed by Margaret Rood. In Perlmutter, S. (Ed.): *Neuroanatomy and Neurophysiology Underlying Current Treatment Techniques for Sensorimotor Dysfunction.* University of Illinois Medical Center, 1971.

Jacobson, Edmund: *Progressive Relaxation.* Chicago, University of Chicago Press, 1959.

Kabat, H.: Studies on neuromuscular dysfunction. II New principles of neuromuscular reeudcation. *Permanente Found Med Bull, 5*:3, 1947·

Kabat, Herman: Central facilitation; the basis of treatment for paralysis. *Permanente Found Med Bull, X* (1-4), August, 1952.

Knott, M., and Voss, D. E.: *Proprioceptive Neuromuscular Facilitation.* New York, Hoeber, 1956.

Lindsley, D. B.: Attention, consciousness, sleep and wakefulness. In Field. J., Magoun, H. W., and Hall, V. E. (Eds.): *Handbook of Physiology.* Baltimore, Williams and Wilkins, 1960, vol. III, pp. 1553-1593.

Moore, Josephine C.: The developing nervous system in physical dysfunction. In Zamir, Lelia J. (Ed.): *Expanding Dimensions in Rehabilitation.* Springfield, Thomas, 1969.

Page, Dorothy: Neuromuscular reflex therapy as an approach to patient care. *Am J Phys Med, 46*:816-835, 1967.

Perlmutter, Shirley: *Neuroanatomy and Neurophysiology Underlying Current Treatment Techniques for Sensorimotor Dysfunction.* Division of Services for Crippled Children, University of Illinois Medical Center. 1971.

Perry, Catherine E.: Principles and techniques of the Brunnstrom approach to the treatment of hemiplegia. *Am J Phys Med, 47*:789-812, 1967.

Phelps, W. M.: The treatment of cerebral palsies. *J Bone Joint Surg, 22*:1004-1012, 1940.

Phelps, W. M.: Factors influencing the treatment of cerebral palsy. *Physiother Rev, 21*:136-138, 1941.

Phelps, W. M.: Let's define cerebral palsy. *Crippled Child, 26*:3-5, 1948.

Rood, M. S.: The use of sensory receptors. In *Approaches to the Treatment of Patients with Neuromuscular Dysfunction.* Dubuque. M. C. Brown, 1962.

Rood, M. S.: Unpublished class notes: Fall 1958, Spring 1959, Summer 1965. Physical Therapy Symposia on "Child with Central Nervous System Deficit": September 1964, May 1965, September 1965.

Semans, S.: Comments made during the Ninth Question and Discussion Period of the Special Therapeutic Exercise Project as reported in *Am J Phys Med, 46*:982-1005, 1967b.

Stockmeyer, S. A.: An interpretation of the approach of Rood to the treatment of neuromuscular dysfunction. *Am J Phys Med, 46*:900-956, 1967.

Tizard, J.: The experimental approach to the treatment and upbringing of handicapped children. *Dev Med Child Neurol, 8*:310, 1966.

Twitchell, T. E.: On the motor deficit in congenital bilateral athetosis. *J Nerv Ment Dis, 129*:104-132, 1959.

Walshe, F. M. R.: On certain tonic or postural reflexes in hemiplegia. *Brain, 46*:1-37, 1923.

Chapter Ten

SPECIAL ADAPTATIONS AND EQUIPMENT

BY WAY OF INTRODUCTION TO THE SPECIAL adaptations and equipment discussed in this chapter, the following should be pointed out. The ideas and equipment have been culled from a number of sources as indicated by the bibliography. It should be understood by the reader that while these ideas and devices are, in the author's opinion, especially well-suited for use by the CP/NI child, they are by no means all those available. In addition to familiarization with these ideas and devices, their inclusion will serve the additional purpose of enabling the reader to gain a better understanding of the basic requirements for equipment and adaptations for the CP/NI and thus be better able to select from the vast number of such adaptations and devices that are now or will in the future be available. It is hoped that this chapter will also encourage those who read it to experiment with adaptations and equipment of their own original design so that an ever increasing amount of this type of aid will be available.

ACTIVITIES OF DAILY LIVING

Plate Stabilizer (ADH)[54]

Plate stabilizers like the ones diagrammed in Figures 52.1 and 52.2 hold plates in position on any smooth surface. Easily put together and attached, they are adjustable and portable, so that the user—the person with weakness, lack of coordination or in-

---

[54]Each of the suggestions in this section are reproduced with permission from the original source; see Sources at end of this chapter.

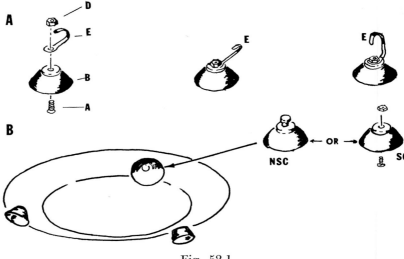

Fig. 52.1

voluntary motion of the arm—may have them at school or home. For adaptations of the stabilizers shown (i.e. deep dish and bowl stabilizers) see Rosenberg, 1968.

STABILIZER WITH HOOK (Fig. 52.1 detail A; Fig. 52.2). Materials: 3 push-on suction cups (B); 3 small hooks or molly hooks (E); 3 small round-head bolts and nuts (A; D).

Method: Put bolt (A) through bottom of suction cup (B),

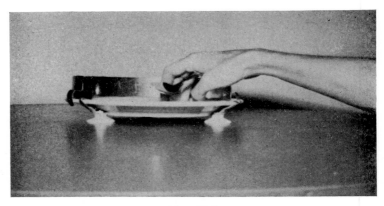

Fig. 52.2

and eye in hook (E), then put nut (D) on bolt (A). Bend hook to fit plate or dish. (NOTE: This stabilizer may be used to hold china plates and taken along when dining out. Since molly hooks can be bent (E), they may be used with a variety of plates, but they will not withstand repeated bending, and work best with thick plates or deep plates with high rims.)

PLATE STABILIZER (Fig. 52.1, detail B). Materials: Plastic plate; 3 suction cups; 3 small round-head bolts and nuts (used only if push-on suction cups are used; must fit hole in suction cup tightly) Method:

1. Set plastic plate on flat surface, and while holding it down push a suction cup under it until cup is depressed in normal holding position. Mark location of cup on plate.

2. Mark plate so that three suction cups can be attached at equal intervals around edge of plate, same distance from edge as determined in step 1.

3. Burn or drill holes large enough to fit bolts or suction cup nipples (NSC) in plate at points marked. Sand edges of holes smooth.

4. If push-on suction cups (sc) are used, insert bolts through suction cup and bottom of plate, then put nuts on bolts. If nippled suction cups are used, push nipples of suction cups through holes in plate. The plate stabilizer using bolts and push-on suction cups is the sturdiest and easiest to use, and its parts may be easily removed, if necessary, when plate is washed. The plate stabilizer using nippled suction cups works well, but with usage the rubber tops of suction cups may wear and break.

Special Spoon (Fig. 53). (ADH)

This spoon with a plastic bowl encourages self-feeding among those whose motions are involuntary. All that is needed is the ability to bring spoon and mouth together.

Since the bowl of the spoon is flexible, there can be no fear of injury to the face, teeth or gums. This flexibility also allows the user to scoop up more food on a single attempt. Its *grip* makes it possible for those whose grasp is weak or erratic to hold a spoon. When eating action has been learned, an ordinary tablespoon or teaspoon may be substituted in the grip.

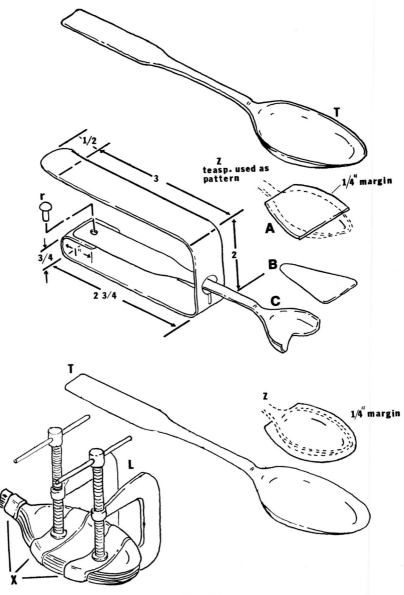

Fig. 53

Materials: three pieces of flexible plastic, 1/32-inch, 2 inches square; Metal iced tea spoon or teaspoon (z); 2 tablespoons (old or worn, used as molds) (T); Adhesive or masking tape; Thin metal strip, ¾ to 1-inch, about 10 inches long; Small rivet or nut and bolt (r) long enough to attach metal strip to spoon handle.

Method

1. Scrape printing from plastic and use teaspoon as pattern (z) to cut pieces of plastic (Fig. 53, parts A, B, and C).
2. Cut teaspoon bowl to shape shown and smooth edges.
3. Drill holes large enough to fit rivet (or bolt) in spoon handle and in metal strip.
4. Drill hole in strip and cut slot, as shown, large enough to allow handle of teaspoon to slide through.
5. Preheat oven to 350 degrees F.
6. Assemble spoons and plastic in order shown. Tape them together and clamp (L) evenly but not tightly enough to force plastic out as it softens.
7. Put spoons in a pan in the oven. As spoons heat, check often to make sure that plastic does not get too soft and run out. When plastic around edges of spoons softens enough to fuse, remove pan from oven and allow to cool.
8. Remove clamps and tape (X), and smooth rough spots on plastic; if there is a smooth bead around edge of spoon, leave it for added strength. (NOTE: If plastic is too thin in places, put a patch on thin spot, reassemble in molds, and re-cook.)
9. Slide spoon handle through grip-handle, and rivet (or bolt) as shown.

Sandwich Holder (Fig. 54). (ADH)

This is a light-weight sandwich holder for persons who can eat sandwiches but who may have difficulty in holding them. All that is required to use it is the ability to grasp the handle of the device and move the arm up and down. The plastic holder encases the sandwich. Each time the metal base is pushed down against the tabletop a new portion of the sandwich is pushed out.

Materials: Square or oblong plastic container (AH) such as hand lotion container (about size of a sandwich) (S); Aluminum

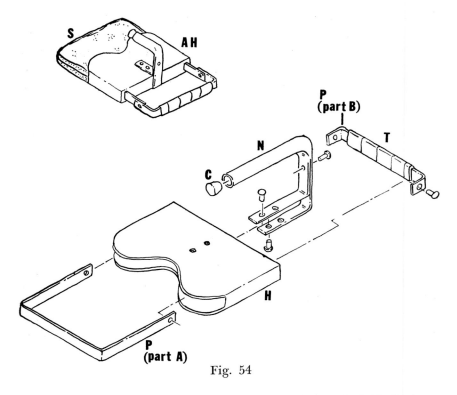

Fig. 54

strip; Aluminum tube; Wood block (size of a sandwich); 7 rivets or small nuts and bolts; Padding (plastic foam strip); Tape; Cork.

Method

1. Cut off top of plastic container about 4 inches from bottom (H). Heat container in boiling water until soft, then force wood block into container to shape it.

2. When plastic has cooled, remove block, and cut open end of container to shape shown in Fig. 54.

3. Cut and bend aluminum strip to form pusher P (parts A and B) as shown. Drill a hole to fit rivets in each end of pusher parts as indicated.

4. Cut two slots to fit pusher parts in closed end of holder (H). Insert pusher (part A) through slots in holder and attach pusher (part B) with two rivets.

5. Tape padding (T) to pusher (part B).

6. Cut tube lengthwise, leaving about 4 inches uncut, then flatten tube where cut. Bend tube 90 degrees at end of cut. Drill a hole to fit rivet close to round portion of tube and install rivet as shown.

7. Bend top half of split tube 90 degrees upward, about two inches from round tube.

8. Drill two holes in top half of split tube and install two rivets to attach top half of split tube to upper side of holder.

9. Bend bottom half of split tube 90 degrees upward around

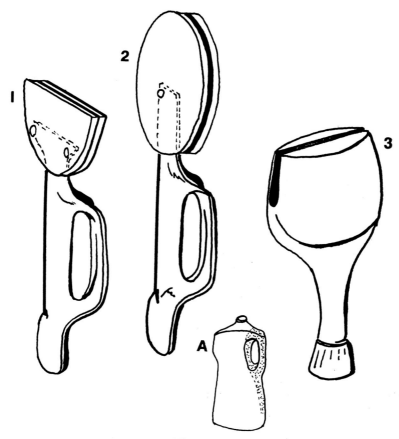

Fig. 55

lower side of holder. Repeat step 6 with bottom half of split tube and lower side of holder.

10. Install cork (C) in end of handle (N).

Holder for Sandwich, Flashcards, Playing Cards (Fig. 55) (PH)

Square handles from 2-quart containers (i.e. fabric softener container, see A) with tongue centered and fixed between two round plastic covers with brass brad can be used to hold sandwiches, flashcards, or regular playing cards. See 1 and 2 in Figure 55. Head and Shoulders bottle (held upside down for dowel-type grip) can also be used for holding sandwiches, playing cards, and flashcards (3).

Portable Drink Holder (Fig. 56) (ADH)

This type of drink holder is used by persons without good arm or hand control. It may be used to hold paper cups, drinking glasses or even bottled drinks, provided that it is placed low enough to allow drinking through a straw. The user can then adapt any handy or available container to hold the cup or glass: a cardboard cylinder, a tin can, or a plastic bottle cut to size.

Materials: 3 suction cups, push-on type; 3 paper clips; 3 leather or rubber scraps; 3 small bolts and nuts.

Method: Drill 2 holes [one to fit bolt (F) and nut (G)] in each rubber or leather (A) scrap as shown in Fig. 56. Bolt one end of each scrap to a suction cup (B). Tie a piece of string (C) through other hole (D), measure length needed, and tie a paper clip (E) on other end of string. Push suction cups firmly on a table, position holder (tin can, part of plastic bottle, cardboard carton or cylinder) and fasten paper clips over its edges.

MODIFICATIONS. String can be tied directly to bolt, and leather scraps can be omitted.

Mouthstick

The mouthstick, like the headwand, has been in use for some time. It is a basic device for use by persons who have control of head, mouth[55] and tongue but who cannot use their arms. Like

---

[55]Caution: Frequent use of this device over a prolonged period may do injury to the teeth, especially to those of children, unless a fitted mouhpiece is used.

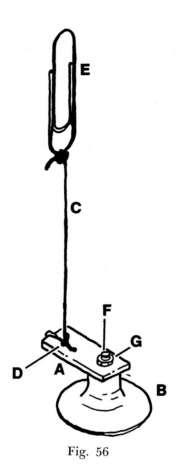

Fig. 56

the headwand, it can be designed and built of several different materials in a variety of ways, and—through the use of interchangeable tips—it may serve many functions.

ADJUSTABLE MOUTHSTICK (Fig. 57) (ADH). Materials: Hanger wire, about 12 inches long (Hw); Stiff plastic drinking straw, about 10 inches long (s); Plastic tape (t); Disposable plastic cigarette filter (pf); Washer, to fit straw (w); Hard rubber strip, ⅛-inch, about 2 by 1½ inches (rs); Rubber tubing (rt), about ½ inch long, to fit over tip of cigarette filter; glue.

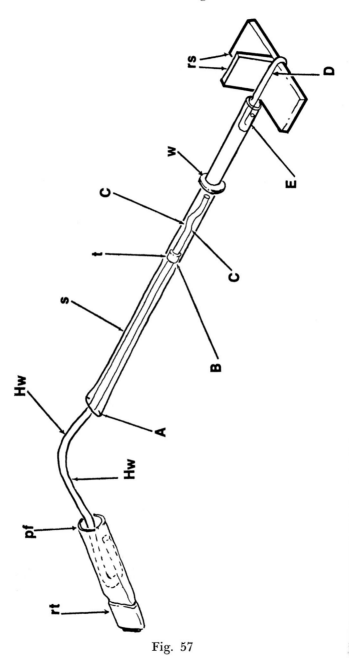

Fig. 57

Method:

1. Cut a 10-inch piece of hanger wire (Hw) and bend it to fit drinking straw as shown in Figure 57.

2. Put wire in straw and dip mouth of straw in boiling water. Flatten mouth of straw to nearly the diameter of the wire (A).

3. Slip wire out other end of straw, apply tape (t) as shown, and reinsert wire in straw. Apply so that taped portion is too big to pass through flattened mouth of straw but small enough to ride easily inside straw (B).

4. Glue wire into plastic filter (mouthpiece, pf), and slip rubber tubing over filter (for tooth comfort).

5. Glue plastic washer on straw as shown (w).

6. Bend a 1¼-inch piece of wire as shown. Bend wire so that two bends firmly touch walls of straw (C). Glue rubber strips (rs) together to form a pusher type tip. Bend end of wire around rubber strip as shown (D). Insert bent end of wire in straw (E).

7. Bend curve so that tip faces down.

MODIFICATIONS. The rubber tip can be replaced by any of the press-on type tips mentioned in *Changing Tips on the Headwand.* Refer to Rosenberg, 1968 for additional suggestions for use of the mouthstick.

Mouthstick made from odds and ends (Fig. 58) (ADH)

Materials: Plastic stirring rod, about 6 inches long (sr); Ball point pen shell (plastic) about 4 inches long, diameter equal to or smaller than that of cigarette (p); Disposable plastic cigarette filter (pf); Plastic glue; Adhesive tape; 2 rubber tile strips; one, ½ inch square; the other 1⅛ inches long and ½ inch wide (rs); Rubber glue; Piece of rubber tubing, about ½ inch long, to fit snugly over tip of cigarette filter (rt).

Method

1. Squeeze small end of mouthpiece (pf) closed, and put rubber tubing (rt) over end of mouthpiece as shown.

2. Glue one end of pen shell (p) into open end of mouthpiece at (A). Insert one end of stirring rod (sr) into open end of pen shell, and tape stirring rod to pen shell at (B).

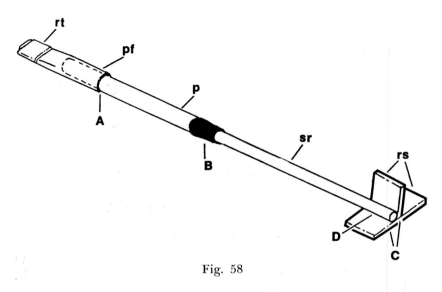

Fig. 58

3. Glue rubber strips together at (C), then glue the strips to end of stirring rod as shown at (D).

MODIFICATIONS: Tip may be made from strips of cardboard, plastic, aluminum sheet or foil, vinyl, rubber tile, or balsa wood. The "stick" can consist simply of a stiff plastic drinking straw, flattened at one end for mouth comfort (no mouthpiece).

Protective Helmet (Urethane Sponge) (Fig. 59). (PH)

Materials: Cotton, gingham, calicos; 1 yd. of 1¼ inch webbed elastic; 1 inch thick plastic sponge to be cut for front and back, cut sponge to fit inside dotted seam allowance.

Method: Front (inside):

1. Place right sides of two front pieces together, pin ends of 2 inches elastic strip to form loop between the two surfaces. Pin one end of 2 inches side elastic between 2 surfaces. Finished side elastic strips will be 1 inch visible.

2. Sew around front pieces leaving notched area open so that sponge can be added. Turn, press, turn in remaining seam allowance and top stitch between notches.

Back (inside): Do the same as for front; however, the two back neck loops should be sewn in when sponge has been added

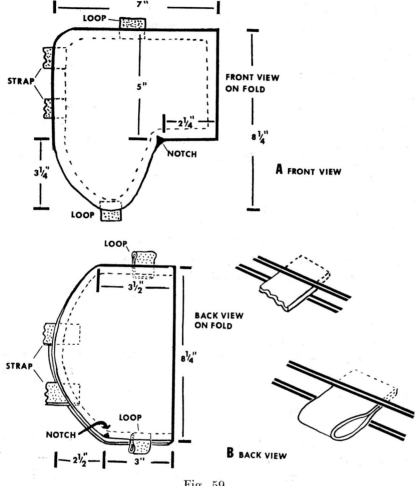

Fig. 59

so that the remaining seam allowance can now be top stitched between notches.

Straps: Cut one 2 inches by 19 inches, finish to size 1 inch by 18 inches. Cut one 2 inches by 32 inches, finish to size 1 inch by 31 inches. Fold straps lengthwise, right sides together. Stitch seam. Turn and press. Then turn in end seam allowance and top stitch. Shorter strap placed through upper loops of helmet and tied in bow. Chin strap (longer) placed through lower loops. Helmet fits head from 19 inches to 26 inches.

Headwand

The headwand can assist its user in a wide variety of activities such as eating, drawing, writing, etc. Good head control is necessary. The headwand shown in Figure 60.1 and 60.2 is commercially available. However, it can be made easily and at little cost and used experimentally to gauge its potential value to the user. Interchangeable tips are used with the headwand to make it adaptable to many functions. See Figures 61.1 and 61.2, *Changing Tips on the Headwand*.

MAKING A HEADWAND Figures 60.1 & 60.2 (ADH) Materials: Aluminum strip, 1 inch, 12 inches long (F); Metal bracket (K); Hanger wire (W); 3 small nuts (n) and bolts (b); 2 rivets (r); Plastic foam (polyurethane) (pf); Velcro tape, about 8 inches (V); Strong cloth, 2 by 20 inches; Plastic upholstery material, 4 by 20 inches; Washer (w); Glue.

Method

1. Measure the user's head from top of one ear to the other, across the forehead and just above the eyebrows. Cut aluminum strip (F) to length measured and drill one hole in it at each end to fit bolts, and two in the middle to fit rivets, as shown in Figure 60.1. Smooth all edges, round ends of strip and clean drilled holes to remove burrs.

2. Shape aluminum strip to user's head and remove. Prepare stiff wire (W) as shown, making sure that its tip will fit into the flared ends of plastic drinking straws used in making tips for headwand. Build up tip (g) with glue or solder. Attach wire to bracket (K) with nut (n) and bolt (b) as shown and rivet bracket to forehead band (F). Glue plastic foam (pf) inside forehead band.

3. Make rear strap (rsA and rsB) from plastic upholstery material, cut and stitched to shape shown in Figure 60.2. Measure user's head for snug fit, and sew opposing panels of Velcro (V) tape to parts rsA and rsB so that loop and hook of the tape fasten rear strap (rsA) just behind forehead band (F).

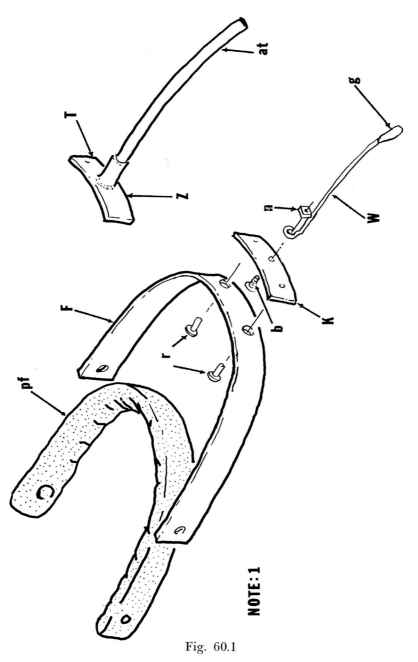

Fig. 60.1

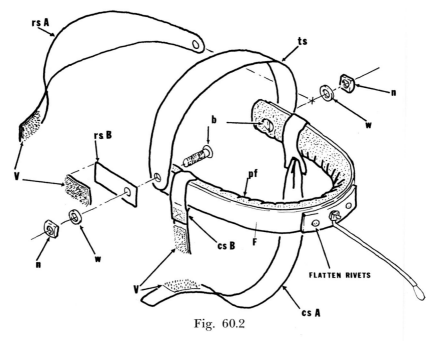

Fig. 60.2

4. Make top strap (ts) from plastic upholstery material cut to the shape shown in Figure 60.2. Measure user's head to assure fit.

5. Make chin strap (csA) from cloth as shown in Figure 60.2, with a buttonhole at one end through which csA can loop to attach to forehead band. Sew a panel of Velcro tape to other end. Sew opposing panel of Velcro to chin strap (csB).

6. Assemble headwand as shown in Figure 60.2. Parts rsA and rsB of rear strap are bolted at non-Velcro ends of forehead band. Chin strap (csA) loops through itself at left temple area of the forehead band as shown and csB is sewn to itself at right temple area of the forehead band. Tab of cloth extending beyond Velcro closure of chin strap allows user with enough reach and control of arm to unfasten it without assistance.

MODIFICATIONS. An alternate protrusion (Z) for the headwand is pictured in Figure 60.1. An aluminum tube (at), slightly bent, is forced into a tubular bracket (T). Bracket is attached to forehead band by rivets, and assembly procedure given above is followed in completion of headwand with tubular protrusion. Tips for this type of headwand are built according to instructions given in *Changing Tips on the Headwand*. Chin strap may be attached to forehead band by heavy-duty, gripper-type snaps or by buckle at left temple area. NOTE: 1. Alternate brackets are illustrated but either may be used. NOTE: 2. Wire may also be welded or bolted to forehead band.

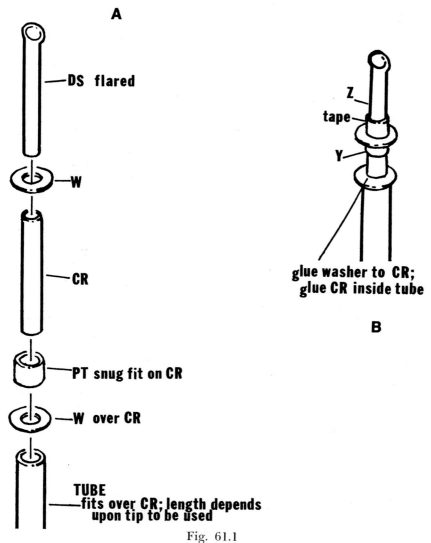

A

—DS flared

—W

—CR

—PT snug fit on CR

—W over CR

TUBE
——fits over CR; length depends
upon tip to be used

Z

tape—

Y—

glue washer to CR;
glue CR inside tube

B

Fig. 61.1

Changing Tips on the Headwand

Tips for Headwand or Mouthstick (Wire Protusion) (Figs. 61.1, 61.2). (ADH) Materials: Metal tube, such as hollow curtain rod (CR); Metal tube, smaller in diameter than tube above and just larger in diameter than a plastic drinking straw; Flexible plastic drinking straw (DS); Washers, to fit smaller metal tube (W); Liquid steel; Plastic tape or flexible plastic tubing (PT).

Method:

1. Make tips for a headwand with wire protrusion from forehead band, as shown in Figure 61.1, details A and B. Force larger metal tube over smaller tube, slip one washer over smaller tube, seat washer at juncture of the tubes, and apply liquid steel to hold washer in position.

2. Flare end of a piece of plastic straw as shown, by heating end of straw and pressing a sharp pointed object larger in diameter than straw into it. Insert other end of straw in smaller tube and glue straw inside curtain rod (at Z). Around joint between straw and tube wrap plastic tape or place tight-fitting tubing over joint. Place washer over tape or tubing as shown, making sure that washer fits tightly. Push plastic tube against washer (Y). *Tips* for shaft devised here are shown in Figure 61.2. Connection between shaft and tips can be made by inserting tips and crimping large metal tube at tip end, by gluing tips in the tube, or by taping tips to tube. If desired, tips will fit into small metal tube, larger tube may be omitted from directions given above. If tips are not to be used with tip changer,[56] washers may also be omitted.

NOTE: Since all tips shown in Figure 61.2 use this holder, only the tips will be detailed.

TYPING PUNCH (Fig. 61.2,A). Cut metal tube to about ½-inch length. Tape (t) stiff wire (w) to tube, and push rubber tip (rt) over end of wire.

---

[56]The tip changer is a rotating device which holds tips for the headwand—for writing, drawing, erasing, turning pages, pushing and other activities. The tips are positioned in the changer so that the headwand can be inserted firmly to attach the tip and remove it. After the tip has been used, the headwand lowers it into its proper slot in the tip changer and moves it into its locked position. The tip easily slips off the wand as the head is raised. For details on materials and construction of this device see Rosenberg, 1968.

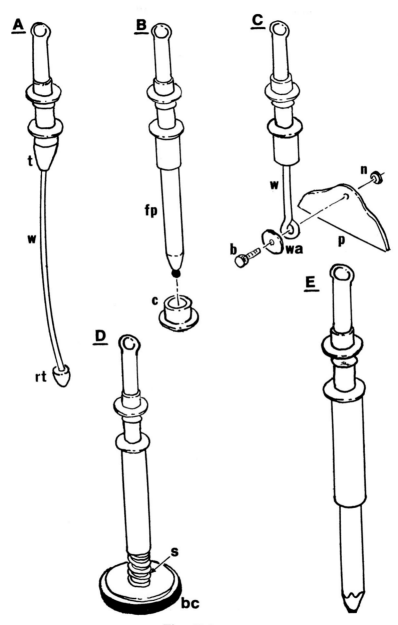

Fig. 61.2

FELT MARKING PEN (Fig. 61.2,B). Cut metal tube to about ½-inch length, insert marking pen (fp) into tube, and crimp tube. Glue marking pen cap (c) to a washer.

FOOD PUSHER (Fig. 61.2,C). Bend a loop in one end of a short piece of stiff wire (w). Wrap tape around the other end of wire. Cut metal tube to about ½-inch length, insert taped end of wire into tube, and crimp tube. Bolt (b) plastic (p) to loop end of wire. Washer = wa; Nut = n.

PAGE TURNER (Fig. 61.2,D). Push spring (s) into end of tube and crimp tube. Push other end of spring through bottle cap (bc) or suction cup and fill cap with Hectograph gelatin.

PENCIL (Fig. 61.2,E). Push pencil into tube and crimp tube around pencil.

Tips for Headwand or Mouthstick (Tubular Protrusion).

Note: Tips to fit the tubular protrusion from forehead band of the headwand are also shown in Figure 61.1, details A and B. The shaft of the tip, however, differs in that a piece of dowel or stiff tube to fit the headwand tubular protrusion is substituted for the plastic drinking straw.

The tips shown in Figure 61.2 are only a few examples, for further suggestions consult Rosenberg, 1968.

Self-Feeding Without Hands (Fig. 62.1, 62.2 and 62.3) (ADH)

The ability to use a headwand (such as in Fig. 60.2) which requires the user to move the head from side to side and several inches forward is all that is necessary to use the feeder shown in Figure 62.2,A. With the *pusher* (Fig. 62.3) in position on the headwand, the user pushes the food into the spoon, then catches the spoon handle with the notch in the pusher and pulls. This raises the spoon to the eating position. The materials cost very little and are simple to put together. Materials: Iced tea spoon or teaspoon (P); Bulldog clip, 2-inch (L); Piece of Lampshade extension post, 2½ inches long (T); 2 bolts, ¼-inch, ½-inch long (Z); Large pants fastener (N); Piece of stiff plastic, 1¼ by 2½ inches (such as plastic container lid) (D); Piece of wire hanger (H), 3 inches long; Plastic drinking straw (if headwand with wire

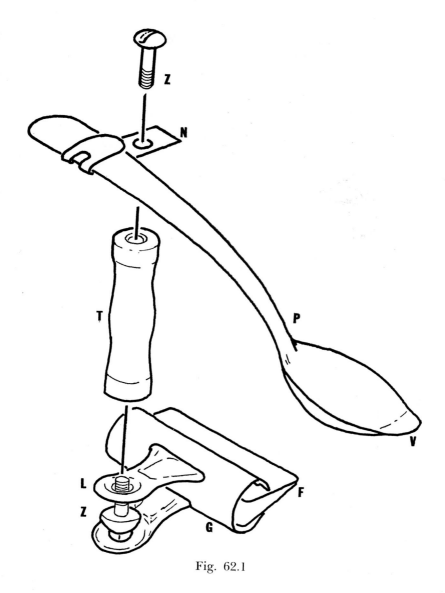

Fig. 62.1

extension is used) (W); Rivet, or nut and bolt (R); Piece of aluminum, 1 by 1½ inches (if spoon holder is to be mounted on right side of plate) (Q); Tubing (U) to fit over wire, 3 inches long.

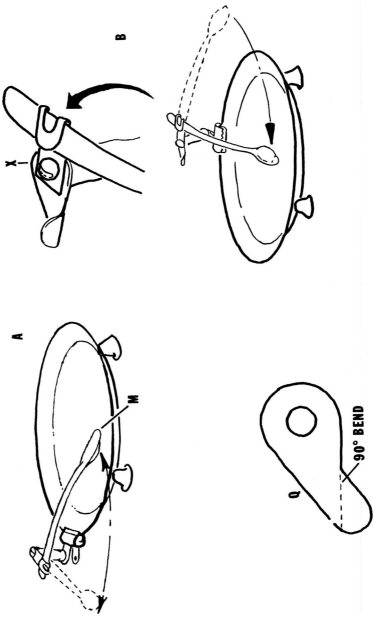

Fig. 62.2

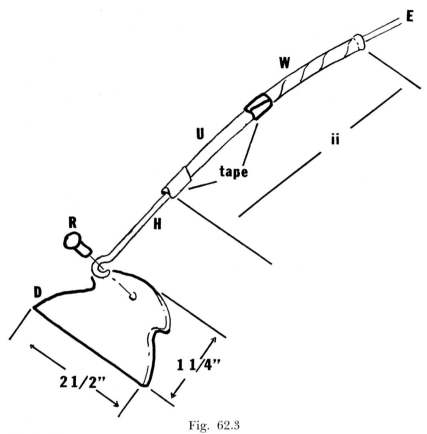

Fig. 62.3

Method

1. Bend jaws of bulldog clip (F) to conform to curvature of plate as shown in Figure 62.1. Bend spring so that jaws remain parallel when closed (G). Enlarge hole in pants fastener (N) to fit bolt. Flatten end of spoon (V) in vise.

2. Assemble bolts, pants fastener, spoon, post and clip as shown.

3. Bend top handle of clip so that, when spoon holder is mounted on plate, the flat part of spoon rests on the plate (M). Tighten top bolt so that, as spoon swivels away from plate, spoon stops in position shown in Figure 62.2, detail A (spoon is mounted for left-hand swing).

4. *If* the spoon holder is attached to right side of plate, a stop

(Q) is required (Q is the right-hand spoon stop pattern); cut aluminum (Q) to shape shown in detail B. This is the right-hand swing spoon mount. Cement stop to post (X) so that handle rests against the stop when the spoon is in its *up* position.

5. Cut plastic (D) to size and shape shown in Figure 62.3. Drill hole to fit rivet (or bolt (R)), and bend wire as shown.

6. Assemble rivet, wire and plastic as shown.

7. If headwand has a wire protrusion (E), prepare the shaft of the pusher tip (ii) as follows: Flare the end of a piece of plastic drinking straw to fit over end of protrusion; tape a small metal tube (to fit wire from pusher tip) to the straw, and then cement or tape pusher wire to tube. When wire protrusion from headwand is inserted in end of shaft, pusher tip is ready for use,

(NOTE: If headwand protusion is tubular, pusher wire may be made longer and bent so that it will fit into and stick in the protrusion. Pusher tips for both wire and tubular headwand protrusions may be adapted for use with the tip changer (see *Changing Tips on the Headwand*).

Combined ADL-Long Opponens Orthosis (Fig. 63). (Kester et al., 1969)

The combined ADL-Long Opponens Orthosis was designed at the Institute of Rehabilitation Medicine to combine the protective functions of a long opponens splint with the utilitarian functions of an ADL splint. It prevents deformities and, at the same time, provides function of the upper extremity. The basic unit of this orthosis is the Rancho-type long opponens splint. (See Figs. 20A, in Ch. 4 *Orthopedic Management in Cerebral Palsy*). The basic unit is modified by removal of the radial hand portion and attachment of an adaptive leather pocket to the palmar bar, thus converting it to an ADL splint. A removable opponens bar assembly (A), including a C-bar, is fitted into the adaptive pocket (B). This device constitutes the long opponens portion of the combined orthosis. For ADL activities the opponens bar assembly can be detached. Various devices can then be inserted into the palmar pocket. The pocket is designed to receive standard eating utensils, toothbrush, comb, etc. A spring clip holder (sch) fits into the

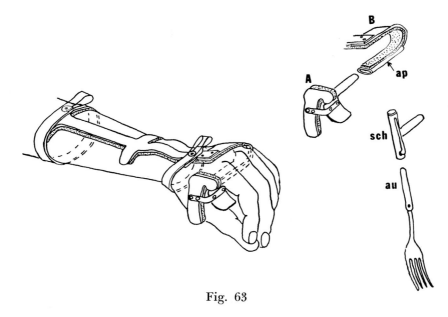

Fig. 63

palmar pocket used to receive adapted eating utensils (au), writing devices and other adapted equipment. The spring clip holder consists of a ⅜-inch I.D. stainless steel tubing with a ¾-inch by 1/32-inch monel blade soldered at right angles to the tubing for insertion into the adaptive pocket. The use of monel permits ease of adjustment to the optimum angle of adaptation placed in the tubing. A partially drilled out ⅜-inch stainless steel cylindrical rod is used to adapt eating utensils and other devices so that they can be received by the spring clip holder. For page turning or typing, a pencil can be placed either in the spring clip holder or through a hole in the adaptive pocket.)

Handles (Fig. 64) (PH)

Assorted plastic bottle handles to hold spoons, forks, typing sticks, crayons can be made from such containers as the one shown in Figure 64, or from ammonia, laundry and dish soap plastic bottles. The hard plastic dispenser tubes from many other plastic bottles (e.g. shampoo) become hard plastic straws. For specific directions for constructing a variety of handles for utensils; games;

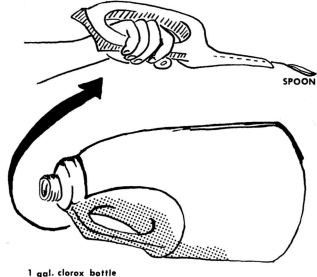

SPOON

1 gal. clorox bottle

Fig. 64

and many other pieces of adapted equipment for the handicapped child made from discarded bottles and containers see Slominski and Griswold, 1970.

LEARNING

Sentence Board (Fig. 65.1) (ADH)

This device can help its user in his ability to associate the spoken with the written word, to group words into sentences, and to read or gauge his potential for these. At the same time, it can stimulate hand use and better coordination. The wooden base of the sentence board has eight built-on channels into which the word blocks fit. Each word from a printed sentence may be written in wax pencil, or be taped on an individual block. The user places the blocks in order as he looks at the sentence or as it is read aloud to him. The user may also form sentences of his own from groups of words provided by the teacher for this sort of practice.

A modification of this sentence board, one for use with letter blocks in spelling exercises is shown in Figure 65.2.

BUILDING SENTENCES. Board (Fig. 65.1). (ADH). Materials:

Plywood, ½-inch by 15½ by 15 inches (base) (Q); 2 wooden strips, ¼ by 1½ by 14 inches (end strips) (V); 2 wooden strips, ¼ by 1½ by 18½ inches (side strips) (Z); 7 wooden strips, ¼ by 1 by 18 inches (divider strips) (K); Wire brads, ½ to 1 inch long; Glue; Wooden blocks, ¾ by 1⅜ by 2 to 5 inches (large dowels, 1⅜-inch or larger, with two sides flattened, may be used).

Method

1. Mark location of divider strips on plywood as shown in Figure 65.1.

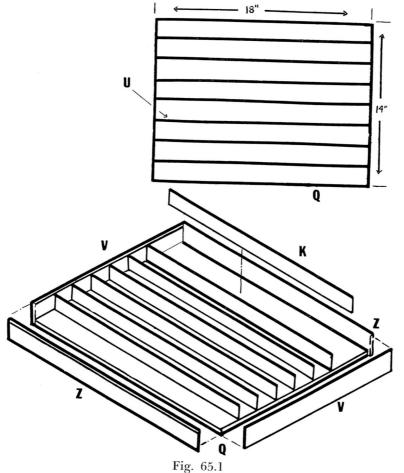

Fig. 65.1

2. Glue and nail divider strips to the plywood on lines marked. Make sure that divider strips are parallel and vertical.

3. Glue and nail side and end strips to base.

4. Cut wooden blocks to dimensions required. Length of blocks may be varied to accommodate words of different lengths. Write words on blocks.

Letter or Number Block Board (Fig. 65.2). (ADH)

Materials: Plywood, ½-inch, 15½ by 15 inches (base) (O); 2 wooden strips, ¼ by 1½ by 15 inches (end strips) (N); 2 wooden

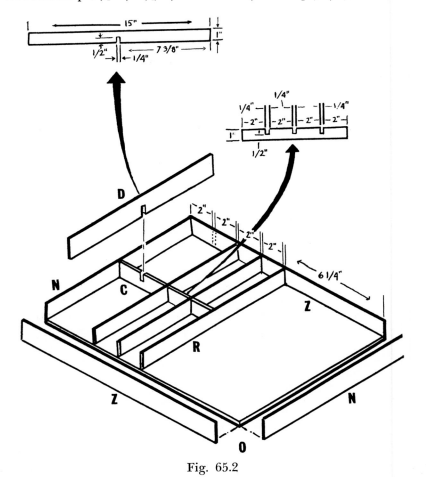

Fig. 65.2

strips, ¼ by 1½ by 16 inches (side strips) (Z); 4 wooden strips, ½ by 1 by 15 inches (divider strips) (D) and end divider (R); 1 wooden strip, ¼ by 1 by 8¾ inches (center strip) (C); Wire brads, ½ to 1 inch long; Glue; Wooden blocks, ¾ by 1⅜ by 2 to 5 inches (large dowels, 1⅜-inch or larger, with two sides flattneed, may be used).

Method

1. Cut notches in divider strips and center strip as shown in Figure 65.2; glue and nail strips to plywood base. Make sure that strips are parallel and vertical.

2. Glue sides and ends to plywood base; nail.

3. Cut wooden blocks to dimensions required. Length of blocks may be varied to accommodate numbers of different lengths. Write numbers or letters on blocks.

Arithmetic

The number board with sponge digits is ideal for use by persons with weak, undependable grasp or aim who are unable to hold pencil or to handle blocks. It presents a possible means whereby those with extremely limited hand use may learn arithmetic or practice solving arithmetic problems. The plastic foam numbers were cut from kitchen sponges purchased at a grocery store. Velcro panels glued and sewn to the backs of the numbers and Velcro panels tacked to the board hold the numbers when they are placed. The softness of the sponge and its light weight make the sponge numbers pleasant to handle, and if a number should be dropped during placement there is no distracting noise. See Rosenberg, 1968, for other adapted equipment for learning arithmetic (e.g. knob digits and magnetic digits).

Learning Arithmetic with Sponge Digits (Fig. 66) (ADH)

Materials: Plywood, ¼-inch, 12 inches square (or large enough to suit reach of user) (PB); 2 suction cups, with attaching bolts and washers; Adhesive-backed blank paper (P), to fit plywood board; Ink or tape (color contrasting with adhesive-backed paper) (PL); 12 strips of Velcro fastener, 1 by 2 inches; Glue; Small staples or tacks (S); Several pieces of plastic foam sponge; Thread.

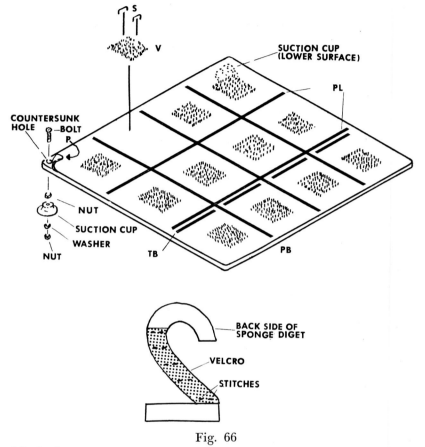

Fig. 66

Method

1. Install a suction cup at top rear corners of board as shown in Fig. 66. Cover board with adhesive-backed paper (P), or paint it. Mark partitioning lines (PL) on the paper with ink, waterproof felt pen, or tape. Glue a strip of Velcro fastener (V), hook side up, in the center of each square. Staple or tack (S) Velcro to board.

2. Cut numeral shapes from sponge. Glue a strip of Velcro fastener to back side of each numeral with loop side up. Sew Velcro to sponge. Total bars may be printed or taped on the playing board, as shown (TB).

Arithmetic Board (Fig. 67) (TA)

A. The Arithmetic Board is used principally to help children with addition and subtraction problems. It is good for children with cerebral palsy because it is concrete, manipulative and holds their attention for longer periods. It can be made of material heavy enough to withstand rough usage. Basswood, balsa wood and hinges are inexpensive. It is simple enough in construction so that a parent can make one for use at home.

B. Under each flap are the numbers from 1 to 10. Below each flap is a blue circle. If the child is to find that $3 + 5 = 8$, he counts three blue circles and raises the flap to find an 8; saying as he does this, "3 and 5 more are 8."

C. Subtraction problems are done the opposite way. For example: $8 - 5 = 3$. The child opens each flap until he has eight opened; then saying, "8 take away 3," he closes three flaps and

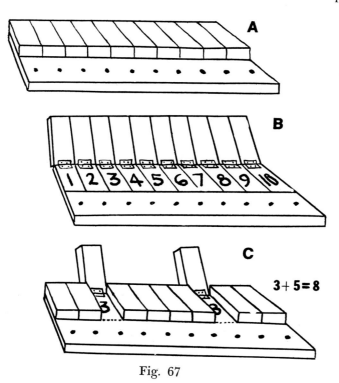

Fig. 67

finds there are five left. Not until the addition procedure is well established and the child has begun to need "The Arithmetic Board" less, should subtraction he started. The Board can also be used for learning to count and recognize the number in its printed form.

Lock Block Board (Fig. 68) (ADH)

This device is used for learning letters, words, or numbers. As the name implies, the blocks actually lock in place preventing displacement.

Materials: Pegboard, 7 by 11 inches (size may be varied to suit user) (P); Tape; 4 suction cups with attaching bolts (may be omitted) (C); Wooden blocks, ¾ inch square (W); Tinner's rivets with ½-inch head (T); Glue.

Method

1. Tape over alternate rows of pegboard holes, as shown in Figure 68.

2. Enlarge exposed holes slightly, and drill ⅝-inch holes touching them. File or cut space between ⅝-inch holes and original holes to form keyhole-shaped holes.

3. If suction cups are to be used, install one suction cup on each corner of pegboard. (NOTE: Wooden blocks ¾ inch square may be used instead of suction cups.)

4. Drill a hole, slightly smaller than shank of rivet, in bottom center of each block. Force shank of rivet into hole, with about ⅜ inch of rivet exposed, and glue rivet to block. Paint or write a letter or number on top surface of block.

Turning Pages

A sponge rubber ball and an adhesive-treated suction cup bolted together make a handy page-turner for the person who can hold a ball in the hand but whose lack of finger control makes turning pages difficult. The device can also be used to pick up small objects. The suction cup sticks to the page because it has been filled with the sticky, gelatinous, but nonstaining filler used in the Hectograph duplicating process. Several other things, such as half of a hollow rubber ball, a rubber crutch tip, a plastic

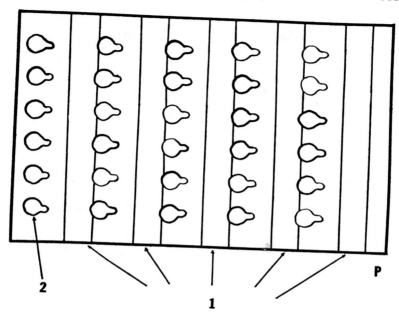

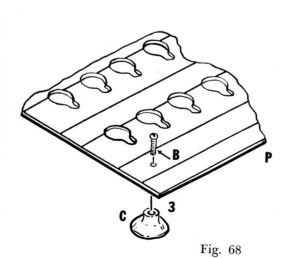

Fig. 68

swivel tip for chair legs, a flexible bottle top, or even a sink stopper, treated in the same way, can be substituted for the suction cup. Page-turners operated by the elbow, by the mouth, and by the headwand have also been devised.

Turning Pages by Hand (Fig. 69.1) (ADH)

Materials: Sponge rubber ball (B); Suction cup (C); Bolt (long enough to extend through ball and suction cup) (Bo) and nut (N); Washer (W); Hectograph duplicator gelatin (H).

Method

1. Place washer on bolt, and force bolt through ball and hole in suction cup. Install nut on bolt, as shown in Figure 69.1.

2. Melt gelatin. Place ball in the mouth of a jar to hold it with suction cup up. Fill suction cup with gelatin and allow gelatin to set for at least one-half hour. Do not use page turner for several hours after pouring the gelatin.

MODIFICATIONS: Wooden dowel and bolt and nut with nail.

1. Drive nail through suction cup and into dowel.

2. Replace suction cup with a plastic swivel tip for chair leg, flexible plastic cap from pill bottle or any such plastic or rubber object which is small and concave.

3. Replace suction cup with half a hollow rubber ball, used without gelatin. This variation of page turner can be used to lift lightweight objects.

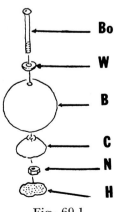

Fig. 69.1

Turning Pages by Elbow (Fig. 69.2) (ADH)

Materials: Suction cup (C); Rubber or leather strip, ⅛-inch thick, about 10 inches long (U); Elastic, 1-inch, long enough to fit around arm in two places (forearm and upper arm) with 1-inch overlap (E); 4 push rivets (R); Small bolt and nut (S, N); Glue; Hectograph duplicator gelatin (H).

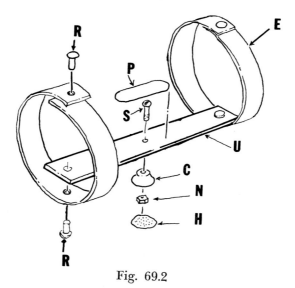

Fig. 69.2

Method

1. Cut 1 inch from rubber or leather strip to make pad. Attach suction cup to strip with nut and bolt as shown. Glue pad to strip over top of bolt.

2. Cut elastic into two pieces that fit arm comfortably. Allow for 1-inch overlap. Rivet to strip as shown. (NOTE: Elastic may be stitched, eliminating the need for rivets.)

3. Fill suction cup with melted gelatin. Allow gelatin to set. Wait several hours before attempting to use the device.

Turning Pages by Mouth (Fig. 69.3) (ADH)

Materials: Suction cup (C); Thin aluminum tube (T); Rubber mouthpiece (M); Spring, to fit inside aluminum tube tightly (S); Small nut and bolt (N); Hectograph duplicator gelatin (H).

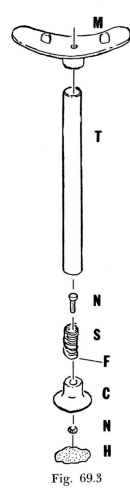

Fig. 69.3

Method

1. Force one end of the spring into the aluminum tube. Attach other end of spring to suction cup with nut and bolt as shown. Bend end of spring (at F) to fit around bolt.

2. Fill suction cup with melted gelatin. Allow to set.

3. Force rubber mouthpiece into or over aluminum tube. Turning Pages by *Headwand* Page-turner Tip: To construct a page-turner tip for use with headwand see *Changing Tips on the Headwand.*

Using Flash Cards

Flash cards are widely-used aids in teaching and learning, but for the person with limited hand use there is the problem of arranging the cards or of keeping them in place. The rack shown in Figure 70 was built to help solve this problem. All that is required is enough use of one hand and arm to grasp a card and place it in one of the slots in the rack, an action which itself may lead to self-initiated hand therapy. Slats atop the base were taken from a discarded venetian blind and nailed to the square lengths of wood which form the base. Strips of adhesive-backed, decorative paper can be used to cover the unfinished wood of the base. Suction cups attached to the corners of the base hold the rack firmly on the table.

FLASH CARD BOARD (Fig. 70) (ADH). Materials: Plywood, ½-inch or ¾-inch, about 12 by 24 inches (size will depend on size and number of flash cards to be held) (PB); 4 wooden slats, about 2 inches wide (from discarded Venetian blind); 3 wooden strips, about ¾ by 1 by 24 inches (S); Finishing nails, about 1 inch long; 3 rubber strips (from discarded innertube), about 1 by 24 inches; Staples (or tape); Brads, about ½ to 1 inch long (19 gauge); 4 suction cups and 4 wood screws with round heads (may be omitted).

Method

1. Use slats and wooden support strips (S) to lay out and mark plywood base as shown in Figure 70, detail A. Drive 1-inch nails into plywood in pattern shown (nails must be close enough together to prevent flash cards from slipping between them, and must extend far enough out of plywood base to hold bottom of cards). Drive nails in the base about ½ inch from edge of slat. Leave about ½ inch of nail exposed (see N).

2. Nail support strips (S) to base as shown in detail B.

3. Staple or tape rubber to front edge of 3 slats, as shown in detail B. Lay slats on support strips, check to see that spacing of slats allows flash cards to be held in the desired position and nail slats to support strips with brads. (NOTE: If necessary for stabilization, suction cups may be installed on bottom corners of base by screwing wood screws partially into base and pressing suction

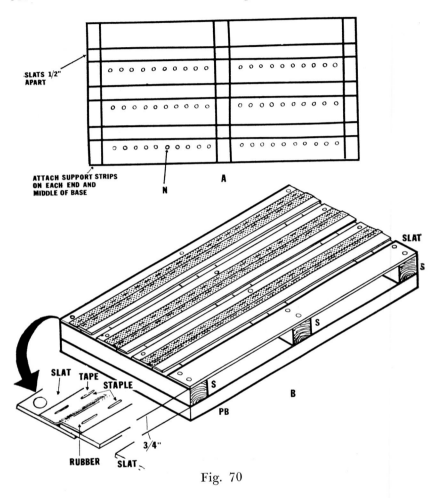

SLATS 1/2" APART

ATTACH SUPPORT STRIPS
ON EACH END AND
MIDDLE OF BASE

N

A

SLAT

S

S

SLAT TAPE STAPLE

SLAT

S

B

PB

3/4"

RUBBER SLAT

Fig. 70

cups onto heads of screws. The unfinished wood and nails may be covered with adhesive-backed paper, or the rack may be painted.)

Writing

A strap-on device can be used by persons who, though able to reach and to control arm motions, have little or no ability to grasp an object manually. The sponge rubber ball, holding a pencil, pen, crayon, or brush, is held to the user's hand by a strap of elastic material fastened with panels of Velcro. The thumb and index finger straddle the writing or drawing instrument to be used, and the fingers are supported comfortable around the ball.

WRITING OR DRAWING WITH A STRAP-ON DEVICE (Fig. 71) (ADH). Materials: Sponge rubber ball (B), to fit hand of user; Bolt the length of ball diameter (C); T-nut, or lock nut and washer, to fit bolt (E); Plastic, semiflexible such as lid of coffee or ice cream container (D); Naugahyde strip (or webbing), 1 by 9 inches (F); Velcro tape; 6 small push rivets (r).

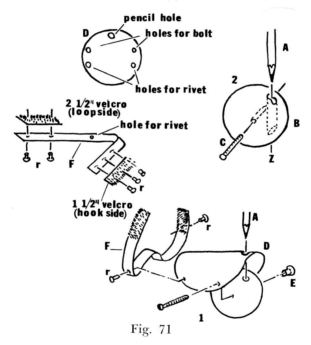

Method Fig. 71

1. Push pencil (A) through ball (B) off center as shown in detail 2, and remove. Run bolt (C) through center of ball at right angle to, and just behind, hole made by pencil and remove. Fit plastic circle (D) over ball, shaping it to curvature of ball (if using plastic lid, first remove rim). Mark locations on plastic of hole made by entry of pencil into ball and those of entry and exit of bolt. Note: Holes for pencil and bolt must be perpendicular (see Z).

2. Separate Velcro tape and cut into two strips as shown. Rivet (r) or stitch tape to strip or webbing in locations indicated.

3. Place plastic over ball as shown in detail 1 and run bolt through ball and plastic, securing bolt with T-nut or lock washer on other side of plastic. Rivet or stitch Naugahyde-Velcro strip (F) to plastic, with mid-portion of strip running under plastic and strip attaching at both sides of plastic.

4. Insert pencil or crayon to be used through large hole in plastic and ball. (NOTE: User places palm of hand on plastic, with index and middle fingers grasping the pencil or crayon. Ends of Naugahyde strip are brought over the back of the hand and fastened by Velcro panels. Strip is adjustable for slight variations in hand size.)

Typewriter Paper Placement

This device can be used by anyone, including headwand and mouthstick users, with enough reach to drop the paper on the rest attached to the machine. It is of particular value to persons with uncontrolled grasp who might wrinkle the paper while attempting to insert it and roll it onto the platen of the typewriter. The guide is constructed of fiber glass and aluminum angle strips, is wider at the back and slants inward to the front so that the paper may be dropped onto a broad area in back and easily guided down by finger, hand, or elbow to the point where it will be picked up by the roller. Mouthstick and headwand users may pick up the paper with a page-turner tip and nudge it into position with a typing punch tip. (See *Changing Tips on the Headwand.*)

Typewriter Guide (Figs. 72.1, 72.2, 72.3) (ADH)

Materials: Aluminum angle strip, 1/16-inch, 1 by 1 by 40 inches; Fiber glass paneling, 1 square foot (Z); six push rivets (r).

Method

1. Cut aluminum angle strip (W) into three pieces and shape as shown in Figure 72.1. Drill holes for rivets in angle strips.

2. Cut the fiber glass paneling to dimensions shown (Z). Position fiber glass and angle strips, and mark locations of holes in

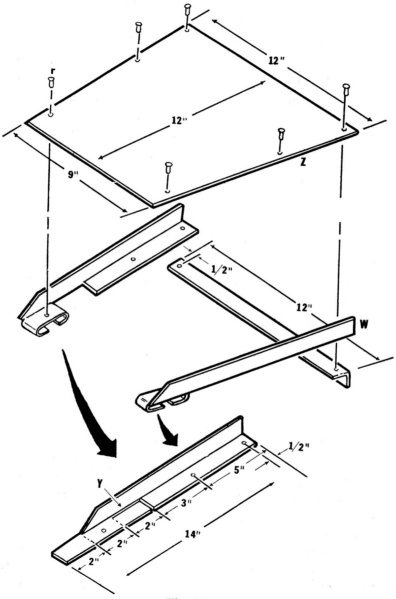

Fig. 72.1

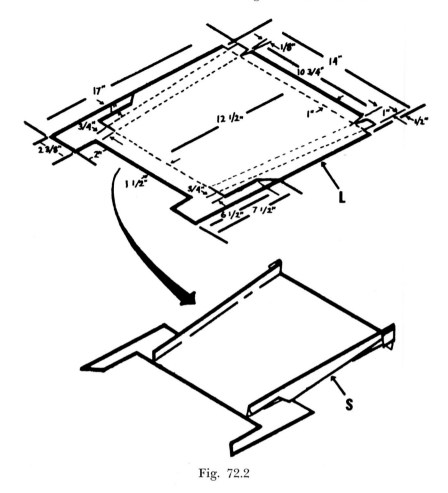

Fig. 72.2

angle strips on fiber glass. Drill holes for rivets in fiber glass, countersinking them so that rivets when installed will be flush.

3. Assemble parts and rivet together as shown. NOTE: Saw out so metal can be bent down (see Y).

MODIFICATIONS:

1. Rivets may be replaced by strong, double-faced tape. If parts are taped together, omit bends in angle strip and cut off strips on each side just below tapered sides. Tape to typewriter paper rest.

2. A one-piece typing paper rest may be made, following pattern and directions shown in Figure 72.2, from a 14- by 17-inch sheet of aluminum. Cut aluminum sheet along solid lines, and mark for bending along broken lines (L). Fold along broken lines (S).

3. A less sturdy paper rest for home use can be made from sheet aluminum, rigid or semi-rigid plastic or cardboard using pattern shown in Figure 72.3. The paper rest is attached to the

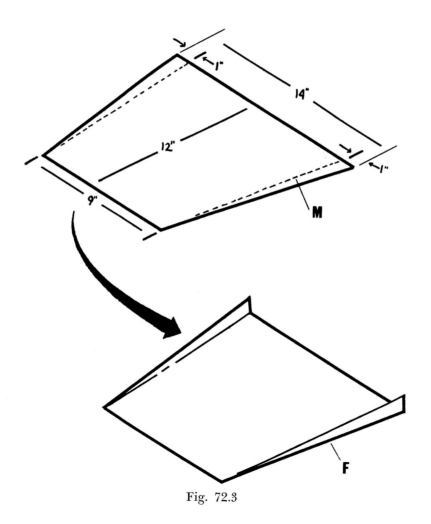

Fig. 72.3

typewriter with double-faced tape. Mark for bending along broken lines (M). Fold along broken lines (F).

Typing Handrest

A typing handrest is useful to the person with a weak wrist in positioning his fingers for typing. It also provides an area to rest the hand on for those who are unable to hold their fingers directly above the typewriter keys. All that is required of the user is enough control of arm, hand and fingers to reach and strike the keys. Constructed of aluminum strips and rods, the typing handrest can be built inexpensively to fit any typewriter. No modifications of the typewriter are necessary to install the shield, and it is easily removed. Since the handrest fits snugly over the keyboard, it does not interfere with the proper placement of the typewriter cover or case.

Typewriter Shield (Fig. 73). (ADH)

Materials: Aluminum strip, ⅛ by 1 by 18 inches; Dowel, ⅜-inch, 4 feet; 10 small, self-threading screws (NG); Plastic steel or plastic wood.

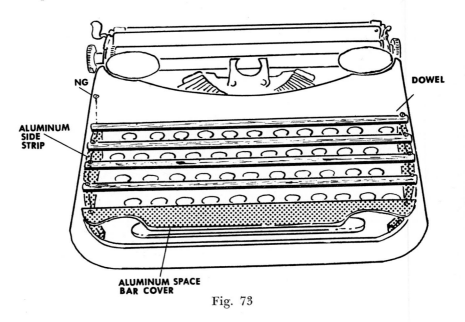

Fig. 73

Method

1. Cut two pieces of aluminum strip to fit in keyboard area between sides of typewriter and keys. Shape strips to fit against sides of typewriter.

2. Cut four lengths of dowel to extend from side to side of keyboard as shown and just a little over aluminum strips on each side. Place dowels between rows of keys and mark their locations on aluminum side strips. Drill holes in strips where marked and corresponding holes in dowels. Use self-threading screws to attach dowels to strips.

3. Shape remaining piece of aluminum strip as shown to extend over space bar of typewriter. Make cutouts in strip so that space bar will be accessible to user. Attach space bar cover to aluminum strip on one side. With handrest in position, push aluminum side strips tight against sides of typewriter. Attach other end of space bar cover to side strip. The device will now stay in position. To remove handrest from typewriter it is necessary to detach space bar cover.

4. Cover dowels and side strips where connected with plastic steel or plastic wood, and paint handrest.

Teaching Machine (**Keith et al. 1967**)

The use of such automated techniques as the Language Master® (manufactured by Bell & Howell, 7100 McCormick Road, Chicago, Illinois) in working with aphasic patients and others is well known. An electric board (See Fig. 6, in Ch. 3 *Learning: Mechanisms and Disorders*) is another type of teaching machine used in treating aphasic linguistic disorders. It can also be used as a motivating and teaching device. It presents stimuli that can be adapted to an individual's grade level and interests, requires an immediate response, and, by means of a light, provides reinforcement for a correct response.

The basic box is constructed of ½-inch plywood. Insulated electric wires on the back of the board are of different colors to facilitate reprogramming. Wires are fastened with thumb screws on the right-hand side so that the pattern of connection can be changed conveniently. Selection of the proper response to a given stimulus makes contacts to complete the circuit and turn on the light. Power is provided by a 6-volt dry cell battery. On the Plexiglas guard covering each card, pictures, letters, or words can be traced with a grease pencil.

The electric board will not signal to the child that he has made the correct response in writing. The child must compare what he has written with the model used on the machine. If the correct response socket was discovered through trial and error and the child did not look at the chosen answer, the board would be of no teaching value. When the child learns the correct response positions on a program, the machine should be reprogrammed. A maximum of seven stimuli and seven responses can be presented at one time. To reduce the number of stimuli presented, slip a piece of paper over the items not wanted. To program the board: select the materials desired (a stimulus card and a corresponding response card).

Applications.[57] In the following examples, the cards described are used merely as illustrations.

Agnosia

VISUAL FORM AGNOSIA. If the child fails to recognize simple common forms, a card containing forms is placed under a Plexiglas® guard on the left, and on the right a card containing similar forms in different order for him to match (Fig. 74.1). The procedure may be varied by presenting the printed word on the right side to be matched with the corresponding form on the left (Fig. 74.1).

VISUAL NUMBER AGNOSIA. If the child is unable to visually recognize numerals: In Figure 74.2 left, numerals are presented for matching with corresponding numerals; printed words may be presented for matching with numerals (Fig. 74.2, center); groups of objects may be matched with numerals or printed words (Fig. 74.2, right).

VISUAL LETTER AGNOSIA. Pictures to illustrate the letter the child is trying to learn (Fig. 74.3, left) may be used; or printed and

---

[57]Terminology employed in the discussion is that used by Halstead, W. C., and Wepman, J. M. in *Manual for the Halstead-Wepman Test for Aphasia.* Chicago. University of Chicago Press, 1949.

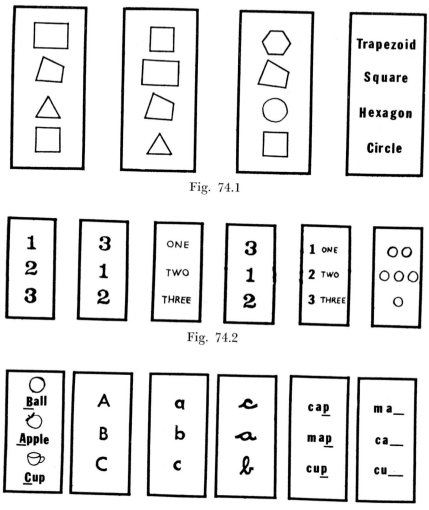

Fig. 74.1

Fig. 74.2

Fig. 74.3

script symbols or upper-case and lower-case letters (Fig. 74.3, center) are matched.

If the child is having difficulty with oral verbal apraxia or auditory recognition: On the left side the stimulus card might contain the words correctly written, on the right side the letter the child is working on is missing from the response words. The

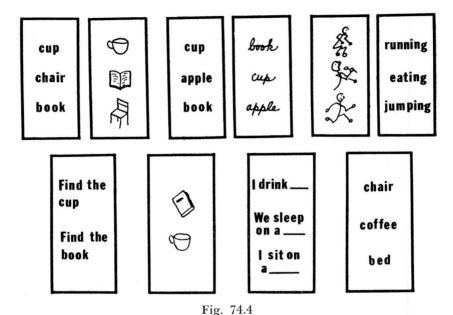

Fig. 74.4

child would match the words, then copy the missing letters on the Plexiglas guard to complete the word (Fig. 74.3, right).

VISUAL WORD AGNOSIA (ALEXIA). Comprehension of the printed word is impaired in this disorder. Pictures (Fig. 74.4, upper left) of objects and matching printed words may be used; printed words and matching script words (upper center), or action pictures and matching words or short phrases (upper right); the child may work at following simple instructions (lower left) or at completing simple sentences (lower right).

Apraxia

This is the loss of the ability to carry out simple voluntary acts and other expressive disorders. For writing apraxia (agraphia) much of the previously suggested material may be adapted to retrain writing. The child may match printed and script words, then copy with a grease pencil on the Plexiglas the words that have been matched. The speech therapist can use the electric board for paraphasia. Difficulties with errors of syntax and articulatory omissions or confusions can be decreased.

In conclusion, Keith and Darley warn that the clinician and teacher must evaluate the effectiveness of this machine for each child because "the machine does not know whether the child has mastered the material the way a human instructor may know through observation and questioning."

Handwriting (Fig. 75) (HT)

The teacher suggests that the colored dots are helpful to the child in writing. The dots can be used for both board work and seat work. Green (G) is for go; blue (B) is for changing directions; red (R) is for stop.

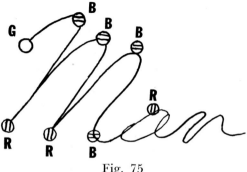

Fig. 75

Tilt-Top Desk-Table (Fig. 76) (TA)

This table has many advantages for use with the cerebral palsied child. It can be raised so papers can be held up my masking tape as a child tries to write if one hand is involved. It also can be arranged for book work or art activity. Wheel chairs can be pushed under it. It is adjustable and can be adapted to the size of children. See Figure 76, for plans and specifications.

ORTHOTIC EQUIPMENT

Arm Control Brace (Fig. 77) (Waylett, 1971)

The cerebral palsy arm control brace (Fig. 77) was developed at Pacific State Hospital (Pomona, California) in their bracing program which was initiated in 1968. The aim of this program was to attempt, through bracing, to improve the upper extremity

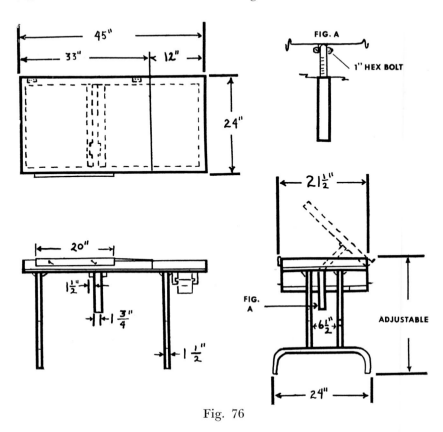

Fig. 76

control of severely athetoid, mentally retarded children in an institutional setting. The basic brace was based on the concept developed at Rancho Los Amigos Hospital in Downey, California.

In addition to the cerebral palsy arm control brace, the authors (Waylett and Lois, 1971) found, as did Garrett (1966) that all patients required the following support equipment to attain partial independence in self-feeding and/or communication activities:

1. TRUNK SUPPORT. A body brace to assist trunk balance and to have a stable point to which the arm control brace could be attached.

2. HEAD SUPPORT. A modified Sayre sling type head support was used. (See Waylett and Lois, 1971 for modifications).

DESCRIPTION OF THE BRACE. SHOULDER: Vertical adjustment

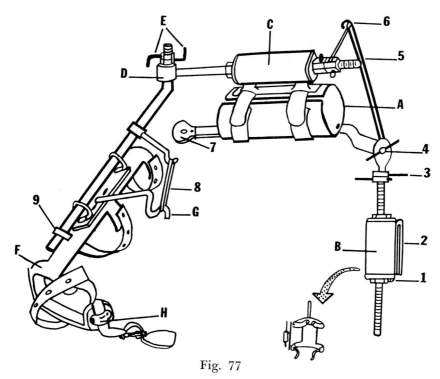

Fig. 77

(4), leather and metal humeral cuff (A) with an adjustable friction joint with stops (3) to control and/or limit horizontal abduction and adduction (*B* is the friction component for control of horizontal abduction and adduction); adjustable external rotation component with rubber band assist (5) with stops and/or friction component (C) for control of internal or external rotation.

Elbow: Adjustable friction joint (D) with adjustable stop (E) for limiting or resisting elbow flexion and/or extension.

Forearm and Hand Component: Forearm cuff (not shown in Fig. 77) or basic long opponens handsplint (F) with supination assist (G) and utensil clip (H).

Upright Chair Friction Feeder (Fig. 78) (Rancho)

This feeder is the same as the standard feeder except ball bearings have been removed from joints and friction discs have been inserted. The feeder is attached to the back of wheelchairs and is used for spastic and athetoid extremities. The friction discs slow down excess movement thereby assisting the child to better control upper extremity movement. (From Rancho Los Amigos Hospital, 7601 East Imperial Highway, Downey, California).

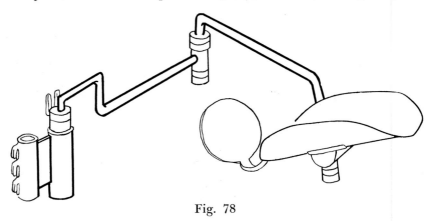

Fig. 78

Spoon Splint to Hold Wrist Neutral (Fig. 79) (PH)

This splint which can be easily constructed by the therapist is essentially the same as the dorsal cock-up splint used in post-surgery treatment of the flexor pronator origin release (See Fig. 16 in Ch. 4 *Orthopedic Management in Cerebral Palsy*).

Method

1. Draw pattern leaving 2 inch overlap of plastic for closure. (Use clorox bottle).

2. Use round-bowl spoon (S) (ice cream or demitasse filed to quarter or dime size).

3. Drill with ⅛-inch bit 2 holes in spoon handle, one at neck, one in stem.

4. Use heated ice pick for holes in plastic (lay drilled spoon on plastic, mark and punch).

5. Use ⅛-inch rapid rivets (r) to attach spoon to plastic. (All shoe repair shops carry these).

6. Pad only if necessary, Use Scholl's ⅛-inch moleskin-covered sponge with adhesive backing.

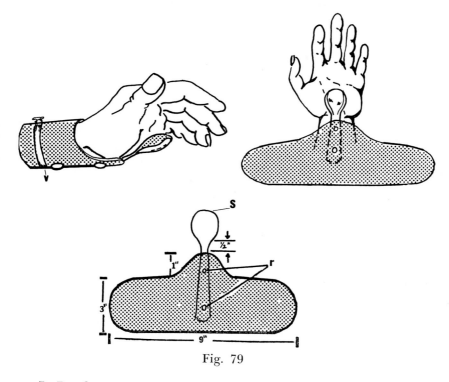

Fig. 79

7. Bend spoon to raise wrist to neutral position.
8. Overlap plastic for wrist closure: velcro, snaps or ties (V).

Roller Chair (Fig. 80, 81) (Finnie, 1971)

This chair is recommended for the spastic quadriplegic who is "unable to sit as he cannot bend at his hips or part and bend his legs" (Finnie, 1970). In addition, she states that "By parting the legs high up it makes it easier for the child to bend his hips and knees and keep his feet flat on the floor and this should enable him to bring his arms forward and use his hands." Miss Finnie warns that the child should not be kept in this chair [in any chair or in any one position] for more than twenty minutes at a time.[58]

[58]Before using this chair or any piece of special equipment such as braces or splints, the therapist and teacher must first consult the child's physician for advice and recommendations.

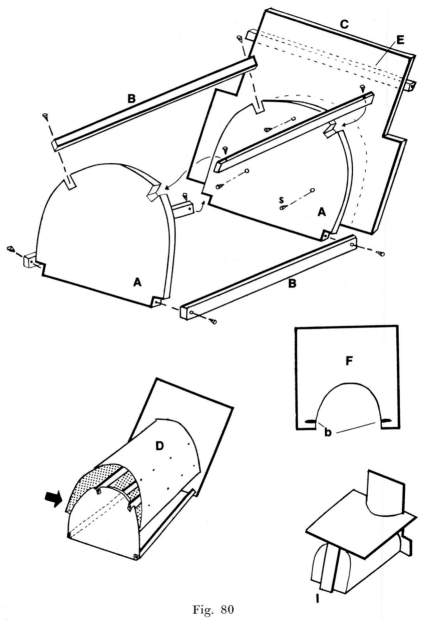

Fig. 80

Fig. 81

Method

1. Two end pieces (A) are cut from plywood ½-inch in thickness. The slots for the braces (B) are 1½-inch deep and ¾-inch wide. The top notches are slanted as shown. The height of the end pieces (A) and, therefore, the "roller" seat (D) is obtained by measuring from the top of the child's knees (when the child is sitting with his knees bent at right angles; feet flat on the floor) to the heel of the foot.

2. Braces (B) are cut from wood to measure 1½ inches by ¾ inches, each is 12 inches long.[59]

3. The backrest (C) is cut from ½-inch plywood. Measurements: 20 inches high, 14 inches wide. This section is secured with three or four ¾-inch wood screws (s). The frame made

[59]Measurements are according to Miss Finnie; however, these may vary according to the child.

from *B* and *A* pieces is covered with ⅛-inch plywood sheeting [or aluminum sheeting] (D) measuring 12 inches wide. This is secured with screws along one edge (indicated in diagram with arrow) with 1½-inch wood screws at ends (fixing *B* to *A*) and ¾-inch screws along the braces at 3 inch intervals. All screws must be countersunk.

4. Attach wood section (E) to back of (C) leaving ends to protrude. This section is used to support cut-out table (F), using two bolts (b) which are attached to cut-out table. The cut-out table can be constructed of Formica with raised edges measuring 24 inches by 24 inches.

5. The leg (1) may be hinged, or two legs may be attached to either side of the table. The slot and back may be covered in foam and vinyl (naughehyde) upholstery material.

MISCELLANEOUS TEACHING SUGGESTIONS AND APPROACHES

Typing Training (Mecham *et al.*, 1966)

The use of the electric typewriter in the educational setting has been advocated for many years. Mecham has devised a *pretyping* perceptal activity which is used as it indicates: before the actual typing sessions are begun. The usual indication for this is to alleviate the frustration the spastic or athetoid may encounter by simply placing him directly on the typewriter even though the motivation is usually high for this activity. The pretyping perceptual activity consists of a chart of the actual typing keyboard: the keys are the size of a penny. The chart is first constructed so that each circle was colored a different shade. Later, it is simplified down to one or two colored circles. The procedure follows something like this: The child is asked to concentrate, visually, on a particular circle; he is requested to "think about touching it" then he touches the circle with his typing finger. Drill is repeated several times a day for five or ten minute periods.

It should be remembered that typing should not be a substitute for writing. It is merely a motivational tool and, in many cases, makes communication much easier. However, there are some children whose only means of communication will be through typing.

One-handed typing techniques for the child with hemiplegia. Fingering for one hand typing for the *right hemiplegic* (the child uses his left hand to type):

qazxsw2

little finger

34edfev

second finger

56tughjbnm

middle finger

89iopl/2kl;',./

index finger

Fingering for one hand typing for the *left hemiplegic* (using right hand to type):

qweasdzxc234

index finger

567rtyfghvbn

middle finger

ui89jkm

second finger

l;'pl/2o-,./

little finger

Mecham cautions that "it is better that the student type with one finger, than destroy motivation by teaching him any typing system." The use of a stylus for typing is indicated when the child has no grasp or inefficient grasp. In placing the typing stylus somewhere other than in the hand, there is one principle to remember (p. 336, Mecham): the further from the hand the typing is performed, the slower and less satisfactory the progress. In other words, the child using the stylus attached to his forehead will have slower progress than the child using a mouth stick.

A cardinal point to make concerning the initial introduction to the actual typewriter: Until the child has developed some independence in the typing process or, at least, has relaxed somewhat, never leave the child at the typewriter to go off to work with someone else. He will need your undivided attention and help initially. Give the child a good chance before you seek an easier way. All the general teaching techniques used with the brain-injured child [environmental stimuli reduction; stimulus value of task should be increased; reward or reinforcement; accurate feedback; repetition; utilization of a variety of sensory modalities; presentation of material in a logical sequence; use meaningful materials; active involvement; success; short periods of time on new activities] apply when teaching typing as do the concepts of normal development.

Generally, as a first lesson plan, Mecham suggests using something familiar such as the child's name. Typing numbers and the alphabet are also suggested as beginning typing subject matter. All children regardless of disability should be instructed to first find the letter key with their eyes, keeping visually fixed on the key until he has successfully struck the key. The occupational therapist may be of assistance if special equipment is needed. Reference is made also to some of the previous suggestions such as the typing guard and headwand with adapted tips.

Word Bingo (TA)

An excellent game for word study. Words are printed on oak tag, 9 on a card for younger children, 15 on a card for older children. Flash cards are made for these same words. These flash cards are shuffled, cut and turned over in order. The game is played like any real bingo game. The flash cards are turned over one at a time, and if the word appears on the bingo card, the child must cover the word with a wooden disc. The winner is the child who first covers a straight line of words, makes an X, covers the card, etc. With young children just learning the words, the flash cards can be held up so that they may be seen for comparison. If the words are fairly well learned, the leader who is holding the flash card, reads it, not permitting the child to see the printed side of the card.

Reading (HT)

To help children interpret sounds of letters, use small white paper cups which have letters printed on the front of the cups. Work on a limited number of sounds at one lesson. Give the letter sound, child drops paper clip in correct cup. This is also helpful to teach letter names by using picture as stimulus. [Adaptations may be necessary for the cerebral palsied child: larger cups secured to table; larger picture and/or letter stimuli on the cup; 1-inch cubes instead of paper clips].

Write words from reading (that children are having trouble with) on slips of paper, fold the paper so the word cannot be seen, fasten with a paper clip. Place words in a glass fish bowl. The child throws into the bowl a piece of string with a small magnet attached and pulls out one of the *fish*. If he can read the word he may keep it; otherwise it must be thrown back into the bowl. Use words from reading of two or three children near same reading level.

PEGBOARDS. Made of one layer of quarter inch pegboard, mounted on a backing of quarter inch plywood. (With backing, if pegs are used, they don't slide through the holes). Pegboards can be used to keep track of vowel sounds in word games. "Put one peg in for every long vowel sound you hear in these words." ant (none), take (1), bake (1), cake (1). This board can also be used for short vowels, too. [Pegboards can be made from insulated ceiling tiles as well].

BELL AND HOWELL LANGUAGE MASTER USAGE. In addition to commercially printed cards use teacher made cards for:

a. Building meaningful sight vocabulary—paste picture on card and write the word alongside of it in manuscript and cursive. Record the word singly and then in a short sentence on the Instructor track. The student listens to the Instructor track and then records what he heard on the Student track.

b. Spelling—record the word to be spelled on the Instructor track. Record the word and spell it on the Student track. The student takes the assigned spelling cards and clips a blank piece of paper over each one. The student puts the cards through on the Instructor track, writes the spelling word and checks his accuracy by playing the card through on the Student track.

c. Dictation and training of auditory memory—the teacher records the sentence within the student's written ability on the Instructor track. The student plays the Instructor track and records what he heard on the Student track. After checking the Instructor track for accuracy of auditory retention, the student writes what he heard. The sentence can be written on the back side of the language master card to allow the student self-correction.

Tile Checkerboard (HT)

Materials: Plywood; Tile 2 x 2 secured from ceramic tile company (discards) two colors; Glue; Checkers.

Method: Place title in shape of checker board. Cut plywood an inch bigger all the way around tile. Glue each tile in place. Let glue get tacky before placing tile down.

Uses: 1. Directionality. Put an x on the third blue tile in the second column. Any number of directions may be developed here. The children enjoy the *feel* of the tile.

2. Number work as "every other". Putting numbers or problems on one color; answers on the other.

3. Standard checker game played. Putting consonants on tile with Marks-a-lot® pen or any felt-tip pen. As they move checkers in play, they must give a word that begins with that letter. If the child doesn't know the letter or word, the other player may get a point for telling the letter or word. It may be played learning the letters, initial consonants, medial or ending consonants. Upper grades play—parts of speech, 95 commonest nouns, etc. All it takes to change the use is a wet sponge and Ajax®. Dolch list can also be taught with it.

Beads on Wire (TA)

A device used by children who cannot handle the materials suggested in the developmental mathematics program. (Rows of beads on a cardboard, plastic discs, sticks, etc.) Ten wooden beads are strung on rigid wire long enough to fit over the child's table. Two or more rows are used; depending on the child's level. In answering "How many" the child can push the required number of beads from left to right. In addition of two and three, he can push over two from one row and three from another and count. In indicating the "fourth" bead, he can push the beads apart and leave a space on either side of the "fourth." Dividing beads into groups can be done in the same way. Answers in subtraction can be indicated by pushing over the required number of beads and taking away the number indicated. The addition may also be used.

REFERENCES

Finnie, Nancie: *Handling the Young Cerebral Palsied Child at Home.* New York, Dutton, 1970.

Garrett, A. L., Lister, M., and Bresnan, J.: New conecpts in bracing for cerebral palsy. *J Amer Phys Ther Assn,* 7:728-733, 1966.

SOURCES

ADH—Rosenberg, Charlot: *Assistive Devices for the Handicapped.* The American Rehabilitation Foundation and the National Medical Audiovisual Center of the National Library of Medicine, printed by Stein Printing Company, Atlanta, 1968.

Finnie, Nancie, Deputy Principal, The Western Cerebral Palsy Centre, London.

HP—*Handbook for Teachers of the Educationally Handicapped.* Published by the Rocky Mountain Special Education Instructional Materials Center, Colorado State College Department of Special Education, Greeley, Colorado.

Keith, Robert L., and Darley, F.: The use of a specific electric board in rehabilitation of the aphasic patient. *J Speech Hear Dis,* 32:148-153, 1967.

Kester, Nancy C., and Lehneis Hans R.: A combined ADL-long opponens orthosis. *Arch Phys Med Rehab,* 50:219-222, 1969.

Mechan, Merlin J. et al.: *Communication Training in Childhood Brain Damage.* Springfield, Thomas, 1966, pp. 332-340.

PH—Slominski, Anita and Griswold, P.: *Please Help Us Help Ourselves.* Cerebral Palsy Clinic, Indiana University Medical Center, Indianapolis, Indiana, 1970.

Rancho Los Amigos Hospital, 7601 East Imperial Highway, Downey, California.

TA—*Teaching Aids for Children with Cerebral Palsy.* The University of the State of New York/The State Education Department Bureau for Physically Handicapped Children, Albany, 1966.

Waylett, Janet, and Barber, Lois: Upper extremity bracing of the severely athetoid mental retardate. *Amer J Occ Ther,* 25:402-407, 1971.

Appendix A

TASK LEVEL EVALUATION

1 Month

Motor
> Hand clenches on contact
> No thumb use
> Lifts head briefly (prone)

Reflex[60]
> Positive supporting response (strong at birth, declines until 4th month)
> Palmar grasp
> Sucking reflex (persists throughout 1st year)
> Tonic neck reflex[61]
> Moro (extension) reflex
> Righting reflexes,[62] neck righting; labyrinthine (faintly present)

---

[60]According to Magnus (1926) there are five principle reflex mechanisms that regulate tone. They are: (1) Tonic labyrinthine reflexes (2) Tonic neck reflexes, (3) Righting reflexes, (4) Supporting reactions, and (5) Segmental reactions.

[61]Actually, the tonic neck reflexes may more accurately be called *attitudes* or *postures*. For instance, the ATNR (assymmetrical tonic neck reflex) appears and is prominent during the first 3 months of life. By the fourth month the head is usually in mid-position. Therefore, symmetrical postures predominate. Presence of the ATNR posture past 6 months may be indicative of pathology or cerebral dysfunction. The ATNR posture: limbs are extended on side toward which the head is rotated. The child's head is turned to the right, the right arm and leg extend with a corresponding decrease in extensor tone and an increase in flexor tone in the left arm and leg. The attitudinal or postural reflexes *maintain* stationary body posture.

[62]There are a variety of these reflexes which emerge as true neck reflexes decline. Origins are in the otoliths, tactile impulses from the trunk and proprioceptive impulses from the neck muscles and cervical spine joints. These neck-righting reflexes gradually disappear, as voluntary activity matures. Should be dissolved when the infant is able to get up directly from the supine without first needing to roll over to the abdomen, and get up on all fours (Paine, 1964):
(1) Labyrinthine: Adjusts the head to gravity (eyes blindfolded). Can be seen faintly in the infant. Held in ventral suspension (hanging from feet) the baby orients head in the horizontal position—the head is adjusted to gravity.
(2) Body righting reflex on neck: With the child in side-lying position, legs are

Eye-Hand
Follows dangling ring (with eyes and head) to midline
Language
Startle response to loud sudden noises (receptive language)
Activity stops when approached by sound
Can be quieted by familiar, friendly voice

2 Month

Motor
Head lifts (prone)
Regards extended arm (TNR)
Head lag when pulled to sitting, lag is not complete
Reflex
Tonic neck reflex (TNR) reaches peak at 2 months
Head comes up from ventral suspension (labyrinthine righting reflex) becomes stronger with each month up to about 4-8 months
Eye-Hand
Follows moving person with or without turning head
Follows, visually, objects past midline
Grasps in pronation
Holds rattle briefly
Language
Babbles, coos
Often looks at speaker and responds by smiling
Special cry for hunger

3-4 Month

Motor
Prone position on forearms—lifts head
Lateral head control
Rolls part way to side

---

turned to opposite side, the head rotates to the horizontal position. Begins to develop about 6 to 7 months.

(3) Neck on Body: Rotation of the neck (head) sideways is followed by rotation of the whole body. Usually disappears around 12 months.

(4) Body on Body: If the child is placed on his side, with head held to the side, the body rights itself to the vertical position.

(5) Optical: Held in ventral suspension, the head orients itself into the horizontal position. This reflex depends on visual clues. Becomes important about 8 months.

These and other reflexes are employed in the newer treatment techniques in physical habilitation. They cause muscle movement without the individual having to attempt any conscious action on his part (Moore, 1969, p. 17). In essence, they *restore* the body to a normal postion.

Slight head lag when pulled to sitting
Supported sitting—head steady, lumbar curve
Moves arms together; now bidexterous making two hand approach
to objects until 24 weeks (4 months)
Supported standing—bears small fraction of weight briefly (support reaction)—foot lifts occassionally[63]
Hands closed loosely
Reflex
Symmetrical tonic neck reflex (head predominately held in midline)
Labyrinthine righting reflex (a prerequisite to lifting head) becomes stronger
Grasp reflex diminishing (more active grasp)
Sucking usually under voluntary control by 4th month
TNR disappearing (abnormal if present at 6-7 months; most prevalent from 2-4 months). See footnote 60.
Moro reflex disappearing
Landau reaction (4 months)[64]
Eye-Hand
Ring, follows in circle while in supine position. Range of vision 180 degrees
Arms become active on sight of toy
Looks from hand to cube—may contact the cube
Splashes with hands in bath
Hands remain open; grasp begins to appear (4 months)
Holds toy (drops toy), outside fingers are strongest, mouths toy
Prefers head in midline for better vision (emerging symmetrical postures)
Language (3 months)
Looks at speaker with eyes; spontaneous social smile
Laughs and uses other vocal pleasure expressions when played with
Often vocalizes with two or more different syllables
(4 months)
Deliberately turns head toward voice source. Smiles at mirror image
Usually frightened by angry voices
Often uses sounds like p, b, or m
Self-care
Anticipates bottle (increased kicking, waving, vocalizations, mouth

[63]Positive adjustment reaction one of which is the positive supporting reaction; crossed extension reaction is included here as well.

[64]Approximate age of appearance; however, there are some who feel this reaction is normal at 3 months. See Mitchell (1962) and Illingsworth (1962). Disappearance is also debatable (See Andre-Thomas *et al.*, 1960, who places the disappearance of this reaction at 7 months).

opening if given at least 2 bottles of milk/day for at least two weeks.

5 *Months*

Motor

Tries to crawl while on abdomen

Lifts head and chest in prone position

Anticipates being pulled up by lifting head from the supine

Reflex

Moro absent (persistence beyond 5 or 6 months is pathological)

Eye-Hand

Pulls ring down while supine

Grasp is squeeze or whole hand

May be unable to actually reach out and grasp a toy but shows he
is trying by "scratching" at table where he sees the object

Language

Recognizes and responds to own name

Usually stops cyring when someone talks to him

Uses vowel-like sounds similar to O and U

Expresses anger, displeasure by vocal patterns other than crying

6 *Months*

Motor

Lifts head when supine spontaneously

Rolls to supine

Lifts head and assists when pulled to sitting

Sits alone momentarily, leaning on hands (sits propped for 30
minutes)

Supported standing—bears large fraction of weight and bounces

Reciprocal leg pattern

Feet to mouth

Reflex

Falling reaction appears and continues (Parachute Reaction)[65]

Sucking reflex may still be present

Reflex grasp may be present in sleep

Equilibrium reactions sequence begins

Eye-Hand

Becoming more visually aware of both gross (people) and fine
(blocks, scribbling by others)

Pats image in mirror

---

[65]According to Paine (1964), this reaction is a valuable physical sign in demonstrating a deficit of integration of movement at a suprasegmental level which affects the upper extremities. It is therefore, a useful diagnostic sign of hemiparesis.

Reaches with one hand
Grasp palmerwise (rings, rattles, cubes, ball)
Resecures dropped objects
Language
Stops or withdraws in response to 'no' at least half of the time
Takes initiative in vocalizing and babbling directly at others
Appears to recognize words like "daddy", "bye-bye"
Aware of strangers
Self-Care
Begins to drink from a cup, prefers bottle, but able to lift cup
Anticipates spoon feeding, sucks food from spoon

7 *Months*

Motor
Reaches one arm for a toy while on stomach
Holds weight while held in standing position (supporting reaction)
While on back, lifts head as if to sit up
Eye-Hand
Rakes pellet with whole hand
Shakes rattle
Holds object in each hand when third is presented drops second
object
Grasps and transfers object (grasp is still in palm but held at radial
side principally by index and 3rd fingers pressed against thumb
—2-finger grasp)
One hand approach to objects
Slaps, scratches table
Language
Appropriately responds with gestures to such words as 'come', 'up',
'high', 'bye-bye'
Gives some attention to music or singing
At least half of the time responds with vocalizations when called
by name
Appears to "name" some things in his own language
Begins some 2-syllable babbling

8 *Months*

Motor
Prone to sitting
Sits erect one minute
Stands briefly, hands held
Trunk pivots, unable however, to crawl
Takes full weight while holding rail or crib

Inside fingers more important

Opposes thumb and first two fingers to hold a block (inferior
scissors grasp—no thumb opposition, just abduction)

Lifts cup by handle

Bites and chews toys (important for feeding)

Holding one toy, will grasp another; does not drop second when
the third object is presented

Language

Two syllables in verbal play

Frequently appears to listen to whole conversations between others

Stops, with regularity, when name is called

Appears to recognize the names of some common objects when
names are spoken

Occasionally "sings along" with some familiar song or music without using real words

Plays "pat-a-cake", "peek-a-boo"

9-10 Months

Motor

Creeps on all fours (reciprocally)

Assumes sitting position from prone

Sits indefinitely with good control

Pulls to standing on furniture

Lowers self to floor

Gets to prone from sitting

Stepping movements when held upright

Reflexes

Sucking reflex disappearing

Eye-Hand

Probes with index finger

Pincer grasps (side of thumb-finger) begins to appear; can pick up
small object

9 months—radial-digital grasps

10 months—inferior pincer grasp (between thumb and tip of index
or middle finger)

Voluntary release beginning to appear

Lifts cup by handle to look for a hidden object

Brings two objects together (such as a cup and a cube) in midline
bimanual play

Takes third cube and retains second

Crude release—doesn't just drop object

Language

Adjusts to words (appropriately responds to bye-bye, where's kitten,
where's the light)

Imitates sounds such as coughing, grunting

Will sustain interest for up to a full minute in looking at pictures in a book if pictures are named

Regularly stops activity in response to "no"

Appears to understand some simple verbal requests (such as giving a toy or other object to a parent)

Uses some gesture language such as shaking head appropriately for "no"

Speaks first words often (da-da, mama, bye-bye, or the name of a pet or toy)[66]

Uses some exclamation like "oh-oh"

Often uses jargon (short sentence-like utterances of 4 or more syllables without true words)

Self-Care

Holds own bottle

Pretends to drink from cup (about 11 mos. drinks from cup which is held for him)

Finger feeds spilled bits of food (munches instead of sucking)

11 Months

Motor

Crawling on soles of feet and palms of hand

Cruises: walks sideways using hands as support by holding on to rails, etc.

Sits and maintains balance while pivoting

Eye-Hand

Beginning concept of *inside* as he begins to place objects *in* other objects

Good pincer grasp with wrist extension

Squeaks doll

Forefinger and thumb more adept

Formboard: associates round role to formboard

Language

Will, on occasion, follow simple commands like "put that down"

Tries, at times, to imitate new words

Appears to understand simple questions like "where is the ball?"

12 Months (1 year)

Motor

Assumes and maintains kneeling balance

---

[66]Some authorities place this skill at 11 months. Research has indicated, however, that delay of appearance of the first word beyond 18 months may indicate a serious physical, mental or hearing handicap (Darley *et al.*, 1961).

Walks with one hand held
Creeps freely on hands and knees
Eye-Hand
Imitates beating, stirring with spoon
Easily releases small objects therefore can place cube in cup but cannot put a small object into a small bottle
Interested in what is inside; likes boxes
Attempts 2 block tower
Pincer grasp between thumb and/or tip of index well developed; child would, therefore, be able to hold objects such as crayon (although it may not be for another 2 or more months that he will actually mark with the pencil or crayon)
Wrist extension
Places peg in $\frac{1}{2}$-inch hole
Language
Uses 3 or more words with some consistency (used to specify an object or situation)
"Talks" to toys and people
Responds frequently by vocalizing to songs or rhymes
Responds with appropriate gestures to several verbal requests demonstrating understanding
Attends and responds to speech with interest over long periods
Makes appropriate verbal response to some requests such as "say bye-bye"
Gives toy on request
Self-Care/Social
Sucking reflex should have disappeared
Finger feeds food from tray
Chews solid foods
Cooperates in dressing
Can drink small amount from cup (self-holding)
May rub spilled food on tray
Can hold spoon and brush it across tray
Interest in taking off hat, shoes, pants
Puts comb to hair, handkerchief to nose
Plays simple games
Repeats a performance laughed at

13-14 Months

Motor
Stands alone momentarily
Eye-Hand
Can pick up pellet (has precise opposition)
Grasps two cubes in one hand (at 14 months)

Reaches near objects with skill—some incoordination present when reaching for far objects

Language

Uses 5 or more true words with some consistency

Uses voice and pointing, gesturing in attempt to obtain objects

Words in jargon utterances

Appears to understand some new words each week

Seems to understand feeling and emotion of most speakers

Attentive for 2 or more minutes in looking at pictures if pictures are named

15-16 Months

Motor

Walks alone several steps

Kneels alone

Falls by sitting

Creeps or hitches upstairs

Rises to standing independently and walks

Stoops and recovers

Eye-Hand

Inserts pellet in bottle

6 or more cubes in cup and out (likes to dump)

Scribbles in imitation (weakly); makes line with crayon

Helps turn pages of a book, pats book

Gets into everything

Throws ball crudely (a favorite pastime)

Builds tower of 2 blocks

Voluntary release matured

Language

Uses consistently 7 or more true words (and gestures)

Use of consonants such as t, d, w, and h more frequently

Carries out verbal request to select and bring familiar object from another room

Recognizes and identifies many objects or pictures when named

Recognizes names of various parts of body

Self-Care/Social

Discards bottle

Takes off shoes

Still prefers finger feeding

Rudiments of toilet training—can sit on toilet seat

May be able to hold cup and spoon awkwardly

May inhibit grasp of dish on tray

17-18 Months

Motor
> Walks alone, seldom falls—runs stiffly
> Upstairs with one hand held (beginning then to be able to stand on one foot with help; beginning to perform such tasks as standing on balance beam with help)
> Seats self in small chair
> Climbs into an adult chair
> Walks into large ball, does not kick it
> Pulls a pull-toy as walks backwards
> Climbs over obstacles

Eye-hand
> Puts 10 or more cubes in cup; release is exaggerated with increase in finger extension
> Scribbles with pencil spontaneously; makes imitative strokes (vertical) with crayon
> Pretends to read (looks at pictures in a book)
> Dumps from large container (plastic milk bottle, coffee can)
> Turns pages, 2-3 at once
> Builds tower of 3-4 blocks
> Throws ball into box
> Accepts 4th and retains 3rd block
> Pulls toy

Language
> Points to eye, nose, ear
> Begins repeating words heard in conversations
> Simple questions comprehended
> Carries out 2 consecutive directions with object such as a ball
> Associates (and remembers) new words by categories (foods, animals etc.)
> Begins using words without gestures

Self-Care/Social
> Removes hat, shoes, mittens, socks
> Unzip large zipper
> Feeds self in part, spills
> Puts on shoes
> Beginning bladder and bowel control (toilet habits regulated in daytime)
> Asks for help when in trouble

19-20 Months

Motor
> Beginning attempts at walking on an undeviating line (this skill

continues to develop until, according to Fields (1969), child is able to walk a 10 foot long line, stepping off one to three times)

Eye-Hand

Interested and able to play appropriately with toys such as pegboard (using large pegs)

Places all pegs (⅝″ sq.) in pegboard

Language

2-3 word sentences imitated

Imitates sounds in environment during play (cars, animals)

Speaking vocabulary of 10-20 words

Points, in response to verbal requests, to parts of body and items of clothing shown in large pictures

Responds appropriately to action words such as "sit down", "stop", etc.

Understands such directions as "give it to me", "give it to him" which contain personal pronouns

21-22 *Months*

Motor

Upstairs holding one rail

Downstairs, with one hand held

Squats when playing

Stands on 1 foot with help (giving child the ability to perform such activities as walking on a balance beam with one foot on beam, one on the floor; or at least attempts to stand on board)

Walks backwards

Eye-Hand

Places 2 blocks in formboard (or may solve entire formboard)

Builds tower of 5-6 blocks

Tries to turn doorknob

Language

Combines two words (two concepts: i.e. "go bye-bye", "mommy come")

Follows 2-3 simple related commands

Recognizes and identifies many common objects and pictures of common objects when they are named

23-24 *Months*

Language

May use, on occasion, 3-word sentences (ie. "There it is")

Refers to self with own name

Selects one item (such as a comb) from a group of five or six items in response to a verbal request

Learning names of animals from book (See: Engelmann, Siegfried:

Give Your Child a Superior Mind. New York, Simon and Schuster, 1966, for learning task age level schedules.)

2 Years (25, 26 and 27 months)

Motor
  Runs fairly well
  Upstairs and downstairs alone, without alternating feet
  Kicks a ball on command
  Gets up by turning to side
  Jumps from bottom step with one foot in the lead
Eye-Hand
  Rotates forearm, can turn knobs
  Turns pages of book singly
  Tower of 7 blocks
  Beginning to learn easy shapes such as a circle
  Adapts to reversal of formboard (4 trials)
  Places 2-3 blocks in row for a train
  Strings 3 1″ beads
  Matches colors (black, red, yellow, blue, green); matches pictures
    (i.e. elephant, chair, doll, wagon); matches shapes (circle,
    square); matches block designs (i.e. two rectangles to form a
    square)
  Removes paper from candy
  Unscrews lid
Pre-Writing
  Imitates vertical stroke
  Crudely imitates circular stroke
  Imitates a "V" (unable to initiate it)

Language
  Usually uses two to three word sentences with pronoun, verb, and
    object
  Frequently uses, correctly, personal pronouns (I, you, he, she, me,
    it etc.)
  Selects, appropriately, pictures demonstrating action (such as a
    picture showing a child running or eating) indicating an under-
    standing of verb forms
  Upon request, points to smaller parts of body (elbow, eyebrow)
  Asks for things by name
  Two-word responses to pictures (a useful index of a child's de-
    velopmental status in language has been the length of the
    responses which he produces when shown pictures or invited to
    play with toys (Brown *et al.*, 1967)

Self-Care/Social

> Holds cup or glass in one hand
> Inhibits overturning of spoon
> Can feed self—may not want to
> Takes off shoes, socks, pants
> Puts both legs in one pants hole
> Verbalizes toilet needs, in daytime, fairly consistently
> Plays alone

2½ Years

Motor

> Can walk on tiptoes
> Jumps with both feet
> Tries to stand on one foot
> Stands on balance board with both feet without help[67]
> Walks in general direction of line drawn on the floor, occasionally
>   steps on line

Eye-Hand

> Grasps too strongly, releases with over-extension
> Tower of 8 blocks
> Places blocks in formboard with no demonstration
> Recognizes through manual manipulation, ordinary objects (i.e.
>   pencil, marble, cube, box, cotton) (Monfraix *et al.*, 1961)
> Adds chimney to block train

Pre-Writing

> Imitates horizontal line, "V" and "H" strokes (holds crayon with
>   fingers rather than with fist)
> Two or more strokes for cross

Language

> 27-30 mos.
>> Repeats two or more numbers correctly, understands concept
>>   of "one"
>> Understands sizes (i.e. little, small, large)
>> Recoginzes names and pictures of most common objects
>> Understands some concepts through functional use (correct
>>   answers to such questions as "What do you eat with?", "What
>>   do you wear?", "What do we cut with?")
>> Can name at least one color
>
> 30-33 mos.
>> Understands common verbs and most common adjectives

[67]Similar tasks appear at approximately the 2 year age level in the Bayley Scales
(Bayley, 1969). According to this Scale, the child attempts to take a step on the
board at approximately 2½ years.

Appropriately answers question "Are you a boy or a girl?"

Discusses, upon request, his own "drawings"

33-36 mos.

Follows 3 simple requests

Understands concepts on, under, front, behind etc.

Uses t, d, n, k, g, ng in words (by 2½ the average child produces 27 different sounds—See Irwin, 1946)

Self-Care/Social

Helps put things away

3 Years

Motor

Runs on toes

Rides tricycle

Upstairs alternating feet; downstairs with both feet on a step

Jumps from bottom step with both feet together

Stands on one foot momentarily

Walks backwards easily

Eye-Hand

Adapts to reversal of formboard, no errors

Tower of 9-10 blocks

Imitates bridge made of 1″ blocks

Good rotation of wrist

Matches 3 color forms

Matches 4 forms (cross, circle, square, star)

Imitates simple two-color block designs

Completes 2 part picture of simple objects (ball, man, tree, etc.)

Imitates train made of blocks

Pre-Writing

Imitates cross

Copies circle

Imitates vertical and horizontal strokes

Traces a square

Language

Y, F, V sounds in words

Can repeat 3 digits

Uses 4 word sentences

Likes to whisper and responds to whisper

Gives full name; tells sex and happenings

Self-Care/Social

Unbuttons accessible buttons

Feeds self, spills little

Undresses rapidly and well except back fastenings

Puts on pants, socks, shoes

Cannot distinguish front and back
Pours well from pitcher

3½ Years

Motor
Stands on one foot for 2 sec.
Motor-incoordination—stumbling, falling, fear of heights (tensional outlets are often exaggerated in the 3½)
Walks on a balance board with two or more alternating steps (Fields, 1969)
Eye-Hand
Builds bridge from model (no demon.)
Hand tremor may be evidenced
Sorts two objects (i.e. red blocks from blue blocks)
Self-Care/Social
Washes, dries hand and face

4 Years

Motor
Stand on one foot (4-8 seconds)
Up and downstairs alternating feet
Skips on one foot
Eye-Hand
Throws overhead
Cut on line with scissors
Saw with hand saw
Holds brush in adult manner
Counts four pennies
Can count, with correct pointing, three objects
Matches 8-10 forms such as octagon, trapezoid, square
Manual (tactile) recognition of 5-7 geometric shapes; the easiest recognized: circle, star; the most difficult: trapezium and hexagon (Monfraix *et al.*, 1961)
Pre-Writing
Copies cross with crayon
Draws rough pictures of familiar things
Picks longer line (3 correct, in 3 trials)
Imitates a square
Language
Can answer simple questions—such as what familiar animals do
Sh, zh, th sounds appear in words
Uses complex sentences
Purpose of communication is to relate experiences and to see information in questions

Articulation errors (l, r, s, z, sh, ch, j, th); has mastered b, p, m, w, and h[68]

Knows colors

Knows 4-5 prepositions such as on, under, front, behind (some authorities place this at 2½ years—See Bzoch *et al.*, 1971)

Five word responses to pictures

5 *Years*

Skips with alternating feet

One foot standing balance over 8 seconds

Walks on long line drawn on floor, heel to toe fashion

Walking board—full length

Runs, climbs onto chairs and tables

Likes to march (to music)

Jumps from table height

Eye-Hand

Uses hands more than arms when catching small ball but frequently fails to catch ball

Prehends and releases with precision

Matches two-color circle   ⊖

Block designs   ▨

Manual recognition of 7-8 shapes (Monfraix *et al.*, 1961)

Can tell how many fingers on each hand

Can name penny, nickle, dime

Likes to copy simple forms

Paints at easel or floor, large brushes and sheets of paper

Can sew using cards (by turning them over)

Places fingers on piano keys, experiments with chords

Manipulates sand making roads and houses

Molds objects with clay

Block building—road, rambling structures, small enclosures

Pre-Writing

Likes to color within lines, can cut and paste, not adept

Copies square

Makes outline drawing, recognizes that it is funny

Prints some capital letters

Draws a recognizable man

Language

Knows most common opposites

Counts ten objects

Repeats 4 digits

---

[68]By the time the child is between 3 and 4 he will be using these consonant sounds correctly in words practically all the time (Davis, 1938; Templin, 1957).

Defines objects in terms of use such as fork, pencil
Some distortion in articulation (r, s blends)
Self-Care/Social
Buttons that he can see
Laces shoes
Dresses self completely
Careless about clothes, motivation may be lacking

6 Years

Motor
Very active, in almost constant motion
Sometimes clumsy (he overdoes and falls in a tumble)
Active body balance in games (skipping and swinging)
Jumps from height of 1 foot landing on toes
Stands on alternating feet eyes closed
Advanced throwing
Eye-Hand
Handles and attempts to use tools and materials
Needs assistance to complete projects, makes a good start
More deliberate, sometimes clumsy
Cuts and paste paper making books and boxes
Likes to use tape
Hammers vigorously, holds hammer near head
Sews using large needle, large stitches
Traced figures—recognizes figures of circle, cross, square traced on
skin with blunt instrument
Manual recognition of 9 geometric shapes (Monfraix *et al.*, 1961)

Block designs   ⊞

Match objects on basis of use, i.e., ball-top (toy); car-motorcycle
(vehicle)
Writing
Uses colored pencils, crayons for drawing
Likes to draw on blackboard
Copies a diamond
Copies printing
Language
Sounds mastered—f, v, s, and z
Seven word responses to pictures
Self-Care/Social
Ties shoes loosely
Dawdles
Boys brush hair, girls need to have hair combed
Not responsible for keeping own clothes

Uses table knife for spreading

7 *Years*

Motor
>   More caution in gross motor activity
>   Activity is variable—active to inactive

Eye-Hand
>   Has runs on certain activities, repeats performance persistently
>   Uses both hands with unequal pressure on piano
>   Can sew straight line
>   Manipulation of tools more tense but more persistent
>   Bats ball 3 times out of 5
>   Recognizes, manually, all geometric forms (Monfraix *et al.*, 1961)

Writing
>   Pencil gripped tightly and held close to point, pressure heavy but variable
>   Copies diamond

Language
>   Can answer questions dealing with likenesses (i.e. describes how two objects are similar)
>   Repeats 5 numbers
>   Sounds mastered—th, zh, sh, I

Self-Care/Social
>   Can tie shoe laces but does not like to bother
>   Washes self fairly completely
>   Uses knife for cutting

8 *Years*

Motor
>   Bodily movement more rhythmical and graceful
>   Aware of posture in self and others

Eye-Hand
>   Uses tools or utensils in household tasks
>   Free stance and movement while painting
>   Dramatic in activity with characteristic and descriptive gestures
>   Increase in speed and smoothness of eye-hand performance with easy release
>   Enjoys being timed but does not compete with time
>   Gap between what he wants to do and can do with hands
>   Beginning perspective in drawing, action figures in good proportion
>   Girls can hem a straight edge

Writing
>   Holds pencil, brush and tools less tensely

Language
Sounds mastered—z, s, r, wh
Eight word response to pictures
Self-Care/Social
Chooses own clothes
Can and will keep shoe laces tied without reminder
Can keep fingernails clean, may be able to cut nails on one hand
Reads on own initiative
Routine household tasks
Bathes self without help
Uses fork and spoon pronately

9 Years

Motor
Better control of own speed but timid of speed in car or sliding or sledding
Interested in own strength and lifting things
Frequently assumes awkward postures
Eye-Hand
Plays ping pong—returning served ball 2 times in succession
Holds and swings hammer well
Saws easily and accurately
Makes finished product
Uses and handles garden tools appropriately
Builds complex structures with erector set
Drawing—beginning to sketch; drawings often detailed; likes to draw still life, maps and designs
Girls—cut out and sew simple garments, can knit

REFERENCES

Items used in the *Task Level Evaluation* were taken from the following:

Battin, R. Ray, and Haug, C. Olaf: *Speech and Language Delay: A Home Training Program,* 2nd ed. Springfield, Thomas, 1968.

Bzock, Kenneth R., and League, Richard: *REEL Scale Receptive-Expressive Emergent Language Scale.* Gainesville, Florida, Tree of Life Press, 1971.

Gesell, Arnold, and Ilg, Francis L.: *Infant and Child in the Culture of Today.* New York, Harper and Row, 1943.

——— and ———: *The Child from Five to Ten.* New York, Harper and Row, 1946.

———, and Amatruda, Catherine S.: *Developmental Diagnosis.* New York, Hoeber, 1947.

————— *et al.: Developmental Schedules.* New York, Psychological Corp., 1949.

Leiter, R. G.: *The Leiter International Performance Test.* California, Author, 1950.

Paine, R. S. *et al.:* Neurologic examination of infants and children. *Ped Clin N Amer,* 7:471-510, 1960.

Appendix B

SWALLOWING PATTERNS FOR DROOLERS

In cerebral palsy, drooling is due to a combination of factors in varying degrees. These include open, relaxed jaw, retracted or protruded; tongue immobility; inability to suck and/or swallow. The following are suggested treatment techniques adapted from Rood answering this problem.

I. Jaw Stability (temporalis, masseter, pterygoids) (Figs. 30-33, Ch. 5)
   A. To encourage *closure*
      1. Brushing (to both sides), (a) Temporalis—lateral to the eyes and above zygomatic arch, in the *hollow,* (b) Masseter—lateral cheek area, and (c) Pterygoids—over and below zygomatic arch.
      2. Pressure
         (i) Stretch pressure to: temporalis; masseter (while child is biting on tongue blade); pterygoid (below zygomatic arch).
         (ii) Resistance to jaw closure while pressure (with fingers) is given to masseter and thumb pushes chin down.
         (iii) Reflex closure—tap under chin.
   Do not force closure as constant pressure on mandible in direction of closure will encourage opening. Ice is contraindicated on these muscles.
   B. To facilitate *retraction* which aids jaw closure
      1. Stimulate temporalis.
      2. Light, quick brushing of lower lip.
   C. To facilitate *protraction*
      1. Pressure to pterygoids under zygomatic arch.
      2. Resist protraction: fingers on pterygoids and thumb on mandible.
      3. Very light, quick brushing to upper lip.
   D. Lip closure (obicularis oris) (Fig. 82).
      1. Brush around mouth (i) lightly brush upper lip to encourage upper lip to go beneath lower teeth, (ii) brush lower lip to encourage it to go behind teeth.
      2. Ice around mouth.
      3. Stretch pressure around mouth with tips of fingers.

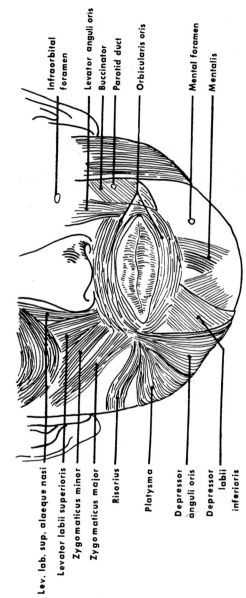

Figure 82. Muscles about the mouth. On the left side of the face the superficial muscles are removed, and the lower part of the masseter is shown. (Reprinted with permission from Hollinshead, W. Henry: *Anatomy for Surgeons*, 2nd ed. New York, Harper and Row, 1968, vol. I.)

4. Resist lip closure with finger tips (push lips apart).
II. Tongue Control
   A. Brushing (use oil paint brush)
      1. Brush the tongue muscles that are used to improve inadequate motions.
      2. Touch the area with the brush in which tongue should move to produce the desired motion (i.e. to facilitate tongue tip elevation, touch hard palate just back of upper teeth.
   B. Ice specific tongue muscles.
   C. Pressure
      1. To inhibit hyperactive gag reflex give pressure to the tongue with a tongue blade or smooth swizle stick. Use *walking* motion: start at tip and work toward back of tongue slowly. If gag reflex is present, you will be unable to work inside mouth (as in brushing); therefore, pressure would necessarily precede brushing.
      2. This pressure will initiate swallowing response with lip and jaw pressure.
   D. Tastes
      1. To facilitate tongue protrusion use bitter tastes (this motion according to Ingram (1962) is the first reaction of the tongue).
      2. To facilitate retraction use sweet, pleasant stimuli.
Let child eat ice as this stimulates the tongue, therefore encourages swallowing and decreases drooling.
See *four* under Swallowing
Often difficulty in swallowing is chiefly due to the inability of the spastic tongue to work the food or liquid to the back of the mouth where the end organs for the swallowing reflex are located (Bosley, 1965).
III. Swallowing. Head stability is a prerequisite, therefore
   A. Brushing
      1. Short and long neck flexors: (i) under chin from ear to ear, (ii) the sternocleidomastoid bilaterally.
      2. Soft palate arch from lateral to midline bilaterally. Do not cross midline.
      3. Brush and ice alternately (brush 2 times and ice 3 times) the V muscles of anterior neck above and below the thyroid.
   B. Ice
      1. V muscles of neck as in number 3 above.
      2. Brief ice in sternal notch produces immediate reflex swallowing.

C. Pressure
   1. Scrub with finger tips (i) over the ears for the long neck flexors and extensors and (ii) occiput where upper trapezius originates (Fig. 83). This will usually lessen drooling.[69]

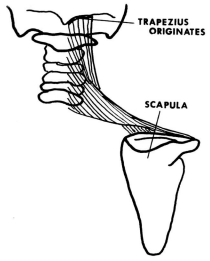

Figure 83. Origin of trapezius muscle (occiput).

   2. Stretch pressure to origin of sternocleidomastoid (where sternum and clavicle *meet* or the sternal notch).
   3. Resisted sucking through a straw (using thick liquid).
   4. Pressure under chin. This causes tongue to retract thereby initiating swallowing.

Reprinted, in part, with permission from A. Joy Huss, M.S., OTR, RPT, Assistant Professor, Occupational Therapy, Wisconsin State University, Eau Claire, Wisconsin.

[69]Use warm, bland liquids to inhibit mucous (acid, cold liquids stimulate the production of mucous secretions. So, avoid milk, citrus juices and sweets—as they increase thickness of mucous and make swallowing difficult and therefore increase drooling. Salty, oily fluids (i.e. meat juices) thins mucous.

As swallowing improves when sucking is efficient, the following stimuli are suggested to produce and encourage sucking: (a) tactile stimulation on lips, above, below, and on cheek, (b) extreme temperatures (cold or warm), (c) odors: ammonia, acetic acid, wakerian, oil of cloves, and (d) tastes—sugar, salt, quinine, acetic acid.

See also under I.D. above.

Appendix C

SOURCES OF MATERIAL FOR VISUALLY IMPAIRED

MAJOR BRAILLE PRESSES[70]

American Printing House for the Blind, Inc.
1839 Frankfort Avenue
Louisville, Kentucky 40206
Braille Institute of America, Inc.
741 North Vermont Avenue
Los Angeles, California 90026
Clovernook Printing House for the Blind
7000 Hamilton Avenue
Cincinnati, Ohio 45231

Prints books and magazines for children, young people and adults in braille. *American Girl, Boys' Life, Braille Variety News, Galaxy, Seventeen, Lion's International Juvenile Braille Monthly,* religious publications, calendars, cookbooks, paper, playing cards.

In addition, *Braille Book Review* (Braille Edition) is embossed bimonthly by the Clovernook Printing House for the Blind. Each issue contains the entire contents of the print editions of *Braille Book Review* and *Talking Book Topics* published by the American Foundation for the Blind.

Howe Press of Perkins School for the Blind
175 North Beacon Street
Watertown, Massachusetts 02172

Aids and appliances, mathematical devices, brailled games, embossed geographical maps are available.

BRAILLE PUBLISHERS

As previously indicated, there is an abundance of braille materials. However, braille materials which can be used with the young child, particularly the young handicapped child, are somewhat scarce. The following sources can be of assistance:

[70]Major braille presses and publishers (Sources: *Directory of Agencies Serving Blind Persons in the U.S., New* York: AFB, 1969. Howard Haycraft, *Books for the Blind,* Library of Congress, Division for the Blind, 1962.)

American Foundation for the Blind
15 West 16th Street
New York, New York 10011

For information regarding educational materials, religious materials, and periodicals in braille, the following pamphlets should be consulted: Educational Materials, Periodicals (Braille), and Religious Materials.

In addition, for information on locating braille materials, both published and hand-transcribed by volunteers, refer to the pamphlet Reference Services.

All of the above mentioned pamphlets are available free on request.

American Brotherhood for the Blind, Inc.
18432 Tophan Street
Tarzana, California 91356

Publisher of *Twin Vision Books* (juvenile titles in a combined print and braille format).

Braille Circulation Library
2823 West Grace Street
Richmond, Virginia

Hadley School for the Blind
700 Elm Street
Winnetka, Illinois 60093

National Council for the Blind
731 Williamson Street
Madison, Wisconsin

New York Association for the Blind
111 East 59th Street
New York, New York 10022

Royal National Institute
224 Great Portland Street
London W.1., England

Volunteer Services for the Blind, Inc.
332 South 13th Street
Philadelphia, Pennsylvania 19107

LARGE TYPE TEXTBOOK PUBLISHERS

American Printing House for the Blind
1839 Frankfort Avenue
Louisville, Kentucky 40206

National Aid to Visually Handicapped
3201 Balboa Street
San Francisco, California 94121

Stanwix House
3020 Chartiers Avenue
Pittsburgh, Pennsylvania 15204
 Specializes in photo-offset, reproduces enlarged books for the first six years of school. Also, monographs on the subject of large type are available. Catalog is available upon request. Books are illustrated, some in color, in 18 to 24 point type. Variations occur in line width, spacing, width or margins and binding.
Harper and Row
49 East 33rd Street
New York, New York 10016
 Publications of the Harper Crest Large Type Editions began in 1966; 18 point type.
Large Print Publication
11060 Fruitland Drive
North Hollywood, California 91604
 Four titles and a book of crossword puzzles are available.
The MacMillan Company
866 Third Avenue
New York, New York 10022
 Titles available include such books as Jack London's *Sea Wolf* and Margaret Mitchell's *Gone With The Wind.*
Ulverscroft Large Print Books
F. A. Thorpe, Ltd.
Artisan House, The Bridge, Antey
Leicester, England
 Nearly 200 titles in newly set type are available at $4 each to libraries, hospitals and institutions: 1749 Grand Concourse, Bronx, New York 10453.
Harcourt, Brace, and World, Inc.
1855 Rollins Road
Burlingame, California
 Limited, recreational; elementary level.
Children's Press, Inc.
Jackson Blvd. and Racine Avenue
Chicago, Illinois 60607
 Type sizes ranging from 10-point to 30-point.
J. B. Lippincott Company
East Washington Square
Philadelphia, Pennsyvania 19105
 Limited, recreation; secondary and elementary.
Field Enterprises Educational Corporation
Merchandise Mart Plaza
Chicago, Illinois

World Book Encyclopedia.
Scribner Large Type Editions
References Department
597 Fifth Avenue
New York, New York 10017

Clothbound volumes for visually limited or difficult readers; contemporary or classic works.
Sightext Publications
P. O. Box 1824
7015 Almeda Street
Houston, Texas 77001

Has a variety of large type publications.
Library Reproduction Service
Microfilm Company of California
1977 South Los Angeles Street
Los Angeles, California 90011

Reproduction of large print textbooks, etc., to specific need of visually handicapped in extended or controlled size; five print sizes; catalog available.
Amsco School Publications
P. O. Box 351, Cooper Station
New York, New York 10003

Enlarged books; will reproduce in large type any material.
Magnum Easy Eye Books
Lancer Books
1560 Broadway
New York, New York 10036

Paperbacks, 30 percent larger than ordinary paperback size, on glare-free paper; unabridged paperback classics—12 point type.
Golden Press
850 Third Avenue
New York, New York, 10022

Viking Press
625 Madison Avenue
New York, New York 10022

MICROFILM

Bell and Howell Company
Micro Photo Division
Duopage Department
1700 Shaw Avenue
Cleveland, Ohio 44112

Dakota Microfilm Company
501 North Dales Street
St. Paul, Minnesota 55103

Economy Blueprint and Supply Company
123 South La Brea Avenue
Los Angeles, California 90036

Microfilm Business Systems Company
5810 West Adams Blvd.
Los Angeles, California 90016

Microfilm Company of California
Library Reproduction Service
1977 South Los Angeles Street
Los Angeles, California 90011

University Microfilms, Inc.
Enlarged Editions Service
313 North First Street
Ann Arbor, Michigan 48107

Volunteer Transcribing Services
617 Oregon Avenue
San Mateo, California 94402

Xerox Corporation
P. O. Box 3300
Grand Central Station
New York, New York 10017

Enlargement of complete books, magazines, sheet music, and other printed material—approximately 2½ times size of ordinary print.

LARGE TYPE DICTIONARIES

Merriam Webster's Seventh New Collegiate Dictionary. Available from Microfilm Company of California. 4 volumes.

Thorndike-Barnhart Junior Dictionary. Available from the American Printing House for the Blind.

Winston Dictionary for Schools. Available from Stanwix House.

Grolier Large Type Dictionary. Available from Keith Jennison Books, 575 Lexington Avenue, New York, New York 10022

VOLUNTEERS

Volunteers Who Produce Books for Blind and Visually Impaired Individuals. Available free on request from the Division for the Blind and Physically Handicapped, Library of Congress, Washington, D. C. 20542

LIBRARIES

Braille books are available from the following:
Cleveland Public Library
Library for the Blind
325 Superior Avenue
Cleveland, Ohio 44114

Free Library of Philadelphia
Library for the Blind
17th and Spring Garden Streets
Philadelphia, Pennsylvania 19130

Iowa Commission for the Blind
Library for the Blind
4th and Keosaqua
Des Moines, Iowa 50309

Jewish Guild for the Blind
1880 Broadway
New York, New York 10023

Nassau-Suffolk Braille Library
Industrial Home for the Blind
329 Hempstead Turnpike
West Hempstead, New York 11552
New York Public Library

Library for the Blind
116 Avenue of the Americas
New York, New York 10013

From *regional libraries*. Besides a hugh variety of brailled volumes, the following is a partial list of magazines which are available, on free loan, in braille: *American Girl, Boy's Life, The Children's Digest, Jack and Jill.*

Talking Books include such titles as: *Jack and Jill, New Outlook for the Blind, Newsweek Talking Magazine,* and *Reader's Digest.*

EDUCATIONAL (TANGIBLE) AIDS

American Printing House for the Blind
1839 Frankfort Avenue
Louisville, Kentucky 40206

Tangible apparatus catalog. The Printing House in conjunction with the National Special Education Instructional Materials Center has developed a national clearing house of instructional materials to be used with the visually disabled child. Consult the Printing House for specific aid.

American Foundation for the Blind   the AFB Regional Office
15 West 16th Street   or
New York, New York 10011

Aids and Appliances Catalog. Non-profit mail order service to provide commercial, adapted or special devices and consultation services. Devices for the partially sighted, as well as the totally blind. Ex.: Braille writing equipment, clocks, watches, games, geographical aids, kitchen aids, math aids, writing aids, etc.

Howe Press of the Perkins School for the Blind
Watertown, Massachusetts 02172

Non-profit organization which produces braille reading and writing devices.

National Society for the Prevention of Blindness
16 East 40th Street
New York, New York 10016

Publications, lectures, posters, films, charts and advisory services. Booklet available entitled: *Suggested Sources of Equipment and Teacher Aids for Partially Sighted Children.*

Tactile Aids for the Blind, Inc.
2625 Forest Avenue
Des Moines, Iowa 50311

Non-Profit organization composed of volunteers who produce and distribute aids. Bookstands, relief maps, clocks, puzzles, magnetic boards, textured blocks, etc. Catalog in print and braille of tangible apparatus and aids.

Michigan State University Regional Instructional Materials Center
218 Erickson Hall
East Lansing, Michigan

Part of the national network of Instructional Materials Centers throughout the country. A recorded aid for braille music, suitcase tutor and talking dictionaries are among the first materials developed.

Creative Playthings, Inc.
316 North Michigan Blvd.
Chicago, Illinois 60601   Games, toys, puzzles, etc.

Stanwix House, Inc.
3020 Chartiers Avenue   Outline maps, world atlases,
Pittsburgh, Pennsylvania 15204   etc.

American Thermo-form Corporation   Thermo-form braille duplica-
8640 East Slauson Avenue   tion; braille thermo-form
Pico Rivera, California 90660   paper.

Consult the following books for additional assistance:

Teaching Aids for Visually Blind and Visually Handicapped Children. Barbara Dorward and Natalie Barraga, 1968. Available from the American Foundation for the Blind.

Techniques with Tangibles. Wilbur Fulker, Charles C Thomas, 1967.

MAGNIFICATION AND LOW VISION AIDS

The New York Association for the Blind (The Lighthouse)
111 East 59th Street
New York, New York 10022

A catalog of optical aids and a guide to selecting the aid according to cause and degree of visual loss. The five sections of the catalog: hand magnifiers, stand magnifiers, headborne magnifiers, distance aids, and miscellaneous devices.

Each aid in the catalog has a symbol equivalency which relates the visual acuity range to the number of dipoters needed to read average print. For example, an individual having corrected acuity from 20/200 to 20/400 might find one of the following aids helpful: cataract hand reader, double lens folding magnifier, folding pocket magnifier, illuminated mangifier, tripod magnifier, etc. The aids may be ordered directly from the Lighthouse Low Vision Services of the New York Association for a very reasonable cost.

American Optical Company
Buffalo, New York

Franklin Institute Projector Magnifier and other magnification devices.

Before ordering any aid or device, be sure to have an accurate diagnosis from a specialist. Seek the advice from a low-vision aids clinic or university medical school before ordering a specific device.

BOOK AND COPY STANDS

Adjustable easel. Wm. J. Bargen, Box 499, Waukegan, Illinois

Study-Stand. Noka Manufacturing Company, 147 Bloomfield Avenue, Bloomfield, N. J.

Desk-easel plan. National Society for the Prevention of Blindness, 16 East 40th Street, New York, New York 10016.

Dictionary table: No. 30 High Style (for large dictionary). G. & C. Merriam Co., Springfield, Massachusetts.

CHALKBOARDS

(Gray-green or blue-green are recommended)

Ezy-Rase Nucite. New York Silicate Book Slate Company, 541 Lexington Avenue, New York, New York.

Hyloplate Lite Site. Weber-Costello Company, Chicago Heights, Illinois.

Slatebestos. Beckley-Cardy Company, 1900 North Narragansett, Chicago, Illinois.

For repainting chalkboards:
> *Endur.* Endur Paint Company, 46 Cornhill, Boston, Massachusetts.
> *"Rite-on" Green.* Sapolin Paints, 205 East 42 Street, New York, New York.

PENCILS AND PENS

Zabco Primary Mechanical Pencil (with large, soft lead). Zaner-Bloser Company, 612 North Park Street, Columbus, Ohio
See local dealers for soft lead pencils.
Esterbrook Drawing and Lettering Pen No. 1: Fountain pen with #2284 point. Esterbrook Pen Company, 350 5th Avenue, New York, New York.
Speedry Brushpen. Gloco Products, 87-52 Lefferts Blvd., Richmond Hill, N. Y.

LARGE TYPE TYPEWRITERS

Remington—No. 17 with Bulletin Type No. 48; Portable No. 5 with Type No. 105 (cuts stencils). Standard with Type No. 105 (cuts stencils).
Royal—Large Vogue; Ampli type (cuts stencils).
Smith Corona—Bulletin Caslen Type, upper and lower case, No. 27; Sight Ease Type No. 47 (cuts stencils); Type No. 67—standard and portable models (cuts stencils); Bulletin Gothic #29.
Underwood—Bulletin type, pitch No. 6, upper and lower case.
Most typewriters are available in electric models also. Use heavily inked ribbon. Keyboard charts—poster size, available from manufacturers.

TYPEWRITING MANUALS

Course of Study in Typewriting for Sight Saving and Braille Classes. Edited by Edith Cohoe. Detroit Board of Education, Department of Special Education, 453 Stimson Avenue, Detroit, Michigan.
New Color Code Typing. Unah R. Winston. Stanwix House, 3020 Chartiers Avenue, Pittsburgh, Pennsylvania 15204.
Touch Typing in 10 Lessons. Ruth Ben'Ary. Six Talking Book recordings read by Richard Harvey. American Printing House for the Blind, 1839 Frankfort Avenue, Louisville, Kentucky 40206. (A mimeographed manual is also available).
A Typing Method to be Used in the Education of the Partially Sighted. Fredericka M. Bertram. San Francisco State College, Division of Education, Special Education Department, College Book Shop.
   Recorded typing lessons are now available through some typewriting companies.

LIGHTING

Better Light Better Sight Bureau, 750 Third Avenue, New York, New York.

The Story of Light and Sight. A study project for 4th, 5th, and 6th grade classes, 1959.

Illuminating Engineering Society, 1860 Broadway, New York, New York.

MISCELLANEOUS INFORMATION

American Library Association
50 East Huron Street
Chicago, Illinois 60611

Has a selective list of reading aids for the handicapped. The list includes information on commercially manufactured equipment, magnifiers, duplicating firms, page turners, projectors and readers, reading stands, talking book machines, talking books, and large-type books.
Division for the Blind and Physically Handicapped
Library of Congress
Washington, D.C. 20542

"That All May Read"—an information brochure describing program of books. Available to borrow is a talking book machine, listing of regional libraries serving each part of the U.S.
Educational Materials Coordinating Unit
Visually Handicapped
Office of the Superintendent of Public Instruction
410 South Michigan Avenue
Chicago, Illinois 60605

Through a contract with the United States Office of Education this project permits the Department of Special Education to demonstrate, among other things, how an office of the Superintendent of Public Instruction can coordinate, produce, and distribute educational material for visually handicapped children and adults (Director is Gloria Calovini, Instructional Materials Center for Handicapped Children and Youth, 316 S. Second Street, Springfield, Illinois.)
Telephone Pioneers of America
195 Broadway
New York, New York 10007

Activities include making books with various objects attached to pages to illustrate the story which is written in braille and large type.
U. S. Office of Education
Washington, D. C.

Various publications are available from Superintendent of Documents, U. S. Printing Office, Washington, D.C. 20402. One is *Educational Programs for Visually Handicapped Children* (Bulletin 1966, No. 6-OE-35070).

Appendix D

HAND UTLILIZATION TECHNIQUES FOR THE CEREBRAL PALSIED CHILD

The following illustrations and advice demonstrate handling techniques which will assist the teacher and therapist in management of the cerebral palsied child in the classroom and clinic. These techniques are also important as proper handling of the child will facilitate correct reactions and movement patterns.

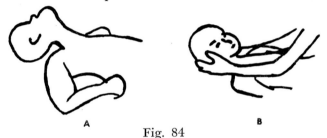

Fig. 84

(a) Some cerebral palsied children push their heads back and at the same time bring their *shoulders up and forward*. Do not try to correct the position of the head by putting a hand on the back of the head, this will only cause the child to push back more.

(b) Place your hands on each side of the head and push upward giving the child a "long neck." As you do this push the shoulders down with your forearms.

Fig. 85

If a child sits on your lap throwing his head, shoulders and arms back, do not try to push him forward as shown in sketch (a).

(b) Illustrates a method of stopping the child pushing himself backward. The forearm comes across the neck and base of skull, the hand and forearm control the shoulders pushing them forward and in.

Fig. 86

Some children cannot raise or hold their head up in mid-line because they are generally too *floppy*. By holding them firmly at the shoulder with your thumbs on their chest, you can give them some stability as you bring the shoulders forward; this will help them to raise their head up and hold it there.

These sketches show how by careful control you can correct the position of the child's arms and at the same time influence the position of the rest of his body. The child in each of the sketches is sitting.

(a) A typical pattern of flexion seen in the *spastic* child. The arms are turned *in* at the shoulders; this is generally accompanied by straight hips.

(b) Hold the child over the outside of elbows and top of the arms.

(c) With *one* movement lift and turn his arms out [external rotation] as you bring him toward you. By handling him in this way, you will facilitate the lifting of his head, straightening of his spine and the bending of his hips.

(d) A typical pattern of extension seen in the *athetoid* child; the arms are turned *out* at the shoulders whether both are bent or one straight and one bent; this is generally accompanied by excessively bent hips.

(e) Hold the child over the outside of the elbows and bring the arms forward. As you straighten the arms turn them *in* at the shoulders [internal rotation at the shoulder].

(f) With *one* movement, the arms still turned *in* at the shoulders and slightly down, bring the child toward you and then gradually lift the arms up. By handling the child in this way you will facilitate the

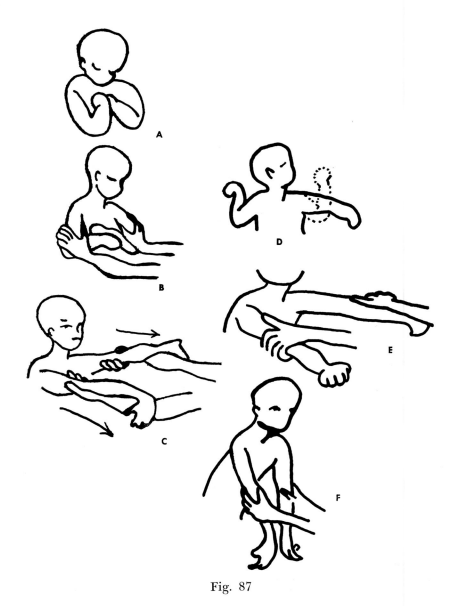

Fig. 87

bending forward of his head, the rounding of his spine, and will modify the excessive bending at the hips.

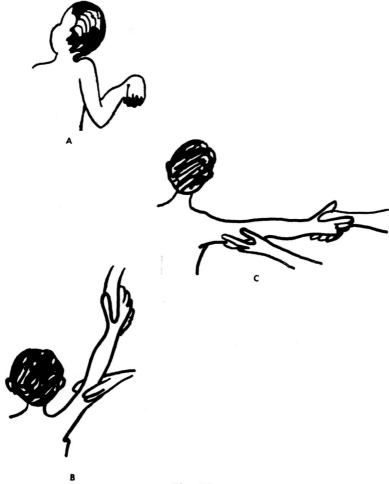

Fig. 88

(a) Shows the arm of a spastic child turned in at the shoulder (which presses down), the head also pulled to this side, the elbow bent, forearm turned in so that the hand faces down, wrist and fingers are forearm turned in so that the hand faces down, wrist and fingers are bent, the thumb lying across the palm of the hand.

(b) and (c) By lifting the arm [above the head], straightening and turning it out at the shoulder and elbow [supinating the forearm or turning the palm up], it will then be found easier to straighten the wrist and open the fingers and thumb.

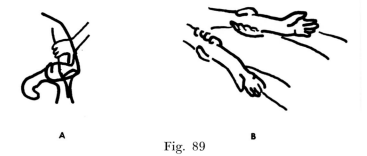

A   B

Fig. 89

(a) Do not try to straighten the child's arm by holding above and below a joint. Trying to stretch a limb in this way will only make it bend more.

(b) By holding your hand *over* the joint you can straighten and turn the limb in or out in one movement.

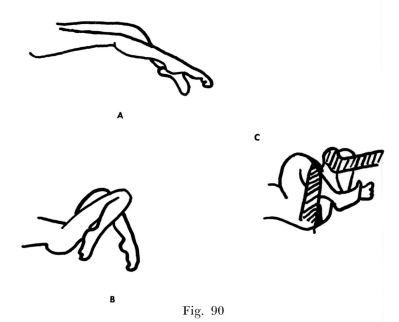

Fig. 90

(a) and (b) Typical positions of the severely spastic child. If we try to bend the foot while the legs are in this position, for example to put the child's shoes or socks on, it will be found to be impossible.

(c) If the hips are bent and the legs parted it will be found that this position will facilitate the bending of the foot.

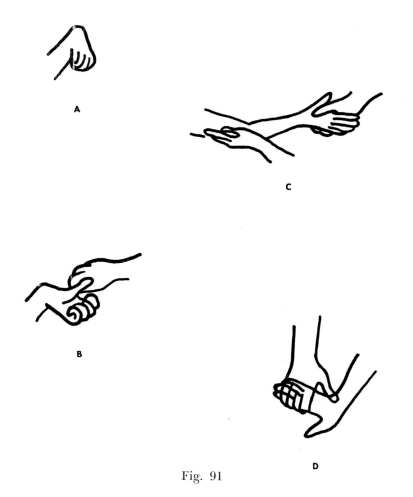

Fig. 91

(a) Typical hand of a spastic child, hand clenched with bent wrist, thumb held across palm of hand.

(b) Incorrect way to straighten wrist and fingers—by pulling on the thumb in this way, the wrist and fingers bend more; there is also danger of damaging the thumb joint.

(c) By first straightening and turning out the arm it is then much easier to straighten the fingers and thumb [to extend the fingers and thumb].

(d) Correct grasp to hold the fingers and wrist straight.

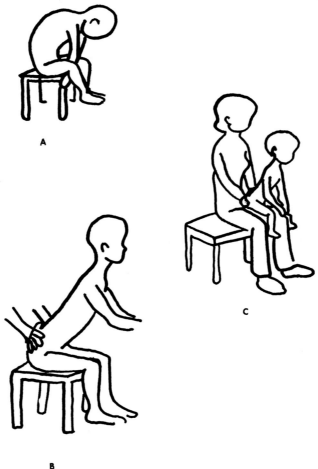

Fig. 92

(a) Floppy child sitting, unable to raise his head and straighten his back.

(b) By placing both hands firmly [pushing down] over lumbar region [lower back], thumbs either side of spine, will give the child a point of fixation and facilitate the raising of his head and straightening of his spine.

(c) This can also be done as the child sits on your lap.

(The preceding figures and legends have been reproduced with permission from Finnie, Nancie R. *Handling the Young Cerebral Palsied Child at Home.* E. P. Dutton & Co., Inc., New York, 1970).

REFERENCES

Bayley, Nancy: *Manual for the Bayley Scales of Infant Development.* New York, The Psychological Corporation, 1969.

Bosley, Elizabeth: Development of sucking and swallowing. *Cereb Palsy J, 26* (6), 1965.

Brown, J. R., Darley, F. L., and Gomez, M. R.: Disorders of communication. *Pediatr Clin N Amer, 14*:725-748, 1967.

Bzoch, K., and League, R.: *Assessing Language Skills in Infancy.* A Handbook for the multidimensional analysis of emergent language. Gainesville, Florida, The Tree of Life Press, 1971.

Darley, F. L., and Winitz, H.: Age of first word: Review of research. *J Speech Hear Disord, 26*:272-290, 1961.

Davis, I. P.: The speech aspects of reading readiness. In *Seventeenth Yearbook of the Dept. of Elementary School Principals.* National Education Asso, 1938, pp. 282-289.

Fields, Ruby D.: Physical abilities of the mentally retarded child. *Phys Ther, 49*:38-46, 1969.

Illingsworth, R. S.: *An Introduction to Developmental Assessment in the First Year,* No. 3 London, National Spastics Society/Heinemann, 1962.

Ingram, T. T. S.: Clinical significance of the infantile feeding reflexes. *Dev Med Child Neurol, 4*:159-169, 1962.

Irwin, O. C., and Chen, H. P.: Development of speech during infancy: Curve of phonemic types. *J Exp Psychol, 36*:431-436, 1946.

Magnus, R.: Physiology of posture. *Lancet* 2:531-536, 1926.

Mitchell, R. G.: The landau reaction (reflex). *Dev Med Child Neurol, 4*:65, 1962.

Monfraix, C., Tardieu, G., and Tardieu, C.: Disturbances of manual perception in children with cerebral palsy. *Dev Med Child Neurol, 3*:544-552, 1961.

Moore, J. C.: *Neuroanatomy Simplified.* Some basic concepts for understanding Rehabilitation Techniques. Dubuque, Kendall/Hunt, 1969.

Paine, Richmond S. et al.: Evolution of postural reflexes in normal infants and in the presence of chronic brain syndromes. *Neurology, 14*:1036-1048, 1964.

Templin, M. C.: Certain language skills in children: Their development and interrelationships. In *The Institute of Child Welfare Monograph Series, No. 26.* Minneapolis, University of Minnesota Press, 1957.

Thomas, A., Chesni, Y., and Ste. Anne Dargassies, S.: *The Neurological Examination of the Infant.* London, National Spastics Society/Heinemann, 1960.

AUTHOR INDEX

A

Abercrombie, M., 46, 51, 215, 216, 217, 218, 219, 220, 221, 223
Achilles, R., 141, 154
Ackerman, B., 186
Adam, A., 213
Adler, F., 179
Agranowitz, A., 55, 56
Allen, H., 191
Annapolle, L., 217
Asher, P., 182
Ayers, A., 78, 93

B

Baker, L., 97, 98, 99, 100, 102
Bakwin, H., 58
Banks, H., 101
Barnett, H., 101
Barr, B., 157, 167
Barr, D., 169
Barr, J., 100
Barsch, R., 176
Bassett, F., 98
Battin, R., 358
Bayley, N., 352
Beakey, A., 182, 216
Belmont, L., 74
Bender, L., 58
Benson, F., 48, 49, 61, 63, 80
Benton, A., 77, 78, 79, 80
Benton, C., 217
Berger, A., 212
Berry, M., 141, 144, 168
Birch, H., 73, 74
Bischoff, R., 207
Blakely, R., 162
Blank, M., 74
Bleck, E., 102
Blencowe, S., 95
Blumberg, M., 154
Bobath, K., 263, 264, 266, 268
Boone, D., 79
Bosley, E., 362
Bowley, A., 9

Boyd, I., 89
Boyes, J., 108
Brachelis, L., 214
Brain, C., 75
Brain, L., 132, 137, 138
Brain, R., 140
Brain, W., 59, 69
Brazier, M., 37
Brock, S., 33, 34, 49
Brodman, K., 33
Brown, J., 75, 351
Brunnstrom, S., 255
Byers, R., 163
Bzock, K., 355, 358

C

Campbell, A., 32
Campbell, M., 157
Cantor, G., 71
Carmean, S., 71
Carroll, R., 106, 115
Carter, S., 230
Cass, M., 155
Chao, D., 236
Churchill, J., 229
Chusid, J., 232, 272
Cicenia, E., 215
Cohen, P., 163, 164
Cohen, S., 176
Cohn, R., 59, 60
Connors, D., 52, 71
Cooper, L., 186
Crane, M., 207
Crickmay, M., 147
Critchley, M., 51, 61, 63
Crothers, B., 136, 229
Cruickshank, W., 53, 316

D

Darley, F., 57, 346
Davidson, H., 76
Davies, E., 155
Davis, H., 168

Davis, I., 355
Deaver, G., 192
DeJong, R., 104
Deleo, G., 215
Denhoff, Eric, 193, 229, 230, 232, 233,
    234, 236, 237, 238, 239, 240, 241, 247
Denny-Brown, D., 264
Doctor, P., 166, 167
Douglas, A., 182
Doyle, J., 167
Duke-Elder, S., 186, 194
Dunn, L., 149
Dunsdon, M., 210
Durham, H., 101
Dwyer, F., 98

E

Eggers, G., 96, 99
Eisenberg, L., 241
Eisenson, J., 54
Eldred, E., 271
Elithorn, A., 51
Engelmann, S., 350
Engle, H., 238
Evans, E., 99, 100, 102

F

Fantle, E., 181, 186
Fay, T., 261
Ferrer, J., 194, 197, 214
Ferreri, J., 71
Ffooks, O., 178
Fieldner, R., 121
Fields, R., 350, 354
Fink, M., 70
Finnie, N., 331, 380
Fonda, G., 209
Frostig, M., 219
Fry, D., 158

G

Gaines, R., 75
Gardiner, P., 187, 192
Gardner, E., 28
Garrett, A., 328
Gassel, M., 73
Gerber, S., 156, 157
Gerrard, J., 162

Gerstmann, J., 64
Gesell, A., 198, 358
Gibson, E., 73
Goldberg, H., 44, 210
Goldner, J., 105, 113, 114
Gollin, E., 74
Goodglass, H., 48, 56, 75
Gordon, N., 231, 240
Granjon-Galefret, N., 61, 137
Green, W., 99, 110, 112
Grice, D., 98
Guey, J., 234
Guibor, G., 180, 182
Gunderson, T., 184
Guttman, E., 137

H

Halacy, D., 45
Hallgren, B., 137
Halpern, D., 122
Halstead, W., 223, 324
Hammil, D., 149
Hannigan, H., 164
Hardy, W., 54, 161
Harris, A., 61
Harris, D., 58
Harris, L., 75
Haufmann, 76
Head, H., 51, 52, 78
Hebb, D., 216
Hécean, H., 48
Hermann, K., 65, 137
Hill, L., 102, 103
Hoberman, J., 155
Hodgsdon, W., 168
Hohman, L., 51
Hollinshead, W., 141, 142, 143, 144, 361
Hoop, N., 74
Hopkins, T., 156
Hortense, B., 56
House, B., 75
Hunziker, H., 236
Huss, J., 247, 273, 363

I

Illingsworth, R. S., vii, 342
Inglis, A., 88, 107, 108, 114
Ingram, A., 97, 131, 132, 133, 134, 135,
    136, 137, 138, 139

Ingram, T., 55, 58, 61, 362
Irwin, O., 148, 149, 150, 151, 353

J

Jackson, A., 157, 167
Jacobson, E., 73, 155, 248
Jensen, A., 71
Jerger, J., 168
Johnson, D., 55, 78
Johnson, M., 61
Jones, M., 72, 202, 220

K

Kabat, H., 155, 250, 251
Kahn, D., 74
Katzin, H., 180, 194, 195, 196
Keats, S., 98, 99, 161, 236, 237, 238
Keith, R., 56, 323
Kendall, P., 120
Kendler, T., 71, 74
Kenny, W., 71
Kephart, N., 77
Kester, N., 302
Kinsbourne, M., 64, 65, 67, 68
Kleffner, F., 56
Knott, M., 155, 250
Koven, L., 154

L

Lamb, D., 102
Lancet, 238
Lassman, F. M., 6
Laursen, A., 37
Leiter, R., 359
Lencione, R., 144, 148
Leven, M., 4
Levine, E., 167
Lewis, 99
Liddell, E., 94
Lindsley, D., 73, 271
Little, W., 88
Livingston, E., 241
Livingston, S., 233, 235
Lowenfeld, B., 209
Luria, A., 68

M

Magnus, R., 340

Malamud, N., 229
Masland, R., 157
Masse, P., 99
Matev, I., 114
Matkin, N., 161, 164
McCarroll, H., 99
McFie, J., 45, 47
McGinnis, M., 56
McGlannan, F., 62
Mecham, M., 76, 146, 334
Mendel, G., 75
Miller, M., 56
Millichap, J., 241
Mitchell, R., 343
Money, J., 61, 63
Monfraiz, C., 52, 352, 354, 355, 356, 357
Montagu, M., 7
Moore, G., 152, 153
Moore, J., 18, 20, 50, 94, 252, 262, 275, 341
Morgan, C., 33, 38
Mortens, J., 102
Mueller M., 208
Myklebust, H., 57, 164
Mysak, E., 140, 146, 147

N

Nadine, C., 76
Nakaono, T., 156
Nathan, P., 33, 44, 50
Neil, G., 69
Nellhause, G., 241
Nelson, T., 46
Nielson, J., 32, 35, 54
Nobach, C., 50
Nober, E., 155, 161
Nolan, C., 202, 207, 208

O

Oakley, D., 47
O'Brien, G., 71
O'Conner, N., 213
Ogle, K., 222
O'Neill, J., 186
Orton, S., 61, 77, 137
Österberg, G., 191

P

Page, D., 262

Paine, R., vii, 55, 62, 163, 240, 241, 340, 343
Palmer, M., 140, 144, 154
Paschall, H., 88, 106, 122
Pearlstone, A., 178, 187, 193
Penfield, W., 32, 48, 140, 230
Perlmutter, S., 269
Perlstein, M., 6, 155, 161, 229, 233, 238
Perry, C., 256
Peterman, M., 235
Phelps, W., 4, 96, 103, 154, 238, 239, 247
Piaget, J., 74, 216
Piercy, H., 59
Plum, P., 237
Poeck, J., 64, 77
Pollock, G., 98, 99, 100, 101, 103
Prechtl, H., 217
Price, L., 58
Pyles, M., 71

R

Rabinovitch, R., 80
Rapin, I., 58
Rapp, S., 239
Rappaport, S., 55
Roberts, A., 56
Roberts, L., 48
Roberts, W., 99
Rood, M., 94, 148, 271, 272, 273
Rosen, J., 164
Rosenberg, C. (ADH), 279, 280, 281, 283, 286, 287, 289, 292, 296, 298, 304, 306, 307, 310, 312, 313, 315, 317, 318, 322
Ruch, P., 26, 27, 37
Rudel, R., 76
Rushworth, G., 89
Russell, W., viii

S

Samilson, R., 94, 95, 105, 106, 112
Sayegh, Y., 73
Schacht, W., 182, 186, 192
Schermann, A., 73
Schonell, F., 60, 210
Sekuler, R., 76
Semans, S., 266, 271

Sequin, E., 57
Shanks, R., 233
Sharrard, W., 102
Shere, E., 73
Sheridan, M., 157
Sherrington, C., 18
Sight Saving Review, 186
Silfverskiöld, N., 97
Silver, A., 61
Silver, C., 97, 98, 101, 102
Skatvedt, 44
Sloan, A., 207
Sloan, L., 234
Slominski, A. (PH), 120, 286, 290, 303, 330
Smith, V., 181
Solomon, P., 214
Sorsby, A., 181
Sortini, A., 161
Soutter, R., 99, 100
Spears, C., 239
Spiker, C., 71
Stamp, W., 111, 119
Stein, I., 112
Stephens, W., 61
Stockmeyer, S., 94, 148, 272
Strayer, L., 97
Subirana, A., 48
Sutherland, N., 216
Swanson, A., 95, 105, 108, 109, 110, 114, 115, 116, 118

T

Tachjean, M., 51, 104
Tardieu, G., 95
Tate, H., 186
Taylor, E., 51
Templin, M., 355
Teuber, J., 44
Thomas, A., 342
Thompson, J., 63
Tizard, J., 50, 51, 69, 192, 275
Tohen, Z., 98
Towbin, A., 5
Travis, L., 140
Tredgold, A., 213
Tretakoff, M., 215
Twitchell, T., 264

V

Veale, H., 166
Vernon, M., 5, 61, 157, 163, 164, 165, 167, 168, 169
Vogt, C., 33
Vulpius, O., 97

W

Walshe, F., 263
Ward, P., 166
Waylett, J., 327, 328
Wechsler, D., 76
Wedell, K., 53
Wepman, J., 56
Werner, H., 58
West, R., 57
Westlake, H., 155
Whitehouse, D., 241

William, R., 107
Williams, D., 215
Wilson, B., 51, 70
Wolfe, W., 154
Wolpert, I., 68
Wood, N., 56
Woods, G., 168, 239

Y

Yarbus, A., 221
Yount, C., 100

Z

Zamir, L., 274
Zangwell, O., 49, 61
Zaporozhets, A., 73, 74, 221
Zeaman, D., 75
Zeman, S., 61

SUBJECT INDEX

A

Ablation, 45
Acalculia, 34, 69
Accommodation (*see* Vision)
Activities of daily living (*see* Equipment and Adaptations)
Adaptation (*see* Equipment and Adaptation)
Agnosia
  auditory verbal, 34, 55, 56
  central blindness (*see* Vision)
    (*see also* Agnosia, visual)
  cortical deafness (*see* Hearing)
  finger, 51, 60, 64, 65, 69
    evaluation of, 65 (*see also* Tests)
  geometric-optic, 35
  simultanagnosia, 35, 68
  tactile-occipital, 35
  verbal, 34, 55
  visual (central blindness) 68, 69
    teaching machine and, 324-326
    (*see also* Vision)
  visual verbal, 34, 55, *68*
Agraphia, 34, 55, 69, 326
Akinetic
  minor motor seizure, 232
Alexia, 34, 69, 326
Alpha motor neuron, (fig) 12, (fig) 13, (fig) 51, 91, 94, 271
Amblyopia ex anopsia (*see* Vision)
American Physical Therapy Association Journal, 264
American Printing House for the Blind, 204, 208
Amphetamines (CNS stimulants) 241
  (*see also* Pharmacological management)
Anacusis (*see* Hearing)
Anoxia, 6, 7, 154, 161
Anticonvulsants (*see* Pharmacological management)
Anxiety
  drug therapy and (*see* Pharmacological management, behavior and)

Aphasia, 46, 54, 55, 56, 63, 74, (table) 138, (table) 165
acquired, 138
anomia (amnesic) 35
Broca's (*see* Aphasia, motor)
developmental
  congenital, 55
  expressive, 138
  mutisim, 58, (table) 138
  receptive, 138
disorders, *54,* 137, (table) 138
motor (expressive) 28, 30, 31, 34, 58, 163
  developmental expressive, 58, (table) 138
  developmental mutisim and, 58, (table) 138
paraphasia, 55
receptive (*see* Aphasia, sensory)
right spastic hemiplegia and, 48
sensory (receptive) 30, 31, 54, 159, 163
specific language disability, 55
teaching machine and, 323
Wernicke's (*see* Aphasia, sensory)
writing defects and, 59
  (*see also* Speech and Language)
Apraxia, 34, 46, 59
  constructional, 46, *58,* 59, 69
  optical, 58
  writing (agraphia) 34, 55, 69, 326
Arithmetic (*see* Mathematics)
Astereognosis, *29,* 51, 52, 71
Ataxia (*see* Cerebral palsy)
Athetosis, 8, 9, 16, 17, 51, 71, 89, 90, 104, 133, 136, 151, 154, 156, 161, 164, 188, 263, 264, 328
causes, 6
deafness and (*see* Hearing)
drugs and, 237, 238
hearing and, 156
management techniques, handling of (*see* Appendix D)
surgery and, 89 (*see also* Orthopedic management)

therapy and, 250 (*see also* Systems of therapy)
tongue and, 141
Attention, 34, 51, 62, 70
Auditory
agnosia, cortical deafness (*see* Hearing)
association areas of brain, 30, (fig) 32, 34
brain, reception center of, 34
hearing and, 158, 164
imperception (auditory symbolic or language) 138, 166
memory (*see* Memory)
nuclei, 162
organization, 48
primary and hearing, 158
processing and hearing, 166
recall, 162
secondary areas of brain, 158
stimuli and cerebellum, 38
temporal lobe and, 30
temporal pattern, 162
verbal agnosia, 34, 55
visual impairments, materials, 206 (*see also* Hearing and Perception)

B

Balance (*see* Vestibular)
Barbituates (sedatives) 240
Behavior
components of, (fig) 17, 18, 21
deafness and, (table) 165
disturbances, 3, (fig) 4
environmental behavior disorders and drug therapy, 237, 239-243
fear/anxiety and drug therapy, 239, (table) 240
hearing and, 163
hyperkinetic behavior and drug therapy (*see* Pharmacological management)
modification techniques and, 70
neural mechanisms and, 45
Bender Gestalt Test, 58, 167
Benton Right-Left Orientation Test, 78-79
Benzedrine, (table) 232, 241, 242

Blindness, 203
central (visual agnosia) 68 (*see also* Vision and Agnosia)
for color, 69
for location of objects, 69
for objects, 68
for space, 69
simultanagnosia, 35, 68
color, 212, 214
tests for (*see* Tests)
damage (brain) and, 214
mental retardation, treatment programs for, 214
Bobath (*see* Systems of therapy)
Body schema
disorders of, 29, 80
finger gnosis, 48
right-left orientation (*see* Discrimination)
Braces (*see* Orthopedic management for specific types)
speech and, 155
therapy and, 246 (*see also* Systems of therapy)
tolerance of and drug therapy (*see* Pharmacological management, muscle relaxation and)
Braille, 202, 203, 205
braillist, 204
catalogs, 204, 206
indexes, 206
libraries, 205
materials, 204
presses (*see* Appendix C)
publishers (*see* Appendix C)
transcribing, volunteer, 206
Brain, 22-39, 43
amygdala, 19
association areas (*see* Cerebrum)
basal ganglia 9, 11, 27, 37, 147, 163, 263
brain stem, 19, 21, (fig) 22, 23, 24, 26, 158, 161, 163, 263, 264
function of, 35
cerebellum, 10, 18, 19, 21, 22, 23, 24, 36, 37, 140
disorders of, 39
function of, 38
cerebrum (*see* Cerebrum)

COEPS, 9, 27, 35, 94
compensation factor, 49
corpus callosum, 23
diencephalon, 7, 23, 27, 35, 36
  dysfunction of, 240
extrapyramidal system (COEPS), 9,
  27, 35, 94
feedback, 21
function of, 24
globus pallidus, 9
hippocampus, 19, 163
hypothalamus, 7, 36
  breathing disorders and, 154
medulla, 23, 26, 35, 36, 140
midbrain, 23, 35, 161, 261, 263
motor strip, 19, 250
nerves (*see* Nervous system)
occipital lobe (*see* Cerebrum)
plasticity of, 49
pons, 23, 26, 35, 36, 162
postcentral gyrus (sensory strip) 26
precentral (motor) area, 7, 26 (*see
  also* Cerebrum)
pyramidal tract, 8, 26, 27, 35, 94
reticular formation (*see* Reticular
  formation)
sensory strip, 26
spinothalamic tract, 272
structure of, 22
thalamus, 7, 19, 36, 37, 43, 62, 69
vermis, 23
Brain stem (*see* Brain)
Broca's area, 28, 34 (*see also* Aphasia,
  motor)
Brodman, 26, 33
Breathing, 152-155
  abnormal patterns, 154
  brain and, 154
  disorders of, 152-155
  hypothalamus, 154
  mechanisms of, 152
  muscles of respiration, (fig) 152, (fig)
    153
  phonation, 153
  resonating system, 153
  respiratory system, 152
  sound production, 153
  therapeutic procedures, 154-155
  vibrating system, 153

Brunnstrom (*see* Systems of therapy)

C

Cataract (*see* Vision)
Celontin, 235
Central nervous system, 15, 16, 22, 24
  angular gyrus, 49
  brain (*see* Brain)
  brain stem (*see* Brain)
  cerebrum (*see* Cerebrum)
  cerebellum (*see* Brain)
  dendritic growth, 50
  feedback and, 21
  function of, 24
  nerves (*see* Nervous system)
  neurons (*see* Nervous system)
  pathways, sensory, 19
  regions of (*see* Brain)
  spinal cord, 22, 24, (table) 25, 37, 39,
    40, (table) 43 (*see also* Periph-
    eral nervous system)
  structure of, 22
  vermis, 23
Cephalocaudal, 252, 259
Cerebellum (*see* Brain)
Cerebral dominance (*see* Dominance)
Cerebral, minimal dysfunction, 62
Cerebral palsy, 3-12, 44, 62, 163
  assessment chart, 264
  ataxia, 8, 10, 132, 136, 156, 210, 233,
    238
  athetosis (*see* Athetosis)
  classification of, 8
  diagnosis of, 8
  definition of, 3
  drooling, treatment of (*see* Appen-
    dix B)
  etiology, 5-7, 157
  flaccid paralysis, 8, 9, 27, 237
  Gerstmann syndrome and, 64
  handling (management) techniques
    (*see* Appendix D)
  hemiplegia, 8, 51, 69, 136, 137, 139,
    151, 229
  incidence, 4, 88
  intelligence and, (table) 133, (table
    134, (table) 135, 164
  mixed, 8, 11
  monoplegia, 8

neuromuscular involvement, types of, 8

orthopedic management and, *(see* Orthopedic management)

paraplegia, 8, 134, 136, 151

quadriplegia, 8, 136, 151, 331

rigidity, 8, 10, 237

spasticity *(see* Spasticity)

sucking, treatment of *(see* Appendix B)

surgery and *(see* Orthopedic management and Vision)

swallowing, treatment and *(see* Appendix B)

tremors, 8, 11

triplegia, 8, 134, 136

Cerebrum, 7, 9, (fig) 17, 19, 22, 23, 24, 26, (fig) 32, (table) 43, 147, 157, 176

Cervicocaudal, 251, 252

Ciliary muscle, 224 *(see also* Muscles, intrinsic eye)

Cochlea, 157, 158, 161, 163

COEPS *(see* Nervous system, extrapyramidal system)

Cognitive process, eye-hand movement and, 221

Color

blindness *(see* Blindness)

perception, 213, 234

tests for color blindness, 214

Communication *(see* Speech and Language)

Conjugate deviation, 181

Consonants, 140, 151, 153, 166

Convulsions, 229 *(see also* Seizures and Pharmacological management)

Corioretinitis, 181

Cortex, cerebral *(see* Cerebrum)

Cortical deafness *(see* Hearing)

Council on Drugs of the American Medical Association, 235

Cranial nerves, 16, 24, (table) 25, 30, 31, 35, 36

Crossed laterality *(see* Laterality)

D

Deaf athetoid, 10, 157, 161

Deafness *(see* Hearing)

Deanol, 242

Decible, 159

Deformities *(see* Orthopedic management)

Derecruitment, 168

Developmental Scale *(see* Appendix A)

Dexedrine, (table) 232, 235, 241, 242

Diamox, (table) 232, 235

Diazepam *(see* Valium)

Dichromatism, 213

Diencephalon, 7, 23, 27, 35, 36, 240

Dilatin, (table) 232, 233, 242

Diplacusis, 159

Diplopia, 184, 190, 233, 235

Dipthong, 153, 166

Directionality *(see* Dominance)

Discrimination *(see also* Perception)

astereognosis, 29, 51, 52, 71

color, 213, 234

deep touch/pressure, 19

dysacusis and, 159

eye movements and, 216

figure-ground, 53, 222

form, *(see also* Stereognosis) 51, 52, 70, 202, 213

phonetic, 60

position/movement *(see also* Perception) 19, 28, 202

surgery and, 104, 105

right/left, 35, 48, 69, 77, (table) 78, (table) 79

sensory, parietal lobe and, 43

sound, 148 (tests for), (table) 150

spatial orientation

athetosis and, 71

body *(see* Discrimination, right-left)

eye movements and, 220

letters and, 76

organization of, 48

stimulus novelty and, 75

stereognosis *(see* Stereognosis)

stimuli *(see* Nervous system)

tactile *(see* Tactile perception)

two-point, 19, 28, 34, 51, 52, 70, 73, 202

surgery and, 104, 105

visual *(see* Perception)

Doman-Delacato System, 260

Dominance

ambidexterity, 61, 137
cerebral, 31, 48, 61, 77, 137
   damage and, 49, 77
   crossed, 62, 211
   delayed, 49, 61, 137
   directionality, 77, 79, 338
   environment and, 48
   eye, 61, 211
   foot, 61, 137
   hand, 48, 61, 137, 211
   language and, 31, 48
   lateral preference, 48
   laterality, v, 48, 49, 57, 61, 77, 137,
      211
   mixed, v, 61, 62
   motor, 31
   non-verbal activities and, 48
   right-left orientation (*see* Discrimi-
      nation)
   sinistrality, 61, 137, 211
   speech and, 31
   tests of, 58
Drooling, treatment techniques (*see*
   Appendix B)
Drug therapy (*see* Pharmacological
   management)
Dysacusis, 57, 157, 158, 159, 161
Dysarthria, 132, 136, 139, 140, 146, 147,
   233
Dyscalculia, 59, 64
Dysgraphia, 55, 61, 63, 64, 130, 136, 137
   agraphia, 69
   parietal, characteristics of, 64
Dyskinesis
   eye muscles and, 181, 224
   speech and, 132, (table) 133
Dyslexia, 55, 61, (table) 62, 63, 64, 130,
   136, 137, 138
   alexia, 69
   developmental, 60, (table) 62, 63, 64,
      130
      ocular skills and, 217
   right-left discrimination and, 64, 69,
      80
   teaching methods and, 63
Dysphasia 55, 130 (table) 134, (table)
   135, 136
   acquired, 137
   classification of, 137

developmental, congenital brain abnormality, 137
specific developmental, 61, 130, 137
Dysphonia, 131, (table) 132, (table) 133,
   136, (table) 138
Dysrhythmia, 132, (table) 133, (table)
   134, (table) 135, 136

E

Effectors (*see* Muscles)
Eighth nerve disorder, 158
Electro-oculogram (EOG), reading and,
   217
Emmetropia, 224
Emotions (*see also* Behavior) 34, 36, 52,
   165, 237
Epilepsy, 3, 137, 229-232, 241
Equinal, 237
Equipment and Adaptations, 279-339
   activities of daily living, 279-304
      feeding (self, without hands) 298-
         302
      handles (for spoons, pencils etc.)
         298-302
      headwand, 292-295
         changing tips on headwant, 296-
            298
         tips for, 298
      helmet, protective, 290-292
      holders, 283-286
      mouthstick, 286-290
      plate stabilizer, 279-281
      splint, combined ADL-Long
         opponens orthosis, 302-303
      spoon, 281-283
   Learning/teaching, 304-327
      arithmetic, 307-310, 338
         arithmetic board, 309-310
         number block board, 306-307
         sponge digits, 307-308
      desk-table, tilt-top, 327
      flash card board, 315-316
      handwriting device, 316-318
      letter block board, 306-307
      lock block board (for learning
         letters, words, numbers) 310
      page turning, 310-314
      sentence board, 304-306

teaching machine (electric board) 323-326
  for apraxia, 326
  for paraphasia, 326
  for visual agnosia, 324
  typing
    guide, 318-322
    handrest, 322-323
    paper placement, 318
    training, 334-336
  writing device, 316-318
Orthotic (orthopedic) equipment, 327-334
  arm control brace, 327-329
  chair, roller, 331-334
  friction feeder, upright chair type, 329-330
  splint, spoon, 330-331
Teaching suggestions-approaches, miscellaneous, 334-339
  beads on wire (for mathematics program) 338
  checkerboard, 338
  reading, 336-338
    Language Master, 337
    pegboards, 337
  typing training, 334-336
  word bingo, 336
Erythroblastosis fetalis, 6, 156
Esophoria, 224
Esotropia (*see* Vision)
Exophoria, 224
Exotropia (*see* Vision)
Exteroceptive stimulation (*see* Rehabilitation techniques, reflexes)
Extrapyramidal System (COEPS) 9, 27, 35, 94
Eye (*see* Vision)
Eye-hand
  cognitive process and, 221
  developmental sequence of (*see* Appendix A)
  performance (*see* Perception, visual)

F

Facilitation (*see* Systems of Therapy, Rehabilitation techniques and Appendix D)
Fay Method (*see* Systems of therapy)

Fear and drug therapy (*see* Pharmacological management, behavior and)
Feeding, (table) 136, 140
Figure-Ground, 53, 222
Finger Naming Test, 64, 65
  differentiation test, 66
  finger block test, (fig) 67, 68
  in-between test, 67
Frequency, 159, (table) 166
Frontal lobe, 8, 9, 19, 26, 31, (fig) 32, 33, 34, 178
  area 4, 26, 33, 254
  area 6, 27, 33
  area 8, 27
  association areas, 27
  damage to, 27
  function of, 33
  lesions, results of, 33
Frostig Figure-Ground Test, 219

G

Gates Test of Reading Ability, 220
Gemonil, (table) 232, 233
Gerstmann Syndrome, 64
Goodenough Draw-a-Man Test, 58
Grand mal seizure, 71

H

Handbook for Teachers of Educationally Handicapped, 327, 336, 338
Hand skills, developmental sequence of (*see* Appendix A)
Handling (management) techniques, cerebral palsy (*see* Appendix D)
Handwriting
  visually impaired and, 212
  writing device, 316-318
Hearing (*see also* Auditory and Speech)
  anacusis, 159 (table) 160
  athetosis and, 136, 156, 161, 164
  auditory agnosia, 34, 158, 169 (*see also* Agnosia)
  cochlea, 157, 158, 161, 163
  conductive loss, 158
  cranial nerves and, 30
  deafness, 30, 155, 157, (table) 165
    aphasia and, (table) 165

athetosis and, 10, 157, 161
cortical, 158, 169
peripheral, (table) 138
word, 34, 55, 138
decibles, 159
defects, 139 (*see also* Hearing disorders)
athetosis and, 10, 136
causes of, 157
incidence of, 157
definitions, 159
degree and extent of, (table) 160
derecruitment, 168
diplacusis, 159
discrimination, 159, 162
disorders, 130, 155-157
associated with kernicterus, 156
dyskinesis and, (table) 133
eighth nerve, 158
high frequency, 58, 136, 160, 162, 163, 164
maternal rubella, 158
dysphonia, 131, (table) 132, (table) 133, 136, (table) 138
dysacusis, 57, 157 158, 159, 161
ear, 157
erythroblastosis, 156
evaluation of, 58
frequency continuum, (table) 166
hard of, 159
hearing aids, 161, 167
high frequency
disorders, 58, 136, 160, 161, 162, 163, 164
sounds, 158, 161, 164, (table) 166
hypocusis, 160
imperception (*see* Auditory)
intelligence and, (table) 133, 164
kernicterus (Rh factor) and, 6, 10, (table) 133, 156, 157, 161, 162, 163, 164, (table) 165
loss
degree and extent of, (table) 160
high frequency, 160, 164, 169
types of, 157
mechanisms of, 157
organ of Corti, 157, 162, 163
peripheral loss, 55
phonemic regression, 159, 160

post-rubella, 166, 168
primary reception of in brain, 30
psychological maladjustment and, 136, (table) 165
recruitment, 158, 159, 161, 162, 168
Rh factor, 6, 10, (table) 133, 156, 157, 161, 162, 163, 164, (table) 165
rubella, maternal and, 156, 157, 158, (table) 165, 166
sound (*see* Sound)
"word deafness", 34, 55, 138
Hemianopia, 69, 73, 192, (fig) 193, 224
contralateral, 31
homonymous, 69, 73
Hemiplegia, 8, 51, 69, 136, 137, 139, 151, 229
Hemolytic disease, 6
High frequency sounds, 158, 161, 164, (table) 166
H.R.R. Pseudo Isochromatic Tables, 214
Hyperactivity, vii, 62, 128
Hyperkinetic behavior and drug therapy (*see* Pharmacological management)
brain damage and, 240
Hypertropia, 182, (fig) 183, 224
Hypocusis, 160
Hypothropia, 182, (fig) 183, 224

I

Imitation synkinesis, 258
Impulse, 14, 15, 19, 30, (table) 43, (fig) 92, 340
Inhibition (*see* Systems of therapy and Rehabilitation techniques, reflexes)
Intelligence
drugs and, 234, 241
frontal lobe and, 33
surgery and, 105

J

Jacksonian or focal seizure, 232
Jacobsen's Principle, 73, 155, 248

K

Kabat technique, 250-255
Kernicterus, 6, 10, (table) 133, 156, 157, 161, 162, 163, 164, (table) 165

Kinesthetic, 19, (table) 20, 28, 70, 75, 202

L

Language (*see also* Aphasia and Speech)
  angular gyrus and, 49
  audition and language-learning, 162
  brain damage and, 49, 162
  delayed, 55
  development of, 34, 49 (*see also* Appendix A)
  disorders, 130-175
  dominance and (*see* Dominance)
  imperception, 166
  nerve regeneration and, 50
  retardation of, 136, 139
  specific language disability, 55
  spoken (*see* Speech)
Language Master, usage of, 337
Laterality (*see* Dominance)
"Lazy" eye (*see* Vision, amblyopia)
Learning (*see also* Behavior and Perception) 30, 42-87
  brain and compensation factor in, 49
  central nervous system processes and, (table) 43, 50
  classical conditioning, 46
  cognitive, 42
  color and, 213
  disorders of, 42-87
  information, transfer of, 52
  motivation and, 43
  perceptual learning, 42, 46
  responses and, 18
  spelling and Gerstmann syndrome, 65
  teaching and, 304-307 (*see also* Teaching-training-treatment methods)
  visual impairments and, 200-228
Leiter International Performance Scale, 164
Lengthening, tendon (*see* Orthopedic management, tendon and Vision, retroplacement)
Librium, 236, 237, 242
Life magazine, 176
Limbic, 26 36
Linguistic disorders (*see* Language)

Listening Test of the Sequential Tests of Educational Progress, 207

M

Marble Board Test, 58
Mathematics, 59, 62, 307-310, 338
Mebraral, (table) 232, 233
Memory
  auditory, 30, 57, 337
  cognitive learning and, 42
  drugs and, 234
  form discrimination and, 70
  immediate and frontal association area, 28
  long-term, 48
  numbers and, 59
  short-term, 70
    non-verbal organization of, 48
  sound, storage of, 30, 34
  speech, motor patterns for, 34
  stereognosis and, 70
  temporal lobe and, 30
  visual (*see* Vision)
  words and, 34, 60
Meningitis, 158
Mental retardation, 3, (fig) 4, 58, 63, 328
  color blindness and, 212
  "organic", vii
  speech and, (table) 133, (table) 134, (table) 135, 136, (table) 138
Meprobamate (*see* Equinal)
Mesantoin, (table) 232, 234
Microfilm duplication, 209 (*see also* Appendix C)
Milontin, (table) 232, 235
Monochromatism, 213
Motor development, sequences of (*see* Appendix A)
Muscles (effectors)
  abdominal, 153
  abductor polliscis longus, 114
  adductor polliscis, myotomy of, 114, (fig) 115
  agonist, 89, 253
    inhibition of, 91
  alpha motoneuron and, (*see* Nervous system)

annulospiral fibers and, (fig) 90, 91, (fig) 92
antagonists, 10, 89, 91, 94, 248, 253, 272
anterior horn and, 91
articulation (*see* Speech)
biceps femoris, 98
cardiac, 20
deformities (*see* Orthopedic management)
dorsal interosseus, 113
drug therapy and, 236-239
electromyograms, 95
extensor carpi radialis brevis, 108
extensor carpi radialis longus, 108
extensor hallucis longus, transfer of, 98
exteroceptors and muscular response, (table) 274
extrafusal (*see* Nervous system)
eye
  ciliary, (fig) 179, 224
  extrinsic, 178, (fig) 180, 181, 185, 190, 194
  intrinsic, 178, (fig) 179, 185, 188
flaccid, 248
flexor carpi radialis, 114
flexor carpi ulnaris, 95, 108, 110, 112, 114, 121
flexor group, 95
flexor pollicis brevis, release of, (fig) 103, 114
flexor pollicis longus, 113
  lengthening of (fig) 103, 114
gamma motoneuron fibers, (fig) 90, (fig) 92
gastrocnemius, 96, 97, 98
hamstring, 99
hypertonia, 94, 263
hypotonia, 95, 263
iliopsoas, 102
involuntary, 9
mastication, 141, 143, (fig) 145
  lateral pterygoid (fig) 142) 143, (fig) 144
  masseter, 141, (fig) 144
  medial pterygoid (fig) 152, 143, (fig) 144
  temporal, (fig) 142, 143, (fig) 144

motor disorders, 48, 58, 59
mouth, (fig) 361
normal, 9, 89, 94, 248
nuclear bag, 89, (fig) 92, 94
nuclear chain fibers, 89
phasic activity and, 95
pronator teres, 109
proprioception, 10, 28, 34, 36, 46
proprioceptors, 18 (table) 20, (fig) 90, 246, 262, 268, 272, 273, (table) 274, 275, 340
  stimulation of, (*see* Rehabilitation techniques, reflexes)
rectus femoris, 98
re-education of, 246, 258
relaxation of and drug therapy, 236-239
respiratory, (fig) 152, 153
semimembranosus, 98
semitendinosus, 98
  transfer of, 100
skeletal, 20, (fig) 93
smooth, 20
soleus, 179
spastic characteristics of, 89, 94, 95, 248, 262, 263, (*see also* Spasticity)
spindles (*see* Nervous system)
stretch reflex, 9, 94, 95, 120, 248
surgical procedures and
  ocular (*see* Vision, surgical procedures)
  orthopedic (*see* Orthopedic management)
  visual (see Vision, surgical procedures)
synchronous activity, (cocontraction) 95
synergies, 256
synergy and the cerebellum, 38
tibialis anterior, posterior, 97, 98, 143
transfers of (*see* Orthopedic management)
trapezius, (fig) 363
triceps surae, 96, 98
types of, 20
voluntary movement and Area 4, 26
zero cerebral, 248
Myelin, 15, 16, 49, 50
  cerebral hemispheres, types of, 23

Myoclonic, minor motor seizure, 232
Myopia, 182, 186, 188, (fig) 189, 190, 197, 211, 225
Myotomy, 88, 106, 114, (fig) 115, 124
Mysoline, (table) 232, 233, 234, 242

N

Nerves (*see* Nervous system)
Nervous system, 13-41, 51, (fig) 57
  afferent, 16, 19, 71
    spinal cord and, 39, 40
  all-or-none principle, 15
  alpha motor neuron, (fig) 90, (fig) 92, (fig) 273
    inhibitation of, (fig) 90, 91, 94, 271
  angular gyrus, 49
  annulospiral ending, (fig) 90, 91, (fig) 92
  anterior horn cell, (fig) 91
  axon, 14, 15, 19,
    collateral growth and, 50
  cell body, 14
  central (*see* Central nervous system)
  coeps, 9, 27, 35, 94
  compensation and, 49
  cranial nerves, 16, 24, (table) 25, 30, 31, 35, 36
  dendrites (nerve cell) 14, 50
  dorsal column-medial lemniscal pathway, 19
  efferent, 14, 16, 18, 20, (fig) 92
    cerebellum and, 39
    spinal cord and, 39, 40
  exteroceptor, 18, (table) 20, 246, (fig) 273, (table) 274, 275
    stimulation of, 260, (fig) 273, (*see also* Rehabilitation techniques,, reflexes)
  extrafusal muscle, 89, (fig) 92, 94, 95
  extrapyramidal system (COEPS), 9, 27, 35, 94
  feedback, 21
  gamma efferent fibers, 89, (fig) 90, (fig) 92, 271, (fig) 273
  glial cells, 16
  golgi tendon organ, 18, (fig) 90, 121
  impulses (efferent), 14, 15, 19, 30, (fig) 92, 340
  interneurons (internuncial) 17

interoceptors, 18, (table) 20
intrafusal, (fig) 90, (fig) 92
ions, 15
motor end plate, (fig 90)
myelin, 15, 16, 49, 50
  cerebral hemispheres, types of, 23
nerves
  cerebral, types of myelination, 23
  cranial, 16, 24, (table) 25, 30, 31, 35, 36
  impulses and, 19
  regeneration of, 15
  resection of, 101
  spinal, 16, 24, 39
neurilemma sheath, 15
neuron, 13, (fig) 14, 16, 37, (fig) 90
nuclear bag, 89, (fig) 92, 94
nuclear chain fibers, 89
peripheral (*see* Peripheral nervous system)
plasticity of, 49
postcentral gyrus, 26
precentral gyrus, 26
proprioceptors, 18, (table) 20, (fig) 90, 246, 262, 268, 272, 273, (table) 274, 275
  stimulation of, 340 (*see also* Rehabilitation techniques, reflexes)
pyramidal system, 8, 26, (fig) 90, 94, 256, 262
receptors, 16, (fig) 17, 18, (table) 20, 272
  growth of, 50
  regeneration of, 15, 50
  relearning and, 16
  resection of, 101
  responses, components of, (fig) 17, 18
  reflex, 21
  voluntary, 21
reticular activating system (*see* Reticular formation)
schwann cell sheath (neurilemma sheath), 15
sensory
  pathways, 19
  strip (*see* Cerebrum, parietal lobe)
spinal cord (*see* Central nervous system and Peripheral nervous system)

spindles, 89, 94, 271
  intrafusal, (fig) 90
  neuromuscular, 18, (fig) 90, 91,
    (fig) 92
  neurotendinous or golgi tendon
    organ, 18, 121
spinothalamic tract, 271
stimulus (stimuli), 14, 38
  novelty of, 75
  preference of, 75
  selection of, 45, 240
  transduction of visual, (fig) 177
stretch reflex, 9, 94, 95, 120, 248
synapse, 15, 50
Neurectomy, 101, (fig) 124
  obturator, 88, 101
  tibial nerve, 96
  triceps, 106
Neuroanatomy, 13
Neurological impairment, vii, 3
Neurophysiology, 13
Neurons, 13, (table) 14, 16, 37, (fig) 90
Neurotomy, (fig) 124
Nystagmus, 10, 181, 182, 211, 225, 233

O

Occipital lobe, 7, 31, (fig) 32, 35, 178
  areas, 31, 178
  functions of, 35
  lesions, results of, 35
  somaesthetic area, 36
Ocular (*see* Vision)
Occupational therapy (*see* Orthopedic
    management, surgical procedures,
    Rehabilitation techniques and Sys-
    tems of therapy)
Olfactory
  temporal lobe impulses and, 30
Ontogenetic, 252, 255
Opthalmologist, 225
Optic nerve atrophy, 181, 182
Optic nerve (*see* Vision, eye)
Optometrist, 225
Organ of Corti, 157, 162, 163
Orthopedic management, 88-129
  abduction splint, 102
  arthrodesis, 106, 112
    subtalar extra-articular, 98
    thumb, 114, 115

bone stabilization, 97, 98
bracing, 96, 118-123, 246
  abduction splint, 102
  ADL-long opponens orthosis, 119
  arm control brace, 327-329
  Australian hand splint, 119, (fig)
    120
  back brace, 122-123
  basic long opponens hand splint
    with C-bar, 111, 119, 121, (fig)
    303
  Boldrey brace, modified, with
    hinged head halter, 122
  contractures and, 118, 119
  contraindications, 120
  Denis-Browne splint, 102
  dorsal cock-up splint, 107, (fig) 108,
    121, 330, (fig) 331
  dynamic, 118
  friction feeder, 329, (fig) 330
  head support, sling type, 328
  klensac ankle, 118
  long leg, 102
    twisters, 119
    with pelvic band, 101, 118, 121
  Miller twister, 119
  orthotic equipment, 327-334
  pancake hand splint, 119, 121
    modified, 108, (fig) 109
  postoperative management and,
    121
  preoperative evaluation and, 121
  scissors gait and, 119
  short leg brace, 118, 119, 121
  short opponens with C-bar, (fig)
    116, 117, 119
  tendon transfers and, 89
  training and, 121
capsulorraphy of thumb, 115
chair, roller, 331-334
contractures
  bracing and, 118, 119
  hip adduction, 88
  prevention of, 118
deformities, prevention of and brac-
    ing, 118
Eggers hamstring transplant, modifi-
    cation of, 99 (table) 124
electromyograms 95

fusion
thumb, 114
wrist, 112
Mustard's iliopsoas transfer, modification of, 102, (table) 124
adductor, 88
adductor pollicis, 114, (fig) 115
myotomy, 106, (table) 124
neurectomy, 101, (table) 124
obturator, 88, 101
tibial nerve, 96
triceps, 106
orthoptic training, 196, 197, 225
orthotic equipment, 327-334
osteotomy, (table) 124
calcaneus, 98
rotation, 101
varus, 102
resection, (table) 124
scissors gait, 100, 101
spasticity (*see* Spasticity)
splints, 118
surgical procedures, 88, 96-118
lower extremity and, 96-103
foot, 96
equinus deformity, 96-97
varus and valgus, 97-98
hip, 100
adduction deformity, 101
flexion contracture, 102
flexion-internal rotation, 99-100
subluxation-dislocation, 101, 102
knee, 98
knee flexion, 99
upper extremity, 103-118
age indications for, 106
elbow, 106
evaluation, pre-operative, 104
fingers, 106-118
sensory defects of hand, 104
types of deformities, 104
wrist, 106-118
fusion, 112
swan neck deformity, 117
thumb-in-palm deformity, 112
tendon
lengthening, 95, 97, 102, 107, 108,

(fig) 109, 113, 114, (fig) 115, (table) 124
abductor pollicis brevis, (fig) 103, 115
adductor pollicis, (fig) 103, 115
biceps, 106
calcaneus, 97
flexor pollicis brevis, (fig) 103, 115
flexor pollicis longus, 114
iliopsoas, 102
triceps surae, 96
z-plastic of hamstring, 99
tenodesis, 89, 118, (table) 124
tenotomy, 101, (table) 124
transfers (transplant) 89, 106, (table) 124
brachioradialis, 115, (fig) 116
Egger's, modification of, 99, (table) 124
flexor carpi radialis, 114
flexor carpi ulnaris, 108, 109, (fig) 110, 112, 114, 121
gastrocnemius, 97
iliopsoas, 102, (fig) 103
semitendinosis, 100
sublimis of 4th finger, 115
treatment, rehabilitation (*see* under specific surgical procedure, this listing)
z-plasty procedure, 99, 114

P

Paradine, (table) 232, 234, 235
Parietal lobe, 26, 28, (fig) 32, 34, 36, 43, 48, 52, 58, 63, 64, 65
areas of, 28, 33
association areas, 29
defects of, 29
discrimination, sensory, 43
principle visual cortex, 178
sensory strip, 26
short term memory and, 48 (*see also* Memory)
visual-spatial and, 48, 58
Partially sighted (*see* Vision)
Patterning, 260
Peabody Picture Vocabulary Test, 149, 208 (visually impaired and)
Peganone, (table) 232, 235

Perception, 19, 21, 30, 35, 42, (table)
43, 44, 46, 221, 223
agnosia (*see* Agnosia)
aphasia (*see* Aphasia)
astereognosis, 29, 51, 52, 71
auditory, 4, 46, 54, 164, 166
central, 46
color, 213
deep touch/pressure, 19
definition of, 223
depth, 10, 184, 222
discrimination (*see* Discrimination)
disturbance/disorders, 3, (fig) 4, 43,
54
dysfunction, 3, 29, 43, 50 (*see also*
specific dysfunctions)
eye (visual)
disorders and, 215
movement and, 210, 216, 218, (fig)
219, 221, 222 (age levels)
figure-ground, 53, 222
form (*see also* Stereognosis), 51, 70,
202, 213
haptic, 74
kinesthetic, (table) 4, 19, (table) 20,
28, 36, 52, 70, 75, 202
learning, 42
manual, 52 (*see also* Appendix A for
age levels)
pain, 69
peripheral, 46, 53
position sense, 19, 28, 202
propioception, 10, 28, 34, 36, 46
sensori-perceptuo-gnosia studies, 47,
50-54
simultanagnosia, 35
somatosensory, 36, 51, 52, 70
space, 213
spatial orientation (*see* Discrimination)
tactile (*see* Tactile perception)
temperature, 69
vibratory sense, 29
visual (*see* Visual perception)
weight, 19
"word blindness," 60
"word deafness," 34, 55, 138
Perinatal, 5, 7
Peripheral nervous system, 15, 16, 39,

92 (*see also* Cranial nerves and
Spinal cord)
damage to, 15
function of, (table) 25, 40
structure of, 24, 179
Petit mal seizure, 232
Pharmacological management, 229-245
anticonvulsants, 229-236
epilepsy and, 229-232, 241
definition/classification, 230
medication used in, 232-236
hemiplegia and, 229
reactions to medication (*see* individual drug name)
seizures, incidence of, 229
behavior and, 239-243
amphetamines (CNS stimulants)
and, 241
barbituates and, 240
drugs and (*see* specific listing)
environmental behavior disorders,
239, (table) 240
hyperkinetic behavior disorders,
239-242
epilepsy and (*see* Pharmacological
management, anticonvulsants)
muscle relaxation and, 236-239
seizure control (*see* Pharmacological
managment anticonvulsants)
Phelps System (*see* Systems of therapy)
Phenobarbital, (table) 232, 233, 236,
242
Phenuron, (table) 232, 234, 235
Phonation, 153
Phonemic regression, 159, 160
Phonetics, 60, (table) 166, (*see also*
Auditory)
Photophobia, 234
Phylogenetic, 255, 260
Physical therapy (*see* Orthopedic man-
agement, surgical procedures and
Rehabilitation techniques)
Pinna, 157
Pleoptics, 197, 225
Postnatal, 5, 7
Post-rubella deafness, 166, 168 (*see also*
Hearing, rubella)
Praxis, 48, 58
Prematurity, 5, 6, 157

deafness and, (table) 165
high frequency hearing impairment and, 161
Prenatal, 5, 6, 137
Proprioception, 10, 28, 34, 36, 46
Proprioceptive neuromuscular facilitation, 155, 250-253
Proprioceptive stimulation (*see* Rehabilitation techniques, reflexes)
Proprioceptor (*see* Nervous system)
Psychological maladjustment (*see* Behavior and Emotions)
drugs and, 239-243
hearing and, 136, (table) 165
Psychomotor seizure, 230
Pyramidal System, 8, 26, (fig) 90, 94, 256, 262

R

Rancho Los Amigos Hospital, 329
Reading (*see* Equipment and Adaptations, Teaching-training-treatment methods and Dyslexia)
Receptors, 16, (fig) 17, 18, (table) 20, 50, 272
exteroceptors (*see* Nervous system)
proprioceptors (*see* Nervous system)
Reciprocal innervation, 248
Recruitment, 158, 159, 161, 162, 168
Reflexes (*see also* Appendix A)
abnormal and speech, 144, 146
alpha-gamma loop reflex system, (fig) 90, (fig) 92
arc, 271
asymmetric tonic neck, 146
automatic, 262
blocking of spinal reflexes, 237
Bobath and use of in therapy (*see* Systems of therapy and Rehabilitation techniques)
Brunnstrom method, use of in therapy, 256 (*see also* Systems of therapy and Rehabilitation techniques)
conditioned, 262
crossed-extension, 261
equilibrium reactions, 264, 269
exteroceptive facilitory-inhibitory responses, (fig) 273
facilitation (*see* Systems of therapy and Rehabilitation techniques, reflexes)
inhibition of (*see also* Systems of therapy and Rehabilitation techniques, reflexes)
drugs and, 237
moro, 262
optical, 341
oral, 144, 146
palatal, 140
pharyngeal, 140
postural, 251, 262-263, 340
primitive, 147, 262
proprioceptive neuromuscular facilitation (PNF) and, 252
regulation of tone and, 340
response, 21, 221 ("orienting-exploratory")
righting reactions, 251, 259, 263, 264, 269, 270, 340-341
spinal cord and, 39, 260
startle, 43
stretch, 9, 94, 95, 120, 248
tonic, 252, 264
labyrinthine, 252, 257, 259, 340
lumbar, 257, 259
neck, 168, 254, 256, 259
training of (Brunnstrom method), 256-258
unconditioned, 221
"unlocking" of, 262
use of in therapy (*see also* Systems of therapy), 252, 256, 261
"Reflex-inhibiting patterns" (RIP's) (*see* Systems of therapy, Bobath)
Reflex, stretch, 9, 94, 95, 120, 248
Refraction, 185, 226
Refractive errors (*see* Vision)
Rehabilitation techniques (*see also* Systems of therapy)
antagonists, reversals of, 250
Bobath (*see* Systems of therapy)
breathing disorders, 139, 152-155
Brunnstrom (*see* Systems of therapy)
brushing, 272, (fig) 273, 360, (*see also* Appendix B)
Cass Method and speech, 155
cerebral palsy hand utilization techniques (*see* Appendix D)

compression, joints, 247, 272, 273, (table) 274
developmental sequence, 247, 254
exteroceptive stimulation, 260, (fig) 273 (*see also* Rehabilitative techniques, reflexes)
facilitation (*see* Rehabilitative techniques, reflexes)
Fay (*see* Systems of therapy)
goal-directed activities, 251
Hoberman Method and speech, 155
icing (*see also* Appendix B), 272
inhibition (*see also* Systems of therapy), 252, (fig) 273
muscle re-education, 246, 258
odors (smell) 273, (table) 274, Appendix B
orthopedic surgery and, 96 (*see also* Orthopedic management, surgical procedures for pre- and post-surgery rehabilitation techniques)
patterning, 250, 260-262
Phelps (*see* Systems of therapy)
pressure, 272, 273, (table) 274
proprioceptive neuromuscular facilitation (*see* Systems of therapy)
proprioceptive stimulation, 259, 261
reflexes
    facilitation of (*see also* Systems of therapy), 250, 252, 257, 259, 272, (fig) 273, (table) 274, Appendix D
    inhibition of (*see also* Systems of therapy), 252, 273, (table) 274, Appendix D
postural, 251
righting, 251
use of in therapy, 256, 341 (*see also* Systems of therapy)
reflexes, use of in speech, 146, 147
repetition, 247, 251, 257
resistance, 247, 251, 254, 259, 270, 272, 360
Rood approach, 85, 92, 148, 155, 252, 271-272, Appendix B
sensory stimuli, (fig) 32, 247, 257, (fig) 273, (table) 274
speech therapy (*see* Speech therapy

and Systems of therapy)
spiral-diagnonal patterns, 251, 253
stretch, 247, 251, 257, 260, 272, 360
swallowing patterns for droolers (*see* Appendix B)
tapping, 257, 259, 360
taste, 273, (table) 274, Appendix B
temperature, 273, (table) 274, Appendix B
traction, joints, 247 (table) 274
vestibular stimulation, 273, (table) 274
Westlake Method and speech, 154
Resection, (table) 124, (fig) 194, 195, 226
Reticular formation (RAS or Reticular Activating System), 19, 35, 36-38, 46, 271
Retroplacement, 195
Reversals, 59, 61, 76, (fig) 77, 211
Rh factor, 6, 10, (table) 133, 156, 157, 161, 162, 163, 164, (table) 165
Right-left orientation, 35, 48, 69, 77, (table) 78, (table) 79
Ritalin, 241, 242
Rood (*see* Systems of therapy and Speech)
Rubella, 6
    speech/hearing disorders and, 136, 156, 157, 158, (table) 165, 166, 168
    visual defects and, 185, 186

S

Saturation effect, 214
Schwann cell (neurilemma sheath), 15
Sedatives, 240
Seizures
    anticonvulsants and, 229-236
    aura and, 231
    types of, 231-232
Self-care, developmental sequence of (*see* Appendix A)
Sensorimotor cortex, (fig) 32
Sensori-perceptuo-gnosia studies, 47, 50-54
Sensory, 38
    disturbances, 3, (fig) 17, 202
    orthopedic surgery and, 104

pathways, 30
stimulus (stimuli) (*see* Nervous system)
Sensory strip, 26
Sequin Form Board, 57
Simultanagnosia, 35, 68
Sinistrality, 61, 137, 211
Soma, (table) 237, 239
Somatosensory, 36, 51, 52, 70
Sound
  discrimination, test for, 148, (table) 150
  frequency continuum, (table) 166
  patterns, storage of, 30, 34
  physics of, 159, 164, 166
  production of, 152
  recognition of, 158
  response to, 164
Spasticity, 6, 8, 9, 27, 52, 53, 89, 90, 95, 104, 140, 262, 263, 264, 267
  characteristics of, 90, 262, 263
  diminishing of by surgery, 95
  drugs and, 236-239
  handling (management) techniques (*see* Appendix D)
  hearing, 156
  sensory loss and, 71
  speech, 151, 154
  surgery and, 90 (*see also* Orthopedic management and Vision)
  teaching-training and, 202 (*see also* Teaching-training-treatment-methods)
  therapy and, (*see* Systems of therapy and Rehabilitation techniques)
Speech (*see also* Language, Aphasia, Hearing and Auditory)
  articulation, 130, 136, 137, 139
  age levels and (*see* Appendix A)
  consonants, 140, (table) 149, (table) 150, 151, 153
  disorders of (table) 132, (table) 133, (table) 134, (table) 135, (table) 136, (table) 138, 139-152
  hemiplegia and, (table) 135, (table) 136, 139
  muscles of, 130, 140
  vowels, (table) 149, (table) 150, 151, 153

brain lesions, 63
breathing (*see* Breathing)
chewing (*see* Appendix B)
cleft palate, 136, 139
comprehension of, 137
diagnostic tests (*see* Tests)
diphthongs, 153, 166
disorders of, 130-175 (*see also* specific disorders)
  articulation, 139-152
  breathing, 139, 152-155
  classification of, 131, (table) 132
  cleft palate, 136, 139
  developmental, 55, (table) 138, (*see also* Aphasia)
  diplegia and, (table) 134
  dyskinesia and, 132, (table) 133
  feeding difficulties and, (table) 136, 140
  hearing (*see* Hearing)
  hemiplegia and, (table) 135, (table) 136, 139
  intelligence and, (table 134, (table) 135
  retardation of language development, 136, 139
  voice, 139
dominance and (*see* Dominance)
drooling and (*see* Appendix B)
dysarthria, 132, 136, 139, 140, 146, 147, 233
dysphasia, 55, 130, (table) 133, (table) 134, (table) 135, (table) 136
  acquired, 137
  classification of, 137
  developmental, congenital brain abnormality, 137
  specific developmental, 61, 130, 137
dysphonia, 131, (table) 132, (table) 133, 136, (table) 138
dysphonia, 131, (table) 132, (table) 134, (table) 135, 136
electric board, use of, 326
expressive, 28
feeding difficulties and, (table) 136, 140
frequency continuum, (table) 166
larynx, 153
mandible, 140, 142

memory for motor patterns of, 34
mental retardation and, (table) 132, (table) 138, 139
motor (expressive) aphasia and (*see* Aphasia)
muscles
    articulation, 130, 140
    mastication (*see* Muscles)
    respiration, (fig) 152, 153
paraphasia, 326
phonation, 130, 131, 153
reflex facilitation/inhibition techniques and, 146, 147
release phenomenon and, 147
resonation, 130, 153
respiration, 130, (fig) 152, (fig) 153, 153
retardation of, 136, 139
Rood approach and, 148, 155, Appendix B
sound (*see* Sound)
sucking (*see* Appendix B)
swallowing (*see* Appendix B)
    stimulation of, 146
temporal fossa, 143
therapy (*see also* Rehabilitation techniques and Systems of therapy) 130, 146, 147, 154
    Cass Method, 155
    Hoberman Method, 155
    Westlake Method, 154
vibrating system, 153
zygomatic arch, 142, (fig) 143
Spelling, 337
Gerstmann syndrome and, 65
Spina bifida, 102
Spinal cord, 22, 24, (table) 25, 37, 39, 40, (table) 43 (*see also* Peripheral nervous system)
Spindles, muscle (*see* Nervous system)
Splints (*see* Orthopedic management, braces)
Squint (*see* Strabismus)
Stereognosis, 19, 34
ataxia and, 10
form discrimination, 51, 52, 70, 202, 213
parietal lobe and, 28, 29
sensory pathway and, 19

surgery and, 104
tactile discrimination and, (table) 20
    (*see also* Tactile perception)
Stimulation
electrical, 45, 255
exteroceptive, 260, (fig) 273, (table) 274 (*see also* Rehabilitation techniques, reflexes)
proprioceptive, 259, 261, (table) 274 (*see also* Rehabilitation techniques, reflexes)
sensory, 257
vestibular, 273, (table) 264 (*see also* Vestibular)
Stimulus (stimuli) (*see* Nervous system)
Strabismus, 178, 181, 183, 184, 185, 186, 190, 191, 192, 211, 219, 221, 223, 226
accommodative convergent, 196
alternating, 182, 224
concommittant, 182
convergent, 196
incidence of, 182
incommitant, 182
results of, 221
surgery and, 193, 194, 195, 196
treatment of, 193, 194, 195, 197
vertical, 182
Strephosymbolia, 59
Stretch reflex, 9, 94, 95, 120, 248
Suppression
impulses and, 9
visual, 197, 226
Surgery (*see* Orthopedic management and Vision)
Swallowing, patterns for droolers (*see* Appendix B)
Synapse, 15, 50
Synergy, 38, 256
Syracuse Visual Figure-Background Test, 53
Systems of therapy, 246-278
    Bobath System, 147, 155, 251, 252, 254, 259, 262-271
        equilibrium reactions, 264, 269
        facilitation, 264, 266, 269
        inhibition, 262, 265, 267
        key points, 265, 267
        postural adaptation, 263
        reflex inhibiting patterns (RIP's),

265, 266, 267, 268, 270, (fig)
376
righting reactions, 264, 269, 270
speech and, 147, 155
"willed movements," 270
breathing disorders and, 154-155
Brunnstrom Method, 79, 251, 252,
253, 255-260
exteroceptive stimulation, 260
facilitation techniques, 259 (*see
also* fig. 88b, and fig. 91c, d,
and Appendix D)
imitation synkinesis, 258
proprioceptive stimulation, 259
quick stretch, 260
reflex training, steps in, 256-259
sensory stimulation, 257
Cass Method, 155
eclectic approach, 246
facilitation techniques (*see* Rehabilitation techniques, under reflexes)
Fay System, 250, 260-262
crossed-diagnonal pattern, 261
homolateral pattern, 261
homologous pattern, 261
unlocking reflexes, 262
Hoberman Method, 155
inhibition techniques (*see* Rehabilitation techniques, under reflexes)
neurophysiological/sensorimotor approach, 147, 246
Phelps System, 247-250
conditioning exercises, 248
Jacobsen's principle, 73, 155, 248
modalities used, 248-250
reciprocal innervation, 248
speech and, 154
principles, basic, 247
developmental sequences, 247, 254,
264, 273
joint compression, 247, 272, 273,
(table) 274
joint traction, 247, (table) 274
repetition, 247, 251, 257
resistance, 247, 251, 254, 259, 270,
272, 360
sensory stimuli, (fig) 32, 247, 257,

(fig) 273, (table) 274
stretch (quick), 247, 251, 257, 260,
272, 360
Proprioceptive Neuromuscular Facilitation (Kabat) Techniques, 250-
255
principles of, 251-253
sensory cues, 251
speech and, 155
spiral/diagonal patterns, 250, 253
techniques used in, 251, 253, 255
Rood System, 85, 92, 148, 155, 252,
271-272, Appendix B
Traditional approach, 155, 246
Westlake Method, 154

T

Tactile perception, 46
after images, 51, 70
discrimination of, 19, (table) 20, 29,
69, 70, 213
manual recognition, 52 (*see also* Appendix A for age levels)
preservation and, 51
sensory pathways and, 19
stimuli, 38, 78
Teaching aids for children with cerebral palsy, 309, 327, 336, 338
Teaching-training-treatment methods,
47, 49, 73
adaptations, 210 (*see also* Equipment and Adaptations)
aphasia and, 55, 56
astereognosis and, 71
ataxia and, 210
back brace, use of in, 122-123
blind, mentally retarded and, 65
blindness and (*see* Teaching-training-treatment methods, visual)
bracing, use of in (*see* Orthopedic
management)
braille materials (*see* Braille)
Cerebral Palsy handling (management) techniques (*see* Appendix
D)
drug therapy and (*see* Pharmacological management)
dyslexia, 63
equipment used in (*see* Equipment

and Adaptations)
general techniques, 336
handling techniques, cerebral palsy
(*see* Appendix D)
hearing loss and, 166
large type textbooks, 365-367, 368
microfilm services, 209, 367-368
miscellaneous suggestions and approaches, 334-339
Peabody Language Development
Kits, 209
pharmacological management and
(*see* Pharmacological management)
programmed instruction, 212
reading, 336-338
reflex-inhibiting patterns, 266
sensory disorders, results of treatment, 71
spatial orientation of letters, 77
sucking, treatment of (*see* Appendix
B)
swallowing, patterns for droolers (*see*
Appendix B)
tangible educational aids, 369-371
teaching machines, 56, 323-326
therapy, systems of (*see* Systems of
therapy)
occupational therapy (*see* Occupational therapy)
physical therapy (*see* Physical therapy)
speech therapy (*see* Speech therapy)
typing
materials for visually impaired (*see*
Appendix C)
training, 334-336
visual disorders
teaching and,
adaptations and considerations,
210
braille (*see* Braille)
equipment (*see* methods/mate-
rials below)
methods/materials, 201, 202, 203
auditory, 206
visual, 208
microfilm duplication, 209, 367-
368

modifications, 201
tangible educational aids, 369-
371
techniques, 201
treatment and,
blind mentally retarded, programs for, 214
non-surgical (*see* Vision, treatment)
surgical (*see* Vision, treatment)
visually impaired, sources of material
for (*see* Appendix C)
Temporal fossa, (fig) 143
Temporal lobe, 30, (fig) 32, 34, 35
functions of, 34
lesions, results of, 35
Wernicke's area, 30
Tendon (*see* Orthopedic management)
Tenotomy (*see* Orthopedic manage-
ment)
Tests
Bender Gestalt, 58, 167
Benton Right-Left Orientation, 78-
79
Finger naming, 64-68
Frostig, 219
Gates Test of Reading Ability, 220
Goodenough Draw-A-Man Test, 58
H.R.R. Pseudo Isochromatic Tables,
214
laterality, 58
Leiter International Performance
Scale, 164
Listening Test of the Sequential
Tests of Educational Progress
207
Marble Board Test, 58
Peabody Picture Vocabulary Test,
149, 208
Sequin Form Board, 57
Sound discrimination, 148
Speech, diagnostic
Integrated Test of Articulation,
148
Short Articulation Test, 148
Syracuse Visual Figure-Background
Test, 53
WAIS, 164
WISC, 62, 64, 164, 219

Thalamus, 7, 19, 36, 37, 43, 62, 69
Therapy (*see* Systems of therapy and Rehabilitation techniques)
Thorazine, 242
Tranquilizers, 236-239
Transfers, muscle (*see* Orthopedic management)
Tridione, (table) 232, 234
Typing training, 334-336

V

Valium, 236, (table) 237, 238
Verbal mediation, 70, 71, 74
Vestibular, (table) 20, 30, (table) 274
Vision (Visual, ocular)
  accommodation, 185, 190, 223
  acuity, 191, 203, 211, 223, 226, 234
    athetosis and, 188, 220
    drugs and, 234
    reading speed/comprehension and, 220
    spastics and, 220
  advancement (resection), 195
  agnosia, 68, 69 (*see also* Vision, central blindness)
  amblyopia ex anopsia, 184, 192, 194, 197, 224
  anatomy of the eye, (fig) 177, (fig) 179, (fig) 180, (*see also* Vision, eye)
  angular gyrus and, 34
  area 17 (*see* Occipital lobe)
  association, 35
  astenopia, 184
  astigmatism, 54, 188, 224
  binocular, 184, 221, 222, 224
  blind (*see* Blindness)
  braille (*see* Braille)
  brain, association areas, 30, (fig) 32, 35, (fig) 177, 178 (*see also* Occipital lobe)
    lesions, results of, 34
    visual cortex, 35, 176, (fig) 177, 180
  cataract, 186, 196, 224
  central blindness (visual agnosia), 68
    for color, 69
    for objects, 68
    for space, 69
    localization of objects, 68

  simultanagnosia, 35, 68
  teaching machine and, 323-326
  cerebrum and, 178
  conjugate deviation, 181
  constructional (optical) apraxia, 58
  convergence, 185, 190, 212, 223, 224
  defects (*see* Vision, disorders/defects)
  depth perception, 184, 222
  diplopia, 184, 190, 233, 235
  discrimination (*see* Perception and Discrimination)
  disorders (defects, impairments) (*see also* individual disorders)
    acuity, 179
    cataract, 181, 185, 186
    causes of, 180
    classification of, 181
    corioretinitis, 181
    extraocular muscles and, 179, 181
    glaucoma, 186
    hemianopia, 31, 69, 73, 192, (fig) 193
    implications of, 179
    optic nerve atrophy, 181, 182
    perceptual, 179, 215, (*see also* Perception)
    reading disability and, 210
    refractive errors, 181, 182, 183, 185
    retrolental fibroplasia, 181, 185
    strabismus (*see* Strabismus)
    structural irregularities, 181, 185
  divergence, 185, 224
  dyskinesia of eye muscles, 181, 224
  E chart, 191
  eccentric fixation, 197
  emmetropia, 224
  esophoria, 224
  esotropia, 182, (fig) 183, 196, 224
  evaluation of visual defects, 192
  exophoria, 224
  exotropia, 181 182, (fig) 183, 197, 224
  extraocular eye muscles, 178, (fig) 180, 181, 185, 190, 194
  eye, (fig) 180, (fig) 189
    anatomy of, 176, (fig) 177, (fig) 179
    cones, 176
    cornea, 188
    fovea, 184, 191, 197, 217, 224

movements, 210, 216, 218, (fig) 219, 221, 222, 225, 226
muscles of (*see* Muscles)
nerves, (table) 25, 178, 179, 225 (*see also* Peripheral nervous system)
retina, 176, 184, 186, 188, 213, 226
rods, 176
structural irregularities, 181
farsightedness (*see* Vision, hypermetropia and hyperopia)
fixation, 217, 220
focus, 224
fovea, 184, 191, 197, 217, 224
fusion, 184, 190, 217, 224
glaucoma and congenital rubella, 186
glossary, 223
hearing and, 164, 165
hemianopsia, 31, 69, 73, 192, (fig) 193, 224
heterophoria, 217, 221, 225
hypermetropia, 188, (fig) 189, 190, 197, 211 (*see also* Vision, hyperopia)
hyperopia, 181, 182, 188, (fig) 189, 224, 225
hyperphoria, 225
hypertropia, 182, (fig) 183, 224
hypophoria, 225
hypotropia, 182, (fig) 183, 224
imagery for objects, 35, 69
impairments (*see* Vision, disorders/defects)
definition of, 203
"lazy" eye, 184, 192, 194, 197, 224
memory, 30, 34, 58, 60, 178
microfilm services, 209-210
microphthalmia, 186
monocular, 222, 225
motor (*see* Perception, visual)
movements, 210, 216, 218, (fig) 219, 221, 222, 225, 226
muscles of the eye (*see* Muscles)
myopia, 182, 186, 188, (fig) 189, 190, 197, 211, 225
nearsightedness (*see* Vision, myopia)
nerves (*see* Vision, eye and Peripheral nervous system)
normal, 191
nystagmus, 10, 181, 182, 211, 225, 233

occipital lobe (*see* Occitipal lobe)
opthalmologist, 225
optic nerve (*see* Vision, eye)
optometrist, 225
orthoptic training, 196, 197, 225
partially seeing, 207
print, types of, 208
reading rate of, 207
patching, 193
pathways, optic, 192
perception/visuomotor skills and eye disorders (*see* Perception)
peripheral field defects, 201
pleoptics, 197, 225
pursuit movements, (fig) 219, 225
recession (retroplacement), 195, 196, 225
refraction, 185, 226
refractive errors, 181, 182, 183, 186, (fig) 187, 188, 191, 196, 223, 226
resection, (fig) 194, 195, 226
retina, 176, 184, 186, 188, 213, 226
retinoscope, 196
retroplacement, 195
rubella and, 185, 186
saccadic movements, 218, 221, 226
space disorientation, 35
spatial ability, 46
squint (*see* Strabismus)
stereopsis, 184
stimuli, transduction of, (fig) 177
strabismus (*see* Strabismus)
suppression, 197, 226
surgical procedures, 193, 194, 195, 196
teaching-training the visually impaired (*see* Teaching-Training-Treatment methods)
treatment, 192-198
amblyopia, 192
cataract, 186, 196, 224
esotropia, 196
glaucoma, 186, 196
refractive errors, 192, 196
strabismus, 193, 194, 195, 196, 197
tunnel vision, 201
visual-verbal agnosia (*see* Agnosia)
visuo-motor skills and, 215, (*see also* Perception)
Visual disorders (*see* Vision)

Visual perception, 4, 35, 46, 48, 51, 75, 164, (table) 165, 178, 183, 213, 215, 217, 242
  central blindness, 68, 69, 324-326
  visual verbal agnosia, 34, 55, 68
Visuomotor (*see* Visual perception)
Vowels, 151, 153, 166, 338

W

WAIS, 164
Wernicke's area, 30, 34, 158
Westlake Method, 45
WISC, 62, 64, 164, 219

Writing
  agraphia, 34, 55, 69, 326
  aphasia and, 59
  mirror (strephosymbolia), 59
  pre-writing, developmental sequence of (*see* Appendix A)

Z

Zarontin, (table) 232, 234, 235
Zero cerebral muscle, 248
Zygomatic arch (*see* Muscles, mastication)